The Ethics of St. Thomas Aquinas

Leo J. Elders

The Ethics of St. Thomas Aquinas
Happiness, Natural Law and The Virtues

The Catholic University of America Press
Washington, DC

Copyright © 2019
The Catholic University of America Press
All rights reserved

The paper used in this publication meets the minimum requirements of American National Standards for Information Science—Permanence of Paper for Printed Library Materials, ANSI z39.48-1984.

∞

Cataloging-in-Publication Data available from the Library of Congress
ISBN 978-0-8132-3198-3

To Ralph McInerny

Benevolentia est principium et radix amicitiae
St.Thomas, *In III Sententiarum*, d.29, q. 1, a. 7

PREFACE

There is a wide variety of opinions about what one ought to do or not to do in certain situations. Almost everyone has some rules of conduct and is sooner or later confronted with questions about the meaning of life, problems related to technological developments, genetical manipulations, the economic order, the use of drugs and similar issues. So the study of the foundations of our moral life is of considerable importance.

In the course of time different ethical systems have been developed such as the ethical thought of Plato, the ethics of Aristotle, Epicurus and the Stoa in classical antiquity. On the borderline between antiquity and the Middle Ages St. Augustine reached profound insights about man's moral life. In their turn the great medieval theologians as well as many philosophers of the modern age elaborated coherent moral theories. In the twentieth century relativism came to the fore. A good number of moralists now felt that in the changing circumstances of life each person must freely determine the rules for his own conduct.

Most authors accordingly no longer saw ethics as a science which helps us to lead a life according to the virtues. The reference to a transcendent rule for moral conduct disappeared and a utilitarian approach began to prevail which sought to evaluate moral goodness with the yardstick of the results obtained, sc. the amount of satisfaction, pleasure or other advantages an action produces. Neo-Freudian psychology considers all conscious acts as inspired by *eros*. On a positivistic view it makes little sense to inquire about the foundations of moral conduct, since moral theory is nothing but a set of rules in use in a particular society which do not need any further legitimation. However, the validity of this view is called in question by the recurrent confrontations with major ethical questions which demand that we determine our position.

It is the purpose of this study to provide a survey of the ethics of Thomas Aquinas in so far as these are based on arguments of natural reason. Certain parts of Thomas's ethics, such as the questions he devotes to the criteria of the morality of our actions and to the natural law are frequently discussed in scholarly publications, but what Thomas writes about the emotions or passions and his study of the individual moral virtues is less known and often remains *terra incognita*. Since this has a high intrinsic value this book aims at making our readers more familiar with it. Accordingly, it presents a summary of the main arguments proposed by Aquinas in the successive questions and articles of the First Part of the Second Volume of the *Summa theologiæ*, while what he writes in other relevant works is also taken into account. Of the detailed and complete treatment of the different moral virtues in the Second Part of the Second Volume the main points at least will be presented. Despite these restrictions we hope that this presentation of the ethics of St. Thomas Aquinas will be of help to those readers who desire to know what the greatest of medieval philosophers has to say about numerous moral issues.

A difficulty one encounters when dealing with the ethics of Aquinas is that Thomas was in the first place a theologian. What he has to say about ethical questions is in large part set forth in theological treatises. This is why some modern students of his thought consider a treatise on his philosophical ethics impossible or, at least, beyond Thomas's own intention. A. de Libera points out that in the last decennia of the thirteenth century theologians of the faculty of theology in Paris addressed a similar critique to some masters of the faculty of arts[1]. The following chapters aim to show that Aquinas did indeed develop a philosophical ethics and that one can put together a coherent and complete ethical theory drawing mostly upon such works as the *Summa theologiæ* which have an unmistakably theological character. Thomas's ethical doctrine will be proposed inasmuch as it is accessible to natural reason. The advantage of such an undertaking is to make a most valuable treasure of wisdom in the field of moral life available to those who restrict themselves to a purely philosophical approach. However, developing a philosophical ethics does not imply that for Aquinas a moral life of such high quality is within reach of man's unaided natural powers only.

On account of the great wealth of subjects Aquinas deals with in his treatises on ethics not all themes will be studied in detail, although an attempt is made to discuss the major questions and to present his main views. The reader should not look for entirely novel interpretations. Our intention is to render as faithfully as possible, even if in a condensed form, what Aquinas has to say regarding ethics. The historical background of most questions is sketched, at the beginning of each chapter, in so far as this is useful for a better understanding of Aquinas's thought. The reader will find references to at least a good number of recent publications on the subject. There are no doubt many manuals on philosophical ethics. The present book finds its justification in the conviction that in teaching ethics it is best to let Thomas Aquinas, one of the greatest of philosophers, guide us regarding the subjects to be treated and the order to be followed. Despite the more than seven centuries which separate our time from his, his teachings have lost none of their truth and surprising actuality. For those who have no opportunity to study the text of Aquinas himself this book offers his main teachings in a shortened, but nevertheless quite complete form, his main teachings.

The text is a translation of the author's *De ethiek van Thomas van Aquino*, Oegstgeest 2001, The Netherlands. Dr. Stephen Theron was so kind as to read the English manuscript and to suggest a great number of corrections and improvements. The voluminous *The Ethics of Aquinas,* Stephen J. Pope, ed., Washington D.C. 2002, presents some 20 scholarly articles by different special-

---

[1] *Penser au Moyen Âge*, Paris 1991, 236.

ists on the main topics of St. Thomas Aquinas's ethics and moral theology and will be helpful for studying in greater detail some of the themes treated here[2].

    L.J. Elders s.v.d.   Boston Mass., September 1, 2004

---

[2] See our review of this important book in *The Review of Metaphysics*, 2002, pp. 673-4.

TABLE OF CONTENTS

Preface		7
Introduction		13
Chapter I	Man's Quest of Happiness	35
Chapter II	Human Acts	47
Chapter III	The Moral Goodness and Badness of our Acts	69
Chapter IV	Passions and Emotions in General	93
Chapter V	The Individual Passions	103
Chapter VI	Habitus	135
Chapter VII	Virtues in General	145
Chapter VIII	Sins and Vices	171
Chapter IX	Laws and the Natural Law	197
	Thomas on the Common Good	226
Chapter X	The Cardinal Virtues. Prudence	229
Chapter XI	Justice	239
	Appendices on War and on Labour	267
Chapter XII	Fortitude	271
Chapter XIII	Temperance	279
Chapter XIV	Love and Friendship	297
Index nominum		307
Index rerum		309
Index of Greek Words		313

INTRODUCTION

The name "ethics" is derived from the Greek word ἠθικός which is formed from ἦθος meaning lair (of animals), place where one stays, custom, character. It is related to the Indo-European *suedh + dhe*, which signifies making something one's own[1]. Aristotle coined the term "ethics" to denote his treatises on human life, in which he expounds how to reach happiness by virtuous living. As he did in the fields of logic, the philosophy of nature, psychology and comparative zoology so here he elaborated a well ordered and fairly complete doctrine of man's moral life. The Presocratic philosophers and the Sophists had made some scattered remarks on ethical questions and Plato had devoted a considerable part of his dialogues to such issues, yet Aristotle was the first to formulate his conclusions about man's moral life in a systematic form. Three of his treatises of ethics are extant: the *Nicomachean Ethics*, the *Eudemian Ethics* and the *Magna Moralia*.

A concise summary of the history of ethics until the age of Aquinas

From the early Greek philosophers we have no more than fragmentary remarks on moral issues. The Pythagoreans taught that good conduct will be rewarded, and bad actions will be punished. They also seem to have prepared the theory according to which virtuous acts hold the mean between excess and deficiency. The Sophist Protagoras deals with the question whether virtues can be taught. His principle that "man is the measure of all things" appears to exclude general rules of conduct valid for all. Socrates dealt with some ethical topics such as virtue, sin, the end of man, but did not reach a clear formulation of the various issues. A well-known theory is his view that no one sins willingly. He stressed the need to avoid excess (μηδὲν ἄγαν) Plato, for his part, discussed such major subjects as the Good, happiness, the moral virtues, the difficulties we meet when we try to do what is good, in particular from the side of the sensitive appetite, τὸ ἐπιθυμητικόν. Well known is the myth of the carriage and the two horses, symbolizing the sensitive appetite, which the coachman tries to keep on the right path. Furthermore, Plato proposed the doctrine of the four cardinal virtues[2]. The way in which man will develop morally depends to a considerable extent on the education he has received, particularly during his early youth[3]. Plato also pro-

---

[1] See A. Eberle, "Zur Etymologie des Wortes Ethik", in *Theol. Quartalschrift* 119 (1938), 168 ff.
[2] Aeschylus already mentions them in his *Seven against Thebe*, v. 610.
[3] *Laws*, Book 7.

fessed the doctrine of virtue as lying between excess and deficiency. Man must lift up his mind to the Good and imitate the god in his life[4].

One of the many innovations Aristotle introduced in his theory of the sciences was the distinction he made between practical and theoretical studies. The philosophy of nature, being a theoretical science, remains outside ethics. As will appear in Chapter One, his ethics is based entirely on the thesis that man's ultimate end is the attainment of happiness and that happiness consists in the practice of the highest and most noble (intellectual) virtue, sc. wisdom in contemplation. He developed the doctrine of the different moral virtues which serve to prepare and to protect contemplative activity and presented the elements of a theory of the criteria of the moral act.

After Aristotle's life time Epicurus and the Stoics presented their respective ethical systems. While Epicurus wants to show that we must try to live without anxiety but with a reasonable amount of pleasure and made this the ideal to be reached the Stoics consider happiness as a state in which reason exercises a perfect control over all the emotions and passions, so that one can live in *apatheia*. Their central idea is that of the cosmic law, present also in human nature, which each man is bound to observe. For Epicurus prudence (φρόνησις) plays a dominant role, whereas according to the Stoics all virtues go hand in hand and are each a particular form of knowledge. Neoplatonism as it arose in the third century A.D. teaches that man must ascend to the First Principle. Through purification from whatever is material and by conversion to what is deepest and most spiritual in his soul, man must leave behind the material world and return to his origin.

The ethics of St. Augustine[5] are based on the quest for happiness, which is to be found in God. The idea of happiness has been impressed on the mind of each human being. All men also have some knowledge of what the main virtues are, for God placed this knowledge in their soul[6]. Through a divine illumination we become aware of the immutable rules of moral behavior. If we observe them we shall attain happiness[7]. Love of the good is the driving force in our moral life. It is of the utmost importance to know what we must love and to possess the right love[8].

---

[4] Cf. E. Schwarz, *Ethik der Griechen*, Stuttgart 1951. Pamela Huby, *Plato and Modern Morality*, London 1972, compares Plato's doctrine with some problems of contemporary morals.

[5] On the first Christian moralists see J. Liebard, *Les enseignements moraux des Pères Apostoliques*, Gembloux 1979 and J. Osborn, *Ethical Patterns in Early Christian Thought*, Cambridge 1976.

[6] *De libero arbitrio*, II, 10.

[7] *De civitate Dei*, XIX, ch. 1: "Nulla est homini causa philosophandi nisi ut beatus sit".

[8] *Sermo* 96, 1, 1: "Cum...nihilque aliud curae esse debeat quomodo vivatur, nisi ut quod amandum est eligatur".

Of the medieval theologians of the twelfth century Peter Abelard must be mentioned as stressing in his *Ethica seu liber dictus Scito teipsum* the inner attitude and intention of the agent. Moral evil and good are to be found not so much in the actions performed as in the intention of the person who acts[9]. Human actions are indifferent as long as we do not take into account the agents' intentions. In this way Abelard defends a distinction between external actions and man's inner attitude[10]. He adds that one must always have the will to submit oneself to the law of God.

Several medieval theologians borrowed moral themes from non-Christian literature[11]. In the twelfth century the study of ethics was associated with that of the liberal arts. Moreover, the masters who taught grammar, poetics and rhetoric were inclined to give a moralizing character to their teaching[12]. A more scientific approach is found in the work of Alain of Lille who, among other things, distinguishes between natural and infused virtues[13]. John of Salisbury examined several themes which had been treated by the ancient authors, such as those of the highest good and happiness. He studied the *De officiis* of Cicero and the doctrine of Epicurus.

An important question concerns the differences between the moral doctrine of the Bible and Greek ethical theories. The Church Fathers adopted a considerable portion of the ethical teachings of the Greek and Roman classical authors. Despite their fundamental criticism of the pagan way of life and its widespread immorality many Christian theologians were convinced that there is a fundamental correspondence between much of what the great classical authors taught and Christian moral doctrine. Especially definitions and distinctions were taken over as well as the doctrines of the virtues and of the natural law. As a matter of fact Christian moral theology up to the end of the Middle Ages accepted the same starting-point as did pagan philosophers, viz. man's quest of happiness.

In the twelfth century the Jewish philosopher Maimonides raised the question of the difference between philosophical ethics and the Torah. He himself wanted

---

[9] *Ethica* 644 A.

[10] See R. Blomme, "À propos de la définition du péché chez Pierre Abélard", in *Ephemerides theologicae lovanienses*, 33 (1957), 319 - 347.

[11] Cf. Ph. Delhaye, "Deux adaptations du *De amicitia* de Cicéron du XIIème siècle", in *Recherches de théologie ancienne et médiévale*, XV (1948), 304 - 331.

[12] Ph. Delhaye, "L'enseignement de la philosophie morale au XIIème siècle", in *Mediaeval Studies*, XI (1949), 77 - 99; id., "La place de l'éthique parmi les disciplines scientifiques au XIIème siècle", in *Mélanges E. D. Janssen. Bibl. Ephem. Theol. Lovaniensium*, I, vol. 2, Louvain 1949, 29 - 44. See also (coll.) *Arts libéraux et philosophie au Moyen Âge*, Montréal - Paris 1969. Seneca, however, had already noted that the liberal arts are not helpful for ethics (*Epist. ad Luc.*, 88, 20).

[13] *Regulae theologicae*, 88: *ML* 210, 666-667. Cf. O. Lottin, *Psychologie et morale aux XIIème et XIIIème siècles*, III 109 - 121.

to remain within the limits of philosophy which, in his view, was highly useful for explaining certain biblical concepts, such as that of the law[14].

During the second half of the twelfth century only two of the ten books of the *Nicomachean Ethics* were known in the Latin West. About 1240 Robert Grosseteste translated the entire work, a translation Albert the Great and Thomas would use. Before that date, William of Auxerre had borrowed certain ideas from the *Nicomachean Ethics*. Somewhat later Alexander of Hales attempted to integrate elements of Aristotle's ethics into his theological writings. Considerable progress was made by St. Albert who, while teaching in Paris, used the *Liber Ethicorum* in his *Commentary on the Sentences*. In Cologne he went so far as to take the daring step of using the *Nicomachean Ethics* as the basic text in a course of theology. He distinguished between a theoretical treatment of ethics (*ethica docens*) and practical questions (*ethica utens*) and argued that one must take man's last end, happiness, as the starting point for setting up rules for moral conduct.

By introducing Aristotle's text into the curriculum of theological disciplines, Albert the Great inaugurated a new era in the study of ethics. Nevertheless Thomas Aquinas was the first to examine all of Aristotle's fundamental tenets on moral life as a whole and to use them in constructing his own ethics. There are frequent references to and long quotations from Aristotle's *Nicomachean Ethics* in the *Summa contra gentiles*, but the most complete treatment of Aristotle's work is found in the Second Part of the *Summa theologiæ* and the *Commentary on the Nicomachean Ethics*, which were both written at about the same time. As R. A Gauthier, the editor of the critical text of this commentary in the *Leonine Edition*, noted, Thomas read in the *Nicomachean Ethics* not so much a doctrine of Aristotle as definite moral philosophy[15].

The sources of St. Thomas's ethics

In our discussion of the various themes we shall refer to the sources used by Aquinas. At this point only some of the more important among them will be mentioned. It goes without saying that Holy Scripture, the doctrine of the Church and of such Church Fathers as John Chrysostom, Ambrose and Augustine exercised a considerable influence upon the moral theology of Thomas and, indirectly, upon his philosophical ethics, inasmuch as these authors indicated the direction in which a solution had to be sought and stimulated the study of certain points. The Fathers of the Church had taken over several of the doctrines of pagan philosophers, in particular as regards definitions and the ordering of the various themes. As we said before, despite their fundamental criti-

---

[14] Cf. Raymond L. Weiss, *Maimonides' Ethics. The Encounter of Philosophical and Religious Morality*, Chicago 1991.

[15] *S. Thomae de Aquino. Sententia libri Ethicorum*, I, 267*.

cism of pagan thought, many of them were convinced that there is a fundamental agreement between much of what these authors had written and Christian moral doctrine. Following the lead of these theologians Thomas notes that what human nature demands in the field of ethics agrees with divine law[16].

The *Nicomachean Ethics* is of fundamental importance for Aquinas. He agrees with Aristotle on the nature of ethics, the role assigned to contemplation, the doctrine of happiness and the virtues. Thomas borrows a good number of definitions and principles from Aristotle, but he delves deeper into the intelligibility of things and points out fundamental structures. He transposes Aristotle's not always strictly coherent theory of prudence in moral life into a moral philosophy strictly based on the first principles[17].

On the philosophical level a second source for Thomas's ethics, besides the works of Aristotle[18], is the doctrine of the Stoa, which Thomas knew through Cicero, Seneca, St. Ambrose and St. Augustine. On many issues Cicero provided important material for Aquinas's synthesis[19]. Seneca is often quoted in questions about such virtues as gratitude, clemency and meekness[20]. In recent years several authors have seen in Thomas's thought a far-reaching Stoic influence, particularly on his doctrine of the natural law. This question will be discussed in the Chapter Nine. However, a careful study of the texts where Stoic theories are mentioned by Thomas shows that in the great majority of cases he discards them after confronting them with the doctrine of the Peripatetics. The most important contribution of the Stoics is to have stimulated further research by those of their theories which deviated from the doctrine of the Peripatetics. In addition to specific Stoic doctrines which he rejected[21] Aquinas also criticized their materialistic epistemology. On the other hand, Thomas, like the Stoics, places natural law in a cosmic context: in the same way as the animals man pos-

---

[16] *Summa contra gentiles*, III, 129: "Ea quae divina lege praecipiuntur rectitudinem habent non solum quia sunt lege posita, sed etiam secundum naturam".

[17] See L. Elders, "St. Thomas Aquinas' Commentary on the Nicomachean Ethics", in L. Elders and K. Hedwig (ed.), *The Ethics of St. Thomas Aquinas*, Città del Vaticano, 1984, 9-49, p. 47.

[18] Part of the *Eudemian Ethics*, known to the medievals under the name of *Liber de bona fortuna*, also provided some material. Cf. V. J. Bourke, *St. Thomas and the Greek Moralists*, Milwaukee 1947.

[19] See C. Vansteenkiste, "Cicerone nell'opere di S. Tommaso", in *Angelicum* 36 (1959), 343-382.

[20] Seneca exercised considerable influence on several Christian authors. See G. Verbeke, *The Presence of Stoicism in Medieval Thought*, Washington D.C. 1981.

[21] The following propositions are examples of such Stoic views: "Omnia peccata esse paria"; "omnes passiones esse malas"; "omnem delectationem esse malam"; bona temporalia non esse hominis bona"; "necessitate quadam vitali hominis vitam duci"; "omnes actus nostros secundum corpora cœlestia disponi".

sesses by nature certain principles which allow him to act in agreement with his being[22].

The nature of ethics

In *Metaphysics* E (VI), ch.1, Aristotle divides the sciences into theoretical, practical and operative disciplines. Theoretical knowledge is subdivided into the study of physical nature, mathematics and theology. Ethics and political philosophy fall under the practical sciences which belong to the domain of practical reason, which formulates the rules of what one must do and indicates how to accomplish one's tasks[23]. At the beginning of his commentary on the *Nicomachean Ethics* Thomas presents this division in the following way: the wise person studies the realm of beings and establishes order in what he does. There is the order found in the physical world, which is the subject matter of natural philosophy, the ordering of the acts of the intellect, which is the task of logic, the ordering of the acts of the will, which is the task of ethics, and the order in the work one does such as building a house, which is established by the arts and crafts[24]. This presentation of the different sciences has the advantage of clarifying from the very beginning the role of ethics and of assigning a place to logic, not mentioned by Aristotle in his division.

St. Thomas defines ethics as the science of human actions in so far as these are ordered to an end. He means freely willed acts according to the order of reason, that is *actus humani*, excluding purely organic processes such as the activity of the vegetative faculties, which are called *actus hominis*[25].

Accepting Aristotle's position on this point Aquinas stresses from the very start of his commentary that man is a social being and belongs to such communities as the family and the political society, societies he needs in order to develop himself and to live a well ordered life[26]. Consequently, the study of man's actions is divided into three branches: ethics which deals with the life of man as an individual; the discipline which considers what one has to do in the context of the family and, thirdly, the science of man's life in a political community. This last discipline completes ethics and aims at promoting the good of all citizens.

---

[22] *In IV Sent.*, d. 33, q. 1, a. 1. Cf. M. Spanneut, "Influences stoïciennes sur la pensée morale de saint Thomas d'Aquin", in L. J. Elders & K. Hedwig. *The Ethics of St. Thomas Aquinas*, Città del Vaticano 1984, 50-79, p. 62.

[23] *Q. d. de veritate*, q. 14, a. 4.

[24] In this text Aquinas also indicated the distinction between the liberal arts and ethics. Liberal arts belong to the productive sciences, but may prepare a person for the study of ethics and help organize his moral life. See G. Verbeke, "Arts libéraux et morale d'après Saint Thomas", in (coll.) *Arts libéraux et philosophie au Moyen Âge*, Montréal / Paris 1969, 653-661.

[25] For an explanation of the term *actus humanus* see *Q. d. de virtutibus*, article 4.

[26] "... ut bene vivat".

As does Thomas himself, we restrict ourselves mainly to the first part. It has been suggested that Aquinas omits to deal with the second and third branches of ethics. But this is not correct. His treatment of the virtues shows that he always considers man in his social life. When dealing with the virtues, in particular with justice, one studies man's duties toward the political society.

In the introduction to his commentary Aquinas makes it clear that ethics is not merely about some insight into what one must do. Aristotle, for his part, had noted that ethics, rather than explaining what virtue is, aims at making us virtuous[27]. Large sections of the *Nicomachean Ethics* consist indeed of prudential reflections on the virtuous life. Nevertheless the treatise also proposes theoretical discussions. It is noteworthy that Thomas weakens Aristotle's statement and writes that the purpose of ethics is not only to give knowledge but also to make us perform good actions, as is the case with all practical disciplines[28]. Nevertheless, ethics is a philosophical discipline and therefore the knowledge it gives is of a general nature in so far as it considers the principles of our actions[29], but, in contrast with the theoretical disciplines, these general considerations are ordered to the performance of good actions. In agreement with this analysis Aquinas writes that ethics studies the different species of acts, as he himself does in the Second Part of the *Summa theologiæ*[30]. However, how one should act in concrete circumstances is not determined by ethics as a science but by the virtue of prudence. Some moralists consider this task of prudence part of ethics itself as a philosophical discipline, but this view contradicts Aristotle's conception of a science. It follows that one may call ethics a theoretical-practical science which studies man's acts from the point of view of his being ordered to a last end[31].

Ethics and the other philosophical disciplines

A next question to be discussed is that of the precise relation of ethics to the other philosophical disciplines. Since ethics considers man's actions, it presupposes knowledge of philosophical anthropology which, according to Aquinas, is

---

[27] *E.N.* 1103^{b}27.
[28] *In I Ethic.*, lesson 3: "Finis enim huius scientiæ non est sola cognitio ad quam forte pervenire possunt passionum sectatores, sed finis huius scientiæ est actus humanus, sicut et omnium scientiarum practicarum".
[29] Cf. *S. Th.* I-II, q. 6, proem: "in universali".
[30] *L.c.* : "Ideo omnis operativa scientia in particulari consideratione perficitur"; *In IV Ethic.*, l. 15, n. 832: "Cognitio rerum moralium perficitur per hoc quod particularia cognoscuntur".
[31] Aristotle is not always very clear as to the nature of ethical science. Some believe that he sees ethics as a deductive science, others think that he formulates general rules from concrete cases. See W.F. R. Hardie, *Aristotle's Ethical Theory*, Oxford 1968, p. 34.

part of the philosophy of nature[32]. But ethics differs from it because it is based on the first principles of the practical intellect, just as the first principles of the speculative intellect constitute the foundation of the theoretical sciences. For this reason there is no real continuity between the latter and ethics, but there does exist a certain relation of dependence. It is impossible to study the ethics of Aquinas without drawing on the insights reached in the philosophy of nature. In classical antiquity this was acknowledged also by many philosophers outside the school of Aristotle, who divided philosophy into three branches, dialectic, the science of nature (which comprised also knowledge about the gods) and ethics[33]. How important the connection is between philosophical anthropology and ethics will appear in the study of happiness as man's last end, but actually also in every single chapter of this book. Finally, in bio-ethics and in the study of the moral aspects of our economic activity the vision one has of man is decisive for the conclusions one draws. A simple example will illustrate the connection with anthropology. Thomas considers lying as to be morally wrong. Behind his argument lies the theory that by its very nature the spoken word must reflect our thinking, a principle of his anthropology.

It is perhaps less easy to determine the relationship between ethics and metaphysics[34]. Obviously the analysis of good and evil is of fundamental importance as is the treatise about God who, according to Aquinas, is the object even of the contemplation constituting the imperfect happiness of man's life on earth. Moreover, the article in the *Summa theologiæ* on the first principles of the practical intellect is developed in analogy with the study of the first principles of the theoretical intellect, which are dealt with in metaphysics. These first principles result from the mind's analysis of our fundamental inclinations. In this way the morality of our acts is connected with and remotely dependent on the ontological order.

More important is the following. St. Thomas's entire moral philosophy is characterized by his doctrine that all things strive to attain the good. Every single choice and all actions must be directed to our real good. The science of ethics helps us to determine what our good is. Now, metaphysics shows that the good, the object of the appetite, is being. It is man's task to reach his fulfilment by uniting himself with the good. For this reason ethics is not just a science which brings us a certain perfection of the appetitive faculties by equipping us

---

[32] Cf. *In I Ethic.*, lesson 19, n. 227: "Unde manifestum est quod oportet politicum aliqualiter cognoscere ea quæ pertinent ad animam".

[33] This division was developed in the Academy, but it was also vigorously propagated by Stoic authors.

[34] W. Kluxen, *Philosophische Ethik bei Thomas von Aquin*², Hamburg 1980, xxxiii, argues that one cannot speak of a real dependence ("Abhängigkeit oder Ableitung") and that the relation between both disciplines is not clear ("als ungeklärt gelten muß"), but this observation would probably have astonished Aquinas.

with the virtues, so as to make us perfect individuals in our environment. The end of man is to be united with the good and with reality as it is in itself[35]. Consequently, according to Aquinas, ethics directs our acts towards our union with reality which, since it is good[36], gives us the fulfilment of our true end[37]. The science of ethics, as it is ordained to help us acquire limited happiness during this life, aims at creating the conditions under which we can unite ourselves with the main object of contemplation, God. Existing beings perfect us[38], and God does so in a most eminent way, for he is the cause of all good things[39]. For this reason Thomas, in his commentary on the *Ethics*, speaks six times of the *bonum intentum*, the good to which man directs himself, while Aristotle writes that moral philosophy concerns what the good man *does (bonum operatum)*[40]. Impossible to affirm more clearly the relationship between ethics and metaphysics and the texts quoted surprise by the light they throw on the way Aquinas conceived the science of ethics. Until the time of Kant a certain dependence of moral philosophy with regard to metaphysics was generally accepted, but Kant caused an upheaval by his attempt to ground metaphysical truths on the ethical categorical imperative.

Ethics and theology

According to Aquinas man has only one last end, sc. the vision of God. Reason discovers that we are ordained to this contemplation of God's being and so it draws the conclusion that our fulfilment as human beings is brought about by this vision, although it does not understand what this vision comprises or how it is to be attained. In view of this position St. Thomas, in his commentary on the *Nicomachean Ethics*, repeatedly states that the happiness Aristotle is speaking

---

[35] *Q. d. de veritate*, q. 22, a. 10: "... est aliquid obiectum animæ secundum quod ad ipsum anima inclinatur secundum modum ipsius rei in seipsa existentis et hæc est ratio appetibilis inquantum est appetibile"; *ibid.*, q. 1, a. 2: "Motus appetitus terminatur ad res"; q. 8, a. 4 ad 5: "Affectus terminatur ad res ipsas"; I^a-II^æ 26, 2: "Appetitus tendit in appetibile realiter consequendum".

[36] Cf. the principle "omne ens est bonum".

[37] *Q. d. de veritate*, q. 21, a 2: "Ratio boni in hoc consistit quod aliquid sit perfectivum alterius per modum finis"; *C.G.* III, ch. 109: "Quælibet voluntas naturaliter vult illud quod est proprium volentis bonum, scil ipsum esse perfectum". Cf. M.C. Donadio Maggi de Gandolfi, *Amor y bien. Los problemas del amor en Santo Tomás de Aquino*, Buenos Aires, 1999, pp. 105-147. The author stresses this being ordered to reality.

[38] *Q. d. de veritate*, q. 21, a. 1: "Ens est perfectivum alterius... non solum secundum rationem speciei, sed etiam secundum esse quod habet in rerum natura, et per hunc modum est perfectivum bonum".

[39] *In I Ethic.*, lesson 1, n. 7.

[40] *Ibid.*, lesson 9.

about as man's end is the imperfect happiness one can reach in this life[41]. These texts have led some Thomists to argue that an authentically philosophical ethics is not possible[42]. If ethics wants to indicate what is man's final end and how this should be reached, it needs to be complemented by theology. Maritain observes that mankind lives *de facto* in the state of fallen nature, whereas a purely philosophical ethics would consider man as if he were living in the state of unspoiled nature. The principles on which ethics is based depend on the science of theology. In this way ethics as a discipline is subordinated to theology[43].

However, Maritain's view runs into considerable difficulties and has been rejected by several Thomists[44]. As a matter of fact, philosophical ethics definitely exists. In order to convince oneself one just has to read the *Nicomachean Ethics*. Moreover, in this work Aristotle pays so much attention to vices and human weakness that it is obvious he does not consider human nature as immune against sin. Where Aristotle's ethics is incomplete, Aquinas perfected it in a masterly way in his commentary where he developed ethics into a coherent science. Ethics has its own first principles, formulated by the practical intellect, which show the way to a virtuous life and a limited happiness, but moral science can also arouse in us the desire of a higher destination. Aquinas applies Aristotle's description of happiness to the imperfect happiness of this life, a happiness which despite its limits is nevertheless fairly stable, since it gives man what he really needs, when his desires are regulated by reason[45].

Yet the collaboration between ethics and theology is desirable. Moral theology benefits from the assistance of philosophical ethics, as clearly appears in the Second Part of the *Summa theologiæ*. Throughout his whole treatise, while elaborating his moral theology, Thomas avails himself of philosophical insights.

---

[41] *In I Ethic.*, l. 9: "Loquitur in hoc libro Philosophus de felicitate qualis in hac vita haberi potest, nam felicitas alterius vitæ omnem investigationem rationis excedit"; cf. *ibid.*, l. 10 : "... felicitas qualem possibile est esse præsentis vitæ" ; l. 17 : "... vitam praesentem, cuius felicitatem Aristoteles hic inquirere intendit" ; *In III Ethic.*, l. 18; *In IX Ethic.*, l. 11, etc.

[42] Cf. J. Maritain, *De la philosophie chrétienne*, Paris, 1933, 101 s.; *Science et sagesse*, Paris, 1935, 327 s.; *Du savoir moral*, Paris, 1936. See also J. Pieper, *Hinführung zu Thomas von Aquin*, p. 211.

[43] "Scientia subalternata theologiæ".

[44] See J.-M. Ramirez, "Sur l'organisation du savoir moral", in *Bulletin thomiste* IV (1935), 423 s.; Th. Deman, "L'organisation du savoir moral", in *Revue des sciences philosophiques et théologiques*, 1934, 258-280 ; R. McInerny, *The Question of Christian Ethics*, Washington D.C. 1993. Cf. also Vernon J. Bourke, "Moral Philosophy without Revelation", in *The Thomist* 40 (1976), 555-570.

[45] *In I Ethic.*, lesson 9: "Hæc felicitas habet per se sufficientiam quia scilicet in se continet omne illud quod est homini necessarium, non autem illud quod potest homini advenire; unde potest melior fieri aliquo alio addito, nec tamen remanet desiderium hominis inquietum, quia desiderium ratione regulatum, quale oportet esse felicis, non habet inquietudinem de his quæ non sunt necessaria, licet sint possibilia adipisci".

These philosophical sections are so complete and coherent that they can stand by themselves. May one isolate them from their theological context so that they become a philosophical exposé of the science of morals? In the past several authors did so without any hesitation[46] and it would seem that their approach is possible and legitimate, although recently objections have been raised against this way of proceeding. The texts of the Second Part which consist of philosophical arguments constitute a coherent whole and, in their explanations, remain at the level of natural reason. This is, moreover, a sign of the correspondence between the insights of philosophical ethics and the moral precepts contained in Biblical revelation. However, the profound meaning of Thomas's Second Part can only be understood if his doctrine of the virtues is integrated with the study of man as the image of God.

The method to be used in the study of ethics

For Aquinas the question of the method to be used in a particular discipline is of great importance. The proper method makes it possible to elaborate analyses and arguments adapted to the subject matter. One must take as a point of departure what is most known to us and proceed to what is less so[47]. In mathematics the first principles happen to be what is best known to us, but in natural science and ethics we cannot proceed from some first principles and so come to understand all that is contained in them, but must consider each time what experience tells us[48]. Contact with experience is of great importance in ethics. On the basis of past experiences one formulates rules and applies them in daily life. In this connection we must also keep in mind that there is a difference between the theoretical and the practical sciences. The former proceed with the help of analysis (*modo resolutivo*) and reduce what is composite to its principles, the latter apply general rules to concrete actions (*modo compositivo*). This is the way to proceed in ethics. However, to determine what one has to do in a concrete case in order to reach a certain end, at the level of deliberation, one uses analysis[49].

---

[46] See, for instance, A.D. Sertillanges, *La philosophie morale de saint Thomas d'Aquin*², Paris 1916, and M. Wittmann, *Die Ethik des hl. Thomas von Aquin*, München 1933.

[47] *In I Ethic.*, lesson 4, nn. 51-52: "Oportet incipere a magis cognitis quia per notiora devenimus ad ignota. Et quia nos ratiocinando notitiam acquirimus, oportet quod procedamus ab his quæ sunt magis nota nobis. Et si quidem eadem sunt magis nota nobis et simpliciter, tunc ratio procedit a principiis, sicut in mathematicis. Si autem alia magis nota sint simpliciter, et alia quoad nos, tunc oportet e converso procedere sicut in naturalibus et moralibus".

[48] *L.c.* : "Quia in moralibus oportet incipere... a quibusdam effectibus consideratis circa actus humanos, oportet illum qui sufficiens auditor vult esse moralis scientiæ, quod sit bene manuductus et exercitatus in consuetudinibus humanæ vitæ". An example: one learns by experience that "concupiscentiæ per abstinentiam superantur".

[49] *S.Th.* I-II, q. 14, a. 2: "Principium autem in inquisitione consilii est finis, qui quidem est prior in intentione, posterior tamen in esse et secundum hoc oportet quod inquisitio consilii sit

23

With regard to the origin of general rules for our conduct Aquinas argues that some of them are known immediately, sc. the first principles of the practical intellect, while other rules result from experience and are obtained by induction. Following Aristotle's account in the *Nicomachean Ethics* II, ch. 7, he distinguishes several types of induction: in mathematics induction helps to formulate a general conclusion such as that numbers are either odd or even[50]. A different type of induction is used in natural science and is based on what is observed. For instance, living beings need nutriments. Induction is also used in ethics: concupiscence becomes weaker the more one resists it[51]. These principles or insights are derived from what normally happens. Finally there are rules or principles used in the various arts and crafts. These are also based on experience and are of great importance because they let us know and understand the properties of the materials we use.

In ethics we use the *modus compositionis*, but this does not mean that analysis (*resolutio*) is totally absent. In order to know man's last end one must use analysis. With regard to the *modus compositionis* the virtue of prudence makes us apply rules to particular situations[52]. The science of morals considers our acts in so far as reason directs them to our end. It does so in agreement with the first principles of the practical intellect and so it adds a moral qualification to these acts which as such are considered in philosophical anthropology. It is not possible, however, to connect all our acts directly with the last end. There are intermediate ends, sc. those at which the different virtues are aiming. In this way the virtues are principles of our actions, although all virtues are practiced in order to reach happiness.

In his commentary on the second chapter of the first book of the *Nicomachean Ethics* Aquinas observes that because of the enormous variety of human actions, ethics provides an approximative knowledge by applying general principles to concrete actions and by proceeding from the simple to the complex. He stresses more than Aristotle the need to follow principles. As we have seen, concrete acts are studied with regard to their effects, as these are produced in most cases (*ut in pluribus*). Aristotle appears to have thought that general rules admit exceptions, while Aquinas tends to ascribe the lack of certitude in the application of rules to defects inherent in man, such as a lack of freedom in our choices or the possibility that a virtuous action may at a given moment be blocked by an obstacle. The classical example of such a situation is that of the

---

resolutiva, incipiendo scilicet ab eo quod in futuro intenditur quousque perveniatur ad id quod statim agendum est".

[50] Thomas writes that this induction proceeds *ex particularibus imaginatis*.

[51] *In I Ethic.*, lesson 11.

[52] For this reason prudence also concerns the appetite. Cf. *In VI Ethic.*, lesson 7, n. 1201: "Est autem considerandum quod... prudentia non est in ratione solum sed habet aliquid in appetitu".

restitution of a dangerous object, which under special circumstances would be wrong, sc. if the owner is in such an emotional state that one cannot hand it over to him without the danger of harm.

What is most knowable in itself is not always so for us. In ethics we cannot deduce all obligations from the principle that good ought to be done and evil avoided, but we must consider the different fields of activity and find out what is to be done in the light of our true end and what the acts lead to[53].

As a result of what we do certain *habitus* are formed, sc. determinations (called virtues) of the faculties to particular sets of actions. In their turn the virtues help the intellect to form a correct judgment as to how we must reach happiness. In fact, in order to know how to act under certain circumstances we must let ourselves be guided by the inclinations to the good which the virtues give us. In the absence of the virtues the intellect will not always or not often form a correct judgment because the appetite, when not informed by the virtues, will cause the intellect to consider something as good which in reality is not so. For the practical intellect to be right means to be in agreement with right appetite[54]. To act correctly one should possess experience and some understanding of what is implied in the various options which lie before us.

An important section of the treatise on the method to be used in ethics concerns the division of the subject-matter. In his commentary on the *Nicomachean Ethics* Thomas writes that one must first study man's last end, happiness, showing in what it consists and by what activity it can be attained[55]. The theme is treated in a general way in the *Summa theologiæ* I^a-$II^æ$ and in greater detail in the II^a-$II^æ$ which examines the different virtues and vices covering the entire field of the morality of human acts.

The study of the virtues is meant to show how man can order himself to his end and strengthen this ordering by performing appropriate acts in the changing circumstances of life. On this approach the first place is not assigned to commands and duty but to man and his freedom. Man's privilege consists in being able to determine, on the basis of his basic natural inclinations, what he should do in different situations.

The *Prima Secundæ* gives concrete indications regarding the division of the subject-matter of ethics. After having determined man's last end Aquinas says that this end is reached by man's actions. These actions must be studied, first in general by examining the aspects common to all actions, next in detail, sc. by considering what is proper to the different species of acts. In the first part of the Second Volume of the *Summa theologiæ* those acts are studied which have a

---

[53] *In I Ethic.*, lesson 4, n. 53: "In moralibus oportet incipere ab his quæ sunt magis nota quoad nos, id est a quibusdam effectibus consideratis circa actus humanos".

[54] *I-II*, 57, 5 ad 3: "Verum autem intellectus practici accipitur per conformitatem ad appetitum rectum".

[55] *In I Ethic.*, lesson 4, n. 43.

direct relation to happiness (and which are exclusively proper to man) along with the factors which determine the morality of our actions. Subsequently the movements of the sensitive appetite are considered which man has in common with the higher animals, in so far as they can influence moral life, sc. the emotions and passions. The treatise on the passions is followed by a study of the principles and causes of our actions. These can be internal principles, such as the virtues, or external, such as. the various types of laws and, at the supernatural level, grace.

After this study of the virtues in general Aquinas examines the different species of the virtues in the II^a-II^æ. By means of two arguments he confirms the traditional division into four cardinal virtues: a) Virtues result when right reason directs our actions in view of our end. By careful consideration of what is involved in a choice the intellect causes a habitus *in itself*, sc. the virtue of prudence. If the intellect is concerned with a good *outside itself,* this good can be in the will and so it causes the virtue of justice,- or it can be a good concerning the passions curbing and mastering them in so far as they incite us to seek immoderately the pleasurable, and so it causes the virtue of moderation or temperance, - or it consists in strengthening us against those passions which weaken or paralyze us and so the virtue of fortitude is caused.

b) The same conclusion is reached by pointing out that each of these cardinal virtues has its seat in one or other of these four faculties: the intellect, the will, the irascible and the concupiscent appetites. All other virtues can be reduced to these four[56]. The treatment of each group of virtues is followed by a discussion of the corresponding vices.

As was pointed out above, the method to be followed in ethics is the *modus compositionis*, sc. the application of norms and rules to concrete actions. How does one come to know these norms? Aquinas distinguishes between first moral principles which the intellect spontaneously formulates on the basis of the fundamental inclinations of our nature (keeping oneself alive, living in community with others, acquiring knowledge, acting for the survival of mankind by procreation, etc.) and secondary principles which are a further determination of the basic norms, as for instance the Ten Commandments are of the precepts to love God and our neighbors[57]. Finally there are norms or rules of conduct such as those that wise people apply, as for instance the rules about warfare. This last group of rules demands much reflection and experience[58]. At times it is difficult to reach certitude as to the question whether a particular action is lawful or not.

---

[56] *Summa theologiæ* II-II, 61, 2: "Aliæ virtutes morales omnes aliqualiter reducuntur ad virtutes cardinales".

[57] I-II 100, 3 ad 1: "Omnia præcepta Decalogi ad illa duo referuntur sicut conclusiones ad principia communia".

[58] I-II 100, 1: "Ad quorum iudicium requiritur multa consideratio diversarum circumstantiarum".

In order to determine what to do one uses arguments in the form of a syllogism. The so-called secondary precepts are conclusions of a syllogism. The use of syllogisms means that ethics is structured as a science, which can be taught to others.

The moral qualification of our acts depends on their conformity with the fundamental inclinations of our human nature. An act which agrees with them is experienced as good, an act which goes against them as bad. Everyone formulates spontaneously the first principle of moral life, sc. the good must be done, evil avoided[59]. These fundamental inclinations have their seat in the will. The formulation of the basic precepts results from the collaboration of the intellect with the will. Therefore these precepts have their seat in the practical intellect. But how do we apply them to our individual actions?

A virtuous person acts spontaneously in agreement with the demands of his human nature. But it is sometimes difficult to know what one should do. The syllogisms mentioned in this connection by Aristotle have as their starting point the end to be reached[60]. Thomas gives the example of a temperate person who aims at moderating his desires and establishing a mean between excess and deficiency. Keeping this in mind this person deliberates how to behave in certain circumstances[61]. However, when one is beset with vices it becomes difficult to take the right decision. The virtue of prudence cannot function when one is not virtuous. In such a case one believes that the pleasure resulting from a particular act is at the moment the greatest good which should be sought. In this way the passions corrupt the insight about the right end[62]. Nevertheless, when one performs a bad action, the intellect is not entirely the prisoner of desire. It knows the general norm as regards what is right in a particular matter. Under the pressure of a passion, however, it formulates besides this principle another judgment. An example: alcoholic beverages are pleasant and one must enjoy them. I am offered a drink. So I accept[63]. The reasoning consists of four stages: in the background there is the principle that evil must be avoided, in this case, getting drunk or becoming an alcoholic. Next the argument quoted, which is independent in respect of this first norm. Because of the presence of this norm the alcoholic is responsible for what he does. It can happen that his addiction is so great that conscious knowledge of the norm disappears. One who always pursues pleasure will consider pleasure his greatest good and without further deliberation seek what brings him the greatest amount of immediate satisfaction[64].

---

[59] I-II 94, 2: "Hoc est ergo primum præceptum legis quod bonum est faciendum ac prosequendum et malum vitandum. Et supra hoc fundantur omnia alia præcepta legis naturæ".
[60] *E.N.* VI 12, 1144^{a}31-36.
[61] *In VI Ethic.*, l. 11, n. 1273.
[62] *In VII Ethic.*, l. 4, n. 1347.
[63] *Ibidem.*
[64] *Ibid.*, lesson 6, 1388-1389.

Several commentators think that according to Aristotle the syllogism is the normal way of deliberation in our moral choices, but other authors have a different view[65]. Thomas for his part is convinced that in every choice a syllogism is used, either explicitly or implicitly. The major proposition formulates the end (frequently subordinate ends) corresponding to the virtues, as in the example of a drink being offered, sc. when I am going to drive home from the party I must be sober. The drink offered would affect my capacity to drive. So I do not accept it.

The example shows how important it is to possess the virtues which are ordained to the end. Thomas speaks of the right *intentio finis*. He means the secondary ends such as "staying healthy", "fulfilling one's social duties" etc. Virtues direct us to the correct ends[66], in particular the virtue of prudence[67]. When placed before a decision one who does not have the virtues risks reasoning differently.

The intellect and the appetite collaborate in our choices and decisions. The intellect must know the truth and the appetite must be inclined to the good, so that it approves what the intellect proposes regarding the means needed to reach a subordinate end. The intellect in its turn is guided in its judgments by the fundamental inclinations of our human nature. The relation of the will to the end is the basis of our moral life in so far as this relation is formulated by the intellect and finds expression in the first principles of moral life.

When the intellect is guided by this order to the good, brought about by the different virtues, it will formulate correctly the proper means to reach the good embodied in the various subordinated ends. The possession of the virtues, therefore, is a condition for a morally good life[68]. Without the presence of the virtues ethics is of little use. To acquire the virtues education and training are of paramount importance.

Ethics considers human actions from the point of view of their being directed to an end. Secondly, it applies principles and rules which indicate the road to be followed and the means to be used. In this respect the role of prudence is of prime importance. But the road to be followed can differ for different persons and also in the different circumstances in which they must act. This variety implies that total certitude about what is best cannot always be reached[69].

---

[65] Cf. W.F.R. Hardie, *Aristotle's Ethical Theory*, Oxford 1968, 240-257.
[66] *In VI Ethic.*, lesson 10, n. 1269.
[67] *In I Ethic.*, lesson 16, n. 189.
[68] *Ibid.*, lesson 3, n. 40.
[69] I-II 94, 4: "In operativis non est eadem veritas vel rectitudo practica apud omnes quantum ad propria".

The intellectual character of Aquinas' ethics

We explained above that the intellect formulates the first principles of the moral order. As Aquinas observes, by its very nature the human will is inclined to act in agreement with the intellect, i.e. to act virtuously[70]. Since it is the intellect's nature to direct man's life the other faculties in their activities must follow the intellect. Consequently St. Thomas formulates this rule: the good of man is to be in agreement with reason[71].

However, human nature is characterized by a certain duality. Man has much in common with animals, but he also possesses an immaterial mind which enables him to distinguish what is right (*honestum*) and what is wrong (*turpe*)[72]. While growing up we have to learn to free ourselves from the domination of our emotions and desires by subjecting them to the rule of reason. In a virtuous person reason and sense-nature function in harmony. The opposite can also happen, however, so that one's reason will then be to a large extent determined by passions, although there always remains some space for free choice[73]. In this case reason is at the service of unchecked passions[74]. If the desire to satisfy our senses is no longer subject to the control of reason then it is no longer an expression of our true nature, since human nature and natural inclinations never direct us to what is morally bad[75]. Aquinas assumes as obvious the distinction between man's reasonable nature and what man has in common with animals. Acting against a particular bodily good may sometimes benefit his higher nature. Outside things are subordinated to the human body, but the body to reason[76].

The virtues enable us to perform actions in agreement with the good of our nature[77]. Vices, on the other hand, lead us to act against our nature, because they are opposed to reason[78].

---

[70] I-II 94, 3: "Cum anima rationalis sit propria forma hominis, naturalis inclinatio inest cuilibet homini ad hoc quod agat secundum rationem et hoc est agere secundum virtutem".

[71] II-II 47, 6. Cf. *Q.d. de veritate*, q. 13, a. 1: "Bonum hominis est secundum rationem vivere".

[72] *In V Ethic.*, lesson 12.

[73] I-II 10, 3.

[74] II-II 135, 1 ad 2.

[75] *In VII Ethic.*, lesson 13: "Unde id quod invenitur in omnibus aut in pluribus, videtur esse ex inclinatione naturæ, quæ non inclinat neque ad malum neque ad falsum". This statement is of great importance. Many authors in Thomas's day and in later ages considered it unacceptable.

[76] II-II 152, 2.

[77] II-II 23, 3: "Virtus moralis definitur per hoc quod est secundum rationem rectam". Cf. II-II 123, 1: "Ad virtutem humanam pertinet ut faciat hominem et opus eius secundum rationem esse".

[78] I-II 54, 3: "... cum sint contra rationem".

To define virtuous and sinful acts Thomas prefers to use the expressions "according to reason" and "opposed to reason" instead of "according to nature" and "against nature"[79]. Reason knows the good of man, the end of human nature, and it tells us which actions are in agreement with the end and which are not[80]. The good of a being consists in the correspondence of its actions with its essential nature. Man's essence is to be a rational animal. Hence those acts will be good which correspond to the right insight of his mind. To deviate from this is to act contrary to one's nature[81]. Yet the expression "acting against nature" is mainly used more specifically by Aquinas to qualify actions which are against human nature in so far as it coincides with that of the animals, as is the case with sodomy[82].

As appears from the above, for Aquinas human nature with its most fundamental inclinations supplies the criterium for morally qualifying any of our actions. With regard to those acts which go beyond our immediate needs, reason must determine which agree and which do not agree with our nature. Since human nature has been created by God, Thomas concludes that whatever is conformable to the order of reason belongs to the order established by God himself[83]. Reason, indeed, is the measure of morality[84]. The acts of the intellect and of the will must agree with the right insight of reason, but reason must also direct us in executing our decisions. To give an example, when responding to an inclination to a good deed, such as helping the poor, an inclination proper to the virtue of pity, we must nevertheless take into account the circumstances and examine if and how we should help. This examination belongs to the virtue of prudence which suggests how in the changing circumstances of life we may reach the good, our happiness, and which means we should use. This is an enormous and never-ending task facing our reason.

The doctrine of reason as determining the morality of our acts is at the very center of Aquinas's ethics. Even if it is true that Aristotle and, to a certain extent, Plato anticipated this doctrine, yet St. Thomas developed it in his own characteristic way. Reason as the cause of the morality of our acts must not be seen as a self-sufficient and arrogant power, for it remains dependent on the order of nature. Aquinas's doctrine should not be confounded with theories of the age of the Enlightenment which made the mind of each human individual, detached from human nature, the decisive factor[85]. Reason formulates the first

---

[79] I-II 18, 5 ad 1.
[80] I-II 19, 3.
[81] *In II Ethic.*, lesson 2.
[82] II-II 154, 9.
[83] I-II 72, 4: "Quæcumque continentur sub ordine rationis, continentur sub ordine ipsius Dei".
[84] *Summa contra gentiles*, III, c. 3: ""Moralium mensura est ratio".
[85] Cf. F. Utz, *Deutsche Thomasausgabe*, Bd. 18bis, p. 360.

principles of the moral order on the basis of the fundamental inclinations of man's nature. We have to do with a natural structure which shows what must be done. The first principles of the practical intellect depend on these natural inclinations and in this way the *ought* follows the *is*. Reason notices that something is a good for us because it is in agreement with our fundamental inclinations. Then it determines which means lead to the end, and which actions avert from it. In carrying out this task reason relies on the virtue of prudence. In its turn prudence makes use of the other moral virtues we acquired by education, personal efforts and practice. Prudence also takes account of our own experience and that of other people. In this way right reason, *ratio recta*, is not a faculty which deliberates *in abstracto*, but it is the practical intellect which collaborates with the will and the virtues. It is an expression of the free human person[86].

The importance of St. Thomas's ethics for our time

Our age is one of pluralism. Views differ as to what is moral and immoral and the previous, often tacit consensus about Christian moral principles has disappeared from public morality. By public morality we mean the set of ideas and rules of conduct which prevails in a certain society. Especially since the eighteenth century philosophers have held different views with regard to the criteria of morality. Utilitarian, deontological, esthetical, emotional and natural law theories began to circulate among the intelligentsia. In daily life, however, people accepted the traditional criteria, mainly guided by Christianity. Since the end of World War II important changes have taken place in respect of what people consider right or wrong. As regards what is called macro-morality criteria have become stricter than in the past. People accept a certain responsibility for the preservation of animal and botanic species as well as a duty to fight the pollution of our natural environment. There is also a measure of agreement concerning our common task to assist people in underdeveloped countries, to promote human rights and to fight the corruption of public officials. Even influential persons in high positions can now be cited and prosecuted for crimes against human rights. Whatever our reservations these views are in general a great improvement, due to education, the insistence of the media on these points and the fear of being unmasked now that judges have begun to prosecute leading politicians and business tycoons for fraud or cruelty.

However, besides this progress one notices real regress at the level of private morality. Extreme subjectivism makes some people neglect the objective character of our obligations. Individual man makes himself and his desires the measuring rod of what he is allowed to do. Objective duties are forgotten. Such in-

---

[86] Cf. L. Elders, "Bonum humanæ animæ est secundum rationem esse", in *Lugano Theological Review*, 1999, 75-90.

stitutions as the family and the state are in crisis. One's personal conscience, detached from all ties with morals and nature, becomes the highest authority which declares what is good and what bad. Many choose free forms of living together above marriage, experiment with free love and homosexual activity and consider freedom from all obligations their highest value. Personal convenience is enough reason to refuse having children or to kill unborn human beings. Many believe they have an unlimited right to dispose of their own bodies, a right which extends from genetic manipulations to suicide and active euthanasia. Faithfulness to others has become an exotic attitude, since we do not know what our feelings will be next month. People live in the "now" of immediate satisfaction. Thefts, violence, public insecurity and drug abuse have increased in an alarming way.

The changes in moral norms are also partly the effect of the technological revolution, increased contacts with people in countries with different customs, the changes in society, increased affluence which allows one to spend considerable amounts of money on purposes other than the immediate needs of daily life, the changing nature of one's work in companies, for example, where one no longer feels integrated, the emancipation of women, the opportunities provided by modern science and medicine for effecting modifications in the human organism, etc. One of the most important developments is the disruption of the natural connection between sexuality and procreation and the resulting sharply decreased birthrate, together with the idea that any form of sexual praxis is acceptable.

We are now living in a world dominated by technology, with the result that the language of nature, which to a great extent is also that of ethics, is no longer understood. Facing the complexities of modern life, aware of the demands made on him, seeing the numerous things over which he has no command, man feels himself powerless and consequently not responsible. Parents are discouraged and let things go because they cannot impose their principles or fight the influences to which their children are exposed[87]. The decline in the practice of religion, caused by the factors mentioned above, in its turn leads to a further weakening of traditional morality.

Aristotle speaks of pleasures which have suspected sources[88]. At present many flaunt their immoral conduct without shame. Doubts are voiced about the value of ethics. According to one opinion moral theory is a product of man's social life and is bound to differ according to the culture and historical period in which people live. Others hold that far from being able to formulate universally valid norms, we can only collect facts about the way certain groups of people

---

[87] The point is argued very well by Michel Anselme in his *La morale retrouvée*, Paris 1998 (éditions Dangles).

[88] *E.N.* 1173^{b}28.

actually conduct themselves and deduce from them some recommendations[89]. There is a widespread opinion that consensus in ethical questions is no longer possible and that one should abandon the ideal of a commonly held moral outlook. Traditional morality is regarded by many as a *Fremdkörper*, which belongs in museums but not in the modern world.

One understands these criticisms better if one keeps in mind that in the past moral doctrine has often been depicted as a set of rules and prohibitions, imposed from the outside on man, reminding him of his duties but restricting his freedom. It is also argued that traditional morality did not see much positive value in sexuality and led to repressed feelings. The same objections are also voiced against traditional moral theology as it was currently taught until the Second Vatican Council. Very often Christians just asked "Is it allowed?". Casuistry reigned. Scarce attention was paid to an invitation to seek the beauty of a life according to the virtues.

On the other hand the difficult situation described above has also led some to look for greater certitude as to man's purpose in life and the best conduct to be adopted. We cannot do away with our human nature and time and again the fundamental principles of moral behaviour resurface in our conscience. J.H. Newman made a striking comparison with the reflection of the mountains on the surface of a Swiss lake. The winds and the waves chase it away, but when the calm weather returns one sees again the image of the mountains in the water. Insight into our fundamental obligations returns when the storms of the passions abate.

Many of us feel the need for rules of conduct which help us to live in a way worthy of man. But where to find this sort of guidance? Must we start our search from the present situation of Western man and try to formulate some practical rules in order to secure a peaceful coexistence with others? Or should we go beyond this and look for true knowledge about our last end so that we can conduct our life under the guidance of right reason? Do we need some help in our task of educating the young? The ethics of St. Thomas Aquinas will provide this assistance.

The ethics of Aquinas is not only a very intelligent doctrine which stresses our personal responsibility - we must establish rules of conduct as free men in conformity with our human nature and see to it that our actions are always reasonable - but Aquinas directs our attention also to our last end, happiness, reminding us that the practice of the virtues is the road to this end. Firstly, according to Aquinas the virtues give unity and coherence to our actions. Our will and appetite stray in all possible directions if they do not acquire a certain stability by means of the virtues. Secondly, the virtues enable us to act swiftly and with a certain perfection. One who does not possess the virtues must each time deliberate carefully what to do in a particular situation. Thirdly, acting accord-

---

[89] See François Dagonet, *Une nouvelle morale*, Paris 1998.

ing to the virtues is also pleasurable, since virtues are stable dispositions in accordance with our nature[90].

Virtues are acquired by repeatedly performing right acts. Youth is the best time of life to begin practicing the virtues, a process which needs to be supported by education and discipline, as Aristotle pointed out[91]. Some simple examples show that this is right. In order to become an experienced pianist one must practice on the instrument from early youth onwards and discipline is needed to persevere. This applies also to the learning of a foreign language. The joy of being able to play well or of speaking the language fluently will be experienced only much later.

What has been lacking in Western culture over the past years is discipline, particularly in education. Some believed that a change in educational policy was necessary. In their view children must be treated as adults and never be forced at all. John Dewey argued that the theory which saw education as the preparation of children for adult life was harmful[92]. But his theory has not brought us any real benefit. When children do not receive clear guidance, they are abandoned to their more superficial inclinations and feelings. It becomes also much more difficult for them to acquire a treasure of solid knowledge in history, geography, languages and the sciences. We see this happening in some schools in our Western countries.

The ethics of St. Thomas stress the need for an education in the virtues. Thus they make an important contribution to a renewed discovery of moral values. There are those who think that a doctrine formulated more than 700 years ago, can have but little to say in a totally changed world. The answer to this is that modern man remains man, is made of the same components as his ancestors, must reach the same end and acquit himself of the same duties. The new possibilities, problems and demands of contemporary society, which have brought about far reaching changes in our way of life, require new applications or further elaboration of certain moral principles. The period in which one lives may have a certain influence on the formulation of such principles. But this does not mean that there are no fundamental rules. Those laid down by Aquinas receive their lasting value from what man is[93].

---

[90] *Q.d. de virtutibus*, qu. 1, a. 1: "... ad tria indigetur: primo ut sit uniformitas in operatione..; secundo, ut operatio perfecta in promptu habeatur... ; tertio, ut delectabiliter perfecta operatio compleatur".

[91] *E.N.* 1103^{a}14 ff. In *Politics* 1334^{b}8-9 Aristotle raises the question whether the young should be educated by arguments or by habituation. Like Plato had done before him he gives priority to habit-forming.

[92] *Recontrruction in Philosophy*, New York^5, p. 147.

[93] See our "L'historicisme en théologie morale", in *Persona, verità e morale. Atti del Congresso internazionale di teologia morale* (Roma, 7-12 aprile 1986), Città Nuova, Roma 1988, 51-59.

CHAPTER I

IN SEARCH OF HAPPINESS

It is a common conviction that most people want to be happy and direct their actions to this goal. Aristotle observes that practically everyone agrees that happiness (εὐδαιμονία) is the supreme good people want to attain. Most understand this as the good life, being successful and free of worries. St. Augustin shares this view and observes that all want to be happy[1]. Later medieval theologians also considered the search for happiness an essential element of the Christian view of man. For St. Anselm it is the key to the understanding of the life of Christians[2]. William of Auvergne writes that only happiness is desirable for its own sake and is the reason for our existence[3]. How important the question of man's happiness was to medieval theologians can also be gathered from the way Alexander of Hales analyzed the *Sententiae* of Peter Lombard: the first book, he says, considers the One who gives us beatitude, the second those who will reach beatitude and those who will not; the third describes the more remote preparation to eternal bliss, while the fourth book deals with the sacraments which prepare us immediately for beatitude. In this manner the whole of theology is studied in the light of the beatitude to be reached by man. Summarizing the period prior to Aquinas Guindon says that Western theologians, far from considering the privileged place given to happiness by the ancients as irreconcilable with divine revelation, saw it as a central doctrine. However the theologians of the Franciscan order, although placing beatitude at the beginning of their treatises on moral theology, organized the latter mainly from the point of view of the law and conscience[4].

St. Thomas goes so far as to state that, because of his nature, man necessarily strives for happiness[5]. Even an author such as Freud noted that all men seek to be happy but that not all succeed in becoming so[6]. Indeed it is commonly understood that reaching the ends we pursue is part of our happiness. When people start to explain what happiness means, however, opinions are found to differ[7].

---

[1] *De Trinitate*, 13, 5: "... quod omnes beate vivere velint".

[2] Martin Grabmann, *Geschichte der scholastischen Methode*, I, 270.

[3] *Summa de vitiis et de virtutibus* (edition Paris, 1674, 109h - 110c).

[4] R. Guindon, *Béatitude et théologie morale chez saint Thomas d'Aquin. Origines, interprétation*, Ottawa 1956, p. 63; 105.

[5] *S.Th.* I 94, 1: "Naturaliter enim et ex necessitate homo vult beaitutudinem". The *ex necessitate* does not exclude spontaniety and free will. Cf. *Q. d. de potentia*, q. 10, a. 2 ad 5: "Voluntas libere appetit felicitatem. licet necesario appetit eam".

[6] *Das Unbehagen in der Kultur* (1930), 24: "Man möchte sagen, daß die Absicht, daß der Mensch glücklich sei, im Plan der Schöpfung nicht enthalten ist".

[7] *Nicomachean Ethics*, 1095a17.

Some describe it by distinguishing between happiness in a hedonistic sense (pleasure) and happiness as possessing such goods as friends, cultural goods, knowledge etc.[8]. In this connection we should mention that Albert the Great distinguished between the happiness of one's daily life (as described in Book I of the *Nicomachean Ethics*) and the beatitude which is given with contemplation (discussed in Book X of this work). St. Thomas Aquinas, however, has not pursued this interpretation of Aristotle's dual treatment of happiness. Book X, he says simply, explains in greater detail in what human happiness consists.

Some authors, however, deny that everyone strives for happiness, since people sometimes sacrifice what they consider their happiness for the sake of duty[9]. Yet this objection loses its force when one considers happiness as the implementation of man's noblest desires, accompanied by spiritual joy or contentment, while taking into account that in this life human happiness remains always limited and incomplete. Moreover, happiness as given with contemplation must not be seen as a smug time of leisure. As Aquinas writes, contemplation is our highest activity, not yielding any practical advantage to those who devote themselves to it[10]. It must also be kept in mind that happiness as the fulfilment of our being, implies also fulfilment of our social nature.

Aquinas's treatise on happiness concerns the very foundations of ethics and, in a broader sense, determines also how one must organize the study of man's moral life. Do we have to develop ethical science as based on obligations or should one set out from man's desire of happiness? Aquinas firmly chooses this latter option, but succeeds in incorporating law and obligations into his moral philosophy based, however, on man's quest of happiness.

The Treatise on Happiness[11] *in the Prima Secundæ of the Summa theologiae*

What does happiness consist in? By what means and in which way can we reach it? In q. 1 of this part of the *Summa theologiae* Aquinas deals with happiness as the final end of human life. In the following questions he asks which objects we must possess in order to be happy (q. 2), by what actions we can attain this object (q. 3), what belongs to happiness (q. 4), and whether we can reach happiness in this life (q. 5).

---

[8] E. Taylor, *Happiness*, London 1980.
[9] Taylor, *o.c.*, p. 35: "It is not true that everyone must want happiness".
[10] *In X Ethicorum*, lesson 10, n. 2097: "Nihil enim homini accrescit ex contemplatione veritatis praeter ipsam veritatis speculationem".
[11] The term *beatitudo* is rendered by "happiness".

Happiness as man's final end (Q. 1)

People desire to become happy. For that reason happiness is an end. Now the end is that for the sake of which or in view of which one acts. The end is the starting-point of man's willed actions but also of all activity in nature. In fact, every action is intended to attain or to realize some good[12]. An action not directed to an end would not have any content and could not even exist. Aquinas formulates the axiom that the end is the first thing the agent is seeking to reach[13]. In all its acts the human will has an object, sc. some good (**article 1**).

Thomas compares this with what happens in nature in general. For in nature all processes are directed to an end. This follows, he adds, from the principle that whatever moves, is moved by some other thing. This other thing, the agent , only moves actively because it is directed to an end or directs itself to an end. Beings which are devoid of intellectual knowledge can only move by virtue of a natural inclination. Man, however, can direct himself to an end (**article 2**).

In the following article St. Thomas explains that human actions depend on the will, of which the object is the good. So our actions are meant to attain or to realize the good. In this way all human acts are constituted as such by being ordained to an end. Sometimes a person seeks to reach a first end which, in its turn, is subordinate to a further end. The end which is directly pursued determines the nature of an action, e.g. as that of building a house or setting up a business. But its moral value depends also on what one finally wants to attain, such as making a living or helping others. This explains why one and the same action can have a varying moral quality[14] (**article 3**).

Having established this Aquinas explains that there has to be one last end of all our actions. If there were not, our acts would never reach a final term and we would not come to rest[15]. This conclusion is important and deserves careful consideration. At first sight it seems that one can have more than one final end in one's life. People can make caring for their own health their goal, but at the same time want to have a comfortable house or enjoy as much entertainment as possible. Nevertheless, Aristotle, who is followed by Thomas Aquinas, argues that in whatever goal we pursue and in whatever we do we want happiness. Other ends, such as those mentioned, contribute to it, whereas happiness itself is never sought for the sake of something else.

---

[12] *Metaphysics* 1094^{a}3.

[13] *S.Th.* I-II, q. 1, a. 1 ad 1: "... finis, etsi sit postremus in executione, est tamen primus in intentione agentis".

[14] I - II, 1, 3 ad 3. Cf. S. Theron, *Natural Law Reconsidered*, Frankfurt 2002, ch. 10, "Ultimate Happiness".

[15] *In I Ethic.*, lesson 9, n. 105.

This conclusion is rejected by several commentators[16]. Aristotle neglected to distinguish, it is claimed, between a comprehensive end on the one hand and a highest end on the other[17]. Yet Aristotle is right. The aspect under which we pursue or do something, or the motive we have, is always a good. The good is desired since it satiates our striving. For Aristotle as well as for Aquinas it is evident that there is an ultimate end[18], in this sense that not only everyone seeks to attain some ultimate end, but also that all have the same ultimate end because of the unity of human nature. St. Thomas understands Aristotle's argument in the following way: What is sought for its own sake and never because of something else is the perfect good[19]. Now, we never seek happiness for the sake of something else[20]. But he corrects Aristotle in his description of happiness. Aristotle was thinking of the imperfect happiness people can attain in this life, but this cannot be the ultimate end, since ultimate happiness must entirely satiate us[21]. Since man's quest for happiness is a basic natural striving, it cannot be in vain, that is, there must be some possibility of reaching happiness[22], even if man cannot attain it by his own efforts. Perfect, ultimate happiness appears rather to be a gift[23] **(article 4)**.

Thomas elaborates this point. Can a person have at the same time more than one ultimate end? This is excluded for three reasons. 1) Man seeks to reach fulfilment, which is his highest good and which satiates his desire. This implies that he cannot, at the same time, pursue something else as a last end, for in that case the first end would not be seen as bringing complete fulfilment of all his desires. 2) Just as the intellect sets out from what it knows naturally, the acts of the will, because of the will's very nature, must have their starting-point in what the will desires. However, in the last analysis this must be one, since nature al-

---

[16] Cf. B. William, "Aristotle on the Good: a Formal Sketch", in *The Philosophical Quarterly* 12 (1962), 289 - 296; A. Kenny, "Aristotle on Happiness", in *Proceedings of the Aristotelian Society* 66 (1965), 93 -102..

[17] Hardie, *o.c.*, p. 28.

[18] *In I Ethic.*, lesson 9, n. 106: "... occurrat statim".

[19] What is sought for the sake of something else is less perfect.

[20] *In I Ethic.*, lesson 9, n. 111.

[21] *Ibid.*, n. 113: "Loquitur enim in hoc libro Philosophus de felicitate qualis in hac vita potest haberi. Nam felicitas alterius vitae omnem investigationem rationis excedit".

[22] H. J. Jaffa, *Thomism and Aristotelianism. A Study of the Commentary by St. Thomas Aquinas on the Nicomachean Ethics*, Chicago 1952, p. 119 ff. rejects this remark as not based on the text. However, when writing his commentary it was obviously Thomas's intention to construct philosophical ethics with the help of Aristotle's principles. His text is more than just a commentary.

[23] However, Thomas adds that one who does not receive this gift is not necessarily unhappy. Apparently he takes into account the fate of children who die without any personal guilt, but have not received Christian baptism. He assumes that they enjoy nonetheless, a blissful afterlife.

ways strives for unity[24]. 3) The acts of the will derive their specification from the end to which they are directed. By "the ultimate end" we mean the end which underlies all human acts and places them in the class[25] of desirable things. Since every class of beings has a first principle and the last end is such a first principle, all our acts can only have one last end. - The difficulties some commentators find with this doctrine appear to be caused by their failure to see what such ends as leading a comfortable life, doing one's duty etc. have in common. Moreover one end is often subordinated to another and is continuous with it (**article 5**).

A next question is whether we do everything for the sake of the last end. At first sight this does not seem to be the case. When playing or seeking entertainment one hardly strives for a last end. Nevertheless the answer is affirmative, since whatever we strive to attain, is sought in so far as it is a good. If it is an imperfect good, as may quite often be the case, it is desired as ordained to the perfect good, because a partial movement in a certain direction is always directed to its terminus[26]. A second argument compares the things we pursue with changes occurring in nature, caused by the First Mover. The objects we pursue attract the will since a first good or end is the basis of whatever is desired. The inclination toward the perfect good and the power of attraction of it operate in every act of the will[27] (**article 6**).

When we consider the last end from the viewpoint of its being desired, all men direct themselves to the same end. However, they do not always agree on what good will bring them perfect happiness. Some seek wealth and comfort, others honour or pleasure. People with a well developed taste can best tell us which wine or dish to choose. Those who have a well educated will should best be able to show us, where our real happiness lies. This remark is not a proof, but a suggestion that we look for happiness in our highest activity. Despite the fact that people may differ in their evaluation of what brings happiness human nature is the same in all. Therefore there is only one and the same good which can make them happy (**article 7**).

---

[24] "Natura non tendit nisi ad unum". This principle is used by Thomas on several occasions (I - II, 1, 7 ad 3; *Q. d. de potentia*, q. 3, a. 15; *Q. d. de malo*, q. 16, a. 5). It rests on the insight that nature strives for an end and does not go into two divergent directions. Thomas can refer to this principle since underlying the acts of the will, which pursue many different objects, there is one fundamental striving, sc. toward the object the will seeks to attain because of its nature.

[25] The Latin text has *genus*, a term which means a class of things which possess the same general nature and which comprises different species.

[26] St. Thomas argues that this principle is evident from what happens in nature and in the work people do.

[27] The recourse to principles drawn from nature is quite striking. Thomas develops his ethics by using facts of experience as his starting-points and applying to human acting the principles apparent in nature.

In the preceding articles some principles derived from what can be observed in nature were used and applied to human actions. This raises the question whether all natural things also strive to attain a last end (**article 8**). Behind this question lies the doctrine that God is the supreme good and the last end and that all beings seek to reach God in so far as they strive for their own fulfilment, which is a participation in God's being. In this sense all things direct themselves to God. This theme receives a detailed treatment in the *Summa contra gentiles*[28]. With regard to the way in which God as the last end is attained, Thomas points out that man can attain this in a way exclusively proper to him, sc. by knowledge and love.

In what does man find supreme happiness ? (Q. 2)

The next question now to be dealt with is: what makes us become totally happy? This question is a classical theme of ethics. Pythagoras is said to have compared the different ends people choose to the goals pursued by those who go to the Olympic games. The athletes take part in them to gain honors, the peddlers and vendors to make money, but the spectators come to admire the beauty of the accomplishments of the athletes. The latter represent those persons who devote their lives to the study and contemplation of nature[29]. Plato likewise writes that people pursue different goals[30], and Aristotle mentions the current theories about what causes happiness: pleasure, honours, wealth. He then argues that man's true happiness lies in the contemplative life[31]. St. Augustine, in turn, devotes several pages to the question of the different ends people pursue[32]. The variety of views about what brings real happiness can be explained by the fact that while people have a natural inclination to happiness, each of them must decide in what he thinks he will find it[33].

In his *Summa contra gentiles*[34] Aquinas discusses several theories about what brings happiness and concludes that supreme human happiness must consist in that activity which is proper to man only, sc. in the contemplation of truth by which he enters into contact with what is above him and is least dependent on

---

[28] Book III, ch. 24. Ch. 25 argues that man can reach God in a way proper to him, sc. by coming to know God's being.

[29] Pythagoras, fragm. 88 : Cicero, *Tuscul. Disputationes*, V, 3, 8.

[30] *Republic* IX, 581 C.

[31] *Nicom. Ethics*, Book I, ch. 3.

[32] *De civitate Dei*, XIX, 2 and 3.

[33] Cf. Thomas, *In IV Sent.*, d. 49, q. 1, a. 3 C: "Quamvis autem ex naturali inclinatione voluntas habeat ut in beatitudinem feratur secundum communem rationem, tamen quod feratur in beatitudinem talem vel talem, hoc non est ex inclinatione naturae, sed per discretionem rationis".

[34] Book III, chapters 26 - 36.

external things. The object of this contemplation is not the material world, but the highest reality, God. Next, Thomas examines what knowledge of God brings us this happiness. It is obvious that what we may come to know about God during life on earth is not sufficient for happiness. Moreover, nothing here on earth is permanent and we are not protected from adversity and disasters. Finally, the perfect virtues required for happiness can only be reached with difficulty and after a long period of practice[35]. St. Thomas can only conclude that perfect happiness is not to be found in this present life, but in after-life during which our immaterial soul continues to exist, even if it cannot reach God, the object and cause of its beatitude, by its own power[36].

In the Second Question of the *Summa theologiae*, I^a - II^{ae} Aquinas considers some answers sometimes given to the question of what human happiness consists in. Material possessions may enable people to live in comfort but they are not an end in themselves. The tribute of honor paid to some people is only a sign of excellency. Thus those who honor us, cannot render us happy. Nor does wielding power constitute happiness, since power is always a means to something else, and so is not itself that final terminus of our striving which is happiness. It is obvious, then, that happiness does not consist in anything outside ourselves, nor in bodily well-being since this is subordinate to the life of the mind. Happiness cannot consist either in pleasure. Pleasure follows upon an act or a good agreeable to us[37]. If this good is imperfect, then so is the pleasure, whereas is the good is perfect, then pleasure is not the essence of happiness but comes in the second place. Since the mind surpasses the body by far inasmuch as it knows the universal, a good of the body cannot constitute our happiness. This holds true also true of the soul itself or whatever is in it, since it is limited[38]. The life according to the mind is what agrees most with our deepest nature, and so we must find happiness in it[39]. The ultimate end is a perfect good which fully sati-

---

[35] Thomas follows Aristotle in the *Nicomachean Ethics* 1177^{b}12. Some modern commentators point out that Aristotle does not make clear the precise relationship between a life according to perfect virtue and contemplation.

[36] *S.cc.G.*, III, chapters 37 - 39; 47 - 48 ; 52.

[37] This point is discussed in greater detail in the commentary on the *Nicomachean Ethics*, Book X. According to Eudoxus pleasure would be the highest good, but Aristotle rejects this view. Pleasure accompanies some good actions, but also some shameful acts. Eudoxus can only mean pleasure which accompanies good actions (*E. N.* 1173^{b}26 ff.). Pleasure accomplishes an action as an added perfection. Cf. *In X Ethic.*, lesson 6, n. 2026: "Delectatio perficit operationem, non efficienter sed formaliter" ; *ibid.*, n. 2030: "... sicut quidam finis, sicut quaedam perfectio superveniens".

[38] Thomas considers the soul and the body separately, because happiness is reached by an activity of the intellect, but also because he has in mind the beatific vision of God which may be attained after the death of the body.

[39] Cf. *In X Ethic.*, lesson 11, n. 2109.

ates our faculties and fulfils our desires. It is reached by the highest activity of the mind[40].

The Second Question closes with **article 8**, which argues that the object of the will is the universal good, as truth is that of the intellect. Nothing can satiate the intellect and the will except the universal good and the source of all truth, God. Referring to a text of Aristotle[41] Thomas writes in the *Summa contra gentiles*, III, ch. 111, that one may assume that divine providence will extend a special care to beings endowed with reason, since they are the only ones who to a certain extent can be said to reach God.

What happiness consists in (Q. 3)

The Third Question examines what happiness is, Question Four what is required for it and Question Five how one actually reaches it. Regarding the first question Aquinas distinguishes between the thing one wants to possess and the state of actually having it. In this latter sense happiness is something proper to man (**article 1**). This is so since activity is our ultimate fulfilment as actualizing our aptitudes. All things are made with a view to their actions[42]. This statement voices a certain critique of the traditional definition of happiness, by Boethius: happiness is the state of satiation caused by possessing a collection of good things[43]. This definition does not say more than that one possesses what is good, but does not explain how one attains happiness (**article 2**). If happiness is consecutive on man's union with the highest good, this union cannot be brought about by the senses, for their objects are the properties of material things, but only by the intellect, even if there will be an overflow of happiness into the lower faculties (**article 3**). While the will rejoices in the good one possesses, the intellect renders this good present (**article 4**).

As St. Thomas had already done in the *Summa contra Gentiles* he shows here too that human happiness must consist in an act of the speculative intellect. The practical intellect directs itself to doing something and organizing things, the speculative intellect is characterized by possessing and contemplating. Yet the practical intellect collaborates in the attainment of happiness by regulating the passions and organizing our life according to the virtues (**article 5**). Our supreme happiness cannot consist in the study of the sciences or of higher creatures (**articles 6 and 7**), but only in the vision of God. The reason is that the desire to know does not find full satisfaction unless when one comes to know the

---

[40] *In X Ethic.*, lesson 10.
[41] *Nic. Ethics*, X, ch. 9, 1179ª24 ff.
[42] Thomas refers to Aristotle's *De caelo* II, 286ª8.
[43] *De consolatione philosophiae*, III, prose 2: "Status omnium bonorum aggregatione perfectus".

First Cause[44]. The knowledge one can acquire in the theoretical sciences does not go beyond the principles material things allow us to know. Man's highest fulfilment can be reached only by what lies above man. However, the happiness one may reach on earth has a certain likeness to perfect happiness. Thus Thomas considers it to be a remote participation in it[45]. As a transitory and preparatory stage this imperfect happiness is a real goal of nature. Thus Thomas can say that one naturally desires it[46]. This imperfect happiness depends on several conditions, such as the state of the body, sufficient external goods, the presence of friends, etc., as is explained in the following Question. Seeking this imperfect happiness is not yet being ordained to ultimate happiness but it puts us on the way towards it.

What is required for happiness (Q. 4)

Question 4 explains in detail what is required for the vision of God, but the explanations belong for the most part to sacred theology, depend on the authority of the Bible as understood by the Church and lie outside our philosophical study. The imperfect happiness on earth consists also in an activity of the intellect, which directs itself to God, the First Cause, and unites itself to Him[47]. Union with God is the goal, since God is the cause of man who receives everything he has from Him. Because of the demands of our life on earth, however, it is impossible to concern ourselves uninterruptedly with this object of contemplation. We can only return to it time and again. Aquinas observes in passing that to attain the (limited) happiness accessible in our present life a good bodily condition is required, since this imperfect happiness consists in acting in conformity with perfect virtue[48]. But a poor physical condition may render a life according to the virtues more difficult (**article 6**). In addition the imperfect happiness of our present life requires some external goods, which do not belong to its essence but are means helpful for securing it (**article 7**). The same can be said of the company of friends, which is so important on account of man's social nature and is dis-

---

[44] Cf. *Compendium theologiae*, ch. 104: "Est igitur finis ultimus intellectualis creaturae Deum per essentiam videre".

[45] I-II, q. 3, a. 6: "... sed participat quandam particularem beatitudinis similitudinem".

[46] *Ibidem*, ad 2: "Naturaliter desideratur non solum perfecta beatitudo, sed etiam qualiscumque similitudo vel participatio eius". Cf. Th. Deman, in *Bulletin thomiste*, 1943 -1944, p. 439: "... l'idée même de béatitude imparfaite, qui dans la doctrine thomiste de la béatitude occupe une place essentielle et incontestable".

[47] I - II, q. 3, a. 2, ad 4: "In hominibus autem secundum statum praesentis vitae est ultima perfectio secundum operationem qua homo coniungitur Deo".

[48] *Nicomachean Ethics*, I, ch. 13, 1102^a5.

cussed in great detail by Aristotle (**article 8**). This imperfect happiness is attained by working oneself up it by starting to secure its basic elements[49].

On reaching happiness (Q. 5)

Human happiness in its proper sense, sc. the blissful knowledge of God's being, lies outside the investigations of philosophical ethics. However, its relation to the imperfect happiness man may attain during life on earth must be further determined. According to Aquinas this imperfect happiness has some particular likeness (*particularis similitudo*) with real, ultimate happiness. He likens this relationship to the way the shrewdness higher animals show in their actions, based on instinct, compares to the prudent behavior of virtuous persons[50]. One should notice, however, the enormous difference: eternal beatitude is of a totally different order. With regard to the limited happiness man may attain in the present life, Thomas refers repeatedly to the *Nicomachean Ethics* 1101^{a}21, a text which, in its medieval Latin translation, says *beatos ut homines*, a wording which expresses a limitation, whereas the Greek text has a different meaning: "We call those happy among people now living, who possess the above mentioned goods". In I -II, q. 5, a. 3 St. Thomas points out that in order to possess real happiness all evil must be excluded and this happiness must be permanent, conditions which cannot be fulfilled during our life on earth. Imperfect happiness can be attained by our own efforts, as we can also acquire the virtues, in the practice of which this happiness consists[51] (**article 5**). This imperfect happiness is a certain preparation for the ultimate bliss which it makes us desire.

How does seeking our final end determine all our actions? (Q. 6)

At the end of the treatise on happiness the question is raised as to how happiness as our last end actually determines human behavior. The answer is that it does so in that in whatever we do, we seek to reach a good and so aim at fulfilling our human existence. Usually something concrete and palpable stands in the foreground as that in which one assumes that happiness can be found: pleasure, satisfaction over having done one's duty, the acquisition of knowledge and the virtues. In all these concrete forms of happiness there is awareness of the fulfilment of one's desire.

---

[49] Cf. A Pegis, "Nature and Spirit: Some Reflections on the Problem of the End of Man", in *Proceedings of the American Catholic Association of Philosophers*, 23 (1949), 62 - 79; B. Ashley, "What is the End of the Human Person? The Vision of God and Integral Human Fulfilment", in Luke Gormally (ed.), *Moral Truth and Moral Tradition: Essays in Honor of Peter Geach and Elizabeth Anscombe*, Portland OR, 1994, 68 - 96.

[50] I - II 3, 6.

[51] I - II 5, 5: "... eo modo quo et virtus in cuius operatione consistit".

As became evident in the previous questions happiness does not have the same meaning for all, although each of us seeks an ultimate fulfilment[52]. Many do not have very high aspirations with regard to acquiring knowledge of the First Cause. Does this mean that Thomas's view that the vision of God is man's ultimate end, is an abstruse theory, having no practical meaning for the majority of people? The fact that only few people explicitly seek God, did not disquiet Aquinas too much. He mentions a number of causes of why it is so difficult to come to see that the knowledge of God is the highest form of knowledge man can reach and that union with God is at the core of his limited happiness on earth. People experience some difficulty in considering spiritual things because of a lack of aptitude[53], or because of other occupations which demand their attention. Others again lack zeal and do not want to travel on the not so easy road of knowledge of and union with God, although by its very nature the human intellect seeks knowledge[54]. As obstacles Thomas mentions the turbulent years of youth, the long duration of this study and the many errors to which people are exposed. Nevertheless, like other natural beings man has an ultimate end which is given with human nature. What is proper to him is that he himself must decide what he will positively choose and that he must then live up to it.

As a last point regarding this treatise on happiness it must be stressed that the quest for happiness has a cosmic dimension, in so far as all things strive to assimilate themselves to God as their First Cause and coming to know God is the end of all intellectual beings[55]. We must finally point out that since man is by his nature ordained to know God, this basic structure of his being constitutes the background of his supernatural vocation. This vocation aims at bringing to fulfilment what one is trying to attain in one's natural inclinations, but cannot reach by one's own powers. In this way the study of happiness helps man to acknowledge more easily his true ultimate end.

---

[52] *In I Ethicorum*, lesson 1.

[53] One might mention here also the difficulties that a mind marked by positivism experiences.

[54] *Summa contra gentiles*, I, ch. 4: "Quem quidem laborem pauci subire volunt pro amore scientiae cuius tamen mentibus hominum naturalem Deus inseruit appetitum".

[55] *Summa contra gentiles* III, chs. 19 and 25.

CHAPTER II

HUMAN ACTS

The philosophy of Aquinas exhibits a high degree of originality in the elaboration of individual themes as well as in the systematic ordering of the various subjects. Yet St. Thomas took over much material from the ancient philosophers and various Christian authors. This is particularly true with regard to the treatise on human acts, which comprises questions 6 to 21 of the *Prima Secundae* of his *Theological Summa*. This exposition is the continuation of the questions on happiness, since man can only reach his happiness by acting. Certain actions are proper to man, while others along with some passions and emotions, are shared with the animals. In this Part of the *Summa* Thomas first examines human acts before considering what is common to man and animals, whereas in the First Part of the *Summa*, when dealing with man's faculties, he first studies the powers man has in common with the animals before turning to the study of the intellect and will. The reason for this reversal is that although the intellect in its operation presupposes the work of the sense faculties, the striving for our ultimate end can only exercised by free acts. The study of the emotions deals with the material man has to work with. In order to reach his end he must bring the emotions under the control of the virtues. This explains why the study of the passions follows that of human acts.

The treatise is subdivided as follows: the study of freely willed acts in general, and of the factors which can reduce or even do away with freedom (Q. 6); the circumstances of human acts (Q. 7); the human will in so far as it directs itself to an end (Q. 8). Q. 9 examines what moves the will, while Q. 10 studies in which way the will begins to act and in which way it is moved. A following series of Questions treats the different stages leading to a free decision, from its first beginning to its execution. QQ. 18 and 19 investigate in what the morality of our acts consists and what determines its quality. In Q. 20 the insights gained thus far are applied to the issue of the morality of our external actions. Q. 21 indicates what the terms "good" and "evil", "praiseworthy" and "meritorious" mean when used to qualify actions. Because of their fundamental importance questions 18 and 19 are studied in a separate chapter.

When are acts voluntary, when involuntary ? (Q. 6)

It is man's task and privilege to direct himself to his end and he does so by voluntary actions. In this connection "voluntary" means the act which proceeds from an intrinsic principle, with at least some knowledge of the end. The term "voluntary" (in Greek ἑκούσιος) is explained by Aquinas as follows: Sometimes a movement in us is caused by what lies outside ourselves. When a movement depends on a principle within us it can be the self-movement of a faculty or a movement caused by something else, as our limbs are moved by the appetite. Whatever moves something or is moved by another, does or undergoes such movement as directed to an end. In order actively to move towards an end some knowledge of the end is required. Beings which know the end move themselves, since they have the principle of their activity within themselves: they are aware of doing something and also of doing something in view of the end. When these two conditions are fulfilled, we speak of voluntary acts.

A voluntary act proceeds from man himself and is performed with some degree of knowledge of the end. Aristotle indicates this directedness to the end only implicitly, in so far as he speaks of "voluntary" when the principle from which the action proceeds lies within the person who knows the particular circumstances under which he performs his act. Thomas added "directed to an end" to the definition, in order to make plain that we speak of human acts in the context of an ethics which directs us to our end (**article 1**).

Aquinas indicates chapters one to three of the Third Book of the *Nicomachean Ethics,* and also some texts of Nemesius[1] and St. John Damascene as a source of his treatment of the subject matter of human acts[2]. What is done under compulsion or in ignorance is not voluntary. The terms "voluntary" and "involuntary" have a rather broad meaning. Aristotle also uses them to denote the activities of children and animals, who are devoid of deliberation and choice and have an imperfect knowledge of the end, which they acquire by sense cognition, in particular by the estimative power[3]. Aquinas adopts this use of the terms, which agrees more with the Greek term ἑκούσιος than with the Latin word *voluntarius*. "Voluntary" in its proper sense signifies human acts as willed, but can be used in a derivative meaning to signify what animals do, when there is a certain likeness with the acts of the human will[4]. What is essential in voluntary acts is that one deliberates on what to do, chooses a particular action among several possibilities and is master of what one does[5] (**article 2**).

Can "not acting" at all be voluntary? The question has its importance in certain cases where civil liability is at stake as, for instance, when one does not help persons in danger. Here moral theology speaks of sins of omission. Aquinas observes that in certain cases the will is able to interrupt this state of not acting, which shows that this not doing anything is voluntary. Often it is our duty to act (**article 3**).

---

[1] *De natura hominis,* c. 32 (edit. by Verbeke and Moncho, Leiden 1975, p. 126 ff.).
[2] *De fide orthodoxa,* II, c. 24 : *PG* 94, 944 ff.
[3] *Nicom. Ethics III, ch. 3, 1111^{b}8-9.*
[4] *S. Th.* I - II 6, 2 ad 1.
[5] I - II 6, 2 ad 2: "... ex hoc contingit quod homo est dominus sui actus quod habet deliberationem de suis actibus; ex hoc enim quod ratio deliberans se habet ad opposita, voluntas in utrumque potest".

Articles 4 to 9 discuss factors reducing or even totally undoing the voluntary character of acts. In his *Nicomachean Ethics* Aristotle deals with this question, insisting in particular on the roles of ignorance and fear. Greek literature mentions such factors as fear, ignorance and the compulsion of irresistible passions which render certain actions no longer voluntary. Is it possible that in certain circumstances our acts are no longer free? Thomas distinguishes between the acts of the will itself, such as wanting something, and acts ordered by the will. With regard to this second group the will may suffer violence. For instance, someone may impede us by brute force from going somewhere. Acts of the will proper, however, proceed from our inmost interior and are not subject to violence from the outside. This is also Aristotle's position. "By **violence** we understand whatever has its origin outside us, that is, which proceeds from a principle without any cooperation whatever of the person who acts or suffers something"[6]. One may drag a person along by force, but if that person consents, there is no question of violence. Violence is directly opposed to the voluntary character of actions. It is a constraint forced upon us from the outside against our will. Consequently violence makes an action involuntary. But a degree of outside pressure, coinciding with what we ourselves want to do, would not be violence[7].

It is not so easy to assess the influence of **fear** on the voluntary character of our actions. Aristotle discusses the problem in the *Nicomachean Ethics,* III, ch. 1 and gives the classic example of the crew of a ship which during a storm is on the point of sinking. To save their lives and the ship the crew cast the merchandise overboard. This is done, because under the circumstances they want to do it, although, absolutely speaking, they do not want to lose the cargo. For this reason this type of action is partly voluntary, partly involuntary, in other words "mixed voluntary"[8]. Nevertheless acts of this kind are voluntary rather than involuntary, for one consents, even if it is for a reason one regrets.

In **article 7** the question is raised whether a violent **sensual desire**[9] can render actions involuntary. In the third objection Thomas quotes a text of Aristotle which says that pleasure and pain distort judgement about our actions[10], but in his answer he argues that desire renders an act voluntary rather than involuntary, for the reason that lust makes us tend to what we desire. Replying to some further difficulties Aquinas notes that sometimes the the will does not at first want a certain pleasure, but supervenient desire may then make the will strive for it. If a desire is so strong that one does not know any more what one is doing, then an action is no longer voluntary, since one's judgment is suspended. In other cases lust may not totally interrupt the work of the mind but only hinder the

---

[6] *Nicom. Ethics* III, ch. 1, 1110^{a}1.
[7] I - II, 6, 5.
[8] *Nicom. Ethics* 1110^{a}11: μικταὶ μὲν οὖν εἰσιν αἱ τοιαῦται πράξεις.
[9] The Latin term is *concupiscentia*.
[10] *E. N.*. VI, 5, 1140^{b}12.

formulation of a correct judgment about a concrete choice. Then, instead of this judgment, a different judgment is formed[11]. However, since the will can refuse to follow the desire for pleasure, its choice remains voluntary. Thomas stresses that an act is "voluntary" when one has the power not to perform it.

Is what is done in **ignorance** voluntary? (**article 8**). According to Aristotle something done under compulsion or in ignorance is involuntary[12]. If we do not have the knowledge required for an act to be voluntary, then the act we perform becomes involuntary. Aquinas distinguishes three cases which had been intimated but not clearly separated by Aristotle: 1) One does not know the consequences of what one does, but if one had foreseen them, one would nevertheless have performed the act. E.g., one did not know that in this particular state it is forbidden to throw used motor oil into the garbage can, but one would have done so all the same if one had known of the law which forbids it. 2) A second type is willed ignorance. One does not want to know about laws and regulations, so as to have an excuse to do certain things. 3) One would not have done something if one had known its consequences or that it was forbidden by law . This last type of ignorance renders an action involuntary.

The circumstances of human acts (Q. 7)

When discussing ignorance Aristotle also mentions the circumstances under which an act is performed, e.g. the fact that a woman with whom one has sexual intercourse is someone else's wife. To indicate what we call the circumstances he speaks of concrete actions (καθ' ἕκαστα). He considers the circumstances from the point of view of the voluntary character of our actions, such as an act done in fear. Ignorance about the circumstances of certain acts can render these acts involuntary[13]. The theory of the circumstances of human acts was further developed in classical antiquity, in particular in the schools of rhetoric. Nemesius uses the term circumstance to signify factors which are attached to the task or main action one is undertaking, such as throwing merchandise over board during a storm at sea[14]. Cicero lists seven circumstances which can be put into verse: "Quis, quid, ubi, quibus auxiliis, cur, quomodo, quando"[15] (Who, what, where, with what, why, how, when). Boethius also mentions the circumstances of human actions[16]. The study of the circumstances of human acts developed

---

[11] An example would be the judgment "I must stop drinking", replaced under the spur of desire by "One more glass will not impair my capacity for driving home by car ".

[12] *E. N..* III, ch. 1, 111p^{a}1. Cf. John Damascene, *De fide orthodoxa*, II, ch. 25.

[13] *E. N.,* III, 2, 1110^{b}33 ff.

[14] *De natura hominis*, ch. 29 (Verbeke and Moncho, p. 121, 6). The Greek term is περίστασις.

[15] *De inventione rhetor.*, I, ch. 24.

[16] *De differentii topicis*, IV : *PL* 64, 1212 - 1213.

further in the Middle Ages after the Fourth Lateran Council, canon 21, had prescribed that confessors must also pay attention to the circumstances under which certain sins were committed[17].

Thomas discusses the circumstances of our actions in connection with his treatment of voluntary and involuntary acts, inasmuch as he considers the circumstances as additional factors attached to every human act. He first explains what circumstances of actions are. The term is derived from the verb "to stand next to something", in the sense of surrounding it. We use, he says, words having a connotation of place to signify what is itself less known than place and local movement. Circumstances are factors which are external to our actions, but nevertheless determine them to a certain extent. What lies outside the substance of things is called an accident. In this way we call the circumstances accidents of human actions. In so far as they have to do with our actions they are also related to ourselves, either directly (such as the place where one does something or the condition of the person who acts) or indirectly through the act, as, for instance, the manner in which one does something. However, the circumstances do not ontologically determine the acting person, as do accidents like quantity or quality do[18].

The advantage of this approach is that only those circumstances are considered which may influence the moral character of our actions. Thus the type of gun with which one kills a person will usually be a circumstance which does not affect the morality of the act. What has no influence is not considered[19]. Occasionally a circumstance can change the specific character of an act, e.g. when sexual intercourse happens to be adultery. In fact, when a circumstance is directly opposed to what right reason considers good it may change the species of the act. Apparently one cannot without qualification apply to circumstances the comparison with accidents[20] (**article 1**). Aquinas notes that Cicero's view of the circumstances of our acts is not quite the same as that of Aristotle. After explaining the difference between these two accounts of circumstances he proceeds to enumerate them. A circumstance can concern the act itself, its cause or its effect. With regard to the act itself, a circumstance can refer to an external condition such as the time when and the place where the act is performed, or the manner in which it is carried out. With regard to the effects or the causes of actions, circumstances can concern the final cause, the material cause (sc. the ob-

---

[17] See Johannes Gründel, *Die Lehre von den Umständen der menschlichen Handlung im Mittelalter. Beiträge zur Geschichte der Philosophie und Theologie des Mittelalters*, Bd. 39, 5, Münster 1963.

[18] I - II, q. 7, a. 1 ad 2 and ad 3.

[19] The purely accidental is not a subject of scientific study. Cf. *Metaphysics* VI, ch. 2, $1026^b 3\text{-}5$.

[20] Cf. Thomas Nisters, *Akzidentien der Praxis. Thomas Lehre von den Umständen Menschlichen Handelns*, Freiburg - München 1992.

ject of the act) and either the main or the instrumental efficient cause. In this way Thomas takes over Cicero's list but adds the object *circa quod*, which Aristotle had mentioned[21], but which Cicero places under the "what" (**article 3**). In the *Quaestio disputata de malo*, q. 2, a. 6, he writes that one can also range the "what" (*quid*) under the *circa quod*. When one destroys someone else's work, one does not just destroy a material thing. One must also take into account what it means for this person (**article 3**).

Among the circumstances the "why" is most important because it concerns the relation of an act to its end. The "what" has the second place since it is what one does and determines the nature of the act. For instance, stealing sacred vessels, used for liturgical ceremonies, becomes a sacrilege[22]. In respect of the "what" as a circumstance, one must notice the difference from what is called the object of our acts, meaning what we have in mind to do. The "what" as a circumstance concerns the effect, i.e. that what brings about. If this hardly differs from what one has in mind, it does not affect the species of the act, e.g. stealing a large or somewhat smaller sum of money is the same kind of action (**article 4**).

How a free act originates (QQ. 8 - 17).

Having examined which acts are voluntary and which are not, and determined the role of the circumstances, Thomas now explains how a free act comes about. His explanations can be rendered schematically as follows:

Acts of the will	The corresponding acts of the intellect
Willing the good in general	Knowledge of the good in general
Intention (tending toward the good)	Application to a concrete situation
Consent	Deliberation
Choice	Judgement limiting us to one option
Execution	Command
Enjoyment	Accompanying knowledge

Eleven of these acts are discussed in questions 8 to 11. However, Aquinas does not treat them according to the chronological order in which they follow upon each other. He first examines the acts by which the will directs itself to a goal, sc. ordering itself to the good in general, enjoying it and tending to it. The same act of the will, he says, is directed to the good in general and turns to a concrete

---

[21] *E.N.* III, 1, 1111^{b}4 (τὸ περὶ τί).
[22] I -II q. 18, a. 10 ad 1.

good and rests in it when it is attained. After that he considers the acts which are related to what is ordered to the end, sc. choice, deliberation, the use of the faculties. Finally, Thomas deals with the acts executed by the will. At first sight this approach is somewhat surprising. Its advantage is that it brings out that in order to understand how a free choice comes about, one has to start arguing from the end which the will pursues. Thomas observes this order all through his ethical writings.

In questions 8 to 17 Aquinas has brought together material from the tradition, ordering it in a novel way. His way of treating this subject is not found in other authors. It clarifies the somewhat hidden zone of the mind where free decisions are prepared.

At a first glance the scheme above may seem complicated. Do we have to believe that a seemingly so simple a thing as making a decision to go shopping presupposes several acts of the will and the intellect? To understand better how a free choice comes about one has to consider that in the process of making such a choice a first and fundamental act of the will develops and unfolds itself in a series of subsequent acts. An example will illustrate what is meant. On a cold day St. Martin of Tours encounters a shivering beggar. His will is directed to the good in general and wants the good of this beggar while he himself knows that something must be done (second stage). He then considers what means to use (third stage), deciding to give the man part of his cape (fourth stage). This choice is executed and, satisfied with the result, St. Martin continues on his way.

The acts of will and intellect involved in a choice are distinguished, but rather than being isolated from each other they are mutually connected. Aquinas reminds us on several occasions that the intellect and will penetrate each other: the intellect knows and comprehends the will, while the will moves the intellect to be active[23]. Moreover, one must keep in mind that the first act of the will, by which it directs itself to the good, is so to say transformed into the acts of consent and choice. One may, indeed, speak of a dynamism of the will. The original act of the will is further determined, just as our concepts are progressive determinations of the first concept of being. For this reason, the successive acts take place, so to say, within the first, which is the will's inclination to the good.

As was observed, St. Thomas does not follow the genetical order of these acts but considers them from the point of view of the end to be reached and the means to be used, subsequently examining the intention and the execution of the act. The will directs itself first to the end and, next, wills the means, required to reach the end. Even if the end and the accompanying satisfaction are only reached later Aquinas deals with them first, since the other acts receive their meaning from the end as being ordered to it..

---

[23] *Q. d. de veritate*, q. 21, a. 3: "Voluntas et intellectus mutuo se includunt. Nam intellectus intelligit voluntatem et voluntas vult intellectum intelligere". Cf. I-II, 17, 3 ad 3: "... actus harum potentiarum supra seipsos reflectuntur".

What our will wills (Q. 8)

Willing the good is nothing else but the natural orientation of the will, which is ordered to the good. Directing itself to the good is as the bud from which the free act flowers. Thus this first act of the will is far from insignificant, as some say it is[24]. At this level there is not yet freedom of choice, but Thomas's concept of freedom is broader than that of freedom of choice and comprises also the spontaneous, naturally necessary orientation of the will to the good[25]. In whatever condition or state one is (during life on earth or in afterlife) one is free to will or not to will with regard to whatever object[26].

Freedom of choice is about things leading to an end. Since this ordering itself to the good in general is the fundamental inclination of the will, it is present in its every single act. Every striving is a striving for the good. The good is what is desirable in things, as based on their perfection. For this reason the "good" is not a tag attached to things by man, but is given with the riches of the contents of things. To direct oneself to the good is not a sign of greed, but an approval of the perfection of things, which pleases the will. The movement towards the good is, in a sense, the very nature of the will. The concept of the good in general, which the intellect places before the will, is abstracted from concrete things, e.g. from something which pleases the senses. In so far as it is general and abstract it is not yet an already realized good, but it determines the direction of all the inclinations of the will. An object presented as evil makes the will turn away from it[27] (**article 1**).

By virtue of its nature the will directs itself to the good which is its end. Since it wills the end it wants also the means needed for it (**article 2**). This raises the question whether by one and the same act one wants the end and the means. The answer is that one can will the end in a twofold way, sc. as such or in so far as it is the reason why we want the means. By the same act one wants to regain one's health and to use the necessary medicaments. In daily life willing the end often goes together with willing the means leading to it (**article 3**).

---

[24] This is the opinion of Jacques Leclercq, *La philosophie morale de saint Thomas devant la pensée contemporaine*, Louvain 1955, p. 300.

[25] *Summa contra gentiles*, III, ch. 138: "Necessitas ex interiori inclinatione proveniens... facit voluntatem magis intense tendere in actum virtutis... Quodsi ad finem perfectionis pervenerit, quandam necessitatem infert ad bene agendum, sicut est in beatis qui peccare non possunt; nec tamen propter hoc aut libertati voluntatis aliquid deperit aut actus bonitati".

[26] *Q. d. de veritate*, q. 22, a. 6.

[27] Thomas speaks of a *noluntas*.

What moves the will ? (Q. 9)

The argument of the previous question has shown that the movement of the will toward the good is of fundamental importance. But what sets the will in motion? In the previous question Thomas spoke of the primary movement of the will to the good. Now the question is asked, how do we explain (assuming that nothing moves itself[28]) that subsequently the will directs itself to some particular good. The question is discussed in articles 2 and following. At this point Aquinas notes only that the will as directing itself to an end moves the other faculties to their respective acts. This is obvious, since we use these faculties when we want to. The particular good, to which they are directed, is comprised under the general good which is the object of the will. The causal influence of the will on the other faculties is a form of efficient causality (**article 1**).

The object which the will seeks to attain is presented to it by the intellect. It determines the will as a formal cause. But this does not answer the question how, from the point of view of efficient causality, the will begins to move itself, for nothing moves itself. One might suggest that the sensitive appetite draws the will toward the desired object. However, since the will is an immaterial power (as is the intellect), the sensitive appetite cannot move the will as an efficient cause. Nonetheless, by pursuing an object which to the intellect appears as agreeable or fitting the sensitive appetite can, if the intellect presents this object[29], provoke an act of the will (**article 2**).

We know from experience that we want not only the end but also the means to attain it. In this sense the will moves itself from willing the end to willing the means (**article 3**). But this does not explain how the will, which at first was at rest, now actually wills something. If one were to say that the deliberation of the intellect leads to the choice of the means, one would not have solved the difficulty, since the will must already actually will this deliberation by the intellect. Since nothing moves itself there is no other solution left than that of an external mover of the will (**article 4**). Since the will is an immaterial power[30], that which moves it as an efficient cause, must itself be immaterial, since a cause and its effect must be adapted to each other[31]. This means that, contrary to what some astrologers say, the celestial bodies cannot exercise any direct influence on the human will (**article 5**).

The question concerning the origin of the acts of the will has not yet been answered. The acts of the will proceed from within the will. Apparently only the

---

[28] This well known axiom - one of the formulas of the principle of causality - plays an important role in metaphysics. In the light of the doctrine of actuality and potency its truth is evident.

[29] The intellect knows and presents the objects, but does not actually move things.

[30] St. Thoms notes that the will lies within the intellect ("voluntas est in ratione").

[31] Cf. the axiom that every agent produces an effect which resembles it.

Creator of human nature and of the human will can make the will actually will something. Moreover, when the will acts it is directed to the good in general. Only God, who is the universal good, can give the will such a movement to the good in general[32] (**article 6**).

On the mode of volition (Q. 10)

By virtue of its nature the will orders itself toward the good in one simple motion. Further acts of the will are derived from this first movement, since in all things that which does not belong *per se* to their nature is reduced to what belongs to them *per se*. The good which lies at the root of this first and the following movements of the will is that which for the will, for the other faculties and for a person as a whole is appropriate and good. This means that one does not want the good as the object of one's will alone, but as fitting to the other faculties, such as the knowledge of the truth, preserving one's life and other things of this kind. All this comes in under the object of the will (**article 1**). This natural movement of the will toward the good does not result from a physical determinism, such as gravity which causes heavy bodies to fall downward. It is an act which sets man's entire intellectual and volitive life into motion and expresses itself in free choice.

Article 2 examines the role of the object which the intellect presents to the will. In an earlier work Aquinas had argued that the root of the freedom of choice lies in the intellect[33]. This point was discussed at the university of Paris. Some Averroists at the faculty of arts attributed efficient causality to the human intellect[34]. Their opinion provoked a reaction on the side of those who tended to consider the will a faculty independent of the intellect[35]. In this article of the *Summa theologiae* Thomas clarifies his doctrine of the *De veritate* by distinguishing between performing an act (*exercitium actus*) and the intrinsic determination of an act by its object (*specificatio actus*).

With regard to its beginning to actually will something the will is not moved by any other power but itself. This is evident, Thomas says, since it is not necessary to continue to think of any particular object and so it cannot be necessary to will it. However, with regard to the influence of the object, there is only one object which determines the will necessarily. Aquinas means the vision of God,

---

[32] The theme of the causal influence of God on the intellect and the will is treated in philosophical theology.

[33] *Q. d. de veritate*, q. 24, a. 2: "Totius libertatis radix est in ratione".

[34] See R. Gauthier, "Trois commentaires averroïstes sur l'*Éthique à Nicomaque*", in *AHLDMA*, 16 (1947-1948), 187 - 336, p 199.

[35] This was the position of Gauthier of Bruges and Gerald of Abbeville. Gauthier argued that the will acts because it wants to use its freedom (*Quaest. disput.*, q. 4 ad 6 : ed. Longpré, *Les philosophes belges*, X, Louvain 1928).

the universal good, by the blessed. Since the will is inclined by its nature to the good, it is irresistibly drawn to God when the intellect sees God as the infinite good. The will cannot not will this object. However, limited goods are not willed necessarily by the will. The will is always specified by the good, even if some objects are only apparent goods[36].

In this connection there is also the question whether the sensitive appetite can move the will, as daily experience seems to suggest. Moreover, as the estimative power helps the intellect to form a judgment, must not the sensitive appetite help the will? Thomas first recalls what he had said before: the sensitive appetite exercises its influence only in so far as its object is presented to the will by the intellect. It happens, however, that a person is so much in the grip of a passion that he considers something a good which under normal circumstances he would not. If, under the influence of a passion, the intellect is fixated on a particular object to such a point that it can no longer deliberate then there is no freedom of choice. In other cases the will addresses itself to the concrete goods which are presented to it, but is not necessarily drawn to any of them (**article** 3).

At the end of the previous question Aquinas concluded that only God can move the will inwardly to its acts. At first sight it would seem that if God reduces the will from a potential state to actual willing he imposes necessity on the will, as the opponents of Thomas's doctrine object. The answer is that one must not look upon this divine motion as a sort of mechanical thrust, which is involuntarily imposed on the will. God moves the will in conformity with its nature, in the sense that under the causal influence of this divine motion the will moves itself freely and its act remains contingent. God can move it in this way, since his efficient causality comprises all modalities of reality and acts in the center of the will[37]. Even if the divine motion causes that the human will infallibly wills a particular thing, this does not make this act of the will necessary[38].

Joy and pleasure as acts of the will (Q. 11)

By its nature the will is inclined to the good. Its nature is to will the good. At the end of this road to the good the reward is joy in the good one has reached or acquired. At this point Aquinas mentions the term *frui* used so often by St. Augustine, who divides things into three classes: things which are good only in so far as they can be used; the persons who use them; goods, finally, which one

---

[36] With regard to the preceding passage one should compare the *Q. d. de malo*, q. 6, where Thomas writes that the object presented by the intellect to the will moves the will as a final cause, but that with regard to beginning to act the will moves itself. "Manifestum est quod voluntas movetur a seipsa ; sicut enim movet alias potentias, ita et seipsam movet".

[37] Cf. *In I Perihermeneias*, I, lesson 14, n. 197: (as a universal cause) "Deus profundit totum ens et omnes eius differentias".

[38] The theme is treated with more detail in metaphysics.

does not use, but enjoys[39]. We find joy in our last end when reaching it. The aim of reaching heavenly bliss is the basic yardstick of Christian morals. One enjoys something when attaching oneself freely to it in love as answering to our desires, as one enjoys eating the fruits of one's own garden which one has long been expecting[40]. This comparison suggests, in veiled terms, that a morally good life on earth is a preparation for the harvest of its fruits in the afterlife. Other things which are not our last end, may be used, but one should not set one's heart on them, as if they were that end. The enjoyment Aquinas is speaking about is an act of the will flowing from sincere love. Animals can enjoy the good only in an imperfect way, because they do not know the good as good and cannot direct themselves to it in a free act (**article 2**).

We can enjoy many things which each time are a terminus of our work and desire. However, in the most proper sense of the term our joy will only be complete when we reach our last end, since other goods we acquire are not the ultimate terminus of our desire (**article 3**).

One reaches one's final goal when this is present not only in one's thoughts and striving, but in reality. Total enjoyment is possible only when one has definitely reached the final end (**article 4**). What Thomas has to say about the enjoyment in the possession of our final end may seem to lack interest. However, he wants to point out that attaining our final end by acting morally will give us an overwhelming joy.

Intention (Q. 12)

In the survey of acts leading to a free choice the act called *intention* is the starting point of the preparation for a particular choice. However, the term intention is used in different senses. It can mean the attention with which one listens to something, but it can also signify the contents of concepts[41] and that which the author of a particular text intends to say. The term can also mean the power transitorily present in an instrument, when used by the main cause (*vis instrumentaria*) and, finally, an act of the will in so far as ordered to further acts. In the **first article** of the present question Thomas indicates that he is using the term in this special sense of directing oneself towards a goal. It is the task of the will to set the powers of the soul in motion. Said in this sense the intention is an act of the will directed to an end which must be reached with the help of certain

---

[39] *De doctrine christiana*, I, 3, 3; cf. I, 4, 4: "Frui enim est amore alicui rei inhaerere propter seipsam".

[40] Thomas connects the verb *frui* with *fructus*.

[41] See, for instance, *Q. d. de veritate*, q. 21, a. 5. This use of the term apparently originated from the Latin translation of the Arab word *ma'ná*, in Avicenna's works. See also *In II Sent.*, d. 38, q. 1, a. 3.

means. The act called intention presupposes the collaboration of the intellect[42]. The reason is that the will strives toward something as it is presented by the intellect. The intention is the link between simply willing the good in general and the act of the will which directs itself to a particular good that is to be attained by certain means[43].

The goal which is the object of the intention, is in many cases not man's last end, but an intermediate goal. In the example of St. Martin it is helping a beggar. When one directs oneself to such an intermediary goal, the will is always ordered to the good in general. When one directs oneself to several of these not-final ends, so that these are in a sense juxtaposed (doing a good job, seeking pleasure, cultivating friendships, being concerned with one's own health), are these particular intentions connected with each other? This will often be the case. If so, they will be inspired by one basic intention such as doing one's duty or seeking pleasure. At any rate, at the origin of all intentions there is the striving for happiness[44]. The more mature and older one becomes the greater the degree of cohesion of the will's different movements (**article 2**).

Is it possible for one intention to be directed to two ends? The answer is affirmative if these goals are ordered to each other and mutually connected. One and the same intention can concern our health and the medicines which might restore it. A somewhat different case would be when, for example, in buying a house one tried to reach different goals which are unrelated to each other, but are connected by our reason, such as the closeness to a subway station, good schools, a safe neighborhood, lower taxes and less noise[45] (**article 3**).

In an analogous way the will can direct itself by one and the same intention to the end and to the means. In certain cases, however, the end and the means are willed separately (**article 4**). From what has been said above we conclude that we form these intentions within the framework of the will's fundamental inclination to the good; the intentions are always directed to a goal. We can only form intentions because of the collaboration of the intellect with the will. Hence animals do not form intentions (**article 5**).

---

[42] *In II Sent., d. 38, q. 1, a. 5.*

[43] In the example we gave at the beginning of the chapter the intention is St. Martin's will to help a poor beggar.

[44] A. Kenny argues that Aristotle accepts the presence of other last goals besides our seeking happiness, for people do not seek happiness in all their undertakings. See his "Aristotle on Happiness", in *Proceedings of the Aristotelian Society*, 66 (1965) 93 -102. His opinion has been refuted in Chapter I.

[45] In this case the intention to buy a suitable house is in a latent way present in the later deliberations. Cf. *In I Corinthians,*, c. 14, lesson 3: "Vis prima, quae movet intentionem, manet in toto opere etiamsi aliquando in aliquo particulari divertat".

The choice of the means leading to the end (Q 13)

Aquinas now deals with the series of those acts of the will which concern the means leading to the end. While in the intention the will directs itself to a goal, the choice of the means leading to the end is a different act. Here the freedom of choice is actualized which consists in willing a determinate course of action relative to the particular good one is pursuing. Prior to this choice the will consents to the intellect's deliberation on the ways and means of reaching this good. Thomas discusses this acquiescence or consent in Q. 16, after having dealt with choice, apparently because the choice projects some light on the significance of consent.

The Latin word for "choice" or "decision" is *electio*, which corresponds to the term προαίρεσις coined by Aristotle in the *Nicomachean Ethics*. In *N.E.* III, ch. 4, he deals with some opinions of his predecessors on what we call choice. According to Aristotle willing, desiring or wanting something (βούλησις[46]) concerns the end, while choice is directed to the means needed to reach the end[47]. The early Christian authors thought that this solution was wrong, since they felt that a Christian chooses God, who, far from being a means, is the last end to which we must order ourselves. Thomas mentions this difficulty in the third article of our question.

Is choice an act of the intellect or of the will? Aristotle stresses the place of the will in our choices, but says that the intellect also plays a role[48]. However, an act (which is one reality) can only belong to one faculty and not simultaneously to two. Choice is a movement of the soul to one good, leaving aside other goods, and for this reason it must be an act of the faculty to which it is proper to want the good, sc. the will. Yet it remains true that it is the intellect which presents the object to the will. Furthermore the intellect directs an act to its end, so that a choice (as an act directed to a goal) receives its form from the intellect. Thomas calls the act of the intellect involved in making a choice a "statement" or "judgment"[49]. This judgment, accompanied by the choice, is the conclusion of a syllogism, sc. of a deliberation. In the example given above St. Martin deliberated how he could help the beggar and reached the conclusion that a good way to do so was to give the man half his officer's cape. So the judgment establishes which means answer best to what the will intends. Thomas says that the choice

---

[46] This is the personal, innermost inclination of man. See R.A. Gauthier and Y. Jolif, *L'Éthique à Nicomaque*, II, 1, Louvain - Paris 1959, p. 192.

[47] *E. N.* 1111^{b}26.

[48] *E. N.* 1139^{a}23: "Η δὲ προαίρεσις ὄρεξις βουλευτική (choice is a striving accompanied by deliberation)

[49] I - II , 13, 1 ad 2: "Conclusio syllogismi qui fit in operabilibus ad rationem pertinent, et dicitur sententia vel iudicium, quam sequitur electio. Et ob hoc ipsa conclusio pertinere videtur ad electionem tanquam ad consequens".

is consecutive to the judgment, although both are inseparably joined together[50]. This choice is a free act, since in it the will directs itself to a limited object, whereas as such it is ordered to the universal good and has a desire so vast that it cannot be satiated by the limited object of its choice. This freedom of choice means that the will is not necessarily bound to the object of its choice, but can also will something else (**article 1**).

The nature of choice is explained in greater detail in the next article. A choice expresses a certain desire. Animals also "desire" certain things. Do animals choose? The difference from what man does is that animals, placed at a particular moment before alternatives, are determined by their nature to this or that object, so that they do not choose. The sensitive appetite directs itself to something concrete: an animal seeks food when it is hungry, warmth when it is cold. Animals of the same species react in a similar manner. The human will, on the other hand, although it is necessarily directed to the good in general, is not bound at the level of a concrete choice to one particular object (**article 2**).

In the next three articles Thomas enquires what the object of our choices is. As was shown in the first article of our question, a choice follows upon the conclusion of a practical syllogism showing what one must do in order to reach a concrete goal. This goal comes first and is not the object of the choice. It is possible, however, that what in one situation is the end is considered a means in a different context. Aquinas gives the example of a person's health which for a physician is the goal to be attained, but may become, in other circumstances, the object of a choice between different possibilities. A chain-smoker may choose the pleasure he finds in smoking instead the care of his health. The same applies to the virtues which are ordered to man's temporal happiness, but can become objects of a choice when vices provide an alternative (**article 3**).

Is the object of our choices always a human act? We are reminded that choices are about what leads to the end. This end can be an activity or a thing (*res aliqua*). If the goal is a thing, there has nevertheless to be a human act to produce, use or enjoy it, as, for instance, a miser enjoys having his money. But whatever leads to a goal is either an action or something which one uses or produces in view of this goal. So it appears that a choice has always to do with actions (**article 4**).

In the course of our life we choose a huge variety of means to reach the goals we set for ourselves. Our choices are always concerned with what is possible. They have to do with actions one can perform. Moreover, one can never attain a goal with the help of something which is impossible. Deliberation, prior to a choice, would lose its meaning if the goal could not be reached. No one directs

---

[50] *L.c., Corpus articuli*: "Ratio quodammodo voluntatem præcedit et ordinat actum eius, inquantum scilicet voluntas in suum obiectum tendit secundum ordinem rationis, eo quod vis apprehensiva appetitivæ suum obiectum repræsentat".

oneself to what is impossible, unless perhaps in thought: "If it were possible, I would want it"(**article 5**).

A last question remains to be answered. If the end is the starting point of a chain of reasoning leading to a judgment and a choice, do not our choices become necessary like the inescapable conclusion of a syllogism? The question becomes even more complicated when one is placed before options of equal value. In such a situation do we still have to choose one object instead of the other(s)? The difficulty is solved as follows: we are able to choose and not to choose, we can want this particular thing or something else. As has been argued before, this is because that the intellect can present the act of doing something, but also of not doing it, as a good. It can also propose various options as desirable or as to be avoided. Only man's complete happiness cannot be presented by the intellect as defective or as bad. However, our choices do not concern perfect happiness. That explains why our choices do not regard perfect happiness, but concern limited and concrete goods. This answers the difficulties mentioned above. Where a particular means is not necessary to reach the end, its choice remains free. As regards a choice between two seemingly equal goods, one is likely to discern in one of them an aspect which makes it more attractive than the other good (**article 6**).

When during the Renaissance and afterwards individualism developed in the West people began to see their freedom as placed in opposition to the rule of the moral law. They believed that the obligations deriving from the law on the one hand and their personal freedom on the other were involved in a struggle in which each tried to dominate. Choice came now to be considered an entirely spontaneous act of the will which no longer depended on the intellect.

The deliberation which precedes a choice (Q. 14)

Among the acts which precede our choices deliberation (carried our with the consent of the will) occupies an important place. Thomas studies this deliberation after dealing with choice, since he believes that the choice throws light on its nature. Aristotle is the first to have discussed deliberation (βούλευσις)[51]. First he determines the object of deliberation. One does not deliberate about eternal and immutable things nor about what happens now in this way and next in another. We deliberate about what depends on ourselves. However, we do not deliberate about our goals but about the means to reach them[52]. Furthermore, a deliberation must be short. If one keeps deliberating and hesitating, nothing is

---

[51] *E. N.* III, ch. 5.

[52] *L.c.*, 1112^{b}11. St. John Damascene follows Aristotle and calls deliberation "appetitus inquirens de rebus agendis, quarum potestas penes nos est" (*De fide orthodoxa*, II : *PG* 94, 946 A).

going to happen. What after deliberation is seen as best or most convenient becomes the object of a choice[53].

In a first observation Aquinas says that at the level of concrete actions there is much incertitude. While scientific research and study have to do with existing things and with what follows necessarily from them, deliberation about what we should do often concerns what is uncertain and precarious[54]. Because of this the intellect only reaches a conclusion after deliberating and the will chooses what the intellect proposes. At this level it becomes clear to what extent the intellect and the will work together and penetrate each other. Aristotle calls choice willing something after deliberation[55] and St. John Damascene calls deliberation a desire which investigates[56] (**article 1**).

The precise object of deliberation must be further determined. Aristotle excluded from deliberation the goals one pursues. He was followed by Nemesius[57]. Indeed the goal we want to reach is the starting-point of a deliberation about the means needed to reach it. This is true when the end is something absolute, such as happiness, but even when it is a more limited goal, such as becoming healthy or rich. However, the latter goals can be compared with other values and in this way become a matter of deliberation. One may also deliberate about one's actions insofar as they are means to the end one has decided to pursue (**article 2**).

The word βούλευσις is rendered in Latin by *consilium*, a term which originally meant deliberation between several persons. St. Thomas argues that regarding what is necessary and general deliberation is much less needed than at the level of concrete actions, where the circumstances are changing all the time. Deliberation should help to bring the intellect to a proper insight (**article 3**). Do we deliberate about whatever we do? Experience shows that neither insignificant things nor what we do according to the norms of the sciences or the rules of the arts are the subject of deliberation. The sciences and the arts indicate the precise way in which one must do something, so that normally no special deliberation is required. (**article 4**).

How do we proceed in deliberating? If we begin our deliberation by considering the causes in order to evaluate their effects, we follow the method of increasing complexity (*modus compositivus*), since the causes are more simple than their effects. In analysis (*modus resolutorius*), on the other hand, we proceed from what is composite to what is simple, for instance, from the particular to what is more universal and from the effects to their causes. In the philosophy of nature and in metaphysics the latter method is used predominantly. Now deliberation starts from the end which will be reached only later on. Next we need

---

[53] *Ibid.*, 1113ª4.
[54] The comparison is borrowed from Nemesius, *De natura hominis*, c. 34.
[55] *E. N.* 1139ª23.
[56] *De fide orthodoxa*, I, c. 22.
[57] *E. N.*, 1112ᵇ11. Nemesius, *De natura hominis*, c. 34.

to determine what we must do for the sake of this end. This explains why in deliberations analysis is used. The various actions open to us are analyzed and evaluated with respect to their relation to the end[58] (**article 5**).

A great number of factors may be involved in a deliberation. Does this mean that one can go on deliberating without end? Thomas notes in which deliberation about a certain course of action is limited. On the one hand there is the goal about which one does not deliberate, but which is taken as the point of departure. On the other hand there are certain principles, rules and other data which one uses and about which one does not deliberate. Such are, for instance, the data of sense-experience (things one sees in one's surroundings, the materials one has to work with, the weather) and factors which play a role but do not depend on our own preferences. The rules of the practical intellect also come in under this heading, e.g., that one has to eat in order to keep alive or that adultery is to be shunned. Among different courses of action which present themselves we may be arrested by the first option which occurs to us as the most obvious one. We decides to choose it, and so deliberation ends. One could of course continue, Aquinas writes, without end in one's search for other possibilities (**article 6**).

Consent as the act of the will corresponding to deliberation (Q. 15)

Deliberation precedes the choice. This deliberation is accompanied and supported by an act of the will called *consensus*. Moral theologians use the term *consensus* to signify agreement with a sinful act, but Aquinas places consent before the choice, sc. the will agrees with the intellect as proposing something (**article 1**).

Since consent is about what has to be done, it is proper to man. Animals are not masters of their appetite, so that they cannot be said to consent to what a putative animal mind might propose (**article 2**). Consent concerns the things one is deliberating about, but not one's directing oneself to the end. By its very nature, as we have stressed, the will turns itself to our last end. Deliberation and consent result from our being directed to the end. They concern possible actions which may help us to reach the end (**article 5**).

Using the faculties to carry out a decision (Q. 16)

A choice is followed by our carrying out what we have decided to do, the will moving whatever other powers of the soul are concerned. One has for instance decided to go from Baltimore to Washington D.C., so one prepares a travel bag,

---

[58] One must keep in mind that deliberation concerns choice. But in ethics as a science general rules are applied to concrete acts and so the *modus compositivus* is used.

walks to the railroad station and buys a ticket. These acts are done under the influence of the will moving the different faculties. For we use our faculties when we want, and by the ensuing acts we intend to attain a good which falls under the object of the will[59]. When we are going to execute what we have decided to do, it is the task of the intellect to indicate the direction[60] (**article 1**).

As in the preceding parts of his treatise on human actions, Thomas also raises at this particular point the question whether animals are free as to the use of their faculties. At first sight the answer seems affirmative, since animals move by themselves. On closer inspection, however, it appears that only what exercises control over a faculty can make it act. Now animals move their members by virtue of a natural inclination, but not, it seems, because they have any awareness of ordering their members to certain activities (**article 2**).

But how far does the control of the human will over the faculties extend? Is it possible to "use" also the last end, in this sense that one directs it to something else? The answer is negative. One only uses those things which are ordered to something else[61]. Thomas nevertheless indicates in which sense one might be said to "use" the end. We must distinguish, again, between the object of our happiness and acquiring or possessing it. A miser wants money in order to possess it. Money is his last end but he considers it as ordered to his possessing it. In this sense one could say that he is "using" his last end (**article 3**).

Is the choice prior to the **use** of our faculties? This unexpected question provides an opportunity for clarifying the interconnection between the various acts involved in a free choice and its execution. The object of our will and our choice is present in the intellect while the will directs itself to it. But this presence of the object in our mind is still imperfect. As a result of its choice the will seeks to possess the object in reality. The use of the faculties follows on the choice . The choice becomes action at the moment one begins to act. One could perhaps speak of an earlier use of the soul's powers by the will in so far as from the very beginning the will makes the intellect become active. Likewise the will's use of the faculties in order to reach the object of one's choice can lead to a further choice of other things needed for it (**article 4**).

The acts commanded by the intellect and the will

Pursuing his explanations Aquinas now discusses the command which is the point of departure of the execution of a decision. The most important themes

---

[59] See above Q. 9, a. 1.

[60] I - II, 6, 1: "Unde manifestum est quod uti primo et principaliter est voluntatis, tanquam primi moventis, rationis autem tanquam dirigentis, sed aliarum potentiarum tanquam exequentium... ".

[61] In the *Sed contra* argument Aquinas quotes Augustine's words in *Quaestiones LXXXIII*, q. 30: "Deo nullus recte utitur, sed fruitur".

under discussion are what commands and what can be commanded. Q. 17 comprises 9 articles and is the longest question of the treatise on the human acts. Thomas argues first that the command is an act of the intellect, which presupposes an act of the will. His reason is that a command directs a person or a faculty to do something. However, directing one to something is the task of the intellect, but since it is a command which must be executed, the will which it is the moving power is involved. For this reason the command is an act of the intellect, presupposing an act of the will by virtue of which the intellect lets other faculties pass to the execution. This is another illustration of the collaboration and mutual penetration of the will and the intellect[62] (**article 1**).

Issuing a command is proper to the intellect. One does not find it in animals. It is true that the appetite moves different faculties but it does so by a natural urge and in this case one can speak only of commands in a remote sense of the word (**article 2**). In fact the execution of a decision and the use of the faculties to reach the goal follow upon the command. But one could say that in the deliberation preceding a choice the will is in a sense using the intellect and this moving or using of the intellect is prior to the command (**article 3**).

In a second group of articles of this question St. Thomas examines which acts of the intellect and the will can be commanded. He first inquires whether the command and the acts which are commanded form one act or are different acts. Referring to Aristotle[63] he writes that in the execution of a command the acts are only carried out by virtue of the command and therefore form a unity with it. The acts of the lower powers of the soul are determined by the command of the higher faculties and form one human act, just as an instrument and the main cause perform together one action. This remark shows to what extent our inner life forms a unity (**article 4**).

The command is an act of the intellect ordering something to be done. The command is addressed in the first place to the will. It commands the will to will and to do something. The intellect does not think just for itself alone but for the entire man and all his faculties. Man commands, as a thinking and willing being, the acts of the will[64]. However, these acts commanded by the intellect, are not the first act of the will which is given with the nature of the will in so far as it orders itself to the good (**article 5**).

Acts of the intellect itself can also be objects of a command, since the intellect can reflect on itself and pass from one act to another. Aquinas distinguishes between knowing an object and performing an act. Performing an act can always

---

[62] Thomas writes that in these cases "virtus prioris actus remanet in actu sequenti" and "virtute manet in ipso (intellectu) aliquid de actu voluntatatis".

[63] He quotes *Topica*, III, c. 2, 1117ª18: "Ubi est unum propter alterum, ibi est unum tantum". The Greek text says that when a good is appreciated because of something else, the two together are not more desirable than one of them alone.

[64] I - II, 17, 5 ad 2.

be commanded. With regard to the object, certain objects are known as immediately evident. Knowing them does not depend on us, as is the case with the things in our environment known through the senses, and with their perception by the mind. Here the intellect does not have to command anything. With regard to the mind's second operation, sc. making positive or negative judgments, the most basic judgments, sc. the first principles, are immediately evident. Their knowledge is not subject to any command. There are judgments, however, which are not totally evident and convincing, with which the intellect can accordingly refuse to agree. Such judgments can be subject to commands, the will being able to choose whether to assent. (**article 6**).

It is not so easy to determine to what extent one has command over the acts of the sensitive appetite. These acts often arise spontaneously, following as they do the impressions of the senses. The sensitive appetite is wholly immersed in the body and is partly dependent on bodily dispositions which are not subject to control by the mind. But in so far as the sensitive appetite is directed to objects present in the cognitive powers, in particular in the imagination, it is possible to control it to some extent, since the imagination is subject to the intellect. There are, however, movements of the sensitive appetite which arise suddenly as they follow immediately on the perception of some object. These movements escape control by the mind. Aquinas ends his explanations by quoting a text of Aristotle explaining that the dominion of reason over the sensitive appetite is not absolute, as that of a master over his slaves, but resembles the way political leaders exercise their power over free citizens, who can refuse to obey[65] (**article 7**).

In this connection Aquinas also raises the question whether the intellect and the will can exercise control over the vegetative functions of the human body. Nemesius denies that this is possible[66]. Thomas explains that these functions are activated by natural inclinations which do not depend on the cognitive faculties. Only those acts which are consecutive on what is in these faculties can be ordered and commanded by the intellect, but not the ones originating from the spontaneity of a natural impulsion. The further an act is removed from matter, the higher the order to which it belongs and so the more subject it is to the command of reason (**article 8**). Experience shows that we have dominion over the use of our limbs as, in a sense, instruments of our faculties. Those bodily movements which are caused by organic processes are not under the command of the intellect and the will. One may think here of our heartbeat, the movements of the lungs etc. Thomas also explains why the sex organs resist control by the mind to a considerable degree. They have a sort of life of their own, directed as they are to procreation (**article 9**).

---

[65] *Politica*, I, ch. 2, 1254^{b}5.

[66] *De natura hominis*, c. 22: "Id quod non persuadetur a ratione est nutritivum et generativum".

The argument of the preceding questions is important since it explains how our choices, which are susceptible of moral assessment, come about. We now pass to the discussion of the morality of our actions.

CHAPTER III

THE MORAL GOODNESS AND BADNESS OF HUMAN ACTS

In the previous chapter the choice of the means leading to the end was discussed as well as the execution of our choices. A choice is made in the light of our perception of the end we want to reach. Since human acts are voluntary, they are qualified as morally good or bad[1]. This takes us to the question of what makes actions good or bad, that is to the criteria of the morality of what we do. At the beginning of the Second Book of Plato's *Republic* two serious young men, Glaucon and Adeimantus, insist that Socrates show them that justice has a solid basis and does not rest on convention and custom, as many of their contemporaries believed. This question led Plato to develop his doctrine of the four cardinal virtues which help man dominate and order the irrational powers within him. The virtuous person acts with his eyes riveted to the idea of the Good[2] which is the model to which we must conform ourselves[3]. Man's supreme duty is to imitate the god[4]. But Plato also writes that we must discover the project which is implicit in our human nature[5], or, simply, that we must follow our nature[6].

Contrary to Plato Aristotle considers ethics a practical science, which does not aim at knowledge but at directing our actions[7]. He shows that human acts, the subject matter of ethics, are much influenced by circumstances. This means that a rigorous science of what one ought to do is not possible[8]. Actually opinions often differ as to how people should behave under changing circumstances. The law is always general and sometimes one has to apply the principle of equity and make an exception to the rule[9]. Aristotle does not speak about the influence of divine commandments on man's moral life, but he does say that the knowledge of God is the yardstick for acting morally and that we should live in conformity with what is highest in us[10]. Our acts are not predetermined by our nature and we must try to reach a balance: acting in the right way lies midway between too

---

[1] Cf. *In II Sent.*, d. 40, q. 1, a. 1: "... et quia actus sunt in genere moris ex hoc quod sunt voluntarii...".
[2] *Statesman* 297 A.
[3] Cf. Diogenes Laertius, *Vitae philosophorum*, III, 78.
[4] *Theaetetus* 176 A ff.
[5] *Ibid.* 172 B.
[6] *Laws* 836 C.
[7] *Nicomachean Ethics* 1095ª5.
[8] *E. N.* 1094ᵇ14 & 23.
[9] *E. N.* V, ch. 14.
[10] *E. N..* VIII, ch. 3.

much and too little[11]. Aristotle added other criteria, such as the behavior of a virtuous, well-educated person who is like a beacon for others to follow. Furthermore, a free and honest person is to himself his own rule of conduct[12]. In other places he speaks of "the eye of the soul", which becomes wise by the practice of the virtues[13]. He also mentions "the right rule" (ὁ ὀρθὸς λόγος), which shows what acting virtuously means. Our reason formulates this rule in agreement with the nature of things and on the basis of our experience[14]. The right rule is not a subjective criterion, but is based on objective facts[15]. Aristotle indicates several factors which determine or co-determine the moral character of our actions.

Epicurus had a different idea of what acting morally means. In his materialistic outlook the goal of man is pleasure, mainly in the sense of freedom from pain and mental anxiety. One must learn to be moderate in one's feelings, seek protection against the outside world and keep oneself aloof from public life, so that one's tranquillity is not disturbed (ἀταραξία). Virtue is subservient to this end and pleasure or delight is the ultimate criterion of our actions (κανών)[16]. In the strict sense of the term Epicureanism has no theory of morality[17].

Zeno, the founder of the Stoa, considered a life, in harmony with oneself under the command of reason as good (ὁμολογουμένως ζῆν). Cleanthes and Speusippus clarified this by understanding the words as meaning a life in agreement with nature, both nature in general and human nature in particular[18]. The Stoics distinguish between several natural inclinations, the first of which is directed to one's own preservation and one's development. There is also an inclination to associate with others which makes us adopt a humane attitude toward them. The good consists in the practice of the virtues, evil in what is opposed to it. Between these two extremes is the vast sector of indifferent objects which a good deal of our daily activities are concerned with. The virtuous life is a life according to the *logos* and manifests itself in the intrinsic coherence of our actions, in agreement with nature[19].

Jewish thought stressed the importance for our moral life of the commandments, given by God, but it added a great number of rules and prescriptions

---

[11] The idea of a balance between too much and too little is found is some treatises of the *Corpus hippocraticum*. See Theodore Tracy, *Physiological Theory and the Doctrine of the Mean in Plato and Aristotle*, The Hague 1969.

[12] *E. N.* III, ch. 6, 1113ª26 ff.; 1128ª32.

[13] *E. N.* VI, ch. 13, 1144ª30.

[14] *E. N.*. II, ch. 5, 1106ᵇ30.

[15] Cf. H. H. Joachim, *The Nicomachean Ethics*, Oxford 1951, 169.

[16] Diogenes Laertius, *o.c.*, X 129.

[17] See J. M. Rist, *Epicurus. An Introduction*, Cambridge 1972.

[18] See Stobaeus, II 75.

[19] See Max Pohlenz, *Geschichte einer geistigen Bewegung*, Göttingen 1947, 116 ff.

which deal with man's daily existence, ritual purity and the ceremonies of religious life. These mandates and rules helped to keep the "chosen people" together and to give it a strong awareness of its exceptional situation, but on the other hand many experienced these rules as suffocating freedom and as devoid of reasonable justification[20]. Confronted with this situation the apostle Paul stressed "the law of freedom" : if one allows oneself to be inspired and moved by the Spirit of God one will spontaneously and freely carry out the will of God. St. Augustine became the interpreter of this new attitude. In search of happiness the Christian acts out of love and complies willingly with what God wants him to do. His well-known saying, *dilige et quod vis fac*[21], is not meant to do away with the commandments but to promote an attitude by which we live spontaneously and in love according to God's commandments. The virtues are considered expressions and forms of our love of God[22].

At the beginning of the twelfth century Peter Abelard stressed the importance of the inner attitude with which one acts. The intention, he writes, is decisive for the morality of our actions. About the middle of this century Peter Lombard deals with this question in the second part of his *Sententiae*. Are our external actions good or bad on account of the intention of the will? The answer is affirmative when by intention we also denote the means to be used[23]. In his treatise on the moral quality of our actions Aquinas, instead of speaking of "intention" and of "the means", divides acts into internal and external acts and studies very carefully the various aspects of the question of what determines that human acts are good or bad, as the case may be.

On the goodness and badness of our actions in general (Q. 18)

While Question 18 deals with the goodness and badness of human acts in general, the next two questions treat the goodness and badness of internal, respectively external actions. Question 18 comprises eleven articles, which shows that we have to do with a complex issue. The first four articles consider the main factors which are decisive for the morality of an act. The following articles deal with more particular themes. Does the goal one seeks to reach determine the moral value of what one is doing? Are some acts neither good nor bad? Do the circumstances sometimes change the moral quality of our acts?

Question 18 is of fundamental importance, since Thomas is passing now from the ontological to the moral order. The **first article** introduces us to this problematic by raising the question whether there are any bad actions at all. To act

---

[20] See Raymond L. Weiss, *Maimonides' Ethics. The Encounter of Philosophy and Religious Morality*, Chicago 1991, 75.

[21] *In Epistulam Ioannis ad Parthos* VII, 8 : *PL* 35, 2033.

[22] *De moribus Ecclesiæ* XV, 25.

[23] *Sententiæ* II, dist. 40.

seems to be something positive and to presuppose a certain perfection. An action means that one has actualized a faculty and enjoys an activity and has reached a certain fulfilment[24]. However, the view that every action is good is contradicted by a quite general opinion that certain actions are bad. To solve this difficulty St. Thomas compares "good" and "bad" as said of actions with good and bad in existing things. There is a relationship between them, since actions are performed by the acting subject and each agent effects something which resembles him. Now if something is affected by evil, then it will lack something of the perfection of its being. To be deprived of sight is an evil, although the person who is blind still possesses considerable ontological goodness. If we apply this to human actions, it appears that an action can be ontologically good but be called bad in so far as something is lacking which it should have had[25]. One should notice, however, that what constitutes the moral character of a bad action is not simply the privation of something which should have been there but that the act was not performed according to right reason. Not nature but reason constitutes the moral order. Reason does so in that it deduces from human nature (also in its social dimension) what one should do. This solves the difficulty raised at the beginning of the article.

The comparison of the moral goodness of our acts with ontological goodness is explained further in **article 2**. Goodness is given with the plenitude of being; things are in some respect bad, when something is lacking. Now the first factor which determines the being of things and their perfection is their essential form. Man's essential goodness consists in being a rational animal. The same applies to our actions. Their nature is determined by the object to which they are directed or are concerned with. To construct a house is determined by building it, writing in making marks. In natural processes defects sometimes occur. A monster is born, because there was a defect in the process of generation. In the case of man, actions are defective when their object, which determines them intrinsically, is at variance with right reason, as is the case when one takes what belongs to someone else. The object is the subject matter the act is concerned with, as considered from a particular point of view. In our example it is a thing, over which another has property rights which must be respected[26]. This means that

---

[24] Aquinas refers to the principle that nothing acts unless being in act. A thing which is in the state of potency, does nothing. In the existentialism of Jean-Paul Sartre morality is held to be the same as being active. Cf. *L'existentialisme est un humanisme*, p. 55: "L'homme n'est rien d'autre que la somme de ses actes".

[25] I - II, 18, 1: "(Actio) dicitur mala, puta si deficiat ei vel determinata quantitas secundum rationem, vel debitus locus vel aliquid huiusmodi".

[26] Bañez points this out in his commentary on I - II, q. 18, a. 2, dubium 1: "Videtur quod obiectum actionis humanae est res illa circa quam versatur actio sub aliqua ratione formali, v.g. obiectum homicidi est homo non absolute, sed ut prohibetur occidi lege naturali, et ita habet rationem obiecti moralis; obiectum furti est res aliena ut prohibita usurpari ab alio"

the object is more than the material thing the action is concerned with, it is this thing as seen by reason in the light of our obligations[27]. When one considers the object by itself, one can feel inclined to think of it as morally neutral. In reality, however, things are placed in a certain position or situation with regard to reason and the natural law. There are also acts which because of their very nature are intrinsically good or bad, because they are concerned with what is necessary for our life[28]. To nourish oneself or to go on a hunger strike belong to this. The determination of the object by reason is not a subjective evaluation, but rests on objective facts. An act is good or bad according as it is ordered to this or that object. This should be understood correctly. Actions which, seen from the outside, seem entirely the same, such as firing a weapon at a human being in different circumstances, may have quite different objects: criminal murder, justified self-defense, the protection of innocent life by neutralizing a dangerous criminal. Thomas calls this being ordered to the object and being determined by it the *substantialis forma*, the essential form of the act[29]. He does not mean the physical structure of the actions. He explicitly says that the object is the *materia circa quam*, that with which the act is concerned and which gives it its specific determination[30]. The object does this in so far as the act is intrinsically ordered to it and is determined by it[31].

Existing things such as living beings and the products of human activity receive their perfection not only from their objects but in part also from additional determinations, such as the state of their organism, their external form, the condition of their faculties. If one of these is defective, its bearer is imperfect or, in this respect, even bad. St. Thomas explains this in the **third article,** applying it to human acts. Here too, besides the acts being ordered to their object, which is fundamental for their goodness or badness, there are accidental determinations which influence the moral qualification of the acts. If some accidental determinations are defective the acts themselves become defective or bad. What is meant are the circumstances of actions, mentioned in the previous chapter, such as who is acting, when and where one does something, etc. The circumstances of

---

(quoted after Th. C. Belmans, *Le sens objectif de l'agir humain,* Città del Vaticano, 1980, p. 255, n. 10). To denote the object Thomas uses such terms as *res, materia, obiectum, terminus vel finis.* Later authors introduced the term *finis operis,* not to be confounded with the *finis operantis,* which is discussed in article 4.

[27] *Q. d. de malo,* q. 2, a. 4 ad 5: "Actus autem moralis... recipit speciem ex obiecto secundum quod comparatur ad rationem".

[28] *S. C. G.* III, 129: "Sunt igitur aliquae operationes naturaliter homini convenientes, quae secundum se sunt rectae et non solum quia lege positae".

[29] I - II, q. 7, a. 4 ad 3.

[30] I - II, q. 18, a. 2 ad 2: "Obiectum non est materia ex qua, sed materia circa quam; et habet quodammodo rationem formae inquantum dat speciem".

[31] *Ibid.,* ad 3: "Et ita ipsa proportio actionis ad effectum est ratio bonitatis eius".

our actions lie outside the essential moral qualification by the object and are accidental determinations of the acts, but they are nevertheless intimately connected with them. Thomas compares this connection to the relation of the so-called *per se* accidents[32] with the essence of things[33] or that of the transcendental properties such as "unity", "truth" and "goodness" to being[34]. The *per se* means that there is no human act without these accidental circumstances, even if the individual circumstances are each time different. Since our acts are necessarily always performed under definite circumstances, the study of the latter has its place in ethics, while accidents belonging to the physical order are not considered[35].

The object of the acts as studied in the second article determines the essential goodness or badness of what we do. In **article 4** Aquinas examines the influence of the motive or the purpose one has when performing an act. The motive or purpose differs from the object as can easily be shown by some examples. One steals money in order to buy a luxury car. We render a service to a person to show our gratitude for what he or she did for us. The goodness or badness which comes with the purpose, is added to that derived from the object. In his treatment of the problem Aquinas presupposes that things are related to their goodness, as they are to their being. Certain things do not depend on others in their existence, so that one can study them by themselves. But there are also things which depend in their being on others. In order to study them, one must consider them in their relation to the things on which they depend. The being of things depends on their efficient cause and on their form, but the goodness of things depends on the end they attain. For this reason human acts, in addition to the absolute goodness which is proper to them, are also called good because of their relation to the end. Aquinas concludes this discussion by speaking of a fourfold goodness of human acts. In the first place, actions have an ontological goodness, as actions In the second place, they possess an essential moral goodness, depending on their object. Next there is an additional goodness (or badness) depending on the circumstances surrounding the acts. Finally, actions have a goodness depending on the goal or end one pursues by them, which is in a sense the cause of their goodness. However, the goal which one seeks to reach is sometimes not a real but only an apparent good. In this case an action directed to such a goal becomes bad. It happens that actions lack one of the four modes of

---

[32] With regard to this term cf. *Q. d. de veritate*, q. 2, a. 7; *In III Metaph.*, lesson 2.

[33] To be able to laugh is a property which belongs *per se* to man's rational nature (cf. *In VI Metaph.*, lesson 3).

[34] I - II, q. 18, a. 3 ad 2: "... sed quaedam sunt per se accidentia quae in unaquaque arte considerantur. Et per hunc modum considerantur circumstantiae actuum in doctrina morali".

[35] I -II, q. 18, a. 3 ad 2. The difficulty which is raised refers to *Metaph.* V, ch. 2, 1026^b4 (no art deals with the per accidens).

being good, for instance when an act which as such is good is directed to a wrong end. An act is not really good unless it is good in every respect[36].

By treating the end by itself, and not as one of the circumstances Thomas follows a different path from other philosophers of his time[37]. What is the point precisely in giving such a particular place to the end? Th. Belmans suggests that in this passage Aquinas has in mind man's last end, sc. God who is the first cause of the goodness of created things[38]. But the answers to the objections as well as a careful analysis of the interconnection of the themes of the entire treatise point in a different direction. What Thomas has in mind are the different subordinated goals one may have when performing an action. These goals will often deserve praise, e.g. to go shopping in order to be able to prepare dinner, helping a poor beggar, carrying out one's daily work, but sometimes they are morally bad as, for instance, to be kind to elderly persons, in order to be able to lay hands on their money.

After having examined what determines the moral qualification of our acts, Thomas discusses some special questions. The first is about the relation of human acts as predicamental accidents to their moral quality. Is an action such as stealing a valuable painting from a museum essentially a physical act, to which the label "theft" is attached? Or is theft a specific act of its own? In other words, does the moral qualification of the act absorb its physical aspects? (**article 5**). The contemporaries of Aquinas opted in favor of the first view: moral goodness or badness are no more than accidental determinations of physical acts[39]. St. Thomas, however, holds the other view, arguing that every act receives its essential determination from its object, as was explained in the second article of this question. Therefore, certain differences with regard to the object will cause a specifically different act[40].

The "difference in the object" Aquinas is speaking about is a difference in the object as it is presented by the intellect (in collaboration with the senses). If a

---

[36] In his answer to the third difficulty St. Thomas quotes the axiom formulated by Ps. Dionysius, *De divinis nominibus*, c. 4: "Bonum causatur ex integra causa".

[37] Albert the Great, *In II Sent.*, dist. 36, a. 6 (Borgnet, 27, 391 f.) considers the end as one of the circumstances.

[38] *O.c.*, p. 90. Belmans thinks that the last lines of the article support his interpretation, sc. : "Quarta (bonitas) autem secundum finem quasi secundum habitudinem ad causam bonitatis". The expression "causa bonitatis" which according to Belmans would refer to God, is repeatedly used by Aquinas to denote a created cause. Cf. I-II 20, 3 arg. 3 ("bonitas actus interioris est causa bonitatis actus exterioris") and *In II Sent.*, d. 40, q. 1, a. 3 ("actus interior et actus exterior voluntatis hoc modo comparantur ad invicem quod uterque est quodammodo alteri bonitatis causa").

[39] This opinion was carried to its extreme by William of Ockham, who considered good and evil as entirely external qualifications of our acts.

[40] Aquinas writes "a certain difference" (*aliqua differentia*), meaning *some*, but not *all* differences. The size of a painting stolen will not cause a specific difference.

thief selects a small painting, so that he can more easily smuggle it out of the museum, such a difference does not change the essence of the thief's act and is called a *differentia per accidens*, while in this context we mean a difference *per se*[41]. Having made this rather technical distinction Aquinas states his thesis: good and evil in human actions result from the essential (*per se*) relation of their object to the intellect. The reason is that the intellect, our rational nature, determines our specific being. What agrees with our rational nature, sc. with our essential form, and therefore with reason, is good, what is at variance with reason is bad. From the wording of the text, sc. the stress on the agreement with one's essential form (*quod conveniat ei secumdum suam formam*), it appears that Aquinas does not see the intellect as reasoning *in abstracto* but as one with human nature. It receives its insights from man's natural inclinations and from further deliberation. The will, as informed by the virtues, provides support.

The thesis proposed in this article is of the greatest importance. Our actions become human or moral acts in so far as they depend on the intellect. A text from Dionysius, often quoted by St. Thomas, illustrates what he says: "The good of man consists in being in agreement with reason, bad is what deviates from it"[42]. Since every human act has an object presented by the intellect, every act has a moral quality. This doctrine clearly shows the intellectual character of Aquinas's ethics mentioned in the introduction[43].

Does not what Thomas writes here about the role of the intellect undermine the comparison with nature? For instance, evil in natural things does not make them belong to a new class of beings, different from that in which it is inherent as a privation, while bad moral acts constitute new classes of acts. - The answer is that even in nature a privation sometimes causes a change of species. A living person and a corpse are specifically different. Moreover, an immoral action is not entirely empty, i.e. without any object. It has an object which is at variance with right reason. The object of an act is what one has in mind to do, such as to take away what belongs to another person. Circumstances may sometimes cause the object to change in species. Adultery has a different object from intercourse which someone not bound by marriage. So acts which belong to the same natural class, can differ in respect of their moral specification[44].

---

[41] Thomas gives the example of colours and sounds which for the senses are different objects, but for the intellect are accidents of the same class.

[42] *De divinis nominibus*, c. 4: "Bonum hominis est secundum rationem esse, malum autem quod est præter rationem". See also *S.C.G.*, III, c. 3: "Moralium autem mensura est ratio".

[43] In *In II Sent.*, d. 40, q. 1, a. 1 Aquinas writes that the end gives the act its specific character. This does not stand in opposition to what he writes about the role of the object. What agrees with right reason is ordered to the end of man.

[44] I - II, q. 1, a. 3 ad 3: "Nihil prohibet actus qui sunt idem secundum speciem naturae, esse diversos secundum speciem moris et e converso".

If the object of an act determines its moral character, what shall we say of the end? Does one have to consider it a secondary circumstance of acts? (**article 6**). At first glance the answer seems affirmative: totally different actions can be directed to the same end. But Aquinas gives a different explanation. The will moves the intellect to deliberate about executing an action in order to reach a goal. One looks for convenient food in order to stay healthy and gain strength. To eat food is one external action[45], acting in view of the end - one's health - is a different act. The end the will pursues is more decisive and, in a way, penetrates the external action. Thus Aristotle writes that who commits adultery to gain a sum of money is unjust rather than licentious[46]. The act of the will lets the external action share in its moral character. The external actions have indeed their own specific character, but derive their general moral value from the end, which is their cause[47]. What Thomas is saying here does not contradict what he wrote in the second article of this question (the object determines the moral value of acts), since the end pursued by the will is the object of the will[48].

However, the relation of the object of an action to the end which one pursues must still be further determined. Does the specification by the end fall under that by the object or is the opposite the case? (**article 7**). This question is not without importance when one must determine the moral quality of actions. In his answer Thomas distinguishes between acts the objects of which are by themselves ordered to the end (cooking a meal is directed to eating the food) and acts where this is not the case (e.g., stealing money in order to buy drugs). In the latter case one commits two sins in one action. As Aquinas writes in his answer to the first objection, regarding its moral character an action may sometimes belong to two different classes[49].

Coming back to the first case, viz. the object of an action being ordered to its end, we must still determine whether the specification by the object falls under that by the end, or if the opposite is the case. In his answer Thomas says that the object is what determines the moral character of an act, because when dealing with the specification of things the form which more precisely determines them, is decisive. The word "tiger" denotes a huge, striped and cat-like being better than "predator". Since the end is more general, it is less precise. This holds the more, the further the end is removed. To steal in order to drug oneself must be characterized stealing.

---

[45] "External" in this connection means outside the will itself as a faculty.
[46] *E. N.* V, c. 4, 1130^{a}26 f.
[47] II - II, 11, 1 ad 2.
[48] "Ita actus interior voluntatis accipit speciem sicut a proprio obiecto".
[49] "... Actus qui secundum substantiam suam est in una specie naturae, secundum conditiones morales supervenientes ad duas species referri potest". An example illustrates this: the same apple may belong to the class of yellow-red objects with regard to its color, but as concerns its fragrance it belongs to a different group.

This conclusion does not contradict what was said in the previous article, sc. that the goal of the will is more determining and, in a sense, penetrates the external act. According to article 6 one who commits adultery to gain money is unjust rather than licentious. In this case, the will determines the external act's moral nature. What was argued there is valid inasmuch as the goal pursued by the will is more general and, therefore, less determined and more fundamental[50]. One can illustrate it by the example of virtuous acts performed out of love of God. These acts remain acts belonging to particular virtues, such as justice or prudence, but they are sustained and inspired by the love of God and in this sense they fall under the virtue of charity. This shows how subtle Aquinas's analysis is and how precisely he gives expression to our experience as well as to people's common conviction.

So far the moral characterization of our acts has been examined from the point of view of their objects and circumstances and of the ends pursued by the will. Thomas now deals with the question whether every action is good or bad in its kind, or whether there are indifferent acts. According to the Stoics there are good, indifferent and bad beings[51]. Indifferent things lie outside our mind, they are the things we can use or which we need in order to stay alive and do our work. Actions aimed at these objects must be called indifferent, i.e. without interest with regard to our real happiness. Among the Christian authors St. Jerome calls such bodily functions as sneezing morally neutral[52]. He was followed much later by Duns Scotus who considers these actions indifferent, because no law tells us anything about them[53]. However, Thomas does not even mention these kinds of bodily movements, since obviously they do not belong to what he defined as human acts. His account takes as its starting-point the relation of the object of an act to the intellect. When the intellect considers something as in agreement with right reason it is good; if not, it is bad. One should notice the difference of this approach from Scotus' appeal to the law. But some actions do not depend on an insight or deliberation of right reason. Examples are picking up a branch or walking without a special purpose in a field. As to their nature these acts are morally neutral. Such acts are human acts, even if the level of consciousness or motivation with which we perform them may not be particularly high. One wants to pick up something or to enter a meadow, but these acts have no immediate relation to the end of our life. Quite a number of actions are of this kind, such as buying unnecessary objects, going to a random vacation

---

[50] Ad 3: "Et secundum hoc genus est causa speciei. Et tanto erit formalius quanto communius".

[51] Cf. *Stoicorum veterum fragmenta*, III, 122 (= Diogenes Laertius, *Adversus Mathematicos*, XI, 59).

[52] *Epistula* 89.

[53] *Oxon.* II, dist. 4, n. 3: "... super quod nulla lex aliquid disponat, id est nec praecipiat, nec vetet, imo nec consulat quod factu expediens sit".

destination, chatting without saying anything of significance, ranging one's books according to their size. One may assume that as people grow older, they become more purposeful in what they do and less inclined to silliness.

Aquinas explains why it is possible for some actions as regards their kind, to be neither good nor evil, by drawing a comparison with a bodily condition. Thus a person may not be not very healthy, but not be sick either[54]. Even if all actions possess an ontological goodness, they do not always possess moral goodness as far as their specific nature is concerned (**article 8**).

The previous article considered actions as such, without reference to the intention of the acting person. A next question is whether concrete, individual acts as such can be indifferent. In Thomas's day this matter was much debated. Bonaventure mentions an opinion which holds that there are no concrete morally neutral acts. This opinion, he thinks, depends on the doctrine of St. Bernard who says that we must give account of every moment of our lives and that, therefore, every single act should be directed to God. But this goes too far, Bonaventure says. There are actions which are not disorderly and bad, although they are not directed to God. They are morally indifferent[55]. However, Bonaventure seems to consider the problem only from the view point of the meritoriousness of our actions.

What was established in the first articles of this question is now applied by Aquinas to the present problem. Not only the object, but also the circumstances, determine the morality of actions. It is unavoidable that every individual act by its circumstances is drawn to the class of either good or bad acts, at least according to the intention of the acting person. The reason is that it is proper to reason to order things. Now an act performed after deliberation will be directed to an end, which will be either good or bad. There is no intermediate solution. Actions which do not proceed from deliberation, such as rubbing one's hands, are not human acts in the strict sense of the term. On the other hand, each act performed with due deliberation agrees with the good of one or the other of the virtues or proceeds from some vice[56].

Medieval theologians wrestled with a problem that had already been formulated by St. Augustine. How do we evaluate, from a theological point of view, acts performed without relation to the supernatural order? One cannot just call them bad, but on the other hand, it was said, they are not good either. Aquinas indicates where to find the solution, sc. by means of his doctrine of the analogy between the natural and the supernatural end of man. Each goal chosen after right deliberation by the intellect is directed to the good at which the virtues are

---

[54] Ad 1: (talis privatio) "non totum bonum aufert sed aliquid relinquit. Unde potest esse aliquid medium inter bonum et malum".

[55] *In II Sent.*, dist. 41, a. 1, q. 3.

[56] See our study "La théorie scotiste de l'acte indifférent et sa critique par Cajetan", in L. Elders, *Autour de Saint Thomas d'Aquin*, tome II, Bruges - Paris 1987, 95 - 106.

aiming[57]. If a person takes good care of his bodily health, he directs himself to the good sought by a virtue. This kind of actions, performed at the level of natural life, must be called good, even if they are directed only potentially to man's supernatural end[58].

According to Aristotle a person who squanders his belongings does not do anything wrong, because he uses his own money and does not harm others, but in his answer to the second difficulty Aquinas notes that any type of conduct that deviates from right reason is wrong[59] **(article 9)**.

Article 9 shows that an action which as such is morally neutral becomes good or bad by being directed to a goal. In this connection a new problem appears: can circumstances determine the morality of actions? This seems difficult to maintain if the object gives acts their species. Moreover, circumstances are like accidents and accidents do not make up the essence of substances. Finally, there are several circumstances, whereas the essence of acts is only one. In his answer Aquinas argues that natural things belong to one species and that one cannot go on adding each time new determinations[60]. But at the level of the mind this is different, since the intellect can consider the object present in it each time from a different angle. In many cases this will not cause a new specific difference in the object, but sometimes a circumstances adds something new, as is the case when one has sexual intercourse with a person already bound by marriage, or when one steals things used in the liturgy[61]. A circumstance which in other situations is accidental in these cases adds a further determination to the object, so that a new species results: what originally was a circumstance, is now part of the object. However, it scarcely happens that two circumstances both determine one object, giving it each a different species. Nevertheless, Thomas does consider it possible that when considered morally one action will belong to more than one species **(article 10)**. In most cases, however, a circumstance will not change the object of an act. A theft remains a theft whether one steals much or little. But circumstances may make immoral acts worse or, on the contrary, give good acts a greater moral value **(article 11)**.

---

[57] Cf. *In II Sent.*, dist. 40, q. 1, a. 5 ad 3: "Omnis actus in aliquod bonum tendens, nisi inordinate in illud tendat, habet pro fine bonum alicuius virtutis eo quod virtutes sufficienter perficiunt circa omnia quae possunt esse bona".

[58] This is stated by Thomas in his reply to the third difficulty.

[59] Thomas stresses the point: "Nos autem hic dicimus malum communiter omne quod est rationi rectae repugnans".

[60] The principle is: "Natura determinata est ad unum".

[61] Thomas writes that theft in a church or chapel "addit specialem repugnantiam ad ordinem rationis". It may happen, however, that a thief does not see any difference from stealing in a profane environment.

The goodness or badness of internal acts of the will (Q. 19)

After these general considerations Aquinas investigates what determines the goodness or badness of the inner acts of the will (Q. 19), before considering the morality of our external actions.(Q. 20).

As was argued above the will inclines towards the object which the intellect presents to it as to its good. At times it happens that this object, while good in certain respects, is contrary to right reason, when taken as a whole and therefore bad. As what is true and not true form the proper object of the intellect, so good and evil are the objects to which the will directs itself. What is good is contrary to evil. In this way specifically different moral acts result in accordance with the object presented. An object not conformed to the right judgment of the intellect is wrong. The will acts badly when choosing it (**article 1**).

We must even go so far as to say that whether the will is good or bad depends only on its object. The will is the foundation and first principle of the morality of what one does. A first principle, however, is simple and not composite[62]. For this reason this first principle can only be the will in its most simple form, sc. as determined by its object. The goodness deriving from the object is the same as the goodness coming to the act from the end, mentioned previously. In the case of the acts of the other faculties the goodness deriving from their objects must be distinguished from that coming to the act from the end pursued.

Aquinas is to such a point convinced of the priority of the acts of the will over the actions of the other faculties and of the will not being exposed to other influences that he even writes that, when the choice of the object (the goal) is right, no circumstance can make it bad. If one objects that one can want to do something that as such is good but at the wrong time, so that this circumstance will make the decision bad, then Aquinas replies that in such a case the will has chosen an object which is not right, sc. to do something at the wrong moment (**article 2**).

The object determines whether an act of the will is good or bad. However, the object does not float down to the will all by itself, it is presented by the intellect. Therefore, in the following articles Thomas considers what makes the object good or bad. The intellect presents the object to the will and so the moral quality of the act of the will depends on the intellect. A difficulty arises however: Aristotle writes that the goodness of what the practical intellect proposes depends on its agreement with right appetite[63], whereas here St. Thomas seems to say the opposite. The explanation is that the intellect acknowledges the fundamental in-

---

[62] The composite has a cause outside itself which brings about the composition, since nothing can put itself together. For this reaason what is simple is first.
[63] *E. N.* VI, ch. 2, 1139ª29 ff. : ὁμολόγως ἔχουσα τῇ ὀρέξει τῇ ὀρθῇ.

clinations of human nature and so the end it proposes to the will is given with human nature. With regard to the means to be used, the intellect must show which of them lead to the end and which do not[64] (**article 3**).

It follows that the intellect does not determine the goodness or badness of the objects without a criterion, since it gives expression to the most fundamental inclinations of human nature[65]. In doing so it formulates the basic principles of moral life, in other words, the natural law[66]. In the **fourth article** of this question these principles are said to rest on God, who is the creator of human nature and the source of order in the world. As will be explained in Chapter IX the order in the world, is called the eternal law (*lex aeterna*). To a certain extent our reason can know this eternal law, but it can also be made known by divine revelation, e.g. the biblical Ten Commandments. While Aquinas stresses the role and responsibility of the human mind, he also refers to the background and the source of our knowledge of the moral law. To illustrate its source he frequently quotes *Psalm* 4, 7: "Some people say, 'who will show us what is right?'. The light of your face has shone before us, Lord". Apparently when defining the end and determining which means lead to it man's reason shares in God's wisdom.

When the intellect presents the object as the good which the will must choose, a further difficulty arises. Our intellect can be mistaken. Certain people consider legitimate what others reject. **Article 5** examines the question of the intellect reaching a wrong judgment, in other words, of an erroneous conscience. Medieval views about **conscience** depended on texts of the ancient philosophers and, to a considerable extent, on Holy Scripture, in particular St. Paul. The Apostle speaks above all of what is called the antecedent conscience, which tells us what we ought to do or not to do. He also mentions the erroneous conscience. A text of St. Jerome, who connects conscience with the so-called *synderesis*, also exercised a considerable influence on medieval authors[67]. In St. Thomas' time views about conscience differed. Many considered it a *habitus*, that is a lasting disposition to an act. Others believed conscience to be a faculty with its own acts. According to St. Bonaventure it is a habitus of the practical intellect[68].

In the modern age treatment of conscience underwent a considerable development. After the rise of casuistry it was even given the place of honour[69]. Conscience was seen as standing between the law and man's free will. With regard

---

[64] Cf. *In VI Ethic.*, lesson 2, n. 1131 (Leonine, p. 237, 109): "Ea autem quae sunt ad finem non sunt nobis determinata a natura sed per rationem investiganda".

[65] I - II, q. 19, a. 3 ad 2: "Rectitudo rationis consistit in conformitate ad appetitum finis debiti".

[66] For a detailed discussion of the natural law see Chapter IX.

[67] *In Ezechielem Prophetam*, 1, 10: *PL* 25, 22 BC. For an explanation of the term *synderesis* see Chapter IX.

[68] *In II Sent.*, d. 39, a. 1, q. 1 & 2 (*Opera omnia*, Quaracchi, II 898-905).

[69] S. Pinckaers, *Les sources de la morale chrétienne*, Fribourg - Paris 1985, 278.

to the law conscience is seen as passive and so does not claim to modify it. It presents the law to the will and plays a role in explaining the law, in order to indicate with great precision where the borderline is between what is permitted and what is prohibited.

Turning now to Aquinas, a first point we notice is that he places conscience in the speculative intellect[70]. The judgment of conscience is the conclusion of a syllogism such as one uses when preparing to make a choice. The conclusion results when a general principle or rule is applied to a particular case. In this judgment of conscience we realize that we stand before an obligation coming from beyond[71]. If the minor premiss is false then so is the conclusion. Considered by itself this conclusion is not part of a decision. A reasoning may take place under the influence of a passion or of the will and outwardly resemble an authentic statement of conscience, although in reality it is not this. People often speak of "following their own conscience" but sometimes the opinion they form results from passions binding the intellect which can no longer reach the correct conclusion. In these cases the true judgment of conscience is repressed[72].

Conscience is the judgment of the intellect about an act one has performed or is on the point of executing. St. Thomas studies conscience in *In II Sent.*, d. 24, q. 2, in the *Q. d. de veritate*, q. 17, and in the *Summa theologiae*. I, 79, as well as in the *Prima secundae*, q. 19, a. 5. He first determines the ontological status of conscience, arguing that it is a conclusion drawn by the mind, a *conclusio cognitiva tantum*[73]. This judgment concerns the moral quality of an act and has an obligatory character. A statement of conscience obliges but does not force us. The will can refuse to follow it, but by leaving aside what the intellect proposes as right, the will is at fault. Even if the intellect is mistaken and the judgment of conscience is erroneous one must nevertheless follow it. In this case this act is not bad unless the intellect's error is blameworthy and could have been avoided. The reason why one must follow one's conscience is that it is our duty to act according to our best insight. This implies that one makes a reasonable effort to know the different aspects of a choice, including the precepts of the laws and the duties resulting from one's state of life.

In this connection St. Thomas mentions different opinions regarding whether one must follow an erroneous conscience. According to some authors one would have to follow an erroneous conscience with regard to indifferent acts, but not a judgement of conscience which tells us to do something which is intrinsically evil. But this opinion is wrong. If the will deviates from what the intellect proposes as the right choice (regardless of whether this object is good or bad), it

---

[70] *Q.d. de veritate*, q. 17, a.1 ad 4: "... in pura cognitione consistit".

[71] Aquinas writes in the *De veritate*, q. 17, a. 4 ad 2: "Conscientiae dictamen nihil est aliud quam perventio praecepti divini".

[72] *Q. d. de veritate*, q. 17, a. 1 ad 4.

[73] *In II Sent.*, d. 24, q. 2, a. 4 ad 2.

becomes itself bad, since it is going to do something which is contrary to the judgment of the mind and which, therefore, is wrong[74]. He concludes the argument as follows: "Consequently we must say that every act of the will against reason, whether the intellect judges correctly or is mistaken, is always bad", i.e. when the will goes against the intellect when it presents something as good or as forbidden[75]. Aquinas then distinguishes between following an erroneous conscience and acting against one's conscience. Conscience is a norm, which depends on a higher norm (it is a *norma normata*), which derives its principles from the order of things. It obliges more than the prescriptions of a civil government since everyone must live in accordance with right reason[76]. Conscience is a judgment of the mind and witnesses to the order present in creation. This is why it has greater authority than what people command us to do. When one follows the voice of one's conscience, against the commands of those in authority, one does not condemn human authority but one judges that in this case one should not obey.

The judgment of conscience aims at providing us with a clear and certain knowledge with regard to the morality of concrete acts. This is why Aquinas does not speak of a doubtful or uncertain conscience. He shows how, in appraising what is morally right and wrong, we may avoid a pervasive legalism on the one hand and an unlimited subjectivism on the other. The intellect and the will must harmoniously collaborate[77].

In article five Thomas speaks more of reason (*ratio*) than of conscience. The term "reason" has a broader sense. The judgment of conscience seems to intervene mostly when we are to perform certain acts which are connected to the commands of moral law. Conscience does not manifest itself when one chooses a profession, buys a car or is looking for a destination for one's holiday travels. In these and similar cases conscience only asks us to acts according to the virtues, to follow right reason and not to lose sight of the true goal of life.

The problem one faces when following a wrong judgment is examined in greater detail in **article 6**. It was established that the will must not deviate from a judgment of conscience, even if it is erroneous. But what is the moral quality of this act following an erroneous judgment? According to an opinion held by many in St. Thomas's day, such a conscience does not oblige when it prescribes acts which as such are bad. But for Thomas himself an erroneous conscience

---

[74] If the intellect errs and presents as bad an object which as such is good, the object becomes bad *per accidens*. This applies also to the case when the intellect presents something bad as good.

[75] I - II, 19, 5 ad 3.

[76] *Q. d. de veritate*, q. 17, a. 5 ad 3: "Omnis enim homo debet secundum rationem agere".

[77] See O. Lottin, *Psychologie et morale aux XIIe et XIIIe siècles*, tome III, 354-406; L. Elders "La doctrine de la conscience de saint Thomas d'Aquin", in id., *Autour de Saint Thomas*, II, 63-94.

binds the will. Can one go one step further and say that the will which follows the intellect in such a case performs a good deed? To answer this question we must first distinguish between the different ways in which conscience can err. If one could and should have known what to do in this particular case then the will following an erroneous conscience has no excuse. If, without any fault, one is mistaken with regard to a circumstance of an action then the will which follows this misconception is without blame[78]. But what shall we say about ignorance concerning what one does? For example, impressed by the devastation caused by modern warfare one could form a judgment that all wars, including defensive wars, are bad, and refuse military service. Many of St. Thomas's contemporaries believed that the will which follows an erroneous conscience, is never morally right since it acts in opposition to divine law. Thomas himself holds a different position. An intrinsically evil object which (without any fault) is presented by reason as good cannot make the act of the will intrinsically good, but this act is not morally bad either. Some modern authors want to go further and say that Aquinas should have thought through his own view with greater consistency. According to them it is sufficient for an act to be considered as morally good in order to become morally good[79]. But according to Aquinas the subjective order cannot to such an extent determine the objective order. He quotes in this connection a saying of Ps.-Dionysius, that any flaw is sufficient to deprive an act of its goodness[80]. The erroneous conscience obliges in the secondary way (*secundum quid*), in this sense that the act one performs following this conscience is objectively neutral, even if the intention of the agent is good.

Whoever follows an erroneous conscience does not oppose himself to God's will, because he experiences the judgment of conscience as the will of God[81]. But if the error is one's own fault a difficult situation ensues. On the one hand one has to follow such a judgment but on the other one sins when one acts in accordance with it, as one does when one does not follow it. To escape from this perplexity one should verify what reason dictates correcting one's erroneous judgment[82].

A final observation on conscience concerns the difference between conscience and prudence. The virtue of prudence makes us seek a course of action in order to reach a good end and always makes us strive for what agrees with our real nature. Prudence does not primarily consider the morality of our actions, but tells us which actions will bring us to the right end. A prudential deliberation takes place at the level of contingent things. Conscience, on the other hand, is a

---

[78] It is an ignorance which makes the act as such involuntary.

[79] Cf. E. d'Arcy, *Conscience and the Right to Freedom*, London 1961, p. 113 ff.

[80] *De divinis nominibus*, ch. 4, § 30.

[81] *Q. d. de veritate*, q. 17, a. 4 ad 1: "per accidens... a lege Dei non recedit".

[82] *Ibid.*, ad 8. Cf. I - II, q. 19, a. 6 ad 3: "Potest ab errore recedere, cum ignorantia sit vincibilis et voluntaria".

speculative judgment and aims at a certain and definitive knowledge. Sometimes it can approve the actions recommended by prudence. This suggests a solution to the problem of a doubting conscience (*conscientia dubia*). Instead of speaking of different options which all seem legitimate one will act according to prudence. Prudence will look for a good or even the best solution. Even if one does not always reach total certitude about what to do one will always act in conformity to the goals of our nature. If despite deliberation doubts persist then one will refrain from acting[83]. This is not a concession to rigorism, for in many cases the doubt as to what to choose concerns things which are neither necessary nor urgent. Moreover, many cases are left to our free choice.

A well known-theme in ethics is the question to what extent the **intention** of the agent, i.e. the goal he pursues, determines the morality of his choice of the means. Aquinas discusses it in **article 7**, while he presupposes what was said in Question 18 on the role of the object. As was mentioned in the introduction, Peter Abelard defended the view that the intention determines the moral quality of our actions[84]. God does not so much consider what people do, as the intention with which they act.

Thomas distinguishes between the intention[85] which precedes the choice and the intention accompanying a choice. The intention precedes a choice when we want something in view of the end to which we direct ourselves. In this case, the order to the end is considered to be the reason and cause of the goodness of what is chosen. One cleans the gutters of the roof to allow the rain water to flow unimpeded to the sewer. The goodness of the act also depends on the goal one pursues and so the intention of the goal determines also the morality of the act. It happens that when doing something one intends a further goal. One supports a charitable undertaking but then thinks of using the donation to obtain some benefits for one's own business. In such a case this additional intention does not impair or undo the original good work of a donation (**article 7**).

Related to the question of the intention is the problem whether the amount of good or evil one has the intention to bring about by one's actions determines the goodness or badness of one's will (**article 8**). In his answer Thomas distinguishes a dual goodness: a first is given with the object, a second depends on the intention of the will with regard to the act it performs. An object can be of relatively little value (cf. the act of cleaning one's house), but when performed with the best of intentions the external action shares in the superior goodness of the intention.

---

[83] *In epist. ad Romanos*, c. 14, lesson 3, n. 1139.

[84] *Scito teipsum*, c. XI.

[85] "Intention" as used here does not have quite the same meaning as the intention we dealt with in Chapter Two. In that chapter "intention" signified an act of the will which started the process of deliberation and directed it, so that a choice became possible. But in the article we are now dealing with it denotes the end which the will seeks to attain by its action.

Concluding his explanations about the morality of the acts of the will Aquinas asks whether in the last analysis their goodness depends on the conformity of the human will with God's will (**article 9**). As we have seen, the goodness of the will depends on the end one pursues. Man's last end and highest good is God. In order to be good the will must be directed to God, i.e. what it wants to attain must also be willed by God. At this point, however, a new distinction intervenes. A person wants to become healthy, while in certain cases it does not seem to be God's will that he be cured. Another example is that of a judge who condemns a criminal to death, while the man's wife and children want him to stay alive. Both sides want a good. The difference is explained by the fact that the human mind can consider the same issue from different points of view. What is good for the one, is not necessarily so for the other. People often aim at particular goods, which are no longer good when considered from a universal point of view. Thus a conflict may arise. The will which directs itself to some particular good is only good when this good is seen in its relation to the common good of the society at large and the good of the universe (**article 10**). The common good must determine the particular good. Man must conform his will to God's will, but this is a general will to be in conformity with God's plan, for he does not know the divine will regarding particular good things he may want to reach. Indirectly this article contains a rebuttal of consequentialism, which teaches that not the nature of an act but its consequences determine its morality. Moreover, Thomas adds, by acting in accordance with one's duty and right knowledge one submits oneself to God's will, since one does what God wills. This is particularly so when one does everything out of love for God and so directs oneself to one's last end.

The goodness and badness of our external actions (Q. 20)

In daily life "good" and "bad" are mostly used to qualify external actions. One person takes care of a sick mother, something which is praised by all; another person steals things, something generally reproved. People are praised or blamed on account of their external and visible actions. These acts, when considered together with their circumstances, do indeed have a goodness or badness of their own which is fundamental. We have to do with acts proceeding from the different virtues or vices. This goodness or badness does not depend on the will, but on the intellect[86], although in the genesis of these acts the will, pursuing a goal, has a decisive role. The purpose which the will pursues also comes first when an act is executed (**article 1**).

---

[86] Q. 20, a. 1; "Bonitas autem vel malitia quam habet actus exterior secundum se, propter debitam materiam et debitas circumstantias, non derivatur a voluntate sed magis a ratione".

This explanation is important since it shows that the intention of the will does not change the goodness of badness of the external actions. This point is elaborated in **article 2**. External actions show a twofold goodness, sc. on account of their objects and circumstances, and, secondly, on account of the will directing itself to an end. In order for an act to be good, not only must the end be good, but also the act itself in respect of its object and the surrounding circumstances[87]. Some actions are bad because of what they are[88] and cannot become good[89]. A good intention cannot make acceptable an action which by itself is bad. But a bad intention can deprive an action which as such is good of its goodness, according to the often quoted axiom of Ps.-Dionysius that in order to be good everything in an act must be good, but that any defect is sufficient to deprive it of its goodness. This article states a central doctrine of natural and Christian ethics[90].

The external action, e.g. gardening, and the decision of the will to perform it are different acts as to their nature, but form a unity. Aquinas distinguishes between external actions which have their own goodness and others which do not. To take a bitter medicine has no other goodness than the one given with the end, sc. to improve one's health, and so it constitutes a total unity with the act of the will. But to eat some delicious fruit has a goodness of its own, also when we eat it for the sake of our health. In this case the external act and that of the will have each their own goodness, but in such a way that the goodness of the act of the will contributes to that of the external action, as the latter does to the goodness of the will's decision (**article 3**).

Does the external action add something to the goodness or badness of the will's act? External actions constitute with the act of the will one moral act, of which they are the accomplishment and end, and in this way they add something to the goodness of the act of the will[91]. If because of circumstances the will cannot proceed to the execution of its decision, then such non-accomplishment is involuntary. Moreover, the will can repeat the same sort of external action, multiply good deeds and thus acquire greater merit. This applies also when the will is engaged intensely over a longer period of time with an external action (**article 4**).

---

[87] Art. 2: "Non sufficit ad hoc quod actus exterior sit bonus, bonitas voluntatis quae est ex intentione finis".

[88] *In I Sent.*, d. 48, q. 1, a. 2 ad 5: "...talia sunt quae per se mala sunt". Aquinas defends the principle "Non sunt facienda mala ut eveniant bona" (*Rom.* 3, 8).

[89] *In II Sent.*, d. 36, q. 1, a. 5 ad 2: "Quod autem est malum ex genere, simpliciter est malum nec bonum fieri potest".

[90] Cf. Servaes (Th.) Pinkaeers, o.p., *Ce qu'on ne peut jamais faire. La question des actes intrinsèquement mauvais. Histoire et dicussion,* Fribourg 1986.

[91] Art. 4: "Unde non est perfecta voluntas nisi sit talis quae, opportunitate data, operetur".

Do the consequences of one's actions add to their goodness of badness? One has organized a sports' event at which an accident happens. Does the accident make it wrong to have organized such an event? It all depends on whether one could have foreseen the accident. If one expects good effects, such as recreation and the fraternizing of the participants, this will increase the goodness, while expected bad consequences can make organizing the competition wrong. As regards the consequences, one may distinguish between those which regularly come with this sort of public gatherings and others which occur only exceptionally. The former add to either the goodness or the badness of organizing such an event, the latter do not (**article 5**).

In the previous articles a distinction was made between the order of nature and the moral order. An act which is of one type ontologically, can sometimes be placed in other categories with regard to its morality[92]. One may go for a walk with a view to one's health, but while one is out one may decide to visit a friend whose house one is passing. In such a case, different internal acts are comprised in one external action.

Annex

Some moralists basing themselves on the distinction between external actions and the acts of the will argued that the will constitutes the moral order when it directs itself by choosing a particular end. According to their view the external action is morally neutral or pre-moral, and is no more than an instrument of the will[93]. However, a great number of such external actions have a natural meaning and goodness, while actions which oppose or destroy what thus amounts to a natural end are bad. One need only think of the acts which concern keeping oneself alive, developing one's intellectual life, participating in the affairs of the community and procreation. When one appeals to the intention of the acting person to make acceptable what is against the natural meaning and scope of the external actions, one exposes oneself to the greatest excesses. Should one approve of torture when it might produce some good results? Those who support this theory try to escape this and similar unacceptable conclusions by saying that one must take into account all the consequences, even those which only may happen in the future[94]. To this we say that taking into account all the consequences im-

---

[92] See article 3 of this question, the reply to the first difficulty.

[93] Cf. L. Janssens, "Ontic and Moral Evil", in *Louvain Studies* IV (1972), pp. 115-156.

[94] One might note in passing that this theory does away also with the moral doctrine of the gospels, while retaining only the commandment of love as specifically Christian. Many of the moral teachings of the gospels express natural duties but these retain their objective value and obligatory character for the Christian. Cf. I-II, 108, 2 ad 1: "Sed ad opera virtutum dirigimur per rationem naturalem quae est regula quaedam operationis humanae et ideo in his non oportuit aliqua praecepta dare ultra moralis legis praecepta (scil. Veteris Testamenti), quae

plies that one do justice to the natural structure and the natural ends of ourselves and of creation. When these are discarded or frustrated, one endangers a natural equilibrium, for nature does nothing in vain.

What does it mean that an act is morally good or bad ? (Q. 21)

In this question Aquinas discusses the terms "sin", "blame" and "praise". "Sin" is not just something that has to do with religious life. Everyone knows what a bad act is. In classical antiquity people considered sin or a misdemeanor to be the transgression of the moral code prevalent in a particular community and the perturbation of man's relation with the gods. In the course of time a second view imposed itself which stressed the moral aspect of such actions. The sinful act is now seen as itself opposed to the will of the gods or the laws of nature. Sin is a lack of respect for the gods and for one's fellow men. Nevertheless the term ἁμαρτία (sin, transgression) also stood for events and actions later viewed as outside the moral order.

In the intellectualism of Socrates ("No one sins willingly"[95]) a bad action is disapproved of and is thought to taint the person who commits it. According to Plato, injustice is the greatest evil for the soul[96], although it does not corrupt the essence of the soul[97]. The soul, however, is anyhow polluted by contact with matter, the body and evil things[98]. Aristotle considers sin above all as a lack of self-mastery (ἀκρασία)[99]. He indicates the solution to Socrates' problem ("Nobody sins willingly") by introducing, in the process leading to a decision, the practical judgment which precedes the choice. If the intellect is influenced by disordered appetite, it will form a wrong judgment. Aristotle distinguishes between ἀτύχημα, damage inflicted unwillingly on an other person, ἁμάρτημα, a fault, often without evil intent but committed by carelessness, and ἀδίκημα, a crime committed out of malice. The Christians laid much stress on the personal aspect of our actions and on individual responsibility. A sin is an act committed against God's will. It is more than a mistake or a missing-the-mark, it consists in a conscious choice[100].

---

sunt de dictamine rationis". See also II-II 10, 10: "Ius autem divinum quod est ex gratia non tollit ius humanum quod est ex naturali ratione".

[95] See Plato's *Protagoras* 345 D.
[96] *Republic* 366 E.
[97] *Republic* 608 C.
[98] *O.c.*, 611 B.
[99] *Ethica Nicomachea* 1147ᵇ23-29. He also uses such terms as ἀκολασία and μαλακία.
[100] See A. M. Festugière, 'La notion du péché présentée par S. Thomas et sa relation avec la morale aristotélicienne", in *New Scholasticism* 5 (1931), 332- 341.- G.E.M. Anscombe exaggerates when she writes that "missing the mark" (not acting prudently) came to be seen as sin in Christianity, as if the concept of sin were entirely absent from ancient moral theory.

Moral evil forms a class within the broader genus of evil. Moral evil or sin is an act which does not agree with the end of man, i.e. with human nature. Activities which proceed from the nature of things are ordered to the end and, therefore, are good. The immediate rule for the will in its choices is the intellect. If the will orders itself to an object in agreement with right insight, its act is good. If it deviates from the right order, it sins. As appears from what was said above, every act of the will deviating from the order indicated by the intellect and from God's eternal law is bad and sinful[101]. To make clear that the will must not follow a judgment of the intellect which does not take into account the order of nature and the end of man, Aquinas writes that the will must agree with both the order of the intellect and with the eternal law.

The first two objections raised in the article are inspired by the theory which considers some acts mere faults or mistakes, such that the person committing them incurs no moral guilt. In this view the intention and the goal one pursues make an action good or bad. Aquinas answers that the person who acts has a twofold goal: a more immediate goal and an ultimate end. A bad act is directed to a goal which removes a person from his true last end.

A bad action deserves reproof, a good one praise (**article 2**). Morally good acts deserve a reward, bad acts must be punished. On account of the now prevailing individualism the question of merit and reward is pushed aside by many as unnecessary and naive, but Aquinas sees man as a member of a community, for which he is responsible and which, in its turn, supports him. Bad actions cause harm to the community, which is, on the contrary, strengthened by the good the citizens do (**article 3**). The good or evil acts we perform also concern God, our last end, to whom in the last analysis all our actions should be directed. A bad action does not acknowledge this order and is opposed to God's governance of the world (**article 4**).

In order to act meritoriously one does not have to keep in mind consciously the good end one pursues. The original intention by which one directed oneself to this end, remains active, even if one thinks of something else, as long as one does not do anything contrary to this end[102].

Cf. G.E.M. Anscombe, "Modern Moral Philosophy" in W.-D. Hudson (ed.), *The is - ought question. A collection of Papers on the Central Problems in Moral Philosophy*, New York (MacMillan) 1969, 175-195.

[101] Thomas defines sin as "actus qui recedit ab ordine rationis et legis æternæ".

[102] Cf. *Super I ad Corinthios*, ch. 14, lesson 3: "In omnibus actibus meritoriis, qui ordinantur ad finem rectum, non requiritur quod intentio agentis coniugatur fini secundum quemlibet actum, sed vis prima quae movet intentionem, manet in toto opere, etiamsi in aliquo particulari divertat; et hic prima vis facit totum opus meritorium, nisi interrumpatur per contrariam affectionem quae divertat a fine prædicto ad finem contrarium".

CHAPTER IV

THE PASSIONS IN GENERAL

Ever since classical antiquity the role of passions and emotions in human life has been discussed by many poets, historians and philosophers. This explains why St. Thomas in his treatise on the passions refers to a great number of authors, such as the Peripatetics, the School of Plato, the Stoics, Cicero and the Fathers of the Church. In Greece a widespread opinion held that people often act badly under the influence of passions difficult to resist. Euripides writes in some of his tragedies that the protagonists do not act freely (οὐχ ἑκών) but are forced (βία)., e.g. driven by a blinding love[1]. According to Plato and the Stoa the passions have their seat in the sensitive and irrational part of the soul. Plato repeatedly speaks of love, desire, concupiscence, lust, but it is difficult to construct a coherent theory of the emotions out of the elements scattered over several of his dialogues. In an often quoted myth he compares the human soul to a wagon drawn by two horses and driven by a coachman[2]. Besides the rational part of the soul, represented by the coachman, there is a fierce and noble force or energy in man, symbolized by one of the horses, whereas the second horse, whimsical and lazy, is a symbol of concupiscence and the lower passions. In another dialogue Plato excludes fear and lust from the rational soul[3]. However, Plato also presents a somewhat different picture of the soul, describing it as the driving-force of all processes. The soul is θυμοειδής, ἐπιθυμητικός and λογιστικός, i.e., it is the source of courage and strength, of concupiscence and desire but also of deliberation. Apparently Plato did not succeed in elaborating a synthesis of his doctrine of the soul. He rejects the opinion that the evil one does under the influence of a passion would not be voluntary[4].

Aristotle gives a detailed description of the passions, which are acts of the soul but also affect the body. He distinguishes between passions, faculties and habits, such as virtues and vices[5]. Such passions as courage, pity, anger, love and hatred cause a modification in our organism[6]. In the passage of the *Nicomachean Ethics* to which we just referred Aristotle mentions eleven passions, three of which do not coincide with the scheme of passions which St. Thomas proposes. Aristotle and the Peripatetics stress the need for self-control and moderation of the passions by our reason. Aristotle's *Rhetoric*, which Thomas read

---

[1] See his *Medea* 1077-1079. Medea knows that what she is going to do is a crime, but her wrath prevails.
[2] *Phædrus* 246 AB.
[3] *Timæus* 69 C ff.
[4] *Laws* 869 E ff.
[5] *E. N.* 1105^{b}20.
[6] *De anima* 403^{a}15-18.

in the translation by William of Moerbeke, provides illustrations of the role of the passions.

According to Zeno, the founder of the Stoic school, emotions develop when our reason fails to give its judgment about what we experience. In such cases the pneuma, which is the energy of the soul, concentrates itself in a passion. The wise man lives in accordance with the virtues and is not moved by passions (ἀπάθεια). Chrysippus elaborates this doctrine in the direction of a pure monism. There is no special part of the soul as the seat of the passions. Under the pressure of the passions the intellect turns to objects devoid of value and is no longer itself[7]. In the days of the Middle Stoa Posidonius stressed that it is important to have some knowledge of the origin of the passions in order to evaluate our actions[8]. He revived Plato's theory of three parts of the soul[9].

Cicero writes that the wise man should not become the prey of fear, desire or anger. He calls the passions illnesses (*morbi*) of the soul, for they are movements of the soul which do not obey reason[10]. St. Augustine, for his part, outlines the positions of the Peripatetics and the Stoa with regard to the passions concluding that they are not very far apart[11]. He distinguishes four basic forms of emotion, sc. desire, joy, fear and sadness, which are all forms of love or of aversion from an evil[12].

Thomas Aquinas inherited a very rich supply of material on our subject in the philosophical literature and with the help of this he elaborated an unsurpassed synthesis[13]. After his first treatment of the subject in the *Quaestiones disputatae de veritate*[14] he devotes 27 questions to the study of the passions in the Second Part of his *Summa theologiae*. Even after more than seven centuries it is almost impossible to improve on his exposition as regards its philosophical and psychological content. Descartes tried to renovate the treatise in his *Les passions de l'âme*. He says that what his predecessors had written about the passions does not amount to very much and is hardly credible, but if we leave aside a number of physiological theories, Descartes himself had little new to offer and, through

---

[7] Cf. Max Pohlenz, *Die Geschichte einer geistigen Bewegung*, Göttingen 1948, p. 146.

[8] Cf. Galenus, *De placitis Hippocratis et Platonis*, ed. Müller, p. 448.

[9] See I. G. Kidd, "Posidonius on Emotions", in A.A. Long (ed.), *Problems in Stoicism*, London 1971, p. 200 f.

[10] *Tuscul. Disputationes*, III, 4, 7; X, 24.

[11] *De civitate Dei*, IX, 4, 1.

[12] *De civitate Dei*, XIV, 7, 2: "Amor ergo inhians habere quod amatur cupiditas est, id autem habens eoque fruens lætitia est; fugiens quod ei adversatur timor est; idque si acciderit sentiens tristitia est".

[13] M. Meier, *Die Lehre des Thomas von Aquin De Passionibus animae in quellenanalytischer Darstellung*. BGPMA, Münster i. Westf. 1912, examined the sources used by Thomas to conclude that the latter's text is "vollinhaltlich abhängig von" his predecessors, but Meier has no eye for the very ingenious elaboration and systematic ordening Thomas introduced.

[14] Q. 26, art. 1 - 3.

his teachers at La Flèche, he depended on Aquinas without being aware of it. He discarded the distinction between the irascible and the concupiscible appetites and used the term "passion" in a broader sense.

Aquinas's treatise on the passions follows that on human acts and their moral evaluation. He begins by pointing out that the passions are common to men and animals. The theme is important in ethics because the passions are the material with which the virtues are concerned with, in particular the virtues of fortitude and temperance, but also justice. Furthermore, the movements of the sensitive appetite are sometimes analogous to those of the will. For these reasons the treatise on the passions precedes treatment of the virtues. This position for the treatise is also explained by the fact that we must first consider what is more general and what man has in common with the animals, before examining what is exclusively proper to human beings. Aquinas chooses this order also in the First Part of the *Summa theologiae*, where he first studies sensitive knowledge before passing to the examination of the intellect and the will.

In modern languages the term "passion" has often a pejorative sense, sc. that of uncontrolled emotion, but for Thomas the passions are dynamic powers and sources of psychological energy at the service of man. While Aristotle emphasized the effect of the emotions on the soul[15] Aquinas adds that they have an effect also on the organism, in particular on the rate of the heartbeat[16], but also on other organs[17]. To a certain extent man can be carried along by the passions[18]. Nowadays the influence of the passions on the glands, blood pressure and the nervous system is widely acknowledged.

In our study of Aquinas's ethics we treat the the passions first in general and then in particular, where we divide the passions into two groups, sc. those belonging to the concupiscible appetite and those of the irascible appetite.

In what part of the soul or in what faculty are the passions to be found? (Q. 22)

The Latin word *passio* (and the verb *pati*) have the general meaning of suffering or undergoing something, in particular as accompanied by the loss of the state in which the subject found itself before, such as losing one's health. However, there is also a form of undergoing in which one does not lose anything. This happens in the cognitive powers when they receive impressions[19]. To suffer or undergo something in the sense of losing a positive accidental determination

---

[15] *De anima* 403ª18.

[16] I - II, 24, 2 ad 2.

[17] *Summa contra gentiles*, I, c. 89: "Omnis passio... secundum transmutationem corporalem fit, puta secundum constrictionem vel dilatationem cordis aut secundum aliquid huiusmodi". See P. Corvez, *Somme théologique des jeunes. Les passions*, p. 201.

[18] *In II Ethic.*, lesson 5, n. 292: "... et quibus homo quodammodo ducitur".

[19] See Aristotle, *De anima* 410ª25: τὸ δὲ αἰσθάνεσθαι πάσχειν τι καὶ κινεῖσθαι.

only occurs in the organism, i.e. in an animal or man seen as a whole. Some passions cause a change for the worse (such as sadness), others bring an improvement or enrichment (such as joy or pleasure) (**article 1**).

After this general introduction Aquinas examines whether the passions have their seat in the cognitive or in the appetitive faculties. The term "passions" suggests that the person affected by them undergoes some influence, e.g. because of outside events, from other people or from changes occurring in himself, so that he gets into a different state. Thomas sees this as a being drawn toward something. The death of a relative or friend may plunge people into sadness. Being drawn to something so as to be riveted by it, e.g. by sadness because of the death of a relative, is characteristic of the appetitive faculties which address themselves to external things or states of the body and are attracted to them, whereas the cognitive faculties draw their objects into the knowing subject.

One might object to this explanation that the will as described in Chapter Two is a dynamic power, which makes choices and carries them out, which seems to contradict what is said here about "undergoing". The solution of this difficulty is that the appetitive faculties are moved actively towards what is outside us in order to reach the things by which they are in a passive way attracted (**article 2**).

A last question remains: do the passions have their seat in the sensitive appetite or in the will? The answer has already been indicated: the passions bring about a change in the organism, something which would not be possible if they had their seat in the will. Texts from John Damascene[20] and Nemesius[21] confirm this conclusion. It goes without saying that these passions are not found in God and purely spiritual beings, but figuratively one may attribute some of these emotions to God inasmuch as his decisions provoke effects which show some similarity with man's way of acting when he is angry, sad or full of tenderness[22] (**article 3**).

The distinction between the passions and their classification

We often find in ourselves or in others a tangle of emotions which are not seldom in conflict with one another. How can we bring about some order and clarity in these manifold inner movements? Plato and Aristotle divided man's sensitive appetitive faculties into a concupiscible and an irascible appetite. Plato speaks of four main passions[23]. According to the Stoics passions are called up by

---

[20] *De fide orthodoxa*, c. 72 : *MG* 94, 941: "Passio est motus appetitivæ virtutis sensibilis in imaginatione boni vel mali".

[21] *De natura hominis*, c. 15 (Verbeke & Mondo, p. 93): "Passio est motus concupiscitivæ virtutis sensibilis in imaginatione boni vel mali".

[22] Ad 3: "... significat simplicem actum virtutis cum similitudine effectus, absque passione".

[23] *Laches* 101 D.

something good or bad presented to us. Consequently they distinguish four main emotions which they called the four strings[24], sc. pleasure, sadness, desire and fear. John Damascene made this theory his own, but Nemesius was perhaps the first to attempt a systematic division of the passions[25] according to their objects, good and evil, which can be either present or absent. Pleasure (joy) and desire concern what is good, sadness and fear are caused by what is bad. Nemesius adds that anger belongs to the irascible appetite, but he does not further explain this. Among later authors St. Albert the Great mentions some divisions of the passions, but he did not succeed in reaching a convincing synthesis. After having given a survey of the passions in some other works[26], Aquinas presents in question 23 of the Second Part of the *Summa theologiae* what one may consider his definitive synthesis.

He takes as his starting point the division of the sensitive appetite into the concupiscible and in the irascible appetitive faculties. The two are specifically different, since the object of the first is the good in so far as agreeable, that of the second something bad in so far as it is saddening or painful. But if the good is difficult to attain, it is the object of the irascible, which does not address itself to it as something agreeable. Thomas adds that nature has given man and some animals this second sensitive appetite in order to help them overcome the difficulties which they encounter and to assist them in their battle to reach some good object or to avoid what is evil[27]. So it helps the concupiscible appetite which rests in the good attained and is pleased with it. Joy and sadness, love and hatred are expressions of the concupiscible, courage and daring, fear and hope are movements of the irascible appetite (**article 1**).

The difference between the passions of the two appetitive faculties is explained in greater detail in **article 2**. To illustrate his view he compares the passions to physical movements, which can be divided into movements toward something and movements away from a thing. In nature there are also contrary movements with regard to one and the same point, such as a movement toward a white colour and a movement away from it. However, in the concupiscible one does not find such contrary movements with regard to one and the same point (either something good or something bad). There is no passion which shies away from the good, nor is there one which seeks what is bad. Emotions which concern the good all tend to it (love, desire, joy), while those concerning some evil are always turning away from it or hating it (hatred, flight, sadness).

The irascible appetite has as its object something good or bad inasmuch as it is difficult to reach or to avoid. Hope makes us strive for some good which is

---

[24] Ariston, fr. 370.
[25] *De natura hominis*, c. 16 (Verbeke, p. 95)
[26] *In III Sent.*, d. 26, q. 1, a. 2; *Q. d. de veritate*, q. 26, a. 4; *In II Ethic.*, lesson 5, n. 293.
[27] In I, 81, 2 Thomas calls the irascible the "quasi proprugnatrix et defensatrix" of the concupiscible appetite.

difficult to attain, while the emotions of despair and discouragement make us renounce it. Consequently there are two contrary passions with regard to the same good. On the other hand, a formidable obstacle or evil which one wants to avoid causes fear, which makes us hesitate, or courage which makes us face a difficulty or danger in order to overcome it. This means that in the irascible there may occur contrary passions both with regard to a good and to an evil.

To all the passions mentioned thus far there are contrary passions. But there is one emotion, anger, which has no contrary. Anger is provoked by an evil already present, which at this particular time cannot be avoided. One can either acquiesce in it and surrender to sadness or rebel against it, without being able to remove it. In this case the feeling of anger will appear (**article 3**).

In the last article of this question Aquinas gives a survey of how these passions originate. If the concupiscible appetite directs itself to some good then love is engendered, which adapts us to the loved object and gives us an inner agreement with it. Its counterpart is the feeling of hatred in respect of an evil. If the good object has not yet been attained, desire will arise. On the other hand, we flee and turn away from an approaching evil. When the good has been reached, joy and satisfaction arise. If an evil is present we experience sadness or pain.

With regard to the passions of the irascible, one feels hope or despair in respect of a good that is difficult to reach, but fears an approaching evil or is audacious with regard to it. If the evil is actually affecting us anger may result. In this way there are six passions of the concupiscible, divided into three pairs, but in the irascible there are two pairs of passions and anger, which stands by itself. Aristotle also mentions eleven passions without, however, proposing a scheme of their division[28]. The passions or emotions mentioned by Aquinas are not quite the same as those distinguished by Aristotle. For instance, Aquinas does not place pity and jealousy under the emotions[29]. He is apparently convinced that besides the eleven types of passions mentioned there are no other basically different emotions. Although he calls pity a *passio* (Q. 24, art. 3), he shows that it is a complex emotion, which presupposes love of one's fellow man, considers his good as one's own, experiences sadness because of the evils which afflict the other and desires to help him out of his painful situation (**article 4**).

The moral qualification of the passions (Q. 24)

According to Aquinas nature has given us the passions as a support and a source of energy. They are also an expression of the corporeal nature of man. As natu-

---

[28] *Nicomachean Ethics*, II, ch. 4.

[29] In his commentary on the *Ethics (In II Ethic.,* lesson 5, n. 293) he uses his own scheme. This shows that Thomas not only wanted to comment on Aristotle's text, but also attempted to propose a universally valid treatise of ethics.

ral movements they possess an ontological goodness. As to their moral value, passions are neutral as long as the will does not intervene by calling them up, or by consenting to them[30]. Involuntary emotions are neither good nor bad morally. Thomas draws a comparison with the body. Movements of our limbs as such are neither good nor bad, but they become so if they follow a command of the intellect and the will, as when we give a hand to help a person, or when we hit him without reason. This is even more true of the emotions which, although they are by themselves morally neutral, are more intimately associated with the mind and the will than are the members of our body (**article 1**).

As we have seen, the Stoics scorned the passions. Cicero for his part was inclined to consider them weak spots or even diseases of the soul[31]. However, Aquinas raises the question whether a passion as such, controlled or commanded by the will, is bad. He sides with the Peripatetics who considered the passions as good as long as they are controlled by reason. It is not true that a passion subtracts itself always from the order of reason[32]. But to the extent that they break away from this control by the mind they make us incline to sin, but in so far as reason regulates them, they are associated with the virtues[33] (**article 2**).

However, the manner in which and the extent to which the passions contribute to the morality of our acts or detract from it must still be determined. Thomas recalls first that according to the Stoics all passions are detrimental to the moral goodness of human acts. This may hold true for unbridled passions, he says, but passions as such contribute to the good of man if they are regulated by reason. The good of man lies in reason as in its root. It will be the more perfect in the measure reason radiates its insights into the other faculties and actions. It is part of man's perfect moral good that the members of his body obey the direction of the intellect. Similarly, man's sensitive appetite and his emotions must be governed by reason. Therefore, we must direct ourselves to the good not only with our will but also with our sensitive appetite.

Passions which originate before the mind judges what to do, can obscure this judgment, so that an act has less goodness. If one helps the poor only because one feels pity for them the act is less valuable than when one does so consciously and with a willed decision. On the other hand, a passion which precedes a sinful action, will diminish its sinfulness[34], since there is less freedom. If one allows one's emotions to develop freely without control by reason, one may

---

[30] Cf. *In II Sent.*, d. 36, q. 1, a. 2, where Thomas speaking of the passions writes: "... in omnibus tamen his non est peccatum nisi secundum quod voluntas aliquo modo circa eas se habet vel imperando eas..., vel etiam acceptando".

[31] *Tuscul. disput.*, III, c. 4.

[32] As 2: "Non tamen oportet quod passio semper declinet ab ordine naturalis rationis".

[33] Ad 3: "... inquantum sunt præter ordinem rationis, inclinant ad peccatum, inquantum autem sunt ordinatæ a ratione, pertinent ad virtutem".

[34] Ad 3: "Passio tendens in malum præcedens iudicium rationis, diminuit peccatum"

easily fall into a state in which one is pulled in different directions, as one sees happening repeatedly in young people.

But with the emotions which follow the choice of the intellect and the will a different situation originates. For instance, being intensively concerned with fighting corruption among politicians will have a repercussion on one's emotional life[35]. In such cases we speak of a passionate zeal for a particular cause. A person can also command consciously certain passions, e.g. anger. If so, the passion enhances the goodness of actions. It happens also that such passions come to dominate without, however, being opposed to the respective virtues[36] (**article 3**).

As was argued above, the passions as such are morally neutral but they can participate in the morality of the judgment of reason and the choice of the will. This moral quality is given with their object that agrees with right reason (or deviates from it). Thomas mentions feelings of shame (fear of what is unbecoming) and envy (sadness over the good others have). In such cases the goodness or badness of these emotions is comparable to that of our external actions.

One might object that these emotions are also found in certain animals and therefore can have no moral character in man. Aquinas answers that the appetite in animals does not obey reason. But since animals follow their instincts, given to them by a higher intellect, sc. God, their actions may nevertheless appear as if inspired by noble moral emotions (**article 4**).

The relations between the passions (Q. 25)

In the final section of his general introduction to the study of the passions Aquinas examines their mutual relations. First he points out that the objects of the passions of the concupiscible appetite are more encompassing than those of the irascible. The reason is that they do not only concern movements towards or from something, but also rest in an object, being pleasure or sadness, which is not the case with the movements of the irascible appetite. One finds pleasure and rest when there is no special difficulty to be overcome. Pleasure and rest are reached at the end, although they are the goal to which one directs oneself from the start. This means that in the order of execution the passions of the irascible appetite precede the passion of pleasure in the concupiscible. Hope comes before pleasure.

However, those passions of the concupiscible appetite which are a movement toward the object are followed by the passions of the irascible. Sadness is fol-

---

[35] An example of this is the love of mystics and saints, which often has an effect on their sensitivity.

[36] II - II, 158, 1 ad 2. Thomas is probably thinking of what happened to Christ when he drove the peddlers out of the temple or let himself be overwhelmed by sadness at the grave of Lazarus.

lowed by anger, desire by hope, which adds to a desire a striving to actually reach the object. So one can say that the passions of the irascible have their starting-point in those of the concupiscible, but that they also have their terminus in (other) passions of the concupiscible[37] (**article 1**). It is a central theme of St. Augustine's theology that all passions originate from love and are forms of love[38]. One might object against this position that desire seems to be prior to love. Thomas, however, defends the absolute priority of love among all the passions in the order of execution. Things which strive for something or incline to it, must to a certain extent agree with it and be fitted to it. For no one strives for a thing which means nothing to him. This being conformed and being fitted to things are the effects of love, which is joy in the good. Love of the good calls up the other emotions. Without this love nothing happens in man's inner life. In this way love is prior to desire and desire precedes joy and pleasure in the good (**article 1**).

However, considered from the point of view of the intention, i.e. from what one seeks to attain, viz pleasure in the good that one wants, this end is prior to the desire and to love, although it is attained last[39]. In his answer to the second ojection Aquinas gives an additional explanation. One might object against the thesis that love is prior to desire that love brings about a certain union with the loved good, but that the desire of it comes earlier than this union and so is prior to love itself. But one must distinguish between the union with the beloved in itself and a certain union which is given with one's conformity with it. The latter is the effect of love and is prior to desire and to actual union. We desire only what is becoming to us (**article 2**).

In the following article Aquinas argues that hope or expectation is the first among the passions of the irascible appetite. The passions which have as their object a good, sc. hope and despair, are by their nature earlier than those whose object is an evil, viz. courage and fear. Hope is prior to despair, and is directed to a good which exercises some attraction, whereas despair comes about not through a good in itself but by its being out of reach. Fear is prior to courage, since fear is a spontaneous backing away from some evil, whereas courage tries to overcome an evil. Hope and despair are earlier than fear and courage, since desire of a good is the reason why one wants to avoid an evil or to overcome it. Anger presupposes the courage to vindicate one's rights and to defend one's position. It appears, then, that hope or expectation is the first movement of the

---

[37] "Sic ergo passiones irascibilis mediæ sunt inter passiones concupiscibilis quae important motum in bonum vel in malum, et inter passiones quæ important quietem in bono vel in malo".

[38] *De civitate Dei*, XIV, c. 7: "Amor ergo inhians habere quod amatur cupiditas est; id autem habens eoque fruens lætitia est; fugiens quod ei adversatur timor est; idque, si acciderit, sentiens tristitia est".

[39] Here the principle applies: "Quod est ultimum in executione est primum in intentione".

irascible appetite. So the order in which all the passions arise is as follows: love and hatred, desire and flight, hope and despair, fear and anger, pleasure and sadness. One or other of these last two succeed to all passions (**article 3**).

Concluding his general treatise on the passions St. Thomas says that, as tradition holds[40], pleasure and sadness, hope and fear are the most important of the passions. The reason is that to move toward the good one directs oneself with love, pursues the good with desire, and then looks at it with hope. With regard to one's confrontation with an evil, one starts with hatred, next one shies away from the evil or flees it and one ends with fear. Pleasure and sadness are so important because they are the terminus of all the other passions (**article 4**).

---

[40] He refers to Boethius, *De consolatione philosophiæ*, I, metr. 7. Cf. also *E.N.* 1105^{b}23; Nemesius, *De natura hominis*, c. 17; Cicero, *De finibus* 3, 10.

CHAPTER V (QQ. 26 - 47)

THE PASSIONS CONSIDERED INDIVIDUALLY

In the following questions Aquinas examines each of the passions of the concupiscible and the irascible appetites. First he studies love, in q. 29 hatred and in q. 30 desire and flight. Next he proposes a detailed treatment of pleasure and sadness (qq. 31 - 39). The last part of the treatise considers the passions of the irascible appetite, sc. hope, despair and fear (qq. 41 - 44), courage (q. 45) and anger (qq. 46 - 47). The order in which each passion is studied is generally as follows: first the passion as such is examined, next its causes and effects while, finally, Aquinas gives some suggestions as to how to avoid what is detrimental in them. The treatise shows a high degree of insight into our emotional life. Particularly valuable are the profound analyses of love[1], desire and lust. The treatise is a clear proof of Thomas's humane approach and throws light on many aspects of human behavior.

THE PASSIONS OF THE CONCUPISCIBLE APPETITIVE FACULTY

What is love? (Q. 26)

In order to examine the nature of love as a passion we must first investigate of which faculty love is an act. Love is directed to what is good and this shows that love is a kind of tending to something. Things have a natural inclination given with their very nature. Plants, for instance, direct themselves to what is fitting to them. An additional group of inclinations is directed to the objects presented in sense-knowledge. In animals these inclinations operate automatically but in man they are subject to a certain control by reason. Finally, in man there is also an inclination to the objects known by the intellect. This inclination takes the form of acts of the will. In all these cases the inclination toward the good begins as a form of love. To love means to be in agreement with or to be adapted to and find pleasure in some good[2] (**article 1**). In a sense, the object places itself in the intention of the appetite which seeks to reach this good. Conformity to the object and the presence of the object in this tendency to it leads to love; moving toward it is desire and resting in it when it has been reached becomes joy and pleasure.

---

[1] His analysis starts with love as it is found in all beings and in the faculties of animals and man which are ordered to actions.

[2] In respect of natural movements St. Thomas speaks of a "connaturalitas appetentis ad id in quod tendit", but the inclination of animals and man to the good is called a "coaptatio ad bonum". As will be shown later, this conformity with and being adapted to the loved object is the basis of a certain presence of the beloved in the lover and of a knowledge which results from connaturality.

In so far as love is a movement elicited in the sensitive appetite it is a passion, but as the first act of the will, by which the will directs itself to the good, it is only in a metaphorical sense a passion, since passions are acts of the sensitive appetite (**article 2**).

"Love" (*amor*) has a general sense, "loving" (*dilectio*) signifies an act of the will by which one wills and chooses the beloved. The Latin word *caritas* means a noble love which directs itself to a good of great value[3], while "friendship" (*amicitia*) signifies a lasting benevolence toward a person dear to us (**article 3**).

In everyday language we also use the words "to love" and "to like" to express our love of material things such as types of food, a particular house, etc. This love which is directed to our own well-being is called "desirous love" (*amor concupiscentiae*), while the love with which one wishes the good of another is called "love of friendship" (*amor amicitiae*). Friendship is love in the full sense of the word, since it loves the good for its own sake, whereas "love of desire" seeks a good in so far as it is useful for something else[4]. This distinction helps to determine what pure love is. It is used in theology to explain the nature of supernatural love as friendship (**article 4**).

How love is born (Q. 27)

The object of love in the strict sense of the term is the good which in the appetitive faculty elicits conformity with and pleasure in this good. The good, as the object of the appetite, elicits love (**article 1**). Since it is presented by the cognitive faculties, these too collaborate in causing love. Thomas notes that, in order to know something perfectly, one should know all that is contained in it but that love must be called perfect when it loves something as it is in itself, even if the knowledge one has of it is imperfect. This explains why it may happen that something is loved more than it is known[5]. Therefore, all tending towards something and all forms of love presuppose some knowledge of it. With regard to the natural inclinations of beings the Creator, who placed these inclinations in them, knows the objects to which they are directed (**article 2**).

A well-known proverb says that everyone likes what resembles him and that like seeks like. If the likeness is real, love of friendship is born. One wills the good of the other as if it were one's own. If in one person this good is potentially

---

[3] In Christian theology the term is used in the sense of the supernatural virtue of love. In some Western languages it has the meaning of unselfish love of one's fellowmen.

[4] "Amor quo amatur aliquid ut sit ei bonum est amor simpliciter; amor autem quo amatur aliquid ut sit bonum alterius, est amor secundum quid". The first is also called benevolent love (*amor benevolentiæ*).

[5] One can like a scientific discipline on account of a vague, general knowledge one has of it, without having really mastered this science. This also applies to the Christian's love of God.

present, but in the other actually, the love of desire arises in the first person or a form of friendship aiming at one's own advantage (*amicitia utilis*). Yet it also happens that one admires or loves another person unselfishly because of certain of his qualities which one possesses oneself only potentially. However, if two persons possess the same capacities or pursue the same activity, one of them may consider the good of the other as a threat to his own good or as an obstacle to what he seeks to attain. In such a case feelings of hatred instead of love may arise (**article 3**).

As appears from the above love is the first passion and the basis of all other passions, since each of these movements results from a certain connaturality with the goal of love. It is also possible that one wants something because of the pleasure it will procure. In this case pleasure is the cause of love. But this pleasure in its turn depends on the fact that its object is adapted to our inclinations in a prior act of love. Every desire also presupposes love of the desired object (**article 4**).

The effects of love (Q. 28).

The subject we must now deal with has been treated by Aquinas with great psychological insight. A vast mass of material he borrowed from spiritual authors has also been incorporated in his text. Six effects of love are successively dealt with. **A first effect is union** with the beloved. As Pseudo-Dionysius says, "love causes unity"[6]. The unity of the one who loves and the beloved is twofold, sc. an actual union by physical presence and a union on the basis of affections. Both love as desire and love as friendship produce this union. Whoever desires something sees it as belonging to his own happiness. Whoever feels real friendship for another person considers the good of his friend as his own. He experiences the other as part of himself (*dimidium animae suae*)[7]. Love as desire leads to union, but friendship is itself this union and bond with another person. Both kinds of love tend to this unity in that they bring the one who loves and the beloved together (**article 1**).

A second effect of love is togetherness **and mutual inherence.** At the level of knowledge the beloved person or object is in the one who loves, inasmuch as it is present in his cognitive faculties. However, the one who loves is not satisfied with a general and superficial knowledge of the beloved and will attempt to understand as well as possible whatever is proper to the beloved, in order to penetrate to its innermost. As regards the appetitive faculties, the beloved object is present in their acts of love, because these faculties are conform to it and find pleasure in it. If the beloved object is present, one rejoices in it. If it is absent,

---

[6] *De divinis nominibus*, c. 4, § 12: *MG* 3, 709.
[7] See St. Augustine, *Confessiones* IV, ch. 6.

love tends toward it, either because of a desire for it or out of friendship, since one wants the good of a friend. Becoming conformed to the beloved object and finding pleasure in it is a very intimate experience, as is confirmed by the way people speak about this effect of love. Not only is the beloved present in the one who loves, but the latter also is in the beloved. The love of desire does not stop short at a superficial possession of the beloved, but wants to penetrate to his or her very core. In the love of friendship the one who loves is in the beloved person inasmuch as he himself seems to experience the good and evil which are his friend's. Friends share joy and suffering and love calls forth a loving response[8] (**article 2**).

Love also brings it about that the loving person leaves himself behind in a form of **ecstasy**. This may happen both at the level of knowledge and in the appetitive faculty. When one leaves behind the mode of knowledge proper to us and is elevated above what belongs to the natural knowledge of the intellect and the senses, one can speak of ecstasy[9]. With regard to the appetitive faculty we speak of ecstasy when it is directed to something else, so that, in a sense, we leave ourselves behind. The ecstasy which comes with knowledge is prepared by love which fills our mind with the thought of the beloved. At the level of our appetite love as desire causes us to go beyond ourselves, but, since we want to acquire a good which is outside us for ourselves this "leaving ourselves behind" is limited. This is different in friendship because here one wants a good for a friend and so one literally goes beyond oneself[10] (**article 3**).

Love calls for **efforts and zeal**. The more intensely one tends to something, the more one will set aside or overcome whatever is contrary to it. A strong love of desire will make us oppose whatever impedes us from obtaining what we desire. This zeal can sometimes turn into jealousy, in particular when this desire concerns material things which cannot in their entirety be possessed simultaneously by several persons[11]. This does not apply to strictly spiritual things, such as the possession of truth. As regards the love of friendship it will bring us to oppose and combat whatever is contrary to the good of a friend (**article 4**).

In literature love is sometimes said to **wound**. Thomas discusses the theme in article 5. Love is the appetite as conformed to some good. Now, nothing suffers damage when it is adapted to something which is fitting and suitable for it.

---

[8] In his answer to the first difficulty St. Thomas summarizes this mutual inherence as follows: "Amatum continetur in amante inquantum est impressum in affectu eius per quandam complacentiam. E converso vero amans continetur in amato inquantum amans sequitur aliquo modo illud quod est intimum amati".

[9] Aquinas speaks also of an "ecstasy" downward, when one lowers oneself to an animal mode of cognition.

[10] "Ille qui amat in tantum extra se exit, inquantum vult bona amici et operatur".

[11] Ad 2.

Rather, it is improved by it[12], whereas love of something which is not good for us will damage and make us worse. For this reason we are very much perfected by our love of God, but loving what is bad causes damage. Besides the good effects of our love of God any intense and pure love of what is good has a wholesome influence on our organism (**article 5**).

In a well-known text Pseudo-Dionysius states that good people do whatever they do out of love[13]. St. Thomas explains the saying as follows: since whatever we do is directed to an end, it is evident that every agent acts because of some form of love, for love is ordered to the good. This is why St. Augustine says that love is **an inexhaustible source of activities**[14] (**article 6**).

Hatred (Q. 29)

Just as all things tend by nature to what is fitting to them, so they turn away from what is detrimental to their good. Love is the conformity of one's appetite with what is known as suitable to one, but hatred opposes and fights what is seen as disadvantageous or contrary to the one who hates. What is opposed to our appetite is considered evil. Yet it happens that something which for one person is an object of hatred, is lovable for others (**article 1**). Love always precedes hatred, because one must first love a good which is appropriate to us before one can feel hatred for what threatens and destroys it. For this reason hatred always proceeds from love. To love something means that one does not want its opposite or hates it, so that love and hatred go together, although in reality love always comes first (**article 2**).

Since an effect cannot be more powerful than its cause, hatred is never more intense than love. Thus one rejects something only for the sake of a good and the inclination to a good is simply more powerful than hatred of the opposite evil. It happens, however, that one perceives feelings of hatred more intensely than love because of the changes which hatred provokes in the organism. Moreover one notices less an already present love than a newly appearing feeling of hatred. One can compare this with a fact of experience: one is more aware of one's love of a friend when this friend is absent than when he is present[15]. Finally, the intensity of love and hatred depends on the good one is concerned with. Hatred of a great evil can be stronger than love of a limited good (**article 3**).

Is it possible to hate oneself? It is natural for all of us to love what is good and, therefore, it must be excluded that someone hates himself simply speaking. It happens, however, that the good one tries to reach is only good in a limited

---

[12] "Amor ergo boni convenientis est perfectivus et meliorativus amantis".

[13] *De divinis nominibus,* c. IV, § 10 : *PG* 3, 708.

[14] *Enarrationes in Psalm. 31*, 2, 5.

[15] Aquinas refers to St. Augustine,*De Trinitate,* X, c. 12: "Amor non ita sentitur cum non prodit cum indigentia".

sense, but is in reality an evil. By trying to reach it one wants for oneself *per accidens* an evil, in other words, this person hates himself. Some people are seeking exclusively the lower goods for themselves and neglect the spiritual. In doing so they show a form of hatred with regard to their own true nature. It is true though that no one wants an evil for himself, unless it is sought under the appearance of a good (**article 4**).

Although truth as such is not the immediate object of the appetite it happens that a certain truth is felt to be opposed to what one would like to be true. What is true can in three ways be opposed to our appetitive faculty: a) One does not want to be true what is true. For example, parents who, against all evidence, do not want to believe that their children have done something bad; b) one refuses to accept a certain doctrine, as some refuse to admit that God exists; c) one can also hate the fact that other people know what one or one's friends have done (**article 5**).

Is it possible to hate something in general? Sense cognition and the accompanying appetite are directed to the concrete and the particular and not to the universal. It happens that because of its specific nature something is contrary to our inclinations and is hated. For example, some people loathe pork qua pork, not because it is meat of a particular animal, but because of its specific properties. The human will, on the other hand, can hate something in general (**article 6**).

Desire (Q. 30)

Desire is one of the most important emotions. Plato paid much attention to desire and to concupiscence. He stressed their relation with pleasure and sensual delight[16]. Aristotle defines desire as a tendency toward what pleases[17]. Pleasure is twofold, since it may concern a good of the sensitive appetite or a good of the will. The sensitive appetite is ordered to the good of man as consisting of body and soul and is called concupiscence (*concupiscentia*) in so far as it is directed to pleasure. But the word "desire" may also be used to denote seeking or longing for what is higher (**article 1**).

Passions are distinguished according as they are in the concupiscible or in the irascible appetitive faculty and in respect of their object. If the good is present, the appetite rests in it. If it absent it draws the appetite toward itself. In the first case pleasure results, in the second desire. Desire differs specifically from love (which is engendered when the object adjusts the appetitive faculty to itself). It also differs from pleasure which is rest in the good one has. Desire differs according to the objects one seeks to attain (**article 2**).

---

[16] *Phaedrus* 237 D.
[17] *Rhetor.* 1370ᵃ17: ἡ γὰρ ἐπιθυμία τοῦ ἡδέος ἐστὶν ὄρεξις.

A desire at the level of our animal nature, such as the desire for food, is called a natural desire. The things which are needed for our life can be desired both by a natural inclination and by a tendency following representations in the senses. Finally, there is the desire caused by an object proposed by the intellect which judges that it is good and fitting. This desire belongs exclusively to man (**article 3**).

Desires seem to be insatiable. With regard to this point Aquinas distinguishes between natural desires and those that are consequent on the knowledge of good objects. The first group cannot be actually insatiable, since nature always tends to what is determinate. But there is a certain infinity in their succession. For instance, one wants to eat again and again. However, the desire which accompanies our intellectual knowledge is really unlimited, because reason can always propose new and greater objects. A person who seeks wealth for the sake of wealth, knows no limit, but the desire for the means needed to reach a certain goal is limited (**article 4**).

Pleasure as such (Q. 31)

Pleasure has a central place in human life. Aquinas devotes four questions to its study. First he defines pleasure, next he examines what causes it and which are its effects. Finally he discusses the morality of pleasure. In the first place the nature of pleasure must be defined. A definition by Aristotle[18] points the way: "Pleasure is the experience of an emotion which places a person totally at once and immediately in a natural state and lets him come to rest". This definition, borrowed from Plato, is not without some difficulties[19]. In his *Nicomachean Ethics* Aristotle even denies that pleasure is an emotion[20], since it is momentary, has no parts and exists in an indivisible "now". St. Thomas answers this objection by observing that, indeed, pleasure is not a movement to some point, in order to attain something. It results when a natural accomplishment is reached, is simultaneous with it[21] and momentary[22], but he argues that nevertheless there is some sort of a process, inasmuch as the appetitive faculty is influenced and changed by the object presented to it[23]. When inanimate things and plants reach the natural state which is becoming to them there is no perception of it but animals perceive it by something happening in their sensitive appetite called pleas-

---

[18] *Rhetor.* $1369^b 33$.

[19] See E. M. Cope, *An Introduction to Aristotle's Rhetoric*, London/Cambridge 1867, 234-237.

[20] *E. N.*. X, cc. 3 and 4, $1173^a 1 - {}^b 4$.

[21] Art. 2, ad 1: "... huiusmodi motus non est successivus nec per se in tempore".

[22] Art. 1: "... consequi naturalem perfectionem est totum simul".

[23] Art. 1, ad 2: "... adhuc remanet immutatio appetitus ab appetibili, ratione cuius delectatio motus quidam est"

ure. The cause of this feeling is the presence of a good that agrees with their nature. When an animal performs an action which is natural for it, without being hampered, it feels pleasure. It follows that pleasure is also an "undergoing of something", although without disadvantage to the body, and therefore it may be called a passion (**article 1**).

When one experiences pleasure, one does not notice that time is passing. Pleasure is, in fact, the terminus of a movement, sc. rest in the good one has reached, but since that good itself is often subject to change, pleasure can also change, in a secondary way (*per accidens*) in the course of time. If the good attained is totally unchangeable the pleasure which comes with will not be subject to time (**article 2**). Joy is a kind of delight which has its seat in man's spiritual appetite, the will. Animals do not feel joy. We can experience joy in whatever we tend to according to our nature, but joy is not always accompanied by pleasure in the sensitive appetite. Joy corresponds to noble desires, as pleasure to concupiscence. Likewise we shall not always perceive joy when we feel pleasure (**article 3**).

In the following articles Aquinas deals with the different forms of pleasure. A first question is whether there is also pleasure in the will, our spiritual appetitive faculty. The will finds pleasure in the good it attains, and this is called joy. While pleasure in the sensitive appetite is accompanied by a change in the body, joy is an act of the will alone (**article 4**). Comparing pleasure with spiritual joy, Aquinas observes that joy in spiritual activities is significantly greater than the pleasure which follows sense-knowledge, since intellectual knowledge is much more perfect. For three reasons spiritual joy is greater than pleasure: a) spiritual goods are better and deserve to be loved more; b) the spiritual faculties themselves are more noble and have a more profound knowledge than the senses. So what causes joy is better known in itself and therefore joy can be more fully perceived; c) the connection between the good which causes joy and the intellect and the will is more intimate, Sense-knowledge remains at the outside of things, while the intellect seeks to know the essence. The union of the senses with the object does not take place all at once, but shows a certain progress, whereas the intellect is united to its object without any change. - However, this holds when one considers pleasure and joy in isolation from their context. In reality the feeling of pleasure will often be more intense, since a) the things perceived by the senses are better known to us; b) as a passion pleasure is accompanied by modifications in the body, something which seldom happens with spiritual joy; c) pleasure is often sought as a compensation for bodily defects and difficulties. In such cases pleasure is noticed more because of this contrast, something which does not happen with spiritual joy, since there is no sadness opposed to it[24] (**article 5**).

---

[24] This does not seem to be entirely true. Thomas comes back to it in q. 35, a. 5.

Thomas then turns to the feelings of pleasure which accompany the activities of the different senses. We experience their activity as something good, both because of the knowledge the senses provide and because of their being useful. Animals experience this pleasure only in the second sense. The pleasure accompanying the activity of the senses is greatest in the sense of sight, but pleasure resulting in the sense of touch from activities serving the survival of the individual or the human species is greatest[25] (**article 6**).

In the preceding articles pleasure was shown to originate from actions in agreement with the nature of the agent Is pleasure possible when actions are not in agreement with the nature of the agent? It depends on what in this case one understands by "nature". For man "natural" names what is proper to him according to his reason, such as a life according to the virtues, the quest of knowledge and contemplation. However, one can also stress in human nature what it has in common with irrational animals. According to both approaches we distinguish an unnatural pleasure from a natural one. Unnatural pleasure results from activities or conduct which deviate from right reason or which are defective from the point of view of our psycho-somatic being. Sometimes defects become a sort of second nature. In such cases the ensuing pleasure is as such unnatural, but is *per accidens* natural for the agent. Homosexual behavior seems to be an example (**article 7**). One form of pleasure can be opposed to another. On a hot day one likes to swim in water of a lower temperature, but on a cold day a hot bath is pleasant. However, the joys which virtuous actions produce, are never opposed to each other, since these actions are all performed in conformity with the same principle, sc. reason (**article 8**).

The cause of pleasure and delight (Q. 32)

In order to experience pleasure we must attain a good which agrees with us and be aware of it. The good agreeing with us is reached by actions, just as is the case with the awareness of pleasure or delight. This proves that pleasure or delight always follow some activity which is conformed to our nature. Even games and entertainment fall under this head since they take away the weariness caused by our work (**article 1**). Yet human life is subject to changes and what does not agree with us today may be pleasant to-morrow. In this sense change can be a source of pleasure or delight. This also applies to otherwise good things we have enjoyed. In certain cases they become too much for us, as, for instance, continued warm and dry weather may become unpleasant. Finally, at the level of our knowledge we may approach things from different angles in order to come to

---

[25] To illustrate this point Thomas quotes *E.N.* III, c. 10, 1118ª18: a lion is not interested in the color of a cow but in the animal as a source of food.

know them better. Therefore, a change of approach can give rise to pleasure (**article 2**).

Expectation and remembering are also sources of pleasure. Pleasure is produced by the presence of a good which agrees with us and of which we are aware. The actual union with a good is more profound and stronger and gives greater pleasure than a union on the level of knowledge or a potential union which has not yet been actualized. In the second place, hope also causes pleasure. One is not only united to a good in one's thought, but also when one expects to reach it. Finally, remembering the good one possessed earlier or a previous union with it, also gives joy. Besides hope, love and desire also cause pleasure, since love brings about a certain union with the beloved, while desire is ordered to pleasure. However, hope gives more pleasure inasmuch as it makes us look forward to the presence of the desired good (**article 3**).

Even sadness can cause some pleasure in so far as it keeps alive the memory of what one loves but one does not have at this moment. Remembering all the difficulties and worries one has been through before can also cause some pleasure (**article 4**). What others do may become a source of pleasure a) inasmuch as this brings us some good, b) in so far as what they do makes us realize better and appreciate what we have and are ourselves, c) inasmuch as we consider what they do as our own good on account of the love we have for them (**article 5**). Doing good to others gives us joy a) when we consider their good as our own, b) if it brings us some advantage, c) when doing good makes us aware of the many good things we possess ourselves, or when it results from the virtue of generosity, and, finally, when we do so at the request of a friend[26]. To punish people can also be a form of doing good, even if often it is not pleasant, in so far one is aware of promoting the real good of the person one punishes, provided one acts with prudence and justice (**article 6**).

Being alike someone or something means that one has a certain unity with him or it. For this reason something which resembles what we have ourselves or want to do ourselves can be agreeable, at least if it does not diminish or undermine our own good. Where that is the case the likeness becomes disagreeable *per accidens*. This may happen: a) when what seemed to be a good for us turns into its contrary. Too much food of a particular type we liked before, may become disgusting; b) if the good which agrees with that of ourselves detracts from the latter by competing with it. When we have almost finished for publication a manuscript on an important and novel subject, it is a considerable disappointment to discover that someone else has just beaten us to it. Finally St. Thomas observes that to be sad, melancholic and, in the case of young people,

---

[26] Aquinas notes that "omnia quae facimus vel patimur propter amicum delectabilia sunt quia amor præcipua causa delectationis est".

organic changes in the body may create a greater desire for pleasure and delight (**article 7**).

To gather knowledge on subjects one likes is pleasant. The more one desires something, the greater the pleasure when one comes to know it better. To wonder (*admiratio*) is a form of curiosity which arises in us when we see something happen without knowing its cause. To wonder about something causes pleasure because it is accompanied by the hope of getting to know its cause. For this reason, what happens seldom, as well as astonishing or out of the ordinary events, causes pleasure. On the other hand, things to which we are accustomed, are pleasant in so far as they agree with us and are, so to say, natural for us (**article 4**).

The effects of pleasure and delight (Q. 33)

Aquinas first mentions an effect of pleasure or delight which at first sight is somewhat surprising, sc. expansion or enlargement. The terms are metaphors used in the Bible[27]. When we have acquired a good which agrees with us we are aware of having become richer and feel "enlarged". Out of love for this good we shall also try to possess it most intimately and enjoy it, so as to "expand" our inner life (**article 1**).

If the good we love is not possessed by us in its entirety, for instance, when it is not totally simultaneous (e.g. a theater performance or a concert) or if acquiring it is a gradual process, as in the case of a developing friendship, the pleasure one experiences produces a desire for more of it. Almost every bodily pleasure causes such a desire for more, since it is protracted over a certain period of time. One should however notice that when bodily pleasure lasts for too long or becomes too intense it may give rise to a certain aversion, because it has gone beyond its natural measure. In such a case one will look for other pleasures. This does not happen in the case of spiritual joys which do not go beyond our capacity, unless one gets tired because of the bodily effort spiritual activity requires. Finally, remembering the pleasure one has enjoyed in the past brings us to desire it again, at least if we are still in the same state or condition. A sick and elderly person will hardly feel a desire for certain things he liked in his youth (**article 2**).

Does pleasure impede the functioning of the intellect? The pleasure one experiences when engaged in intellectual work obviously does not impede the functioning of reason. Bodily pleasure renders the work of the mind more difficult for three reasons: a) it distracts our attention and makes us concentrate more on our sensations, in proportion to their intensity; b) excessive pleasure goes against the order of reason and hinders it from acting in agreement with the vir-

---

[27] Cf. *Jesaiah* 60, 5 and *2 Cor.* 6, 11 (*"cor* nostrum dilatatum est").

tue of prudence; c) sometimes bodily pleasure is accompanied by changes in our organism and faculties such as the imagination, so that the activity of reason is paralyzed (**article 3**).

Closing his account of the effects of pleasure St. Thomas deals with the question whether pleasure perfects our acts. Aristotle discussed this theme in Book X of his *Nicomachean Ethics*. In a twofold way pleasure perfects our acts, a) inasmuch as it is a good which is added and is complementary to them, b) in so far as because of this accompanying pleasure one is more intensely engaged in acting and does so with greater zeal. - Several quotations from the *Nicomachean Ethics* illustrate this argument and show in particular that pleasure is the fulfilment of an action[28]. An action causes pleasure as an efficient cause, while pleasure perfects an action in the manner of a goal that is reached (**article 4**).

The moral value of delight and pleasure (Q. 34)

The issue of the moral goodness of the passions concerns above all pleasure, which in Antiquity was viewed with distrust by many philosophers. While Democritus, Aristippus and Eudoxus taught, each in his own way, the goodness of pleasure, at least if sought with moderation, Antisthenes, a disciple of Socrates and the first of the Cynics, totally despised any search for pleasure. Plato, for his part, fought the doctrine that the good and pleasure are identical[29]. He rejected the type of pleasure of which one should feel ashamed, drew attention to pleasure's connection with pain and worries, and spoke of the real joy and pleasure of the mind[30].

According to the Stoics it is impossible to control the passions, once they have taken hold of us. For this reason they must be suppressed and extirpated. The position of the Ancient Stoa was formulated by Chrysippus. The passions originate because of the weakness of reason (the *logos*) in us, which yields to them when over-impressed by external things and so renounces setting up a rule of conduct. Philosophy teaches us how to find a cure for our passions. Its goal is to free us from them and help us reach the state of *apatheia*, which, however, does not mean total insensitiveness.

The Epicureans chose a much more positive approach. The goal of moral life is to find the peace of the heart which goes together with moderate pleasure. Unlimited passions cause misery and so the passions must be bridled. Epicurus himself pleaded in favor of a reduction of the passions and desires to their most simple form[31].

---

[28] *E. N.*, X, c. 4, 1174^{b}24.
[29] *Gorgias* 495 A.
[30] *Republic*, XI.
[31] Cf. M. Rist, *Epicurus. An Introduction*, pp. 100 ff.

With regard to Aristotle's view, two texts deal *ex professo* with pleasure. In the *Nicomachean Ethics,* Book VII, cc. 12-15 pleasure is said to be an unhampered act or activity, while in Book X, cc. 1-8 Aristotle argues that pleasure or delight result from an action which has been performed in conformity with nature. In this second treatise on pleasure Aristotle tries to overcome the antagonism between the theories of Antisthenes and Aristippus, sc. refusal of pleasure and hedonism. According to hedonism all forms of pleasure are the same and good, but Aristotle argues that a certain type of pleasure is morally bad, while other forms are good. Their moral value depends on the actions which cause them.

Some authors consider all types of pleasure as bad, hoping perhaps to help those who are always seeking pleasure to temper their desires. Their argument is false, for no one can live without some sensory and bodily pleasure[32]. Thomas gives two arguments to defend the goodness of certain kinds of pleasure: a) The first starts from the good in which one rests and through which one experiences pleasure. When the good in which the appetitive faculty finds rest is conformed to right reason then the pleasure or delight which accompany this rest are morally good. b) A second argument is based on the actions one performs. If an action is good, the pleasure which follows is also good[33]. One should distinguish between natural and moral goodness. Pleasure or delight are good if they are consequent on a morally right choice of the will. Thomas explains this in his answer to the first objection. If the appetitive faculty rests in what is contrary to reason, the resulting pleasure is bad. But even if pleasure, consequent on a morally good act, is so intense that it impedes the use of reason, it need not be bad, for it is reasonable to interrupt now and then the activity of reason as one does during one's sleep[34] (**article 1**).

The Epicureans considered all pleasure as such good. They did not make a distinction between "good for a certain person" and "simply good". It happens that something is not good as such but is or seems to be good for a certain person, a) when this person is now in a particular state which makes a certain action desirable (e.g. taking an otherwise dangerous medicine) or b) when a certain person considers something good which is not so as such. In this case the pleasure, accompanying his or her particular action, is only apparently good and actually morally bad, since it is not conformed to reason. This does not prevent it from being perceived as agreeable by the sensitive appetite and possessing ontological goodness (**article 2**).

---

[32] Q. 34, a. 1: "Cum enim nullus possit vivere sine aliqua sensibili et corporali delectatione...".

[33] Cf. *E.N.* X, c. 5, 1175^{b}27-34.

[34] Art. 1, ad 1: "Nam et ipsa ratio hoc habet ut quandoque rationis usus intercipiatur".

Can pleasure increase indefinitely or is there a maximum pleasure, given with a perfect rest in what is best[35]? Sensual pleasure is imperfect because it is connected with the beginning and end of activities. In respect of spiritual pleasure, the delight which results when one reaches the last end, God, will be greatest. It is best for anything to reach its last end (**article 3**).

Since pleasure or delight accompany our acts one might wonder whether pleasure is a yardstick determining the moral goodness of what one is doing. Sensual pleasure cannot be such a measure, because it is present both when the will is good and when it is bad. From the fact that a person finds the food he is eating delicious one cannot deduce anything as to his moral attitude. But whoever rejoices in virtuous deeds, will be a good person, while one who finds pleasure in bad actions, is morally bad[36]. Thomas concludes his treatise on pleasure and delight by recalling that pleasure completes our actions and that, for this reason, an act is not entirely good if it is not accompanied by pleasure in the good one attains. Goodness depends on whether one reaches the goal. Since pleasure and delight are, in a sense the goal of an action, the goodness of pleasure is in a sense the cause of the goodness of an action[37] (**article 4**).

Suffering[38] and sadness as such (Q. 35)

By stressing so strongly the need and value of pleasure and delight Aquinas could give one the impression of favouring a kind of spiritual hedonism and of having no eye for suffering, pain and sadness, which visit us so often in the course of life. But the series of five questions devoted to this issue show the opposite. With regard to the two terms *dolor* and *tristitia*, mentioned in the title of Q. 35, Cicero observes that while the Greek language has one word, πόνος, in Latin two terms are used, sc. *labor* and *dolor*, to denote weariness, because of the efforts one makes on the one hand and the pain suffered on the other[39].

The Greek philosophers scarcely studied sadness and suffering in a systematic way. Panætius wrote a *Letter* to Quintus Aelius Tubero on the theme of how to keep suffering under control, but this is now lost. The Bible, on the other hand, mentions suffering frequently, as does St. Augustine whose works are an important source for Aquinas's treatise. Thomas first examines suffering and sad-

---

[35] Art. 3 ad 3: ""Delectatio non habet quod sit optimum ex hoc quod est delectatio, sed ex hoc quod est perfecta quies in optimo".

[36] Art. 4: "Est enim bonus et virtuosus qui gaudet in operibus virtutum, malus autem qui in operibus malis".

[37] Art. 4 ad 3: "Cum delectatio perficiat operationem per modum finis... , non potest esse operatio perfecte bona, nisi etiam adsit delectatio in bono; nam bonitas rei dependet ex fine. Et sic quodammodo bonitas delectationis est causa bonitatis in operatione".

[38] The Latin word *dolor* signifies both pain and suffering in a general way.

[39] *Tuscul. Disput.* II, 15, 35.

ness as such, asking next what their causes and their effects are and what means one can use to combat them. Finally the question is raised of how to evaluate suffering and sadness morally.

Thomas first shows that suffering is a state of feeling. Pain or suffering seems to be something of the body rather than of our senses. But this opinion, he says, is not true: we suffer when some evil strikes us, i.e. when it is closing in on us, just as pleasure and delight are triggered off by the presence of some good. In both cases we must become aware of the presence of either a good or an evil by a cognitive act, but good and evil as such are objects of our appetitive faculty. Suffering and sadness as passions, therefore, are the reaction of the sensitive appetite to an evil which is present (**article 1**).

The title of Q. 35 has two terms, sc. suffering and sadness. What is the difference between the two? One must distinguish between the perception of the external senses and the acts of the internal senses. The latter are concerned with more objects than are the former, sc. not only with present but also with past and future objects. Pleasure which follows an act of the internal sense-faculties is called joy, and suffering resulting from an internal act of cognition is called sadness. One speaks of pain with regard to certain experiences of the sense of touch, but not so as regards those of other external sense-powers. Thomas explains this by saying that even where their objects are not conformed to these other faculties they are not against their nature. A distasteful mixture of colours or unharmonious sounds are not against the nature of sight and hearing, as is a potentially damaging touch. It is true though that owing to his spiritual faculties a person can feel sad because of the presence of distasteful objects (**article 2**).

The passions differ according to the objects which elicit them. Since the objects of pleasure and suffering are opposed, the respective passions are also opposed. This does not contradict the fact that sadness can become the occasion for a greater desire for pleasure or delight. It also happens that in order to reach a form of pleasure one willingly sustains pain. Finally, suffering sometimes causes a certain pleasure in a secondary way, e.g. when saddened by the absence of a friend one recalls his love and kindness (**article 3**).

Sadness and pleasure are opposed when they concern the same thing. For example, some people are happy with the good results of, say, the Liberal Party in a national election, while others are saddened by them. Rejoicing about the good results of one's children at school but grieving because of the death of a relative are unrelated rather than opposed emotions, while rejoicing about the good in a particular society but feeling sad about some evil developments in it are not opposites but amount to the same emotion (**article 4**).

Are some forms of sadness opposed to the joy contemplation gives? Nothing is contrary to contemplation as such and so no one is ever saddened by contemplation as such, but one can regret certain obstacles which render contemplation difficult. However, the subject one is considering can give rise to sadness if it is itself a sad one[40] (**article 5**).

Is it better for us to avoid sadness and suffering than to seek pleasure? The inclination to pleasure as such is stronger than the aversion from suffering and sadness. The good which we want to reach can be totally convenient to us, while the evil we try to avoid is never in all respects unfitting to us. In addition, the good is sought for its own sake, while one turns away from an evil because it deprives us of a good, i.e. because of something else. It happens though that one tries to avoid sadness rather than to find pleasure. An example is when one tries to help a friend to overcome his sorrow rather than finding joy in one's friendship with him. One can also forgo the pleasure some delicious but unhealthy foodstuffs give, in order to avoid sadness about one's worsening health. It happens also that one does everything in one's power to get out of a difficult and painful situation, rather than being concerned with seeking pleasure (**article 6**).

When comparing bodily pain with spiritual suffering we see similarities and differences. Both are acts of the appetitive powers but in different respects. a) The cause of pain is the presence of an evil that affects the body, while spiritual suffering is caused by something which goes against the appetitive faculty. b) Pain results from a perception of the exterior senses, in particular of the sense of touch, whereas mental suffering is the result of what the imagination or the intellect present to the appetite. Mental suffering is more directly opposed to the appetite than pain, since pain is experienced as contrary to the appetite in so far as it is caused by some damage done to the body. For this reason suffering is more intense than pain. This follows also from the fact that the perceptions of the mind and of imagination are at a higher level than what the sense of touch experiences[41]. For this reason suffering is more intense than pain in the external senses[42]. Spiritual suffering can be caused by many more things, since our interior cognitive faculties extend to more objects than the external senses (**article 7**).

Nemesius speaks of four types of sadness, sc. acedia, anxiety, jealousy and pity[43]. This is not a division of a genus in its species, but the listing nevertheless has some value. When looking at the cause and the object of sadness, one can consider the sadness of another person as one's own (pity), or deem the good of another as saddening for oneself (jealousy), while if one considers the effects of sadness one can speak of anxiety if there seems to be no escape from a threat-

---

[40] Contemplation as such is never bad since it deals with truth which is the good of the mind (ad 2).

[41] It is true though that one does not suffer because of representations but because of what is represented (*"de re cuius est similitudo"*).

[42] Spiritual suffering and bodily pain can also occur together. In this case spiritual suffering becomes stronger.

[43] *De natura hominis*, c. 19.

ening evil. Sadness can finally lead to a certain paralysis of the powers of our soul (acedia) **(article 8)**.

What causes sadness and suffering (Q. 36)

Is it the loss of a good or, rather, the presence of an evil which makes us suffer? Considered in themselves being deprived of a good and the presence of an evil amount to the same thing, but since, at the level of our knowledge, we perceive this privation as something in itself we experience an evil as contrary to a good. This makes our will feel more keenly the privation of a good than the presence of an evil. But we suffer because an evil is present, and, on the other hand, one feels pleasure in the good when one acquires it. Therefore, when one looks at it from the point of view of the object, the presence of an evil is more properly the cause of suffering than the loss of a good. With regard to the love because of which both pleasure and suffering arise, suffering regards the absent good rather than the evil which is present **(article 1)**.

Love makes us tend to what is good and avoid evil[44]. When some evil is present, sadness arises. So love is the general cause of sadness. Desire is the first effect of love, and so it is also a cause of sadness **(article 2)**. All things tend to unity in that they try to have whatever perfects them. If this is not possible then this inclination causes suffering. By "unity" here is not meant just any union but the cohesion which constitutes the perfection of a being. Separation from what is suits us causes suffering, whereas removal of what is detrimental is experienced as good **(article 3)**. An evil which is present causes suffering or sadness. Therefore, what inflicts this evil on us is the cause of suffering. Since suffering is against our inclinations we do not seek it ourselves but it is forced on us **(article 4)**.

The effects of suffering and sadness (Q. 37)

Pain and sadness influence human life. A first effect of suffering is that it renders the work of the mind difficult. Since all our faculties are rooted in the soul, an intense concentration on one faculty prevents us from using the other powers with ease. Pain claims our attention, demanding that we remove what is contrary to our inclinations. Pain makes it practically impossible to study since this demands a considerable effort. But there are exceptions, such as when interest in study is so strong that one does not let one's attention weaken. Physical pain impedes intellectual work more than does spiritual suffering **(article 1)**.

---

[44] Art. 2, ad 1: "Inclinatio appetitus ad bonum consequendum est causa inclinationis appetitus ad malum fugiendum".

Suffering depresses the mind and prevents it enjoying its work as it would like to do by paralyzing its activities. If the evil is so great that there is no escape left one can no longer find any relief and distraction (**article 2**). Sadness, for its part, does not always lay hold on the mind to such an extent that it paralyzes all inner and outer activity. A less pervasive sadness may be the reason why one does one's work less well than otherwise. But sadness may also energize people making them seek to remove its cause (**article 3**).

Thomas believes that of all the passions sadness does most harm to our body and he explains this as follows: there is in the body a certain dynamism which goes out from the heart and spreads through the entire organism. Such passions as love, desire and pleasure strengthen this dynamism[45], unless their intensity is too great. But some passions which make us avoid an evil or turn us away from it are opposed to this dynamic process. This is the case with fear, despair and above all with sadness which burdens the mind. Anxiety and anger are always accompanied by sadness and damage our organic life, as does stress (**article 4**).

The means to be used against suffering and sadness (Q. 38)

In view of the detrimental effects on the body of sadness as a passion, we look for means to overcome this emotion. Just as rest helps when one is tired, forms of pleasure and delight are a means against sadness, whatever its cause may be[46]. The pleasure which softens sadness need not be of the same kind as our suffering, for, just because of what they are, pleasure and delight are opposed to any type of sadness. Thomas adds a remark on the sadness one feels when one is dealing with something about which in the past one rejoiced in the company of a friend, because now this friend is absent or has died. However deep our sorrow may be, after a lapse of time joy in what one is doing now and love of oneself will gain the upper hand (**article 1**).

Commenting on a text of St. Augustine[47] Aquinas notes that weeping and similar expressions of one's sadness soften our suffering, since our sorrow no longer remains shut up within ourselves but in a sense moves to the outside and dissolves. These visible manifestations of suffering are appropriate as bringing some alleviation in suffering. Aquinas quotes a general principle: "Every effect agrees with its cause and, therefore, conformable to it"[48]. By making one's sorrow visible one does what is fitting to the state in which one finds oneself, and this is helpful (**article 2**).

---

[45] Aquinas speaks of a *quædam motio*.

[46] Q. 38, a. 1: "Quælibet delectatio remedium affert ad mitigandam quamlibet tristitiam ex quocumque procedat".

[47] *Confessions*, IC, ch. 7: "In solis gemitibus et lacrimis erat ei aliquantula requies".

[48] Art. 2, ad 1: "Omnis effectus est conveniens suæ causæ et per consequens delectabilis"

A friend who shares our suffering consoles us, for sorrow is a certain burden and when a friend comforts us we have the feeling that he shares our burden. In addition, on such occasions one may notice that a friend really likes us. This also will give us some joy and so diminish our sadness (**article 3**). Likewise study and contemplation can contribute to lessening our suffering. Contemplation of the truth gives a great joy and thus meditating on divine things or on future happiness can bring us relief in our trials. The joy we experience in our higher faculties seems to reach the lower appetite[49] (**article 4**).

One can also reduce sadness as a passion by whatever promotes the vitality of the body. Thomas mentions a remark of Augustine on the wholesome effect of baths. To this one may add rest, enjoyment in the beauty of nature, moderate exercise etc. (**article 5**).

The moral qualification of sadness and suffering (Q. 39)

Sadness as such is bad, for it concerns an evil which is present which impedes us to find satisfaction in what is good. On the other hand, it is right that one feels sad at the presence of some evil. If this were not the case one would be insensitive or one would not consider this evil an evil at all, something which would be wrong, if it really is an evil. For this reason it is right to be saddened by a present evil. However, reason must judge whether a certain sadness, as regretting an evil, is justified before sadness can have a moral value[50].

Aquinas intimated already that there is a certain natural goodness in sadness. Apparently it is useful (*bonum utile*), but is it also intrinsically valuable (*bonum honestum*)? Sadness can be caused by a correct judgment about an evil which is present and is contrary to the inclination of the will. In this case feeling sadness as such is morally good (*bonum honestum*), but must evidently remain subject to the rule and the measure of reason, as other emotions must obey reason[51]. Sadness because of something good which one detests is morally bad. Being angry and sad because of an evil which is a punishment for our sins is not wrong, as long as one does not oppose God's justice in governing the world (**article 2**).

---

[49] Art. 4, ad 3: "In viribus animæ fit redundatia a superiori ad inferius. Et secundum hoc delectatio contemplationis, quæ est in superiori parte, redundat ad mitigandum etiam dolorem qui est in sensu".

[50] This is the meaning of the sentence: "Sed quia sermones morales sunt in singularibus quorum sunt quæstiones, illud quod est ex suppositione bonum, debet bonum iudicari, sicut quod est ex suppositione voluntarium, iudicatur voluntarium, ut dicitur in *III Ethic.*, et supra habitum est (q. 6, a. 6)". Cf. art. 2: "... per rectum iudicium rationis, et recusatio mali est per voluntatem bene dispositam detestantem malum".

[51] Art. 2, ad 1: "Omnes passiones animæ regulari debent secundum regulam rationis quae est radix boni honesti".

In so far as sadness makes us avoid a present evil (at least if this should be avoided), it is useful. However, what is contrary to a good must be avoided because of what it is. Sadness because of sins committed is useful, since it helps us to avoid them in the future. One can also avoid something which in itself is not bad, but may become an occasion of doing something wrong. If this has the form of a certain aversion to a life in luxury, it can be quite useful. Sadness about things that should be avoided is helpful, since it helps us not to do anything bad[52] (**article 3**).

In the preceding articles the theme of the moral value of sadness was dealt with. The question remains as to the moral significance of bodily pain. Pain, like sadness, is not the greatest of human evils. Both concern either an apparent evil (which in reality is a good) or a real evil. It is worse to abandon a real good than to be wrongly saddened by the presence of an apparent evil. On the other hand, sadness about a real evil is not at all the worse thing which can happen to us. It is worse not to see that it is an evil or not to have the will to avoid it. The will which rejects what is evil and seeks to avoid it is definitely good. For this reason sadness and pain are not the highest evil, since they are always accompanied by some good. That which damages what is more important in us is worse than that which is opposed to what is less so. For this reason evils affecting the soul are worse than bodily pain (**article 4**).

THE PASSIONS OF THE IRASCIBLE APPETITIVE FACULTY

After examining the different emotions of the concupiscent appetite Thomas considers the passions of the irascible. He devotes nine questions to them (QQ. 40 - 48). The first question deals with hope and its counterpart, despair, the four following questions with fear. Question 45 examines courage and daring, while the last three questions deal with anger. This somewhat unequal treatment is due to the particular difficulties involved in the study of some of these passions.

Hope and despair (Q. 40)

Aquinas analyses successively hope as such, going on to ask in which faculty of the soul hope has its seat and whether animals have hope or expect certain things. Is despair contrary to hope? Is hope based on experience? Are young people and the intoxicated more inclined to hope? Finally Thomas raises the question of the relation of hope to love and of the influence of hope on our activities.

---

[52] Art. 3: Sicut ergo delectatio de bono facit ut bonum avidius quæratur, ita tristitia de malo facit ut malum vehementius fugiatur", Ad 2: "Quodlibet fugiendum redditur magis fugiendum propter tristitiam".

To understand what hope is, one must consider it from the point of view of its object. Now this object is manifestly some good, since evil is feared and not hoped for. Moreover, the object of hope is something that lies in the future and that is to be attained with considerable effort[53]. What can be reached easily is not an object of hope. Finally, there must be a real possibility of reaching this object. One does not hope for something out of reach. Hope presupposes that one desires the good one hopes to attain, so that desire lies at the root of hope, as all passions of the irascible appetite presuppose those of the concupiscible appetite. When the good one desires to obtain is difficult to reach the irascible appetite comes to our help with the passion of hope[54] (**article 1**).

Hope is an act of the appetitive faculty. The cognitive powers place within themselves what we come to know, while the appetitive faculties tend and move towards these objects. So hope is a movement of the appetite toward an object presented to it which can be attained in the future, albeit with difficulty. Hope can be based on our own strength or ability or on that of someone else. In this second case one speaks of expectation and of looking forward to something rather than of hope. The solid confidence one has of reaching what one is hoping for gives firmness to one's hope (**article 2**).

To a certain extent we gather what goes on in animals from their visible behavior. When a retriever sees a faraway hare, he does not pursue it, due to a natural instinct which tells him that there is no chance to catch it. This suggests that in certain animals hope and despair may occur. Although animals have no idea of what lies in the future, they move themselves toward it, moved as they are by a natural desire, as if they could foresee it (**article 3**). This remarks serves to stress that hope is a positive force which helps us to direct ourselves to something difficult to reach.

The passions of the irascible appetite are either directed to an object or move away from it. When one considers a certain good as not within reach, one turns away from it. This is called despair, when one abandons all attempts of attaining it. In this way the appetite is *per accidens* directed to a certain evil, sc. the non-attainability of an object although one somehow still desires it (**article 4**). But what precisely are hope and expectation based on? Aquinas takes as his starting-point his description of the object of hope as a good which is difficult but not impossible to reach. Therefore, the cause of hope can be that which makes a thing actually attainable for us or makes us think that it is. In the first place, whatever increases our power is a cause of hope, such as wealth, physical strength and authority. Experience also is such a factor, if it shows how one can

---

[53] Q. 4o, a. 1 ad 2: "... cum arduitate et difficultate adispiscendi". This makes hope differ from plain desire.

[54] *Ibid.*, ad 3: "... obiectum spei non tantum addit possibilitatem super obiectum desiderii, sed etiam arduitatem quæ ad aliam potentiam facit spem pertinere, scilicet ad irascibilem, quæ respicit arduum".

more easily reach something. In the second place, whatever gives us the conviction that we can attain something is a cause of hope. Expertise and persuasion (by others) are such causes, because they suggest that something lies within our reach. Obviously experience can also point the other way and suggest that something we believed to be within reach is impossible to attain. Experience not only provides reliable knowledge but becomes also a lasting disposition in us (*habitus*) which makes it easier for us to do a certain kind of work. Reason contributes to the rise of hope in us in so far as it shows that something is possible. Stupidity and inexperience may make us think that something impossible is as yet possible and so generate false expectations. Elderly persons know by experience that certain things are impossible and so their hope extends to fewer things (**article 5**).

Youth and bodily strength are a source of hope for three reasons, according to the three aspects which characterize the object of hope (as a good, as lying in the future, as difficult to attain but not out of reach). Young people have only a short past behind them and little to remember, so they easily turn to the future. They possess strength and a spirit of enterprise to undertake what is difficult. Since for the most part they have not yet suffered many disappointments they believe more easily that something is possible[55]. A somewhat similar attitude may be found among those who have been drinking, sc. they have the feeling of being strong but lack insight into the dangers or difficulties which await them. For similar reasons stupid persons may cherish great expectations (**article 6**).

In so far as hope is directed to a good we desire and love it is itself caused by love. One hopes only for something one likes. If our hope is based on the knowledge that another person will make it possible for us to reach what we hope for then this makes us love this person and we begin to consider him as good for us. It also happens that we put our hope in someone because we believe that he likes us[56] (**article 7**).

The last article deals with the question whether hope is useful. Does hope promote what we undertake or, rather, is it an obstacle? Hope as such has a favorable influence on our work. It directs us to a difficult object that we see as lying within reach. In addition, hope also gives us some pleasure, for it calls up, in our expectation, a certain presence of a good[57]. But pleasure in what we do promotes our work (**article 8**).

---

[55] Art. 6: "Unde et iuvenes, propter inexperientiam impedimentorum et defectuum, de facili reputant aliquid sibi esse possibile. Et ideo sunt bonæ spei". Cf. ad 3: "... non solum experientia sed etiam inexperientia est causa spei".

[56] Art. 7 : "Ex hoc autem quod amamus aliquem, non speramus de eo nisi per accidens, inquantum scilicet credimus nos redamari ab ipso".

[57] See Chapter IV, q. 33, a. 3.

Fear as such (Q. 41)

Aquinas considered fear so important a passion that he devotes four questions to its study. First he examines fear as an emotion. After sadness fear shows best the typical properties of a passion, since it has an effect on the organism and as such is detrimental rather than advantageous. Fear concerns an evil and so it must be a movement of the appetite which is directed to what is good or recoils from what is evil. Since fear is accompanied by a reaction in the body and refers to some evil which threatens to get the better of us, it is obviously a passion which one suffers and which has its seat in the sensitive appetite. Sadness because of the presence of an evil afflicts us more than fear, which concerns some approaching evil. If one objects that the sense-powers have no knowledge of what lies in the future, the answer is that on account of what manifests itself to its sense powers an animal can hope to reach a future good or can fear a threatening evil (**article 1**). Fear has a specific object, sc. a future evil which is difficult to avoid or to resist. This is what makes fear a special passion. Fear must not be confused with aversion or fleeing, for it concerns an evil from which it is difficult to escape. It is related to sadness insofar as the object of fear, when present, causes sadness (**article 2**).

If by a natural emotion one understands a passion to which nature moves us, one can call certain forms of fear natural, such as fear of a natural evil which threatens us. But fear of an evil which is contrary to our desires simply is not a "natural" fear for, generally speaking, we call an emotion natural when it tends to reach a good or to avoid what is bad for us, since that is given with our nature. Other passions too go far beyond the range of natural inclinations or sometimes are even opposed to them. So out of fear one sometimes does not combat an evil, although our nature wants us to oppose it (**article 3**).

As appears from the above, fear is a complex emotion, which can be subdivided into several kinds. There is fear of the difficulties we may run into in our actions and another sort of fear in respect of things surrounding us. With regard to the first we may be afraid of the extra effort we may have to make, so that aversion from work and inertia result. Another type of fear arises when we are afraid that others will discover a misdemeanor or crime we have committed, or it concerns the anticipated bad effects of a sin one is going to commit. In this way shame is a form of fear. Evils which threaten us from outside can be beyond our strength in three ways, sc. if the evil is very great, if we are not familiar with the evil which threatens us or if an evil could not be foreseen and appears all of a sudden. All these three situations can cause fear (**article 4**).

The object of fear (Q. 42)

In order to determine more precisely the nature of fear Aquinas first examines whether its object is something good or bad. Some texts of Aristotle, St. Augustine and the Bible seem to present the good as the proper object of fear. St. John Damascene, on the other hand, says that fear concerns a future evil[58]. Fear, indeed, makes us turn away from an evil but is not a movement towards a good. One wants to get away from an evil, since it deprives us of a good. Finally, something which as such is a good can frighten us, if it can become the cause of an evil for us. One fears God because he punishes sinful behavior and people are afraid of exposure to sunlight since it may cause skin cancer (**article 1**).

Certain forms of evil thwart our personal desires, others are natural evils such as death. Dying is natural to man, even if it is sometimes caused by violence at the hands of others, just as some disasters which are otherwise natural evils such as flooding or avalanches (claiming victims) may also be due to human interventions. It happens that some future evil is not perceived as affecting us, in particular when it is still so far away or so small that it does not scare us. On the other hand, an evil which approaches with ineluctable necessity may be perceived as already present. In order to fear an evil people must have some hope that they can escape from it[59] (**article 2**).

Do we fear that we may commit a sin? Fear concerns a future evil which is difficult to avoid. However, only that which does not lie within our power is frightening. The will is the proper cause of the sins one commits and for this reason the possibility of sinning is not something which frightens us. But one may fear what seduces or moves us to sin. In such cases one fears a seductive power rather than the sins one might commit. Thomas points out that any evil we fear always has a cause which lies outside ourselves[60]. This means that one also fears to be punished (**article 3**).

One fears an evil which is approaching from the outside. In this way one can also fear fear. However, fear is subject to our will to the extent to which the sensitive appetite obeys reason. So one can shake off or suppress feelings of fear[61]. From what has been said it appears that fear may take on different forms (**article 4**).

A threatening evil from outside which is unusual or which shows up suddenly seems greater. On the other hand, if one has to cope with an evil for a longer pe-

---

[58] *De fide orthodoxa*, c. 12: *MG* 94, 929.
[59] Art. 2. Cf. Aristotle, *Rhetor.*, II, c. 5, 1383ª5: "Ad hoc quod aliquis timeat, oportet adesse aliquam spem salutis".
[60] Art. 3 ad 3: "Et ideo semper malum quod timetur est a causa extrinseca".
[61] Art. 4: "Subiacet autem voluntati, inquantum appetitus inferior obedit rationi; unde homo potest timorem repellere".

riod it does not seem so terrible any more. If one anticipates a threatening evil or one has become familiar with it over a prolonged span of time it is no longer so dreadful, just as one feels pain less if the pain stays with one a long time. What comes to us suddenly does not allow us to take appropriate measures to prevent or counteract it. Obviously, whatever increases our strength will also give us more hope and will diminish fear, since it makes it easier for us to resist the evil (**article 5**). An evil which strikes us, from which there is no escape, is perceived as lasting. There does not seem to be an end to it and this is the worse among the objects of fear[62] (**article 6**).

The cause of fear (Q. 43)

For St. Augustine there is no doubt that there is no other cause of fear than the prospect of losing what we love or of not attaining what we hope to possess[63]. In this connection Aquinas examines in which way love is the cause of fear. That which is the cause of the object of a passion is also the cause of this passion itself. However something can be the efficient cause of the object or a disposing cause. The efficient cause brings the object towards us. In this way something which gives us the representation of an approaching evil is the efficient cause of fear. On the other hand, a particular disposition in us can make us to see something we are confronted with as fearful. So love is the cause of fear, since we begin to feel fear when there is a danger that we are going to lose what we love[64] (**article 1**).

A person who is weak cannot easily withstand a threatening evil. So a lack of strength is a cause of fear. But it may also happen that a person loses any inkling that he is facing a real evil or even feels no love for a good which risks being destroyed by an evil. This serious anomaly results in a lack of fear. The evil which is threatening or difficult to avoid is the efficient cause of the fear which it provokes, and the more so the greater the evil it is[65] (**article 2**).

The effects of fear (Q. 44)

Aquinas deals with the effects of fear in four articles, A first effect is its well-known constrictive and paralyzing action. If a threatening and scarcely avoid-

---

[62] Art. 6: "Mala autem quae postquam advenerint, non possunt habere remedium, vel non de facili, accipiuntur ut perpetua vel diuturna. Et ideo maxime redduntur timenda".

[63] *Liber octoginta trium quæstionum*, Q. 3: *ML* 40, 22.

[64] Q. 43, a. 1: "Et hoc modo amor est causa timoris; ex hoc enim quod aliquis amat aliquod bonum sequitur quod privativum talis boni ei sit malum et per consequens quod timeat ipsum tanquam malum".

[65] Art. 2: "Ex hoc enim quod aliquid quod apprehenditur ut nocivum, est virtuosum, contingit quod eius effectus repelli non potest".

able evil approaches we feel the insufficiency of our own strength. Our appetitive faculty withdraws since it feels itself powerless. This is accompanied by a tightness in our chest. The opposite happens with angry people, who react vigorously and courageously. When one fears one is inclined to be silent, whereas sadness makes people manifest their feelings by crying or complaints. When one is mortally frightened the body heat goes inward and one becomes pale like a corpse (**article 1**).

When we are facing difficulties or have to carry out an important task, we do not always completely trust our own ability but seek counsel and help from others. For the same reason fear makes us solicit advice. Our own capacity to deliberate quietly is not enhanced by fear nor by any other emotion. Rather, it decreases. When one is strongly affected by a passion one will represent something as greater or smaller than it really is. For instance, when one loves someone, the beloved can seem better than she or he is. When one fears something, it might be just as bad as it seems or worse. An invasive fear may considerably reduce our capacity to deliberate (**article 2**).

It is well-known that fear can make people tremble and shake. The control of the body diminishes, something which Aquinas attributes to a lack of bodily heat (**article 3**). In addition fear can also hinder us from doing our work. On the other hand, a not so overwhelming fear can make us check painstakingly what we have to do and execute our tasks with greater care. But this no longer applies when a very intense fear impedes us from reflecting (**article 4**).

Aquinas does not devote any question to the moral value of fear. The reason is that fear arises spontaneously when one is confronted with a threatening and considerable evil, which one cannot surmount. But what causes this evil does, of course, have a moral value.

Courage (Q. 45)

Fear's counterpart is courage. Fear makes us flee from a threatening evil which we do not have the strength to resist[66]. But courage make us confront and oppose this evil, since it makes us feel stronger[67]. Courage differs from hope, since courage refers to a threatening evil, while hope is directed to a future good (**article 1**). Courage follows on hope, since when someone expects to be able to triumph over a frightening evil he fights it with courage. Fear, on the other hand, is followed by despair. One gives up since one fears the difficulties connected with the good one was hoping for. This is why hope is prior to courage, as fear is to despair. Courage is an effect of hope. Although overcoming a threatening

---

[66] Q. 45, art 1: "Timor enim refugit nocumentum futurum propter eius victoriam super ipsum timentem".

[67] *Ibid.* : "Audacia aggreditur periculum imminens propter victoriam sui super ipsum periculum".

evil is something good, the immediate object of courage is nevertheless the evil that one is confronting (**article 2**).

Whatever gives us hope or chases fear away is a cause of courage. Hope brings it about that despite difficulties we nevertheless believe we can accomplish something difficult by our own strength, experience and ability, with the means at our disposal or thanks to the help of others, in particular of friends and of God. The absence of fear also helps become courageous. This will be the case when one does not need to fear anything from others if one has no enemies. Another factor which helps us become courageous is the disposition of our organism, e.g. a strong heart and much energy. Aquinas finally quotes an observation of Aristotle's: "Those who have little experience of dangers and of failure are usually more courageous"[68]. They are not aware of their own weakness nor of all the difficulties they will have to face. Those who have suffered unjust treatment, however, often show greater courage since they trust that God will put them in the right (**article 3**).

Aristotle observes that courageous persons sometimes show greater courage at the beginning of their action than at a later stage[69]. Thomas uses this text as a starting-point for some further valuable remarks on this emotion. As a passion courage follows upon what the sense-powers present us. However, the sense-powers do not compare things with each other nor do they represent the different aspects and circumstances. The result is that a first impression does not allow one to know all the factors which can cause difficulties in a particular undertaking, so that courage easily arises. But if it turns out, when dealing with the issue, that greater difficulties arise than one could initially foresee, zest to continue will be less. Our reason, on the other hand, examines the different aspects of an issue or an undertaking. This explains why persons possessing the virtue of fortitude seem to be slow at first. This is because they do not act as driven by emotions merely but with deliberation. Hence they do not encounter unforeseen difficulties. Their will is directed to the good and perseveres, while others, who are led only by the passion of courage, base their action on hope which excludes fear. Thomas also points out that the object of courage consists of something good and something bad, sc. opposing an evil presupposes that one hopes to reach some good. However, if the difficulties turn out to be greater than one had expected then hope decreases. Finally Aquinas notes that anger about what has been done to us, increases our courage. This remark prepares the transition to the next series of questions which deal with anger (**article 4**).

---

[68] *Rhetor.*, II, c. 5, 1383^{a}28.
[69] *E. N.*, III, c. 7, 1116^{a}7.

Anger as such (Q. 46)

The first of the series of questions dealing with anger comprises eight articles. Aquinas first examines where anger has its seat and whether it is a separate passion. A difficulty is that anger seems to arise from several other passions: from sadness because of what has been done to us, from the desire to straighten this out and from hope of revenging ourselves. If there is no such hope because the person who wronged us is too powerful then we feel sad instead of becoming angry. Anger is a passion which arises because of an evil which is present. The other passions of the irascible appetite all contribute to anger, the passion which makes itself felt most[70]. Anger arises from contrary passions, sc. sadness and hope, but has itself no opposite (**article 1**).

To understand better what anger is, its object must be determined more precisely. The object of love is the good. Thus one wants a good for oneself or someone else. But the object of hatred is an evil, since one wants some evil to befall another person. In the case of anger it is different again. On the one hand, anger implies that one wants to revenge oneself on someone else and perceives this as a good thing to do. On the other hand, it addresses itself to a person or a thing perceived as an evil. Therefore, anger is a passion which is composed of opposite emotions[71] (**article 2**).

The passions of the irascible appetite differ from those of the concupiscible appetite in that their object , the good, and the evil opposing it - are accompanied by a certain difficulty. However, Thomas specifies here, anger concerns two objects, revenge and the person on whom one wants to revenge oneself. Both objects must entail certain difficulties in order to give rise to anything describable as anger. This means that anger is a passion of the irascible appetite. In the first article Aquinas had written that anger arises from sadness and desire, emotions which are not constitutive parts of anger but its cause (**article 3**).

It is a well-known fact that people can become so angry that they no longer deliberate. Nevertheless anger is always accompanied by a certain use of reason, since to revenge oneself one must compare the evil one has suffered with whatever one wants to inflict on someone else[72]. Yet in anger as a passion it is not reason which commands revenge. The irascible appetite can pass to the act of revenge by itself. In actually revenging oneself anger keeps one from respecting the rule of reason[73] (**article 4**).

---

[70] This also explains the use of the term *irascible* for the sensitive appetite, whose acts are fear, hope, anger etc..

[71] In *In III Sent.*, dist. 26, q. 1, a. 3 ad 5 Thomas writes that anger is composed of courage, sadness and hope.

[72] Animals can make a certain comparison using their estimative power.

[73] Art. 4, ad 3: "... non observat regulam rationis".

Is anger as a passion more natural than desire? Aristotle thought so[74], but Aquinas says that the question must be considered from the point of view of the causes of the passions. One can consider the cause of an emotion both from the point of view of its object and from that of the person in whom the passion arises. Considered from the first viewpoint desire is more natural than anger, but considered from the side of the person, anger is more natural in one way more natural, desire in another. Reason is more involved in anger than it is in desire. Thus what is specifically human and hence natural, sc. reason, comes more to the fore in anger (**article 5**).

Comparing the passion of anger with that of hatred, Aquinas notes that both persons in anger and those who hate someone wish an evil to happen to him. There is a difference, however, in so far as the person in anger is convinced that the evil he wants to inflict is a just retribution. Inflicting an evil under the aspect of a good is better than just wishing someone evil, as those who hate a person do. Moreover, those in anger want the other person to know why they are seeking revenge. A final difference is that hatred lasts longer insofar as it proceeds from the conviction that the person one hates is dangerous to oneself[75] (**article 6**).

What anger tries to accomplish, sc. revenge for an injustice one has suffered, falls under the virtue of justice. But if this is correct, how do we explain that animals also appear to have this passion. Aquinas replies that, moved by instinct or representations in their imagination, animals may act in a way which resembles what man does by reason. Moreover, in man anger may also result from a representation which indicates that one has been wronged or suffered damage from someone. In this way people may become angry at animals, plants and inanimate things, as animals do at whatever thwarts or hurts them. But anger motivated by reason is not concerned with inanimate things which cannot commit any injustice and do not suffer (**article 7**). In fact, anger has different forms. St. John Damascene[76] and Nemesius[77] distinguish between a sudden flash of anger, long-lasting anger and being enraged. Considering the effects of anger St. Gregory the Great distinguishes between anger which paralyzes one's speech, anger which make one use strong language and anger which expresses a person's grudge clearly[78] (**article 8**).

---

[74] *E. N.* VII, c. 6, 1149^{b}6. The Greek text, however, is more subtle than its Latin rendering. To have an angry and fretful character is more natural than desiring things which are not necessary.

[75] Hatred may be directed to individuals or to a whole class of things, perceived as opposed to oneself (art. 7 ad 3).

[76] *De fide orthodoxa*, II, c. 16: *MG* 94, 933.

[77] *De natura hominis*, c.21 : *MG* 40, 692.

[78] *Moralia*, XXI, c. 5 : *ML* 76, 194. Gregory seems to be inspired by the *Gospel according to Matthew* 5, 22.

The consequences of anger and how to fight this passion (Q. 47)

As we found Aquinas explaining above, anger makes us want to inflict damage on someone else who has been unjust to us. As we seek our own good, so we also ward off threatening evils. However, an injustice committed against others does not concern us, unless it is in one way or another also directed against ourselves, e.g. if it harms our relatives and friends, or damages or shows contempt for certain things which are dear to us[79]. One tries to revenge oneself insofar as one thinks that it is justified on account of the injustice committed against us. However, people can damage others either out of ignorance or out of passion or by a deliberate choice. In the latter case the injustice is greatest, since it is committed willingly or out of malice. This explains why we are angrier at those whom we suspect are hurting us on purpose. Their behavior expresses a certain contempt, which contradicts the excellence we seek to attain for ourselves. If the unjust treatment we suffer or the damage inflicted are not inspired by contempt then they are felt to be less serious. To forget the good that others have done or the support which we have received from them can also be a sign of disrespect. This is likewise the case when one does not take into consideration the situation of the other person, e.g. his sadness because of a tragic event in his family. Since animals also want to attain a certain excellence, they too become angry at whatever hinders or impedes them (**article 2**).

Those in a high position may easily become angry when what they excel in is despised or considered of little interest[80]. An evil which saddens us may also make us angry. This explains why people who struggle with certain defects quickly get angry when attention is drawn to them (**article 3**). Gratuitous disrespect or contempt shown to a person will easily provoke his anger. If the one who despises us has himself certain defects his behavior will probably make us even angrier. Thus the learned feel provoked when an illiterate person despises them. But if the culprit acknowledges his mistake and excuses himself then he honors them, thus calming their anger. When those who have offended us die our indignation eases off, for the dead cannot be affected by any retribution. Moreover, we know that they have already been visited by a much greater evil than the one we wanted to inflict on them (**article 4**).

---

[79] Q. 47, art. 1 ad 3: "In id quo maxime studemus, reputamus esse bonum nostrum. Et ideo, cum illud despicitur, reputamus nos quoque despici, et arbitramur nos læsos".

[80] However, a person conscious of standing far above his critics will be less inclined to anger in such cases (art.3, ad 2).

The effects of anger (Q. 48)

As Aristotle shows[81] and as has been explained above[82], pleasures and distractions are helpful against sadness and anxiety. Since anger makes us seek to revenge the injustice done to us, this revenge, when carried out, will give pleasure and take away sadness. Moreover, already before one actually revenges oneself one enjoys it somewhat in anticipation (**article 1**).

By a disposition of human nature the passions direct themselves with greater intensity to what is opposed to us, the more it is present. Anger is a strong reaction against an evil done to us and is accompanied by a vigorous reaction in the body, e.g. a sudden flush or an accelerated heartbeat. But this accession of heat differs from the warm feeling love gives us and which is tender and sweet, while the effect of anger is bitterness. Since in the course of time our memories become less distinct the memory of the evil we suffered will also become weaker. The same holds true of friendship, which will lose its intensity if it is only feeding on memories. Aquinas furthermore notes that if one becomes successively angry at several persons, one's anger in respect of the first will diminish, in particular when the injustice done to us later is more serious (**article 2**).

Although in its proper activity the intellect does not use the senses it nevertheless needs their collaboration. When the senses are hampered in their operation the activity of the intellect will also be hindered, as happens when people are drunk. So since anger provokes a strong reaction in the body it hampers the work of the mind more than the other passions do, even if, as was said above, a certain rational reflection is required for anger to develop[83]. In his answer to the second objection here Aquinas points out that concupiscence or lust like to work in a hidden way, since what they pursue is something dishonest or disgraceful, whereas anger comes out into the open, the more so where reason does not sufficiently intervene to remind us what should be kept hidden (**article 3**). In the final article of this question Thomas mentions yet another aspect of anger. Because anger hampers the activity of the mind, it happens that people who are very angry become speechless. On the other hand, anger shows most on person's eyes and face, which give expression to what is going on his heart. In extreme cases anger can even paralyze the use of our limbs and cause death (**article 4**). This last article of our question closes the treatise on the passions considered individually and Aquinas now passes to the study of the principles of human acts.

---

[81] *Ethic. Nicom.* VII, c. 14, 1154^{b}27. Cf. Thomas, *In VII Ethic.*, l. 14: "Delectatio corporalis propter sui superabundantiam est medicina contra tristitiam".
[82] Q. 38, art. 1.
[83] Q. 46, art. 4.

CHAPTER VI

THE PRINCIPLES OF OUR ACTS

After studying the passions which often accompany our deliberations and choices and which must be ordered by reason Aquinas now investigates, where we can find some support in the numerous decisions we must take and the tasks we must carry out. Human beings are endowed with free will and can choose what they are going to do[1]. But they are also creatures of habit and from early in the morning until late at night they perform their actions all the more easily because of dispositions acquired in the course of their lives. When washing oneself and dressing, while preparing meals and eating or when using a language we continually follow particular dispositions we have acquired earlier. Each of these dispositions helps us to proceed along a certain path in our psyche, nervous system and muscles and so facilitates performing complex activities. In moral life there are also acquired dispositions, sc. the virtues and vices, analogous to those just mentioned, which make it much easier to act for the good in the various fields of our tasks and obligations, or for the worse. Finally, there are also rules of conduct which are imposed on us from without and which, in ethics, are called "laws". The latter are external principles of our acts.

This does not mean that our intellect and will are entirely determined by virtues and vices to whatever action we perform. They remain open to different options, since the will continues to be free, but such permanent dispositions exercise a certain pressure, so that acting in conformity with them comes easily and is pleasurable[2]. The study of the virtues and vices presupposes that one is acquainted with the doctrine of the faculties or powers in man. In a general introduction Thomas discusses the category of realities to which the virtues belong, sc. that of lasting dispositions at the level of the mind, in Latin called *habitus*. As in other fields Thomas first considers the more general and what is common, before dealing with what is more particular. He thus proceeds in a more systematic way than Aristotle did in his *Nicomachean Ethics*[3].

The treatise on the *habitus* is a *novum*[4] in the work of Aquinas[5]. It comprises six questions: the nature of the *habitus* (Q. 49), the soul and the faculties as the

---

[1] Cf. *Q. d. de veritate*, q. 24, a. 4: "... habet in se unde possit agere".

[2] See *S. Th.* I-II 55, 1.

[3] Cf. M. Wittmann, *Die Ethik des hl. Thomas von Aquin in ihrer systematischen Aufbau dargestellt und in ihren geschichtlichen, besonders in den antiken Quellen erforscht*, München 1933, 218 ff.

[4] On the following pages the Latin term *habitus* will be used (also as a plural), for which there is no real equivalent in contemporary English.

[5] O.H. Pesch, "Die bleibende Bedeutung der thomanischen Tugendethik", in *Freiburger Zeitschrift für Philosophie und Theologie* 21 (1974), 359 - 391. See also E. Schockenhoff,

seat of the *habitus* (Q. 50), the coming into being and disappearance of the *habitus* (QQ. 51 - 53), the divisions of the *habitus* (Q. 54). The articles go into details and Aquinas brings long quotations from his sources, in particular from Simplicius' *Commentary on the Categories*. This points to the importance he attached to the matter.

The nature of the habitus (Q. 49)

The term habitus is derived from the Latin verb *habere* and means a disposition to a particular, customary way of doing something, sc. a permanent disposition[6]. Health is such a disposition of the body. But in this treatise Thomas speaks mainly of habitus in so far as they are dispositions of the faculties, by which these are ordered to particular actions, although not totally determined[7] (**article 1**). A habitus is a determination or disposition of something in accordance with its nature or opposed to it. An illness is a disposition not in conformity with our nature, while health is conformed to it. The term habitus refers to a disposition which is durable. A science which one has mastered is a durable disposition, but superficial knowledge is not and can easily be lost[8]. By mentioning that some habitus are according to our nature, but others not, Thomas laid the foundation for his treatises on the virtues and the vices, placing them within the larger genus of the habitus (**article 2**).

In a more remote sense *every* habitus is ordered to action in so far as it determines beings which by their nature are meant to act. But there is a group of habitus which are directly ordered to acts, sc. those which are present in those faculties which by their very nature are principles of actions[9]. This means that the primary function of a habitus present in a faculty is to assist it in acting (**article 3**). What is required so that a substance can be determined by a habitus? In the first place it must have a potential capacity for a further determination. Secondly, it must be capable of being determined in different ways. Finally, different factors or components must collaborate in order to bring about this determination. This last condition is apparent in such habitus as health or beauty, to which different factors contribute. Habitus in our faculties are caused by acts of the same species and are strengthened by repeating them. As has been shown in

---

Bonum hominis. Die anthropologischen und theologischen Grundlagen der Tugendethik des Thomas von Aquin, Mainz, 1987, p. 202.

[6] The Greek word for habitus is ἕξις. Cf. *Metaph*. V, c. 20, 1022^{b}10. In the Latin West the concept became known through Boethius' treatise *In Categorias Aristotelis: PL* 64, 242 A, but at first not much importance was attached to it.

[7] St. Thomas quotes the commentary of Simplicius on the *Categoriae*, c. 9.

[8] In this article Aquinas indicates that dispositions and habitus are specifically different, but in the *Q. d. de malo*, q. 7, a. 2, ad 4, this is not explicitly stated.

[9] Art. 3: "Manifestum est autem quod natura et ratio potentiae est ut sit principium actus".

Chapter II, several acts work together in order to make a free choice come about. Likewise to produce a habitus various acts collaborate and determine the faculties (**article 4**).

The seat of the habitus (Q. 50)

At first sight the detailed study of the question as to where the habitus are located may seem of little interest. However, the answers help us to distinguish better between the different moral virtues. A first question is whether some habitus have their seat in the body. In his answer Aquinas points out that inasmuch as a habitus brings a substance into the required disposition for acting it would seem to be in the soul, which is the principle of all activities which are not immediately given with nature[10] and only in a more remote sense in the body, in so far as the soul acts using the body. However, a habitus which is not ordered to action, but gives a certain disposition, can have its seat in the body, e.g. health and beauty, but such habitus are not very durable, exposed as they are to influences which provoke changes in the body (**article 1**).

The habitus ordered to actions have their seat in the soul, i.e. in the faculties by means of which the soul acts. These faculties are prior to the habitus[11]. There are no *natural* habitus in the essence of the soul itself, because the soul is the primary formal cause which constitutes human nature. At most, Thomas writes, one could speak of some dispositions in the body ordered to the soul[12] (**article 2**).

To the extent that the senses and the sensory appetite act by virtue of their nature, they are not determined by habitus, since their activity is given with their very nature and is already determined. But in man, in so far as the senses follow commands of reason they can be directed to different objects and so there is room for habitus, such as dispositions in sight or hearing which make one like particular shapes and colors or sounds. The sense-faculties of animals do not follow orders commands of reason and so there are no habitus in them. Only when animals are trained by man, can habit forming in their faculties occur to a certain extent. In man the sensory appetitive faculties are subject to reason and

---

[10] Activities which are given with one's nature are natural and one does not need a habitus for them, for natural processes are determined to one kind of thing, as is digestion. A habitus is first required when a subject is capable of a variety of acts.

[11] Art. 2 ad 3: "Unde est posterior potentia". The concept of a habitus not ordered to action is used elsewhere by Aquinas to explain man's participation in God's nature by supernatural grace.

[12] Most likely are meant the dispositions in the biological material of human beings by which the soul receives its individuality (the so-called *dispositiones praeviae*). Aquinas acknowledges the possibility of a supernatural habitus determining the human soul in its innermost.

will, while the cognitive sensory faculties present this material to reason and so precede intellectual knowledge. At best one could speak of a certain formation of habit under the direction of the intellect and the will, in such internal senses as memory and the estimative sense (called *cogitativa* in man). But this kind of determination does not take place in the external sense powers (**article 3**).

In the intellect, however, several habitus are formed. Besides the habitus of the first principles one acquires a considerable knowledge through experience or study. This knowledge becomes habitual, when the mind turns to other things. It is so to say slumbering, but can be used again at a later moment. Even if the object of such knowledge is a material reality, it does not mean that its habitus has a mixed corporeal-spiritual structure and is also in the body. The reason is that a habitus disposes a faculty for a special kind of action, in this case for actual knowledge. Since the intellect is immaterial, the respective habitus of the intellect are also immaterial (**article 4**). Each faculty able to perform different acts needs the corresponding habitus in order to be well disposed to them and to act with ease and pleasure. Since the human will can act in different ways (on account of its nature it is not determined to just one kind of action[13]), there are also habitus in the will (**article 5**).

How the habitus originate (Q. 51)

The question of the origin of the habitus is of fundamental importance in ethics, since it concerns directly the origin of virtues and vices[14]. A first question will be whether we possess certain habitus by nature. Aquinas distinguishes between the habitus which dispose a subject in view of a certain form and those which dispose the faculties in view of their acts. There are, indeed, in the intellect and the will certain dispositions which are partially by nature and partially the result of influences from without. Thomas means here the first principles of the speculative and of the practical intellect[15]. The latter are studied in ethics since they are the basis of natural law. Together they constitute a set, sc. a permanent determination of the intellect, which uses these principles in all later judgments and reasoning. One may add that human beings have individually varying natural dispositions in the organs of sense-cognition, which explains why some can

---

[13] However, by its nature the will is always directed to the good, but this can take different forms. Cf. art. 5 ad 3: "Sed quia hoc bonum multipliciter diversificatur, necessarium est ut ad aliquid determinatum bonum rationis voluntas per aliquem habitum inclinetur, ad hoc quod sequatur promptior operatio".

[14] In Book II of his *Nicomachean Ethics* Aristotole claims to show how we acquire the virtues and become morally good persons.

[15] These are the first principles of the speculative intellect such as the principles of contradiction and causality and those of the practical intellect such as "the good must be done, evil avoided", etc.

more easily devote themselves to intellectual work than others. - As regards the appetitive faculties, one can at best speak of a natural inclination of these faculties to certain good objects which are in conformity with human nature[16]. But such inclinations are not yet a habitus. Finally, there may also be in the body some dispositions to virtues (or vices), e.g. to gentleness or to chastity but these cannot be called habitus in the strict sense of the term (**article 1**).

The first article left the question pending of how the habitus are ordinarily produced in the faculties. It appears that many of them are not a product of our nature. In order to throw some light on the problem of their origin St. Thomas first notes that when a thing works entirely by itself (like the sun radiating its light and warmth) there is no question of the formation of a habitus, because such activities are intrinsic to the nature concerned. The sun always acts in this way. But in human beings the situation is different. The acts of our appetitive faculties arise in so far as these faculties are moved by the objects which the senses and intellect present to them. This presupposes that there is an inclination of these faculties toward the good and that they are open to its attractive force. The intellect, for its part, is moved in its thinking by the first self-evident principles. In so far as the faculties are moved by something else, they undergo a causal influence and a disposition may be formed in them, which we call a habitus. This happens mainly by repeated actions[17]. In this way the moral virtues arise in our appetitive faculties in so far as these are influenced by the intellect which directs our acts so as to be in conformity with reason. The intellect forms the habitus of a science, when in its study of a subject matter it proceeds from the first principles. But at this point a difficulty must be solved. An effect cannot be more valuable than its cause. Now a habitus, e.g. the virtue of justice, seems more valuable than the preceding act, for a virtue causes the acts proceeding from a faculty to be better. The solution is that the cause which forms the habitus is best, as the rule of reason for the moral virtues is better than these virtues themselves and the first principles better than the sciences based on them (**article 2**).

Could a single act ever be sufficient to cause a habitus in a faculty? Here one must distinguish between the cognitive and the appetitive faculties. With regard to the latter, in order for a single act to produce a habitus this act would have to overcome and actualize the entire capacity of such a faculty. Since the appetite is drawn in different directions the intellect, with its judgment that a certain act should be performed, cannot overcome the potentiality of the appetitive faculty and so cannot bring about that from now on it will always perform an act in the same way, as if it had become its second nature. A plurality of acts are required

---

[16] Thomas speaks of *seminalia virtutum*, an expression one finds only in this article and in I-II 63, 1.

[17] Art. 2: "... multiplicatis actibus generatur quaedam qualitas in potentia passiva et mota quae nominatur habitus".

in order to secure this result. As regards the cognitive faculties Aquinas reminds us that the intellect[18] can be forced by a single proposition to accept a conclusion. When something is not evident one must examine it further, before reaching certitude. With regard to the lower sense-faculties an act must be repeated before something can become impressed deeply on them. Our memory provides a good example of this. By repeating to oneself the facts one wants to store in one's memory these will be preserved (**article 3**). Finally Thomas recalls that God can place certain habitus in man which give him the capacity to perform acts directed to an end which lies beyond the reach of his natural powers, a theme which is of great importance in the theology of divine grace (**article 4**).

Intensifying a habitus (Q. 52)

After it has been established that habitus are formed by acting repeatedly in a certain way, we must now deal with the question how a habitus, and in particular a virtue, can become stronger or more intense. In matters outside the order of quantity "growth" must be seen as becoming better[19]. However, the perfection of a form can be considered in two ways, sc. in itself or regarding the manner in which a subject participates in it. It is obvious that forms admit degrees of perfection, e.g. one can have a greater or lesser knowledge. With regard to a subject's participation in a form several explanations have been proposed as to how this can intensify, four of which are mentioned here by Aquinas. His own solution is as follows. What makes up the specific nature of a thing is fixed and does not allow any more or less[20]. This applies both to substances and to the nature of such qualities as whiteness, heat etc. considered in themselves But things whose specific nature consists in being directed to something else, can become greater or smaller, preserving their nature, while the thing toward which they are directed remains the same. In this way an individual movement can get faster or slower and some processes more or less intense. Our own health can also become better or less good, while it remains the health of the same body, unless when one understands by anyone's health the perfect condition of his or her body. When considering a quality according to the degree in which a subject partakes in it, we see therefore that we can possess certain qualities in a higher or lower degree, but not others. With regard to the disposition of a certain matter to a particular form a person can be more or a less well disposed. But the different the numbers, for example, have no more or less[21]. Considering a habitus

---

[18] Thomas speaks of the *intellectus possibilis*, that is the intellect which receives the cognitive impressions (the *species intelligibiles*).

[19] St. Augustine, *De Trinitate*, VI, c. 9: "In his quae non mole magna sunt, idem est esse maius quod melius".

[20] If this were the case, a different species would come about.

[21] In Aristotle's view numbers as 2, 3, 4 etc. are each a species. Cf. *Metaph.* VIII, 1043^{b}35.

from the viewpoint of its being directed to something, its becoming stronger or weaker can be conceived in two ways: a) in so far as this habitus itself extends to more things, as when one's health is diffused in all the members and organs of the body or when a science deals with a broader subject, b) insofar as a subject partakes in it. This depends on the state of this subject, which is given with its nature or results from habituation. In the following articles these conclusions are applied to the virtues[22]. In his answer to the second objection Aquinas observes that, when looked upon from the point of view of its nature, a habitus is not a closed entity, as are the species of the numbers, and that therefore it can become stronger or weaker (**article 1**).

Intensification of a habitus cannot be caused by adding more of the same form. Such an addition would change its species. Nevertheless in certain accidents such an addition does take place. A movement may become faster, a voyage longer, while they remain the same because of their being directed to the same terminus. However, a movement can become more intense, to the extent that its subject engages itself more intensely in it and carries it out faster. Knowledge - such as the habitus of geometry - becomes extended further when one learns new truths. It can also become stronger in persons who have a clear mind and are quick at seeing the legitimate implications (**article 2**).

Acts of the same type cause the same habitus. However, it is up to our free decision whether we use a habitus or not, or whether to perform acts opposed to it. It may also happen that an act we perform, e.g. of the virtue of fortitude, is less strong than was the habitus as acquired earlier. In such a case the habitus does not become stronger, but rather weaker. Acts which correspond with the degree of intensity of a habitus or are more intense will further intensify it (**article 3**).

The waning and disappearance of habitus (Q. 53),

Do habitus disappear? At a first sight it is not obvious what factor could cause them to do so. Particularly regarding immaterial habitus of the intellect and will there would seem to be a difficulty. In his answer to this question Thomas explains that a form can be damaged by its contrary as well as by the disappearance of the subject in which it is present. This means that a habitus in a perishable subject and any habits caused by something to which something else is opposed can disappear. So the habitus in the intellect and will cannot disappear by the corruption of their subject, since the soul is imperishable. But it happens that by processes in the body the sense faculties which accompany the acts of the habitus in the intellect can no longer accomplish their task and so these habitus in the mind are no longer of any use. But their roots in the mind are not affected.

---

[22] See Q. 66, a. 1.

Likewise nothing is opposed to certain habitus of the mind, such as concepts and the complex of first principles. However, something can be opposed to the conclusions reached in certain sciences. A fallacious argument can undo a correct conclusion reached earlier and so destroy the habitus. Moral virtues which have their seat in the sensory appetite can be opposed and hence neutralized by a judgment of the intellect proceeding from ignorance, passion or a deliberate choice. The same applies, *mutatis mutandis,* to vices (**article 1**).

Just as a habitus can grow stronger, so it can also become weaker under the influence of the same causes by which it is destroyed, since becoming weaker introduces corruption. Although a habitus as such, not being something composite, does not lose any of its parts, it becomes weaker with regard to the degree in which a subject partakes in it. Thus whiteness as such does not change, but a surface can become more or less white (**article 2**).

A last question is whether through a person's not acting in conformity with an already present habitus, this habitus can diminish and disappear. By not acting in conformity with a particular habitus one can weaken it *per accidens,* inasmuch as this not-acting allows other influences to affect the particular habitus. One can observe this in the virtues and in scientific knowledge. If one does not act virtuously, the passions will easily gain the upper hand, so that the virtues decline. Similarly, if the mind does not actually use the habitus of science which it has acquired, then it will be swamped by all sorts of images in the imagination and so become less capable of deliberation and reasoning (**article 3**).

The differences between the habitus (Q. 54)

A first question is whether there can be several habitus in one faculty. A faculty, because of its specific nature, is directed to one kind of act. Just as a body cannot have different shapes at the same time, so it would seem that a faculty cannot be determined simultaneously by different habitus. In his response Aquinas distinguishes between those habitus which determine a subject's natural condition and those habitus which dispose the faculties to certain acts. With regard to the first type, different habitus can be present in one subject at the same time, provided this subject has a variety of parts or aspects. Thus there are in the body the habitus of health, strength and beauty among others. The same applies to the habitus which are located in the faculties. A faculty can perform different acts because of the variety of objects to which it directs the acts[23]. There are indeed wholly different objects, such as the abstract objects of the mathematical sciences on the one hand and physical bodies on the other. Similarly we distinguish between justice in inter-human relationships and justice in governing the

---

[23] In q. 51, a. 2 St. Thomas drew attention to the difference of such acts from entirely natural activities of a physical body, which is determined to one type of activity.

commonwealth. For this reason a plurality of habitus are possible in the faculties, by which these are inclined to different types of acts. The difficulty raised here disappears if one keeps in mind that the specifically different objects of the various virtues yet possess a generic unity and fall under the same generic object. The difference from bodies which at one particular moment can have only one shape, is that this shape is their external limit, whereas a habitus stands at the origin of a series of acts. On the other hand a faculty cannot perform more than one act at the same time (**article 1**).

What differentiates habitus? The enquiry is preliminary to understanding how the moral virtues are differentiated. We can consider a habitus either as a form or as an entity and its nature will depend on the efficient cause which produces it. As was explained in the first article, the habitus stand in a certain relationship to our nature and one can tabulate the different habitus according to what they bring about. If, for example, they produce acts that are in agreement with our nature, they are good, if not then they are bad. This first division separates virtues and vices[24]. Within this comes the distinction central to ethics, according to the objects to which the virtues are directed and which are their external formal causes[25]. Thomas does not mean here the object as a concrete thing. For instance, money as such does not determine the nature of justice. It is the formal aspect of the object which does so, in this case money in so far as it is the property of people or is used by them (**articles 2 & 3**).

One further query concerns the internal unity of a habitus. A habitus can have different objects provided these have a certain aspect in common. For instance, one can order the virtue of justice to the employees of a factory and one's domestic staff. However, within the range of the virtue of justice in general (and the other cardinal virtues) we distinguish subordinated habitus which are either subspecies of a virtue or dispositions used by that virtue[26]. But what governs the unity of the habitus of a *science*? Does it consist of a collection of concepts and conclusions? One may reply that the different concepts etc. must be considered as the elements out of which the habitus of a science is made up, but that this habitus itself is a simple and unified determination of the intellect (**article 4**).

---

[24] St. Thomas adds that theology studies those habitus which dispose a person to acts in conformity with a higher nature, meaning the theological virtues and the infused moral virtues.

[25] Cf. Cajetan, *In Primam Secundae*, q. 54, a. 2, II.

[26] These are the *partes integrales, partes subiectivae* and *partes potentiales* of the four cardinal virtues.

CHAPTER VII

ON THE VIRTUES IN GENERAL

Introduction

Treatment of the virtues occupies the central place in the ethics of both Aristotle and of Aquinas. Virtues are durable dispositions in our faculties which prompt us to act in conformity with our last end according to the right insight of the intellect. The virtues facilitate the performance of moral acts and give us a certain pleasure. By a life according to the virtues man shows that he has been made according to the image of God and is on his way to his final end. For the Greeks the apprenticeship of the virtues was one of the most important purposes of education and Aquinas's ethics also consists for a considerable part in a study of how to live according the virtues[1]. However, in later centuries considerations of the law, of obligations and of human freedom came to dominate. Virtue was hardly touched upon in the treatises on moral theology[2]. After the middle of the twentieth century, the situation changed and some authors began to stress the importance of a study of the virtues for moral life. In particular Alasdair MacIntyre[3], Joseph Pieper[4] and Servais Pinckaers[5] deserve praise for their efforts to place the virtues at the centre of ethics[6].

The term ἀρετή used by Plato and Aristotle to signify virtue has a long history. Originally it meant excellence and strength. In Plato's dialogue the meaning of the word evolves from that of the correct knowledge about what one should do to that of a moral attitude. In *Gorgias* 503 D ff. virtue is depicted as a relationship or an ordering which makes an action balanced. Plato mentions different virtues and distinguishes between perfect virtue, a gift of the gods, and the imperfect virtue one can acquire by habituation.

Aristotle knows the use of ἀρετή in the sense of bodily strength[7], but he says that in the proper sense of the term virtue is a habitus of the soul[8]. He distin-

---

[1] The scientific study of the virtues occupies most of the Second Part of the *Summa theologiae*.

[2] Lalande, *Vocabulaire technique de la philosophie*[5] (1947), p. 1203, notes that the term *vertu* is disappearing from everyday language.

[3] *After Virtue. A Study in Moral Theory*, London 1981.

[4] His treatises on the moral virtues are well-known.

[5] *Les sources de la morale chrétienne*, Fribourg/Paris 1985.

[6] For a survey see Romano Cessario, O.P., "Virtue Theory and the Present Evolution of Thomism", in D. Hudson and S. Moran (ed.), *The Future of Thomism*, Notre Dame Press, Notre Dame IN, 1992.

[7] *Rhet.* 1360^{b}20 ff.

[8] *E. N.* 1102^{a}16.

guishes between virtues of the intellect and moral virtues. The first are five in number but can be reduced to wisdom (σοφία) and prudence (φρόνησις)[9]. He defines moral virtue as a disposition which makes us act with deliberation and directs our choices; it lies midway between excess and deficiency, as a wise person would determine this[10]. The correct mean cannot be calculated mathematically, but must be adapted to the different individuals. Aristotle admits that it is not easy to find the correct mean of our passions and desires as well as in the use of natural goods. In his ethical theory the virtues do not cover the entire field of man's activity, but only that of the passions and of social obligations. We acquire the virtues by performing morally right actions.

The Stoic doctrine of the virtues had a considerable influence during the first centuries of our era and up into the Middle Ages. In Stoic monism the virtues are living powers and forms of a fundamental striving (ὁρμή). Although Zeno spoke of several virtues he considered them an expression of the same fundamental dynamism of the soul. Thus, whoever possesses one virtue, also has the others[11]. This implies that there is only perfect virtue. which the wise man possesses, since his entire life is governed by reason. Consequently he is consistent in his actions and lives in perfect harmony with the cosmos and with his own nature.

St. Augustine developed his well-known doctrine of love as the root of the different virtues. Relying on Augustine Peter Lombard defines virtue as a good habitus of the mind, which makes one to live in the right way and which one cannot use for bad actions. It is caused in us by God[12]. But shortly before him Peter Abelard had described the virtues as habitus acquired by man himself, while Hugh of St. Victor places the virtues again in a theological context, connecting them with divine grace[13].

In organizing his text Thomas does not follow theological principles so much as a rational ordering of the material. By far the greater part of the text on the virtues and vices in general concerns the virtues which man can acquire for himself. But Thomas also deals with the infused virtues which are essential for the supernatural life of Christians. He considers the acquired natural virtues an essential part of man's moral life[14], so that we may consider the detailed questions about the acquired virtues as part of his philosophical ethics. The four cardinal virtues - prudence, justice, fortitude and temperance - treated by Aquinas in the

---

[9] *E. N.* 1139^{b}17.

[10] *E. N.* 1106^{b}36 ff.

[11] We cannot discuss here the differences between the views of Zeno, Cleanthes and Chrysippus.

[12] *Sententiae*, II, d. 27, c. 5.

[13] *De sacramentis christianae fidei*, I, 6, 17.

[14] The treatment of the acquired virtues makes it possible to determine the nature of the infused virtues, which are analogous to the acquired virtues in the natural order.

Second Volume of Part II of the *Summa theologiae*, will be discussed in the final chapters of our study,.

The first and general part of the treatise on the virtues deals with five themes. What are the virtues? Where are they to be located in man? How do we divide them? What is their origin and cause? Finally, what are their properties, i.e. in which way are they a mean and how are they mutually related, etc. We must keep in mind that acquiring the virtues is not just a private affair of individual citizens. A good and acceptable moral order in society is only possible when its members are up to a certain point honest, i.e. virtuous citizens.

The definition of the virtues (Q. 55)

It is generally agreed that a virtue is something good and positive. The virtues render our activities and emotions in agreement with right reason or, according to some, with our duty and with the law. The virtues cover the vast field of our emotions, our work and our inter-personal relationships. But it is not so easy to say what a virtue is. Is virtue a power or capacity to act? Does it consist in acting honestly and durably in conformity with divine law?[15]. Do virtues concern man's daily life or are they directly ordered to eternal life? The difficulties mentioned in the first article of q. 55 give expression to the many uncertainties concerning the concept of virtue. Referring to a text of Aristotle's[16] Thomas shows that virtues are habitus. He does so by stressing the generally acknowledged fact that a virtue is something valuable, sc. an improvement and accomplishment of our faculties. Since the purpose of the faculties is to act, their perfection must consist in their being adapted to and capacitated for those acts which are fitting to them. Contrary to natural functions such as the activities of vegetative life and the perceptions of the external senses, man's rational faculties, the intellect and the will, are not determined to one type of acts but can go in different directions. But by the different habitus they are ordered to certain acts. Thomas acknowledges that the term virtue is used in different senses. St. Augustine, for instance, understands virtue as the *ordo amoris*[17], rather than as a single habitus at the origin of a particular set of acts (**article 1**).

There are, as we have noted, various kinds of habitus ranging from such bodily dispositions as health to the first principles of the intellect. Certain faculties

---

[15] St. Augustine and Peter Lombard seem to favor this approach. Augustine writes that virtue is the order love brings with it (*ordo amoris*), sc. the enjoying of what deserves to be enjoyed and using (and not enjoying) things which are meant only to be used (*Liber 83 quaestionum*, q.30).

[16] *Categoriae*, c. 6, 8^{b}29.

[17] *De moribus Ecclesiae*, c. 15; *De civitate Dei*, XV, c. 22.

or powers concern the being of things[18], while others, exclusively proper to man, are ordered to actions and derive from the soul, the principle of life[19]. The human virtues Thomas is here concerned with belong to those faculties which have their roots in man's spiritual soul and, therefore, are habitus directed to actions (*habitus operativi*). One might object against this conclusion that the virtues make us resemble to God and therefore also concern our ontological being. But God's being is wisdom and love and that therefore our most perfect assimilation to God will be achieved by whatever makes us capable of performing acts of wisdom and love (**article 2**).

Since the virtues perfect our faculties they are directed to the best and highest that is attainable by these faculties. This means that virtues are directed to the good and not to evil since moral evil is a defect and failure or weakness in the acts of the faculties. Therefore, virtues are good habitus which work what is good[20]. This is not contradicted by what St. Paul writes, sc that virtues find their perfection in weakness (*2 Cor.* 12, 9). Paul means that a virtue shows best what it is by making us act well in difficulties despite personal weakness (**article 3**).

The first three articles of this question prepare the ground for a definition of virtue. A text of Peter Lombard, derived from St. Augustine[21], serves as a guideline: a virtue is a good quality of the mind, by which one lives right, which no one uses for something bad and which God causes in us without us. Thomas sees this proposition as a definition according to the four causes, and finds it excellent. He notes that the material cause (the matter or the object of the virtues) has not been indicated in the definition, since that is impossible when speaking about virtue in general[22]. Instead, Peter Lombard tells us where the virtues have their seat, sc. in our mind. The definition is of infused virtue and so cites God as their efficient cause. This is different in the case of the virtues acquired by our own efforts which have their seat also in the mind. Nevertheless the sensory appetite can also be called a seat of virtue in so far as it shares in the operation of reason (**article 4**). St. Thomas himself states succinctly that moral virtues are defined by the fact that they enable us to act in agreement with right reason[23].

---

[18] Thomas speaks of a *potentia ad esse*, which belongs to the level of matter and the body. He means the aptitude to certain further determinations such as health and bodily beauty.

[19] Thomas mentions the group of faculties or operative powers which animals and man have in common without discussing them further. At this point he wants to speak only about *human* virtues as belonging to specifically human faculties.

[20] "Virtus est quae bonum facit habentem et opus eius bonum reddit".

[21] *Sententiae*, II, d. 27, c. 3.

[22] The matter or object the virtues are concerned with is each time different.

[23] *S. Th.* II-II, q. 23, a. 3: "Virtus moralis definitur per hoc quod est secundum rationem rectam".

The faculties in which virtues have their seat (Q.56)

Since the virtues are positive powers, sc. dispositions directed to actions, they will be located in those faculties which, by themselves, do not yet make us act rightly. One must add that the virtues direct us to what is best for us, sc. to our true end. This end either exists in our actions themselves or in what we obtain by them[24]. Since we act by means of our faculties, the virtues must be habitus of the faculties. One can also put it this way: the virtues have their seat in the soul in so far as this is determined by its faculties (**article 1**).

A virtue such as prudence which gives us the right knowledge of what must be done so that our acts are morally correct[25], engages both the intellect and the will. This raises the question whether a virtue can be in more than one faculty. Faculties are ordered to objects which belong to one class of beings (even though themselves differing in kind objects may differ in kind)[26]. Since each virtue has an inner unity it is impossible for it to be found in two different faculties. But within one faculty different virtues are possible. Thus the will, for example, can possess such virtues as justice, piety, pity etc. which dispose it to morally good acts with regard to the different objects of these virtues. Although it is impossible that a virtue be found in different faculties its influence can nevertheless extend from the faculty in which it has its seat to other faculties, rather as the will moves itself and other faculties (**article 2**).

Virtues are dispositions to good actions and so the moral virtues consist essentially in making us seek the good[27]. If so, can moral virtues have the intellect as their seat? Aristotle speaks of intellectual virtues such as the understanding of first principles, but also of the habitus of the different sciences. This use of the term "virtue" agrees with its original meaning in Greek, but our word "virtue" is hardly apt to express this sense. In his answer to this question Aquinas points out the difference between the typical habitus of the intellect and those of the other faculties. To have mastered a foreign language, a habitus of the mind, does not mean that one has become a good person. Moreover such habitus do not exclude that one makes mistakes if distraught. But virtues such as justice make one actually to do what is just and to be considered a good person.

Purely intellectual habitus such as those of the different sciences have no connection with the will[28]. However, virtues are dispositions which make us act

---

[24] Thomas writes : "Bonum consistit in operatione".

[25] Prudence is the *recta ratio agibilium*. Cf. *E. N.*, VI, c. 5, 1140^{b}4.

[26] The will, for instance, is directed to the good, but this comprises a great variety of things, and even things which under one aspect are a good, but as such are evil. The intellect, on the other hand, is directed to being as true and has different habitus, each of which approaches the truth of being in a different way.

[27] Art. 2 ad 2: "Sed essentialiter in appetendo virtus moralis consistit".

[28] "... absque omni ordine ad voluntatem".

rightly. Since all human acts depend on the will which moves the different faculties, the moral virtues must have their seat in the will or in the other faculties in so far as they are moved by the will[29]. The intellect is also moved by the will and therefore, in so far as it is ordered to the will, it can be the seat of authentic virtues. This is the case with supernatural faith and, above all, with the virtue of prudence, inasmuch as the intellect recognizes the natural order of the will to the different goals which people pursue and in view of this gives practical indications for acting[30]. This is the task of what is called the practical intellect. The habitus of the sciences, however, have their seat in the speculative intellect (**article 3**).

The moral virtues have their seat in the appetitive faculties in so far as they belongs to our rational nature. This raises the question of whether the irascible or concupiscible appetite could be the seat of virtues? One would be inclined to give a positive answer insofar as a virtue like temperance seems to belong to the concupiscible, courage or fortitude to the irascible appetite. However, St. Thomas makes a distinction between these faculties as such , and the aspect under which they are subject to reason. In these faculties as such there are no virtues, for we do not speak of virtues in animals, although they do possess appetitive faculties. But in human beings these faculties are subject to reason and will with which they collaborate and, therefore, they can be the seat of virtues. A further reason for this is that the intellect and the will when using these appetitive faculties cannot perform really perfect acts, unless these faculties are well disposed. For instance, emotions in these faculties may at times be in conflict with reason. Therefore, there must be in these appetitive faculties a capacity for the virtues, by which they can obey the intellect and the will[31] (**article 4**).

In the sensory powers habitus can be formed, but these are not virtues in the strict sense of the term. Each virtue is ordered to a class of good actions and, for

---

[29] Cf. *Q. d. de virtutibus*, q. 1, a. 8: "Manifestum est autem quod ipsa voluntas in quantum est potentia ad utrumlibet se habens in his quae sunt ad finem, est susceptiva habitualis inclinationis in haec vel in illa".

[30] Such goals are to stay alive, to take care of one's own well-being and that of others, to work for one's spiritual development, to live in society, etc.

[31] "Ideo virtus quae est in irascibili et concupiscibili nihil aliud est quam quaedam habitualis conformitas istarum potentiarum ad rationem". Cf. *Q. d. de virtutibus*, q. 1, a. 8: "Irascibilis autem et concupiscibilis naturaliter sunt obaudibiles rationi. Unde naturaliter sunt susceptivae virtutis". Thomas speaks of a first movement (*inchoatio*) towards and a beginning of the virtues which comes with our human nature. Some persons have in addition a special capacity for certain virtues. - This thesis that there is a natural disposition to the virtues rests on man's spiritual nature as such which is presupposed to this discussion of the *Prima Secundæ*. But if one considers the actual conduct of people, a remark at II-II 29, 1 seems to be closer to the truth: "Appetitus sensitivus plerumque tendit in contrarium rationis appetitus".Cf. S. Theron, *Natural Law Reconsidered*, pp. 171-172.

this reason, it is located in those faculties which must perform these good acts[32]. However, human knowledge does not reach its fulfilment in sense-cognition, which has a preparatory role and influences the intellect more than that it is influenced by it[33]. This explains why one does not find any virtues in the sensory powers (**article 5**).

Can the will be the seat of virtues? A general principle prepares the answer: a virtue is necessary when the nature of a faculty is not sufficient to make it perform good actions. Although the will directs itself to the good presented to it by the intellect and does not need a virtue to do so, it needs a particular virtue, sc. justice, to pursue a good which lies outside our personal good, as is the good of our fellow men[34] (**article 6**).

THE DIFFERENT CLASSES OF VIRTUES (QQ. 57 - 62)

In a series of questions Aquinas now examines the different kinds or classes of the virtues: intellectual virtues, moral virtues, theological virtues. The themes will be discussed in so far as they can be considered under philosophical ethics.

The intellectual virtues (Q. 57)

A first question which has already been answered implicitly is whether the habitus in the speculative intellect should be called virtues? In so far as they help the intellect to carry out its work correctly, one may call them virtues, though in the full sense of the term they are not, since they are not directed to a correct moral use of the other faculties or even of the sciences[35]. They are directed to the knowledge of the truth. Virtues of the will such as justice, on the other hand, enable us to act rightly and to use the sciences responsibly. In this article an important truth is indicated, viz. that when one really possesses a virtue one acts in conformity with it. As long as one has to struggle with less perfect inclinations and desires, one does not yet possess perfect virtue[36] (**article 1**).

In **the second article** Aquinas considers the three habitus of the speculative intellect in detail, as Aristotle presented them, sc. wisdom, scientific knowledge and the habitus of the first principles. Related to this topic is the question whether arts or crafts can be called virtues. By art we mean the required habit-

---

[32] "Unde oportet quod virtus sit in illa potentia quae est consummativa boni operis".

[33] Art. 5 ad 1: "Virtutes autem sensitivae apprehensivae magis se habent ut moventes respectu intellectus".

[34] In this connection Thomas also says that God is the supreme good which transcends the limits of our human nature. The will directs itself to God when moved by the supernatural virtue of charity.

[35] Using a distinction made by Augustine Aquinas speaks here of *usus bonus*.

[36] See below q. 58, a. 3 ad 2 where self-control and perseverance are studied.

ual knowledge of how to carry out certain tasks. In this field good results are not due to an intervention of the will and the inner attitude with which one carried our a task does not make a difference. For this reason here we do not speak of virtue (**article 3**).

The next three articles deal with the virtue of prudence. Does prudence differ from art? Prudence, like art, belongs to the practical intellect. An art is the habitus of right knowledge required to make something or accomplish a certain task. (*recta ratio factibilium*).It is directed to activities which use or work on material outside of ourselves, whereas prudence is concerned with our own actions. In theoretical knowledge the starting-points must be certain and true in order to allow us to reach the right conclusions. In a similar way prudence must be directed to the right goals. This presupposes that our sensory appetite is well disciplined, something which is not necessary for art[37]. A person can be a good artist or technician, yet lead a morally bad life. This shows that prudence is not an art (**article 4**).

The virtue of prudence is absolutely necessary for man. In order to lead a good moral life, one must act morally. In order to do so, one must set out from the right insight and not from some emotion or urge. This implies that one has one's eyes directed to a good goal and orders oneself to it in the right way. Now the virtues bring it about that, in the different fields of our activity, we direct ourselves to good ends. The virtues are concerned with what is contingent, where we must find the way and the proper means in order to reach the goal in the right manner. But in order to direct our acts to the goal in the proper way, we must use our mind. To do so we need a habitus or disposition in the intellect facilitating it, sc. the virtue of prudence. This shows that this virtue is most necessary (**article 5**).

Aristotle mentions three virtues which assist prudence, sc. the capacity for investigation and deliberation (εὐβουλία), the capacity to judge in conformity with the prevalent customs and rules (σύνεσις) and, finally, a disposition which, where there are no rules, helps to set a course of action according to the best insight of reason (γνώμη)[38]. Thomas further explains the function of these three assisting virtues[39]: owing to the preparatory work done by these assisting virtues prudence can indicate a certain way of acting in a concrete case. Prudence itself has parts, such as the knowledge of what happened earlier in similar circumstances, a sharp grasp of the situation and of the particular goal one is

---

[37] "Ars non praesupponit appetitum rectum".

[38] *E. N.*, VI, c. 11, 1143ª23.

[39] Art. 6 ad 3: "Distinguuntur autem synesis et gnome secundum diversas regulas quibus iudicatur: nam synesis est iudicativa de agendis secundum communem legem; gnome autem secundum ipsam rationem naturalem, in his in quibus deficit lex communis". Cf. II-II, qq. 48 ff.

pursuing, and, finally, it must anticipate the consequences of what one wants to do[40] (**article 6**).

The difference between the intellectual and the moral virtues (Q. 58)

The treatise of the virtues is centered around the moral virtues. Question 58 considers whether every virtue is a moral virtue, next whether the moral virtues differ from the intellectual virtues, and whether besides these two groups there are other virtues. Finally the question is examined whether a moral virtue is possible without the support of the intellectual virtues and whether the latter are possible without the moral virtues.

In his answer to the first question[41] Aquinas draws attention to the original meaning of the Latin word *mos* (from which the words "moral" and "morality" are derived). *Mos* has a dual meaning, sc. usage or custom and, second, a natural inclination to do something[42]. While the Latin word *mos* has these two meanings, the Greek uses two terms, sc. ἔθος and ἦθος[43]. St. Thomas argues that *moralis* in the expression "moral virtues" signifies primarily the inclination to do something. The words "custom" and "usage" express something related to this, since by repeatedly doing something it becomes so to say a second nature for us[44]. However, the inclination to act is most properly present in the appetitive faculties. For this reason not every virtue is said to be a moral virtue, but only those which have their seat in the appetitive faculties (**article 1**).

Explaining how the moral virtues differ from the intellectual virtues Aquinas recalls that in a certain sense the intellect is the principle of whatever we are doing, while the other faculties, each in its own way, follow it. The limbs of the body carry out the orders of the intellect immediately, but with the other faculties this is somewhat different[45]. The appetitive faculties do not always follow reason but can oppose it[46]. It happens that strong emotions impede the right judgment of the intellect[47]. This situation shows how necessary it is that there

---

[40] For a more detailed treatment see II-II, qq. 48 ff.

[41] In q. 56, a. 3 the character of the intellectual virtues has already been discussed.

[42] In this second sense we speak of the nature and behavior of animals, e.g. of a lion.

[43] Both words have the same root, but their meaning became somewhat different: ἔθος signifies mainly custom and usage, while in most cases ἦθος denotes the moral character of persons.

[44] "Consuetudo quodammodo vertitur in naturam rei et facit inclinationem similem naturali".

[45] Socrates believed that when the intellect has true knowledge we act virtuously and that bad actions are to be reduced to mistaken knowledge. However, experience belies his optimism.

[46] II-II, 29, 1: "Appetitus sensitivus plerumque tendit in contrarium rationalis appetitus".

[47] In such cases the judgment about what one should do will be determined by a passion and so be opposed to true insight into one's obligations.

are virtues in the appetitive faculties which enable us to act in agreement with right reason[48]. Consequently, because of their different function the moral virtues must be distinguished from the intellectual. The former are virtues because they are in agreement with right reason, a statement characteristic of the moral doctrine of Aquinas[49]. So virtues are not automatisms, blind forces or habits, but share in the knowledge of reason and are themselves filled with intelligibility. This does not mean that they carry some part of reason in themselves, but that they receive guidance by the intellect through the virtue of prudence[50] (**article 2**).

Is there a third class of virtues besides the intellectual and the moral virtues? A virtue is a habitus which makes us act in the right way. There are two principles of human acts, sc. the intellect and the appetitive faculties which are the moving powers in man. For this reason any virtue must be a determination and fulfilment of the one or of the other of these faculties. If a virtue perfects the speculative or the practical intellect, it is an intellectual virtue. If it perfects the appetitive faculties, it is a moral virtue. As to the virtue of prudence, it is essentially an intellectual virtue, but it has in common with the moral virtues that it directs the will to perform acts capable of reaching a goal and so it can be ranked also under the latter.

In his answer to the second objection St. Thomas discusses self-control and perseverance. Self-control has its seat in the intellect and is a habitus which makes the mind oppose certain passions which threaten to drag us down. Self-control or continence is not a virtue in the full sense of the term, since it goes together with the presence of passions one tries to control, whereas the presence of virtues in the full sense of the term is not compatible with experiencing difficulties in exercising the control of the emotions. Following Aristotle St. Thomas argues against some of his contemporaries that self-control or continence is not yet perfect virtue (**article 3**).

In the preceding articles the connection between the intellectual and the moral virtues was stressed. Are moral virtues possible without the intellectual virtues? Evidently one does not have to be a philosopher, theologian or scholar to live virtuously, but without prudence there is no moral virtue. For the practice of virtues entails that a) one makes the right choices as directed to the proper end, something dependent on the moral virtues, b) that one uses the right means to reach the end. But this is possible only when the intellect gives the required in-

---

[48] "Sic igitur ad hoc quod homo bene agat, requiritur quod non solum ratio sit bene disposita per habitum virtutis intellectualis, sed etiam quod vis appetitiva sit bene disposita per habitum virtutis moralis".

[49] "Ita habitus moralis habet rationem virtutis humanae inquantum rationi conformatur".

[50] Ad 4: "Recta ratio quae est secundum prudentiam, ponitur in definitione virtutis moralis, non tanquam pars essentiae eius, sed sicut quiddam participatum in omnibus virtutibus moralibus, inquantum prudentia dirigit omnes virtutes morales".

formation and indicates the road to be followed, which is the task of prudence and the virtues associated with it. Without prudence there cannot be any moral virtues. Prudence presupposes that the first principles of our acts are present in the intellect, such as "the good must be done, what is bad avoided", "one must respect one's parents", etc. However, in order to possess the virtue of prudence it is not necessary to be highly intelligent or proficient in one's undertakings. Those who are not can nevertheless be prudent. In his answer to the last objection raised in this article St. Thomas stresses once more the connection between the mind and the moral virtues. Although it is true that certain natural inclinations can be a starting point for the virtues (it is natural for children to respect their parents and for people to trust others), these natural inclinations must nevertheless be shaped and accompanied by reason in order to move in the right direction. In short, it is not sufficient that at the outset a moral virtue directs us to what is in agreement with right reason it must constantly be accompanied by reason, as Aristotle says[51] (**article 4**).

From the above it appears that the intellectual virtues (other than prudence) can be present without one having the moral virtues, but that this is not possible for prudence. Prudence enables us to act rightly, not just by telling us how we should act in general but by giving concrete indications in individual cases. For the first requirement the first principles of the practical intellect offer guidelines, but for the second one must have the right attitude with regard to concrete situations. Judgments can be warped easily by emotions, so that moral virtues are required in order to allow one to judge correctly. In this connection Aquinas quotes the principle "as a man is, so will the end seem to him"[52]. Being directed by the virtues to particular ends precedes the work of reason indicating the means to reach this end (**article 5**).

The relation of the moral virtues to the passions (Q. 59)

This theme has two parts: Thomas studies first the relation to the emotions (q. 59) to pass next to ask to what extent the distinctions between the moral virtues depends upon the passions (q. 60). Are the moral virtues themselves emotions? One might be tempted to see whatever movements there are inside man as making up one class of realities. But Thomas give three reasons why the identification of the virtues with passions is impossible: a) a passion is a movement, while a virtue is a principle of movement; b) passions as such are neither good nor bad, but good when they are in agreement with reason and bad when they

---

[51] *E.N.* VI, c. 13, 1144^{b}21. Art. 4 ad 3: " (et ideo virtus moralis) non tamen solum est secundum rationem rectam, ut Platonici posuerunt, sed etiam oportet quod sit cum ratione recta, ut Aristoteles dicit".

[52] *E.N.* III, c. 5, 1114^{a}32.

are not[53], whereas virtues are directed only to the good; c) even if there would be a passion exclusively directed to the good, it would differ from the virtues since a passion begins in the appetite, whether or not we suppose it ending in the intellect, whereas a virtue starts from reason and has its terminus in the appetite. situation Hence Aristotle defines virtue as a habitus leading us to a deliberate choice of the mean (between excess and deficiency), as a wise person's reason would determine it[54].This must be so understood as that virtue itself is not a mean among the various passions, but enables us to determine it. If it is objected against this conclusion that pity is both a passion and a virtue one may answer with St. Augustine that pity is an act of a virtue, if indeed it follows reason and takes into account the requirements of justice[55] (**article 1**).

The Peripatetics and the Stoics differed on whether a virtue could coexist with a passion. While the Stoics excluded all passions from the wise man, Aristotle held that feelings of fear or sadness may easily arise in a virtuous person because of outside events. As long as passions are regulated by reason they can go together with the virtues. Unregulated passions are not compatible with the virtues (**article 2**).

This conclusion answers the question whether moderate sadness can go together with the possession of virtues. Man is composed of soul and body and an evil which affects his bodily being can sadden also a wise person, since it concerns the loss of a good. A virtuous person can also feel sad about minor shortcomings in his moral life or be depressed by the evil he sees in his environment. It is unreasonable to say that a prudent and virtuous person should never be sad. He can be affected by an evil that his reason sees and condemns for what it is, and which has a repercussion on the sensitive part of his being. In the foregoing articles it was shown that virtues make the sensory appetite follow reason. Therefore, it is even virtuous to be moderately saddened when we are affected by an evil. Moreover, sadness as an emotion moves us to try to avoid evil as much as possible (**article 3**).

Are all moral virtues concerned with passions? The moral virtues confer a certain perfection on the appetitive faculties by ordering them in conformity with reason. This means that there are virtues in respect of everything which can be ordered by reason. But reason orders not only the emotions of the sensory appetite but also the acts of the will (which is not the seat of passions). Therefore, not every moral virtue concerns the passions. If one objects that, according to Aristotle, the moral virtues have to do with pleasure and sadness[56], Thomas answers that not every moral virtue deals with these emotions as with its own

---

[53] "Bonum enim vel malum hominis est secundum rationem vel praeter rationem esse" (I-II 24, 1: Dionysius, *De divinis nominibus*, c. 4).

[54] *E.N.*, II, c. 6, 1106^{b}36.

[55] *De civitate Dei*, IX, c.6.

[56] *E.N.* II, c. 3, 1104^{b}8.

object. But it is true that pleasure accompanies every morally good act and that bad actions will lead to sadness **(article 4)**.

A final query concerns the co-existence of moral virtues and passions. If one considers the passions and emotions as irrational movements then it is obvious that perfect virtue does not go together with passions. But if by passions one understands all the movements of the sensory appetite, one must hold that the moral virtues are concerned with the passions as their proper subject matter and that if there were no passions then the virtues would not be possible. It is not the task of the virtues to render the faculties of the sensory appetite superfluous, but they must see to it that the latter be subordinated to reason and follow its rule. However, moral virtues which do not concern the emotions but acts of the will can be without any ties to the passions. This is the case with the virtue of justice. Nonetheless, righteous actions will produce joy in the will and, since the lower faculties follow higher ones, this joy may often redound in the sensitive appetite, so that pleasure arises **(article 5)**.

How the moral virtues are distinguished from one another (Q. 60)

The theme of this question was already mentioned at the beginning of q. 59. A first enquiry concerns whether the moral virtues are one single virtue. If the intellect, on which all moral acts depend, is one faculty, and the end to which all acts are directed is also one, must not the moral virtues be just one virtue? Thomas replies in the negative. It is true that right reason determines the morality of all our acts, but the influence of the intellect on the appetitive faculties adapts itself variously to the different objects to which the appetite directs itself. In this way a plurality of moral virtues originate in the appetite. Moreover, these virtues are directed each to different goals, even if the final end is the same **(article 1)**.

The question of the division and the number of the moral virtues was a problem for Albert the Great[57]. In the second article Aquinas proposes a new and original solution. The moral virtues can be subdivided in a) virtues which concern the different emotions. These virtues make that the emotions are in agreement with the end of human life. They are the virtues of fortitude and temperance which are mainly concerned with movements within us, b) virtues bearing upon actions affecting what is outside us, i.e. our relations to others, sc. the virtues that come in under justice[58]. However, it happens that a lack of temperance or fortitude leads to unjust actions, e.g. when out of anger one treats another person unjustly **(article 2)**.

---

[57] *De bono*, tr. 1, q. 6, a. 1 (Geyer 28, 80).
[58] Justice is used here in a broad sense as concerning whatever obligation to others we may have (art. 3 ad 1).

Does the virtue of justice regulate all our actions with regard to our fellow men? These actions may have a common object, sc. what from an objective point of view should be done[59], but this can vary. Obligations towards one's parents are not the same as those with regard to society at large. Likewise, the obligation of a promise is not the same as that of an officially signed business deal. Therefore we distinguish between justice in the strict sense of the term and obligations related to piety, gratefulness, religion, etc. (**article 3**).

More than one virtue is required to order our passions, since some passions are located in the irascible, others in the concupiscible appetite. On the other hand, some of them are opposed to others, such as pleasure to sadness, fear to courage. In these cases one virtue determines the mean to be sought. When several emotions are in the same way opposed to our reason or, on the other hand, tend to the same good then one virtue regulates them. This explains why mutually opposed passions of the concupiscible are the matter of one and the same virtue. But the situation is different for the passions of the irascible appetite, some of which concern an evil, others a good. So we distinguish the virtues of fortitude, magnanimity and gentleness (which has to do with anger) (**article 4**).

There is a difficulty in the conclusion of the last article. How can a single virtue regulate different passions? Aquinas answers that the virtues are determined by their relation to the intellect, the passions by that to the appetite. This explains why the objects of the passions call for different virtues in the appetite. Since the acts of the intellect and of the appetite are not the same an object which calls forth different passions, need not always lead to different virtues, and *vice versa*. It is also possible that the object of one passion, comes in under more than one virtue, as is the case with pleasure.

In the following section of the fifth article Aquinas examines how the virtues can be distinguished from one another. A first principle to help us distinguish the virtues is that passions affecting different appetitive faculties are always the object of different virtues[60]. Where the objects of various passions differ and hence have a different relation to the intellect, in so far as they are something of our body, our mind, of material things external to us or concern our relations with others, they will be each time the matter of a different virtue. The good of which the perception by the sense of touch (and taste) is accompanied by pleasure and which has to do with the continued existence of the individual person or the survival of the species is the object of the virtue of temperance. The pleasure which accompanies the use of the senses of sight and hearing is not so intense and need not be controlled by a virtue.

A good which is not perceived as such by the senses but by our internal faculties, such as money or honour, may be difficult to attain and so become the

---

[59] Thomas calls this "secundum ipsam convenientiam rei in seipsa".
[60] See article 4.

object of the irascible appetite. The virtue of liberality (*liberalitas*) concerns financial matters inasmuch as they are the object of desire, pleasure or love. With regard to possessions one wants to use for important projects for the public benefit, the virtue of *magnificentia*, sc. public patronage, will govern one's actions. The virtue of moderate ambition (*philotimia*) will exercise a moderating influence regarding such goods as the honors we seek. In respect of recognition and honor which one may want to obtain by outstanding actions of the virtue of magnanimity must guide our desire.

The good in our daily relations with others belongs to the virtue of affability or gentleness. As regards what one says and does, there is the virtue of truthfulness. Our behavior in sports and play is regulated, Aristotle says, by spiritedness, to which we may add a sporting spirit.

Aristotle mentions a total of ten virtues all of which concern the passions, sc. fortitude, temperance, liberality, public patronage, magnanimity, proper ambition, friendliness, gentleness, truthfulness, and spiritedness. Later on in his *Ethics* he adds justice which governs our dealings with others.

In this article Thomas gives a well-argued explanation of the list of virtues Aristotle presents in Chapter Seven of Book II of his *Nicomachean Ethics*. What is new in his explanation is that it considers the virtues from the point of view of the intellect. "Since reason brings about a certain order in man's lower parts, and extends its knowledge to what lies outside man, an object of a passion will have a different relation to the intellect according as it is known by the senses, by the imagination or by the intellect. This relation will also differ according as it belongs to the soul, the body or to what lies outside man. Consequently different virtues will result"[61]. The intellect must govern all emotions and human acts and, to this effect, it uses the virtues, which impose the authority of reason in the will and in the sensory appetite. Only in this way will our activities be directed to our last end (**article 5**).

The cardinal virtues (Q. 61)

In the *Republic* 428 A - 429 A, Plato mentions four important virtues, prudence, fortitude, justice and temperance (in Greek σοφία ἀνδρεία δικαιοσύνη and σωφροσύνη). These virtues regulate the movements of the appetitive and concupiscent part of man. The doctrine of the four main virtues must be considered a permanent achievement of Greek ethical thought. However, in Aristotle's works these four virtues do not have the privileged place Plato assigns to them.

---

[61] "Et quia ordine quodam ratio inferiores hominis partes regit et etiam se ad exteriora extendit, ideo etiam secundum quod unum obiectum passionis apprehenditur sensu vel imaginatione, aut etiam ratione et secundum etiam quod pertinet ad animam, corpus vel exteriores res, diversam habitudinem habet ad rationem, et per consequens natum est diversificare virtutem".

Aristotle uses a different division[62], as we have seen in the previous question. The Stoa, however, maintains the doctrine of the four main virtues but considers three of them as forms of prudence. According to Cicero[63] prudence manifests itself in the choices we make, fortitude in the courage which helps us to face difficult situations while justice is the will to give to everyone what he is entitled to and temperance is concerned with abstaining from lust.

The Christian authors have taken over this doctrine of the virtues. If one practices them inspired by love, they belong to the supernatural order[64]. Aquinas noticed accounts of the four cardinal virtues in the philosophical writings of his predecessors and accepted this division, arguing that all the other virtues rest on these four. The name "cardinal virtues" goes back to St. Ambrose's *De officiis ministrorum*. The term *cardinal* recalls the way in which the ancient Romans measured land: they distinguished square lots, the sides of which measure 700 meters[65]. It is noteworthy that at this point Aquinas no longer upholds the order of the virtues as elaborated by Aristotle.

At the beginning of the question Thomas stresses that he is speaking now about human virtues. One can distinguish between perfect and imperfect virtues. The first effect that our inclinations have the right direction, render us capable of acting well and make us accomplish good deeds. Imperfect virtues, on the other hand, give the aptitude to act in a morally correct way, but do not demand that all inclinations are directed correctly and do not necessarily cause a faculty to perform only good actions. The virtues which give the right direction to the fundamental inclinations are more perfect and primary. These are the moral virtues and prudence, which as the only one among the intellectual virtues is, in a sense, also a moral virtue. The cardinal virtues, indeed, are moral virtues (**article 1**).

How many moral virtues are there? Their number can be determined either by the number of subjects (faculties) in which they are or according to their different definitions, which depend each time on how the intellect sees them. This good they bring about can consist in the deliberations of reason itself, which are governed by the virtue of prudence. But reason can also regulate other things: thus the order in our dealings with our fellow men is brought about by justice. In so far as the passions move us in a direction contrary to the order of reason they must be regulated and governed, which is the task of the virtue of temperance.

---

[62] *E.N.* II, c. 7 & c. 8 and elsewhere in his works.

[63] *De finibus*, V, 67.

[64] Cf. O. Lottin, "Le traité d'Alaim de Lille sur les vertus, les vices et les dons du Saint-Esprit", in *Medieval Studies* 12 (1950), p. 34.

[65] The starting point was the *cardo maximus* and served as the point of reference. So the four cardinal virtues are like beacons between which our moral life must develop. See O. Hilltbrunner, "Die Schrift "De officiis ministrorum" des hl. Ambrosius", in *Gymnasium* 1964, 174-189.

In so far, finally, as an emotion such as fear threatens to prevent us from doing what we should do, the virtue of fortitude must intervene.

When on the other hand the question of the number of the moral virtues is determined from the point of view of the faculties in which they are located, the conclusion stands that there are four main virtues. Thus reason is perfected by prudence, the will by justice, the concupiscible appetite by temperance and the irascible by fortitude. All other virtues can be reduced to one or other of these cardinal virtues, both as regards the faculty in which they are and as regards their essential definition (**article 2**).

One might object against the theory of the four main or cardinal virtues that many spiritual authors consider humility and patience more important. On a closer inspection, however, one can distinguish between a less and more perfect way in which the proper essence of such virtues as prudence, justice, temperance and fortitude is realized. Prudence reaches its greatest perfection in the command of reason, justice in our relations with our equals, temperance in the repression of violent passions (lust in the sense of touch), fortitude in situations of a threatening danger. In this sense the four cardinal virtues are primary because of their objects. Other virtues, which are subordinated to them, can under a particular aspect come close to this object and so occupy the first rank, as is the case with humility or patience. However, if one considers what the four cardinal virtues are[66], then all other virtues are subordinated to them. One can, for instance, call fortitude every virtue which strengthens us in order to resist the emotions (**article 3**).

In a sense one could say that every virtue possesses something of the four above mentioned cardinal virtues: all must be accompanied by correct knowledge (prudence), make us do what we should do (justice), make us keep the right measure (temperance), make us steadfast when doing our duty and accomplishing difficult tasks (fortitude). In this way the four cardinal virtues work together[67].

However, it is a mistake to reduce the moral virtues to a single virtue, as the Stoics did, since each of them is directed to a particular matter, to which its name corresponds. If the objects differ then so do the virtues. But there is a mutual influence of the virtues on each other. A person who can master his desires, something quite difficult, will more easily keep the right measure in situations in which courage is required. In this way fortitude is moderated by temperance and

---

[66] The Latin term used by Thomas is *ratio formalis*.

[67] "Cuiuslibet enim virtuti morali, ex hoc quod est habitus, convenit quaedam firmitas, ut a contrario non moveatur, quod dictum est ad fortitudinem pertinere. Ex hoc vero quod est virtus, habet quod ordinetur ad bonum, in quo importatur ratio recti vel debiti quod dicebatur ad iustitiam pertinere. In hoc vero quod est virtus moralis rationem participans, habet quod modum rationis in omnibus servet et ultra se non extendat; quod dicebatur pertinere ad temperantiam".

temperance fortified by fortitude[68]. As has been noted before, the Stoics consider the moral virtues manifestations of the same *logos* and let the virtues coalesce, a position rejected by Aquinas (**article 4**).

In the last article of this question Thomas takes up some further interrogations with regard to the four cardinal virtues. Does God possess moral virtues? Is Macrobius[69] right when, referring to Plotinus, he calls these virtues "social" and says that they purify the mind and are exemplary?

Aquinas gives Macrobius's somewhat confused text a good sense. The model of all things is in God, therefore also of the virtues. His intellect may be called prudence, his self-possession temperance. God's immutability is his fortitude and his action in conformity to the eternal law justice. A person who possesses these virtues will behave himself in the proper way in civil life. Inasmuch as the cardinal virtues assist us on our journey to moral perfection they have a purifying function. If our prudence reaches a high degree of perfection and directs us to be spiritually united with God as often as possible, if our temperance no longer knows any earthly desires and our justice is allied permanently with God, then these are virtues of a purified soul. Thus the last article of this question shows how a life according to the virtues has its model in God and how by living according to them one makes progress on the road to perfection (**article 5**).

On the cause of the virtues (Q. 63)[70]

In Greek literature of the fifth century B.C. there is often question of the opposition between nature (in the sense of the permanent nature of things) and law (in the sense of customs and positive civil laws)[71]. According to some authors human behavior is a question of custom and tradition, so that moral evaluation of acts is socially determined, while for others nature is the proper measure and authentic norm of conduct. Connected to this debate is the question whether the character of certain persons determines their conduct to such an extent that there is hardly any room for improvement by education, or whether human nature indicates some fundamental moral rules, so that people's behavior can be im-

---

[68] Clement of Alexandria speaks of the mutual intertwinement of virtues (ἀντακολουθία) (*Stromateis* 4, 26).

[69] An author inspired by Neoplatonism living in the first half of the fifth century, perhaps a high official of the empire in Spain or North-Africa. His *Commentarii in Somnium Scipionis* (a well known text from the sixth book of the *De republica* of Cicero), enjoyed a certain authority in the Middle Ages. See J. Flamant, *Macrobe et le néo-platonisme à la fin du IVe siècle*, Leiden 1977.

[70] Q. 62 treats the theological virtues, faith, hope and love, and lies outside the scope of our study.

[71] See F. Heinimann, *Nomos und Physis*, Basel 19435. Cf. L. Elders, "Nature et moralité", in *id.*, *Autour de saint Thomas, II*, Paris/Bruges 1987, 23-45.

proved by training? Plato writes that we must follow nature[72], but he also says that no one has such a perfect nature as to know right away and without any effort what to do and to have the power and the desire to do always what is best[73]. By obeying the laws (and by a proper education) individual persons can acquire the virtues[74]. Aristotle allows for a certain influence of a person's character and natural disposition on his conduct, but says that we are also responsible ourselves for virtues and vices[75]. Nevertheless a good natural disposition is of considerable help in acquiring the virtues[76].

In the first article of this question Aquinas examines the issue. Aristotle acknowledges that there is a kind of natural aptitude for the virtues, but nevertheless holds that the virtues only develop and are perfected by repeatedly acting according to them. It is not true that one must already have a virtue in order to act virtuously[77]. The word "natural" in "natural aptitude" can be explained in two ways, sc. as being in agreement with one's specific, rational nature oras being natural for some particular persons, on account of their inborn character. In both ways the virtues are something natural for man, at least in the sense of his having a certain aptitude to acquire and develop them[78]. Our human rational nature gives a group of first principles to the intellect, some of which are for speculative thought, others for practical action. The principles of the practical intellect are seminal for the virtues. Moreover, there is also in the will a certain inclination to any good which agrees with the intellect.

With regard to the inborn character of individual persons, it is obvious that some people are less well disposed to certain virtues than others. The sensepowers may be helped or hindered in their activities by the state of the organs in which they are situated since this state redounds upon our spiritual faculties which collaborate with the sensory faculties. One person will be more gifted for study, another for courageous behavior, another again for temperance and self-control. But such a natural aptitude does not mean that from the very start these virtues are already present in a fully developed form. We must acquire them by acting repeatedly in conformity with the objects of the different virtues in the changing circumstances of our lives[79] (**article 1**).

In the chapter on the habitus it was shown that habitus are acquired and strengthened by the respective acts. Therefore, the virtues of the natural order are caused by our acts in so far as these follow the right rule of reason. St. Tho-

---

[72] *Laws* 836 C.
[73] *Laws* 875 A.
[74] *Ibid.* 955 D.
[75] *E.N.* III, c. 7, 1114^{b}21 ff.: καὶ γὰρ τῶν ἕξεων συναίτιοί πως αὐτοὶ ἐσμεν.
[76] *Ibid.* 1114^{b}6-12.
[77] *E.N.* II, c. 3.
[78] "Secundum quandam inchoationem".
[79] St. Thomas adds that the theological virtues are given by God.

mas adds that by one act contrary to an acquired virtue this virtue does not disappear. The reason is that not acts but habitus are directly opposed to habitus. Although, according to Christian theology, one cannot remain free from serious sin without the help of divine grace, one can nevertheless acquire the virtues, by which, generally speaking, one can avoid what is wrong, in particular in what is most directly opposed to right reason. To the question how individual acts can cause the virtues, which seem more perfect than acts, he replies that the first principles on which they rest are of a higher order than the acts which conform the appetite to reason (**article 2**). The last two articles of this question concern the supernatural virtues.

The mean of the virtues (Q. 64)

The last part of the treatise on the virtues in general comprises four questions on certain of their aspects or properties. A first property is that the virtues allow us to perform acts which hold the mean between two extremes[80]. Aristotle confirms this explicitly in his definition of moral virtues. They are dispositions which make us choose acts which are midway between extremes[81].

A moral virtue perfects the sensory appetitive faculties with regard to some particular matter. Reason indicates here the right order and measure. Inclinations and desires are good when they are marked by measure and rule, but bad when they deviate from them. A deviation occurs when the facultie go beyond this measure or fall short of it. The good of a moral virtue consists in its being tuned in to the measure of reason[82]. Now between too much and too little there is a mean which corresponds to the right measure.

---

[80] The theory of the mean between extremes had been developed by Alcmaeon and was used by the ancient physicians. According to several treatises of the *Corpus hippocraticum* the human body is a system of four contrary elements in a certain equilibrium. In order to stay healthy one must preserve this equilibrium. Plato speaks of an equilibrium in the universe and in the human soul. Aristotle developed the theory of a balanced distribution of cold and heat in the human body (in particular between digestion and respiration) and in the external senses, which are midway between contrary qualities. See Th. Thracy, *Physiological Theory and the Doctrine of the Mean in Plato and Aristotle,*The Hague 1969.

[81] *E.N.*, c. 6, 1106^{b}36. Aquinas omits the last part of the definition in his *sed contra* ("a mean with regard to us which is rationally determined and as a wise person would determine it"). Some commentators understand "rationally determined" as determined by reason, others as determined by a norm. Cf. W.F.R. Hardie, "Aristotle's Doctrine that Virtue is a Mean", in *Proceedings of the Aristotelelian Society* 65 (1965), p. 183-204. In the *corpus articuli* Thomas combines both explanations: reason imposes measure and a rule. Cf. also the answer to the first difficulty: "Virtus moralis bonitatem habet ex regula rationis".

[82] "Et ideo patet quod bonum virtutis moralis consistit in adaequatione ad mensuram rationis".

In his answer to the second and third objections Aquinas reminds us that the circumstances of acts help to determine the mean. The virtue which makes us sponsor public institutions or initiatives by means of donations is inclined to go to a maximum, but on account of certain circumstances (there are also other institutions or initiatives which deserve to be supported) we look for the right measure. Aquinas avails of the opportunity here to neutralize an objection against Aristotle's doctrine, viz. if virtue consists in a mean, one should seek moderate sexual pleasure and not live in total continence as persons do who devote their life to God. Likewise total poverty seems an extreme. Aquinas answers that, as is the case with the virtue of public patronage, in seeking pleasure or practicing poverty one must follow the rule of reason, which sets the measure of what is right in view of the goal to be reached. In fact those who live a celibate life are not without joy and pleasure, while as regards poverty it is obvious that one must have enough food and shelter to remain alive and to be able to work (**article 1**).

In this first article it becomes clear that the concept of "the mean of the virtues" must not be seen as a quantitative determination. In his answer to the third objection Aquinas points out that in the last analysis the mean is something proper to reason (a point he elaborates in article 2), not in the sense that it would be within reason itself[83], but so that reason indicates what the mean is for a particular matter. A moral virtue consists in making us act in agreement with right reason. In questions of justice the mean is that to which the parties are entitled and which is equitable. In this case the mean is an objective fact which must be determined by reason. For the other moral virtues the mean is determined with regard to ourselves. Here the mean is not the same for all, since people are different as regards their needs and tasks (**article 2**).

In the following article Thomas enquires whether the intellectual and theological virtues have a mean. In respect of the former one could call the knowledge of the truth, that is the affirmation of that which is, the mean, while affirming what is not and denying what is would form the extremes. Thus as regards to prudence, its insights must rest on truth and so keep the mean. Since it directs the other virtues prudence must impose on them the mean indicated by reason. While prudence establishes what the mean is in the different fields of our activity, the moral virtues help us reach the mean, in so far as they are led by prudence. With the theological virtues it is different. They have no mean since God, who transcends whatever we can do, is their measure. One can never love God enough or sufficiently place one's trust in Him. Yet, in a sense, even here we are subject to restrictions, since our forces are limited (**articles 3 & 4**).

---

[83] "... quasi ipse actus rationis ad medium reducatur".

The relations between the moral virtues (Q. 65)

One might think that one could practice one particular virtue without possessing the others. Sometimes persons who are otherwise virtuous do not seem to possess a particular virtue such as fortitude, magnanimity etc. It also happens that someone is prudent in a limited field, but not in other domains. However, this is contradicted by Cicero[84], St. Ambrose and St. Augustine: if one does not have one particular virtue, one does not possess the other virtues either. The theory of the virtues being intertwined and one goes back to the Stoa, especially to Chrysippus, for whom a virtue is a ἡγεμονικὸν πῶς ἔχον, that is a form of the rational principle in us[85], a theory which is obviously related to Stoic monism.

In his answer St. Thomas distinguishes between perfect and imperfect virtue. In its imperfect form a virtue is a tendency in a person to some virtuous action, while in other fields this same person shows that he does not yet possess the respective virtues. Such an inclination may originate from a person's constitution, character or from a certain habituation. A perfect virtue, however, is a habitus which inclines us to perform good actions. In their perfect form the virtues are interconnected, as all authors hold. This is quite obvious since the virtue of fortitude is not possible without temperance, justice or right insight. Aquinas adds that when one looks at it from the point of view of the matter of the virtues, the same conclusion imposes itself: the moral virtues must bring us to make the right choices. For this prudence is required, because in a choice one must not only direct oneself to the proper end, but also choose the proper means which lead to this end, something which is the task of prudence. However, prudence cannot exercise its influence in the field of the other virtues if not assisted by them.

If one exercises oneself in a particular field of behavior, e.g. by mastering one's anger, one acquires a certain disposition which helps not to become angry easily. But this disposition does not yet have the character of a virtue. In daily life one will have to exercise oneself in different types of activity, which fall under the virtues. By doing so one acquires the respective habitus. Even if one does not have the opportunity to practice some of the virtues, one will acquire a disposition for using them when the occasion presents itself[86]. This last remark applies to a virtue like the patronage of public or charitable organizations and institutions which not everyone can practice.

---

[84] *Tuscul. Disput.* II, c. 14: "Ecquid nescis... virtutem, si unam amiseris... nullam esse te habiturum".

[85] See *Stoicorum veterum fragmenta*, III, 307, 75. Cf. Max Pohlenz, *Die Stoa. Geschichte einer geistigen Bewegung*, I, 127. Clement of Alexandria spoke of an intertwinement of the virtues.

[86] Aquinas writes "in proxima potentia" and "illud habere dicimur quod in promptu est ut habeamus" (art. 1 ad 1).

Whereas the different sciences deal with subject matters which need not be related, the passions and actions which are the objects of the virtues do have such a relation with one another. All passions originate from love and hatred and find their terminus in pleasure or sadness. Likewise the acts which are the matter of the moral virtues are related to one another and to the passions (**article 1**).

Opposing himself to an opinion which in his time was widely diffused, Aquinas writes that the moral virtues, in so far as they lead us to a good which does not lie beyond our natural powers, can be acquired by our actions and can exist without supernatural love[87]. But without this supernatural love they are not perfect, since they do not lead us to our last end (**article 2**). The following articles of this question deal with the relation of the theological virtues with each other and with the moral virtues and will not be discussed here.

Are all virtues of equal value? (Q. 66)

If one considers the specific nature of the virtues then they are not all equal since the cause is better than its effect and those effects are more eminent which are closer to their cause. Reason being the cause and root of the good in man[88], a virtue such as prudence, which is closest to reason, has more goodness than the other moral virtues. For similar reasons justice is a more eminent virtue than fortitude or temperance, and fortitude more eminent than temperance.

This question of whether virtues are equal can also be raised with regard to the same virtues as present in different people. As such these are equal, since whoever possesses a virtue, has whatever it comprises. It is possible, however, that one person possesses a virtue in a higher degree than another, or acquires it in a fuller sense later in life. One can see this in the fact that one person is better disposed to attain the mean between extremes than another, because he has a better opportunity to practice it or has a better natural disposition. The Stoics were mistaken when they argued that only those who are best disposed possess the virtues[89]. In order to possess a virtue it is sufficient only to approximate to the mean[90] (**article 1**).

---

[87] "Virtutes morales prout sunt operativi boni in ordine ad finem qui non excedit facultatem naturalem hominis, possunt per opera humana acquiri. Et sic acquisitæ sine caritate esse possunt".

[88] "Causa et radix humani boni est ratio".

[89] According to them a virtue is something absolute, which (like true or rectilinear) knows no more and less. The virtue of man and woman, of free citizens and slaves, of humans and of the gods is the same. One has it, or one does not have it at all, since its essence is unchangeable knowledge. Cf. Seneca, *Epist.* 92, 24: "Non intenditur virtus". See M. Pohlenz, *o.c.*, p. 127.

[90] "Sufficit prope medium esse".

Another question is whether the different virtues which are simultaneously present in a person are equal to each other. They are not equal as regards their specific essence. In respect of their intensifying or weakening, they are, since all the virtues grow or decrease at the same time in a proportionate relation, just as the fingers of the hand of a child grow in the same proportion. Aquinas adds that for those authors who think that the four cardinal virtues are general conditions for our acts a person only possesses equal virtues when these general conditions are present[91]. One may also consider the question of the equality of the virtues from the point of view of prudence. Prudence will be present in a proportionally equal way in all the virtues of the same person. As regards the matter of the virtues it is possible that one is more inclined to the acts of one virtue than to those of the other virtues (**article 2**).

Considered as such, a virtue is the more important the more eminent its object is. The object of the intellect is more eminent than that of the appetite, since it is universal, while the appetite is directed to concrete things. For this reason the intellectual virtues are nobler than the moral virtues. But when one considers the question from the point of view of our actions then the moral virtues rank more highly, since they make us act well and, secondly, since they realize more fully what is implied in the term virtue (sc. a capacity to act)[92]. The moral virtues are more durable than the intellectual since, living as we do in society, we must practice them day after day (**article 3**).

One may call a virtue greater the greater the good it brings about as reason determines it (*bonum rationis*). In this respect justice is the most important moral virtue. This follows from the fact that it has its seat in the will, the rational appetite, and is directed to actions which concern not only the acting person himself but also his relation to others. When one compares fortitude and temperance, fortitude is more noble since this virtue subjects man's most powerful inclination, sc. to keep oneself alive, to the control of reason (**article 4**).

As justice is the most important moral virtue, so wisdom is the greatest intellectual virtue on account of its object, God, the First Cause. When studying a cause, one must also consider its effects, and so wisdom as the knowledge of the ultimate causes is the yardstick for evaluating the other intellectual virtues. Prudence, on the other hand, deals with human affairs and is therefore subordinated to wisdom. Prudence shows how to reach the end, happiness, but wisdom considers the end itself. It is true that the knowledge of the ultimate end which wisdom gives us in this life is imperfect; it is only a first approach toward this future happiness. Although in this life we can only acquire a very limited

---

[91] He refers to St. Augustine, *De Trinitate* VI, c. 4: "Quicumque sunt æquales in fortitudine, æquales sunt in prudentia et temperantia".

[92] Art. 3, ad 2: "Secundum virtutes morales dicitur homo bonus simpliciter et non secundum intellectuales, quia appetitus movet alias potentias ad suum actum... Unde per hoc etiam non probatur nisi quod virtus moralis sit melior secundum quid".

knowledge of God, this knowledge is more valuable than whatever else we may come to know[93] (**article 5**)[94].

Do the virtues remain after death ? (Q. 67)

According to St. Augustine Cicero denied that the virtues remain present in the separated soul[95]. In fact the material substratum of these virtues, sc. a certain inclination in the appetitive faculties in respect of the passions, disappears in death. There will no longer be any desire for food and drinks or of sexual pleasure, nor the challenge to resist threatening dangers nor any need for an equitable exchange of goods. However, the formal element of these virtues, sc. the order of reason, remains. Reason knows best what is proper to and suitable for the separate soul as St. Augustine explains in a beautiful text[96]. The moral virtues remain present in their roots. But justice, which has its seat in the imperishable will, remains in its essence (**article 1**).

But what about the intellectual virtues after our death? According to Avicenna[97] no concepts would remain in the intellect (*intellectus possibilis*) when the soul no longer turns to sense-objects, but Aquinas rejects this view. Concepts are received in the intellect according to its spiritual nature, and therefore they are immaterial and imperishable. But what is stored in the imagination is lost. Since the habitus of the intellectual virtues are made up of concepts they remain after death (**article 2**)[98].

---

[93] Art. 5, ad 3: "Sed tamen illa modica cognitio quae per sapientiam de Deo haberi potest, omni alii cognitioni praefertur".

[94] In the last article of this question St. Thomas explains why love is the greatest among the theological virtues. Although faith, hope and love are equal with regard to their object, love gets closest to its object, God.

[95] *De Trinitate* XIV, c. 9.

[96] *De Trinitate* XIV, c. 4: "Prudentia ibi erit sine ullo periculo erroris, fortitudo sine molestia tolerandorum malorum; temperantia sine repugnatione libidinum, ut prudentiæ sit nullum bonum Deo præponere vel æquare; fortitudinis ei firmissime cohærere; temperantia nullo defectu noxio delectari" (the quotation is from XIV, c. 9, 12).

[97] *De anima*, pars 5, c. 6.

[98] The last articles of this question discuss whether the theological virtues remain intact after death.

CHAPTER VIII

VICES AND SINS

Introduction

The treatise on vices and sins is the counterpart of the chapter on the virtues. It comprises 19 questions running from Q. 71 to Q. 89 of the first volume of the Second Part of the *Summa theologiae*. The subject-matter of the entire treatise is well ordered. Vices and sins as such are dealt with first; next Aquinas determines how to distinguish between sins and presents a comparative study of sins. Finally, after discussing the question of the seat of vices and sins he studies the causes and effects of sins.

In nature, in human acts or in man made things evil is the privation of a quality which a subject or an action should have. A blind person or a letter full of spelling mistakes are each deprived of what they should have had. Evil is real, sc. a real absence or lack of something, but it does not have an existence of its own, existing as it does only in a subject. Evil in nature occurs at the level of their substantial being (the corruption of things) or of the accidents (the privation of accidental qualities) and as a lack of serviceability in respect of other things[1]. The evil in human acts is twofold, sc. a) a defect which occurs in the action itself, e.g. a wrong argument, a poorly executed job. This may be caused by insufficient talent for a certain type of activity, by some damage inflicted on the faculties or by a lack of attention or knowledge about how to do something. b) We speak of moral evil when a human act is deprived of what it should have, sc. the proper order to man's real end as determined by reason.

In classical antiquity one finds archaic ideas about sin, which is seen as an act producing undesired effects. It is a transgression, possibly without any guilt, of customs, rites or a generally accepted code of conduct[2]. Later a more precise idea of sin comes to the fore as a violation of the rights of others, caused by pride (ὕβρις) which leads to blindness (ἄτη). Similarly in Israel the terms for sin did not at the very beginning have a religious connotation[3]. According to Socrates bad actions result from ignorance (οὐδεὶς ἑκὼν ἁμαρτάνει). Aris-

---

[1] In this sense earthquakes, hurricanes etc. can be called an evil, since the required order to the end is lacking, sc. the usefulness or serviceability which man may expect from nature. In *Q. d. de malo*, q. 1, a. 1 ad 1 St. Thomas calls this lack of serviceability "an evil for others". Punishment is another example: it is a good for society and for re-establishing the violated order of justice, but an evil for the person who is punished.

[2] The Latin word *scelus* signified originally an involuntary transgression of a tabu, *vitium* a transgression of the rules in the games in honour of Jupiter. See *Hasting's Encyclopedia for Religion and Ethics*, "sin".

[3] See Kittel, *Theol. Wörterbuch zum N.T.*, under ἁμαρτάνω.

totle was inclined to measure moral evil by its effects, in particular those on others, even if he sees a lack of measure in acts which do not possess the right mean[4]. St. Thomas is very clear about the fact that moral evil lies in the act itself, in so far as it is not in agreement with right reason[5]. Moral evil is not a subdivision of ontic or ontological evil[6], but a form of evil in its own right. It consists in ordering an act to a goal which is contrary to what right reason considers fitting and correct[7]. Since the will chooses an action directed to the wrong end, it is the root from which evil proceeds[8]. In the modern Western world the awareness of sin is declining. The reasons for this phenomenon could be the extravagant subjectivism which encourages people to decide themselves what they are going to consider to be good or bad according to their more superficial desires. Other factors might be the waning of the awareness of God as our creator and legislator and, finally, psychological theories which suggest that one should follow one's inclinations without restraint.

Vices and sins as such (Q. 71)

Ethics does not study each individual act as such, but deals with what is general and common. Virtues are the principles of morally good acts, but bad habitus the causes of morally evil acts. This is the reason why Aquinas begins his treatise on sin with a discussion of the vices[9]. The question comprises six articles. A vice is contrary to a virtue and must be studied as such. One can study a virtue, a) for itself (a disposition which gives our faculties the aptitude to certain acts); b) in respect of what a virtue brings about, a certain goodness which renders man more perfect in a way which is fitting to his nature, c) in respect of that to which a virtue is ordered, sc. good actions.

---

[4] Cf. James J. Walsh, *Aristotle's Conception of Moral Weakness*, New York & London 1963.

[5] *S. Th.* I-II, 18, 9 ad 2: "Nos autem hic dicimus malum communiter omne quod est rationi rectae repugnans".

[6] *Q. d. de malo*, q. 2, a. 5 ad 2: "Ens simpliciter non convertitur cum bono moris, sicut nec cum bono naturae".

[7] *S.C..G.* III, c. 9: "Moralium autem mensura est ratio... Quod igitur in moralibus sortitur speciem a fine qui est secundum rationem, dicitur secundum suam speciem bonum; quod vero sortitur speciem a fine contrario fini rationis, dicitur secundum speciem suam malum". Cf. *ibid.*, c. 10: "Vitium morale in sola actione consideratur, non autem in aliquo effectu producto".

[8] *Ibid.* III, c. 10: "In actu igitur voluntatis quaerenda est radix et origo peccati moralis". - Aristotle points out that animals live in agreement with their natural inclinations (τῇ ὀρέξει ζῇ). Animals and children before having the use of their reason cannot act morally.

[9] Cf. A.M. Festugière, "La notion du péché présentée par S. Thomas, I-II, 71, et sa relation avec la morale aristotélicienne", in *The New Scholasticism* 5 (1931), 332-341.

With regard to the first point, the vices are opposed to the virtues. As regards the second point, b), a certain malice is opposed to virtue, inasmuch as a virtue means a certain moral goodness. In respect of c) sins are contrary to good actions to which the virtues are ordered. If a person has a vice, it means that he does not possess the disposition which is fitting to his nature (**article 1**).

In the first article we have just summarized Thomas stresses that a virtue is a good disposition in conformity with our human nature[10], while vices are bad dispositions. This point is elaborated in the second article. As opposed to the virtues, vices are dispositions which counteract what is according to our nature. In this connection "our nature" means primarily our rational nature, determined by the presence of reason[11]. Virtue makes us and our acts to be good. Since vices are opposed to the order of reason, they go against our nature. In his answer to the fourth objection Aquinas stresses that God's plan and intention regarding his creatures, called the eternal law (*lex aeterna*), is the ground-plan for the order our reason must impose. It follows that what is contrary to reason is also contrary to God's plan[12]. If vices are contrary to nature, how do we explain, that one finds them more frequently in people than the virtues? One would expect that what is natural predominates. The answer to this difficulty lies in man's dual nature, sc. his rational and his sensual nature. Since the sensual part comes first and the intellect begins its work with the help of the material collected by the senses, one can understand that a good number of people move predominantly at this first level and frequently act in opposition to the order of reason[13], although not without a judgment and decision of the mind (**article 2**).

Is a vice worse than an act proceeding from it? Virtuous and sinful acts are at a higher level of actuality than the habitus of which they are acts. For instance, it is better actually to do what is good than to be capable of doing it. Likewise people are not punished because of a vice they have, but because of their bad actions. On the other hand, a habitus is more permanent than an act, and from this point of view a habitus is a greater evil than a bad action (**article 3**).

Natural things act with necessity, so that they do not act contrary to their specific nature. Man, however, is capable of virtuous behavior when he wants to but can also perform acts contrary to it. As a habitus is not produced by only one act

---

[10] Even if the virtues are not conferred on us by nature, they make us to be inclined to what agrees with our nature (ad 1).

[11] Cf. Dionysius, *De divinis nominibus*, c. 4: "Bonum autem hominis est secundum rationem esse et malum hominis est praeter rationem esse".

[12] Cf. *S.C.G.* III, c. 122: "Non enim Deus a nobis offenditur, nisi ex eo quod contra nostrum bonum agimus".

[13] Ad 3: "Ex hoc autem vitia et peccata in hominibus proveniunt quod sequuntur inclinationem naturæ sensitivæ contra ordinem rationis".

so it is not destroyed either by a single act[14]. Obviously sinful acts against a virtue do not exclude, at a different moment, virtuous acts in conformity with it (**article 4**).

A difficult question is whether a sin is always an act. There are sins of neglect, when one sins by not doing what one should do, and this seems to suggest a negative answer to our question. But some authors believe that even here a positive act of the will is required, although there is no external action. The solution is that a sin of neglect (in the sense of not doing something one is supposed to do) as such does not require an act. Someone neglects his wife without giving much thought to it and without willing it explicitly. However, when one asks what is the cause of such conduct there must always be some act. One fails to do what one can and must do. If this neglect is within our power, it is also willed[15], either directly (one does not want to do something) or indirectly (one wants to do something else, e.g. to go out with one's friends instead of staying home with one's wife and children). In this last case, the act of the will, directed to something else, may have only an accidental relation (*per accidens*) to the neglect. One goes out at night, sleeps over and fails to wake up in time for one's work. In these cases it is better to say that the sin of neglect is formally speaking without an act (**article 5**)..

The final article of this question examines the relation of a sinful act to the will of God. In Christian tradition sin is mostly defined as a transgression of the law of God. For instance, St. Augustine says that "Sin is something said or done or a desire contrary to the eternal law"[16]. St. Thomas reminds the reader that sin is a bad *human* act, therefore a voluntary act. An act is wrong when it does not have the right measure and is not adapted to its rule. This rule is in the first place human reason, and more remotely God's plan governing all things (the eternal law). Theologians see sin primarily as an offence against God, philosophers as an act which is contrary to right reason. The flaw in a sinful act is that it does not agree with the end of man. Since such an act is opposed to the right insight of reason, it is also an offense against God (**article 6**).

---

[14] This does not apply to the infused virtues which are removed by one serious sin against them.

[15] Even not expressly willing something can be said to be willed. Ad 2: "Unde etiam non velle potest dici voluntarium, in quantum in potestate hominis est velle et non velle".

[16] *Contra Faustum*, XXII, c. 27: "Peccatum est dictum vel factum vel concupitum contra legem aeternam".

Distinguishing between sins (Q. 72)

A person who commits a bad action directs himself to some object he wants to attain[17]. For such a person the fact that his act deviates from right reason and the rule of conduct to be observed is secondary. Since the nature of an act depends on that to which it is directed and not on something secondary, the species of sins depend on their objects (**article 1**).

Every sin, therefore, consists in an act which is directed unreasonably to a transitory good[18], which one desires. One may look for pleasure in a good one is unreasonably seeking (such as being unduly honoured) or desire bodily pleasure of the sense of touch (**article 2**). The object of our acts is the subject matter they are concerned with[19]. But, our acts are subordinated to the end which the will tries to reach and this ultimately determines the nature of the sin (**article 3**).

Medieval theology distinguished between sins against ourselves, against God and against our fellow men[20]. The theme provides Thomas an opportunity for an important clarification. There is a threefold order in man: he must follow the insights of his reason in so far as his actions and emotions must be in agreement with the rule of reason. Secondly, he must also live in conformity with the law of God. Thirdly some obligations are derived from his being a member of society. Deviations, therefore, will be sins against oneself, against God and against others. It is true that right reason and the law of God coincide for the most part, but there are commandments which lie outside the range of natural reason, such as those concerning supernatural faith. By transgressing them one is considered to act against God. There are acts which are concerned with ourselves and not with our fellow men. If they are contrary to right reason, one sins against oneself. Finally, one can also sin against others. In this answer of Aquinas we notice the partial equalizing of the order of reason and divine law[21]. This implies that a philosophical ethics is possible (**article 4**).

The nature and the amount of punishment one exposes oneself to for wrongdoing has no influence on the kind of sin one commits[22]. This is because the eventual punishment lies outside the intention of the one who acts and what is

---

[17] A quotation from *De divinis nominibus*, c. 4, § 19 points out that no one performs an action to seek evil, sc. a privation of a good, as a privation ("nullus intendens ad malum operatur").

[18] On countless occasions St. Thomas uses the definition of sin as "aversio ab incommutabili bono et conversio ad commutabile bonum", which stresses the deviation from man's last end, God, and a turning oneself in an irrational way to transitory goods. The definition is inspired by Augustine: God is immutable, creatures mutable. Cf. *De libero arbitrio*, II, 19, 53.

[19] "Materia circa quam".

[20] St. Thomas refers to Isidore, but according to the *Leonine* the reference is to a work by Hugh of St. Victor.

[21] "Quæcumque continentur sub ordine rationis, continentur sub ordine ipsius Dei".

[22] It may, though, deter one from sinning.

per accidens has no decisive influence. One must, however, distinguish between serious and lesser sins[23]. Thus explains Thomas, in the disorderliness of a bad action one can distinguish between a disorder with regard to the last end and that in respect of what comes after the end. When one turns away from one's last end, God, one commits a serious or mortal sin, but when this disorderliness concerns the manner in which one acts, while the order to the last end remains intact, one speaks of venial sin. The two kinds of sin differ greatly with regard to their relation to the end, but they agree in so far as they concern objects which determine the nature of the sin. So both can belong to the same species (**article 5**).

A further question, again, is whether doing something and failing to do it belong to the same kind of sin. Here one must distinguish between the material act and what is formal in it. To kill some one by poisoning him or with a weapon are different material acts, but formally they will belong to the same species. A negation is always based on some positive reality that is its cause. Aquinas gives the example of a miser who steals out of avarice, and refuses to help others. The difference between doing something which is wrong and failing to do what one should do, explains why some positive and negative commandments are mentioned together in the Bible, not as concerning different virtues but as denoting degrees in the practice of one and the same virtue (**article 6**).

One can also speak of sinning "by one's words, one's thoughts and one's works"[24]. Aquinas understands the expression as denoting the stages a sinful act can go through. It is thought out in our innermost, manifested sometimes in words and gestures and carried out in what one does (**article 7**). As we have seen, the distinction between sins depends on the object to which one directs oneself. Thus objects which have too much of something and others which have too little of it, differ specifically e.g. aversion from pleasure and indulgence in pleasure differ in type (**article 8**). Circumstances do not determine the kind of sins if the disorderly circumstances proceed from the same motive as the sin itself: someone who is avaricious will accept money from persons from whom he should not do so, and at times and in places where this is not correct. It happens, however, that acting under disorderly circumstances proceeds from different motivations, so that the species of the sin varies accordingly, e.g. to eat only delicious meals can result from gluttony, but overeating may have a different motivation (**article 9**).

---

[23] "Peccatum veniale" and "peccatum mortale" in Catholic moral theology.
[24] Cf. St. Jerome, *Super Ezechiel*, 43, 23: *ML* 25, 446.

The relation between sins (Q. 73)

All virtues move us in the same direction because they follow the right insight of reason. So they are connected with each other through the virtue of prudence[25]. But one who sins, seeks a good without taking into account the rule of reason. This means that the objects, to which one directs oneself, bear no connection with each other, and can even be opposed. Therefore, sins need not be connected. As was argued in the treatise on habitus, a single contrary action does not remove the respective habitus. By repeated actions, however, a vice is produced which destroys the respective virtue and so removes also prudence and with it all the other virtues in their perfect form, since they all rest on prudence. However, certain dispositions to virtuous actions may survive, but these are no longer real virtues (**article 1**).

This does not mean that as the virtues are connected with each other, so also sins are. According to the Stoa all vices would originate from a lack of self-control, that is from an inclination (εὐεμπτωσία) to weakness and to the emotions[26]. But this viewpoint is not right. Sins are directed to different objects and are not deprived of all reasonable insight and of whatever is positive[27]. One can remove oneself in different degrees from right insight and so sins will be more or less serious (**article 2**).

A sin is more serious if one's not following the right insight concerns a more fundamental principle in the order of reason. This happens when the end from which one deviates is more important. Things outside us are ordered to man, man himself is ordered to God. For this reason, transgressions against outside material things are less serious than what is done against man himself (e.g. murder), and these sins, in turn, are a lesser evil than what is done against God, e.g. blasphemy. Notwithstanding this conclusion one can compare sins with each other inasmuch as they deviate in a lesser or higher degree from our last end (**article 3**).

Sins which are directly opposed to the virtues are greater the more important are the virtues are to which they are opposed. On the other hand, the virtues will restrain all inclinations to evil which are at variance with them, so that it happens that a less serious sin will also be opposed to a virtue (**article 4**). Sins of the spirit are more serious than those of the body. In the first the aversion from

---

[25] Prudence is the *recta ratio agibilium*.
[26] *SVF* III 421. Cf. Cicero, *Tuscul. Disput.* IV, 22: "Omnium autem perturbationum fontem esse dicunt intemperantiam quæ est a tota mente et a recta ratione defectio sic aversa a præscriptione rationis, ut nullo modo appetitiones animi nec regi nec contineri queant". In his *Paradoxa ad Brutum*, III, 1 Cicero writes that sins can differ but that the fact of sinning remains the same ("... ipsum quidem illud peccare quoquo verteris, unum est"). It is transgressing a limit. How far one goes after that, does not make a difference.
[27] Absolute and total evil would destroy itself. Cf. *E.N.* IV, c. 11, 1126ª12.

God is primary, in the second the conversion to transitory things holds the first place. Moreover, the inclination to sins of the body is greater in human beings than that to sins of the spirit and so their culpability is less (**article 5**).

With regard to the causes of sinful actions one must distinguish between the will to commit a sin[28] and factors which seduce the will to sin. As regards the will itself, a sin will be the greater the stronger the decision is to commit it. As to other factors, the wrongness of the chosen end makes the sins thus originating proportionally more serious, while factors which impede the free decision of the will, such as ignorance, weakness, violence or fear diminish the sinful character of an act (**article 6**). Circumstances can aggravate sins in three ways, a) by making the sin to be of another species (sexual intercourse with the wife of some one else), b) when a wrong act is repeated under different circumstances, e.g. when hindering others by making excessive noise, first at one's own house, later in the vicinity of a nursing home, c) if they co-determine what one does they can aggravate an offence. The gravity of theft is increased with the value of the stolen object (**article 7**).

If an action causes damage to others the sin becomes more serious the greater the damage one inflicts. If one did not foresee nor intend to harm others one's culpability is less, unless one neglected to consider the consequences of one's actions or when the damage follows directly upon what one does. An example of the latter case would be to wage a campaign of slander against a high official so that he loses his position. The bad consequences as such do not make the sin greater. What is decisive is the lack of agreement with right reason. If this should be increased by the bad consequences then these consequences render one more guilty (**article 8**).

Does a sin against someone become greater according to the rank of the person against whom it is committed? This person is, in a sense, the object of the sin. As was argued before, it is in the first place the object which determines the species and the seriousness of a sin. If the object concerns a more important human end then a sin against it will be more serious. Our main ends are God, we ourselves and our fellow men. Whatever we do, is done for the sake of one of these three ends. To the extent that the person against whom one commits a sin stands closer to God (e.g. is more virtuous or more devoted to God's service), a sin against him will also be directed more against God. A sin against ourselves, in the sense of being against those who are intimately related to us, is the more serious, the closer the relation or the greater the obligations we have towards these persons. As regards our fellow men, a sin against them is the more serious the greater the number of people it affects. Causing damage to one's own possessions is less sinful than damaging things which do not belong to us. But acting against one's own good, in so far as this good is not rightfully subject to our

---

[28] This is called by Thomas the tree which produces bad fruit (after *Matthew* 7, 18).

free disposition, e.g. when one commits suicide, is worse than killing someone else (**article 9**).

A final enquiry concerns the effect of the standing of the person who sins upon the seriousness of his act. Sins committed after deliberation are more serious when these acts are performed by persons of higher rank. They could have more easily refrained from sinning because of their knowledge and virtue. Sometimes there is a considerable contrast between what one might expect from someone and what this person actually does, e.g. when a high ranking officer in a company, who already enjoys a high salary, steals company money at the expense of small investors. His bad example as an officer can have an especially damaging effect (**article 10**).

Where do sins occur?(Q. 74)

When studying the habitus and the virtues Aquinas also discusses where they are located in man, in particular, in which faculties. Similarly he also examines the question of where sins occur. In a first observation he highlights the difference between immanent and transient actions. Writing a letter is a transient action which goes from a human being to the paper upon which he writes and which receives the action. Another group of actions such as those of the cognitive and appetitive faculties remain in the person who performs them. The acts of the virtues and sins belong to this second group. Consequently, the faculty in which the act originates, is also where it is located. Since moral acts are voluntary, the will is their first principle and so both virtuous acts and sins are in the will (**article 1**).

Since the will moves the other faculties to their actions these are implicated in the sinful act and so sins can also be said to be in these faculties[29]. One must understand this conclusion in the light of St. Thomas' doctrine that the faculties are not externally juxtaposed to each other, but that the more high-ranking faculties include the lower ones[30]. However, one cannot say that those members of the body which are used in sinful acts are the subject of these sins, for the members of the body are not principles of our actions. Moreover, an action of these

---

[29] "Unde non sola voluntas potest esse subiectum peccati, sed omnes illae potentæ quæ possunt moveri ad suos actus vel ab eis reprimi per voluntatem".

[30] Cf. *Q. d. de veritate*, q. 21, a. 3: "Voluntas et intellectus mutuo se includunt". The will contains the sensory appetitive faculties, as the senses are a kind of participation in reason (*S.Th.* I, 77, 7). The rational soul calls forth in the matter (which is to be the organic body) these sensory powers and actualizes them. Cf. L. Elders, "*Contineri* as a Fundamental Structure of St. Thomas' Ontology", in *Aquinas* 18 (1975), pp. 58 -79.

members is directed to what is outside and is not immanent. The physical act by which one takes the purse of someone else, is not a moral action[31] (**article 2**).

This is elaborated in the following articles. Sins can be located in the sensory faculties (the so-called *sensualitas*). The reason is that in man these faculties are in contact with the intellect and naturally follow its commands. Therefore their acts can be voluntary and so when these are contrary to right reason, sin can be ascribed to them. Although one could never totally submit all movements of our unruly sensory faculties to the control of reason it is nevertheless possible to avoid each of these movements taken individually (**article 3**). Can these movements, which are so difficult to control, become serious sins? No, says Aquinas: the subordinate faculties as such cannot deviate from the end, but are subject to reason and the will[32]. But an irregularity in the sensory faculties can lead to a serious sin in our reason and will (**article 4**).

In the preceding articles Thomas spoke of what is higher in man and of the *ratio*, to which the lower powers are subordinated. He now determines the role of the intellect and will as possible subjects of sins. The intellect has a twofold activity, sc. knowing the truth and directing the other powers in man. Both activities can become sinful. Thus error in the knowledge of truth can be caused by sinful neglect. Again, the intellect can command the other powers to act sinfully or not refrain them from turning to what is wrong. In these cases the intellect is guilty. In his answer to the second objection Aquinas explains the relation of the intellect to the will on this point. In a sense the will precedes the act of the intellect and moves it, but the intellect, for its part, also exercises a causal influence on the will and is the principle of its act. So one may call an act of the will reasonable and an act on the intellect voluntary (**article 5**). If reason does not immediately prohibit irregular acts in the sensory appetitive faculties or suppress them it commits a sin. Although disorderly lust is located in the sense-powers the responsibility for it rests with the mind (**article 6**).

The next article shows that the intellect reaches a decision and gives directions in two stages. It first forms a general judgement on the basis of already present knowledge. It can go further and consider what a given act means in the light of the first principles[33]. The final decision and choice are reserved to the

---

[31] However, the external action is connected with the sin. It is the the result of the sinful act within one's innermost and shares in its disorderliness. In this broader sense a sin is more than a wrong decision. See *Q. d. de malo,* q. 2, a. 2: "Et sic patet quod peccatum est in plus quam culpa... Quæ quidem difformitas invenitur non solum in actu interiori sed etiam exteriori". But, Thomas says, theologians speak of sin in so far as it involves guilt (*culpa*). This is how he himself speaks in the *Summa theologiae*.

[32] "Inordinatio autem a fine non est nisi eius cuius est ordinare in finem. Unde peccatum mortale non potest esse in sensualitate, sed solum in ratione".

[33] Thomas speaks of the *ratio superior*, which considers an act in the light of God's commandments.

intellect at this second stage (**article 7**). A problem related to this is whether pausing over the thought of a sinful act is itself sinful? One can distinguish here between entertaining the thought on the one hand and taking pleasure in it on the other. The first action need not be wrong and can be justified. In the second case, however, one consents, to a certain extent, to a wrong action. To take pleasure in the thought is a sin, the malice of which depends on what this thought is about and on the degree of consent (**article 8**). The last two articles examine whether sins can occur in the *ratio superior*, the intellect which judges human actions in the light of the law of God.

On the causes of sins in general (Q 75)

The causes of sin are discussed in a long series of questions. We shall deal with the subject in so far as it belongs to philosophical ethics. Generally speaking evil is not the direct (*per se*) result of an act, since it is a privation, whereas actions effect something which is positive. But in so far as a sin is an act, its ontic content can have a direct cause (*causa per se*). As regards its disorderly character, it has, as do all other privations, a cause which produces it *per accidens*. A privation of something which should have been present happens only when there is a cause which impedes the full effect from coming about. This is why evil has a cause which is defective or, in other words, a cause *per accidens*. This defective cause is, with regard to sins, the cause of sins as acts. When the will directs itself to some passing good without being guided by the rule of reason it directly causes the sin as an act, but it causes the disorderly aspect of it in a secondary way (*per accidens*), without really intending it. The lack of order in the sinful action originates from a lack of order in the will. In his answer to the third objection St. Thomas writes that not observing the rule of reason as such is not yet a sin, but that there is a sin as soon as the will begins to act. In this way a sin is not caused by another sin, but by a positive act, from which a good is absent (sc. the right order to the rule of reason)[34]. One should not look for a further cause for this not paying attention to the right rule of conduct. Here the freedom of the will is sufficient. The will is the cause of sins in so far as it is defective, and this being defective is purely negative[35] (**article 1**).

To commit a sin, however, can be a complex act. We distinguish between the immediate cause of a sinful action (the intellect and the will, sc. man in so far as he is free) and remote causes, sc. sense-perception and the sensory appetitive

---

[34] *Q. d. de malo*, q. 1, a. 3: "Culpa voluntatis non est in hoc quod actu non attendit ad regulam rationis vel legis divinæ, sed ex hoc quod non habens regulam vel mensuram huiusmodi procedit ad eligendum".

[35] *Ibid.*: "Huiusmodi autem quod est non uti regula praedicta, non oportet aliquam causam quaerere, quia ad hoc sufficit ipsa libertas voluntatis per quam potest agere vel non agere"; "defectus ille est negatio sola".

faculties. If the latter are inclined to a particular object the will can influence the intellect in its favor, as will be shown in q. 77, a. 1. The intellect can neglect to consider the correct rule of conduct to be observed, so that the will commits a sinful act. So it appears that some internal acts precede a sin (**article 2**). Our free will alone is a sufficient cause of the sinful act because no outside agent, except God, can influence the will. But outside agents can try to influence the intellect by persuasion or by proposing attractive objects to the senses. But these influences do not compel us. (**article 3**).

A sin can be the cause of other sins and this in the four genera of causality: as an efficient cause one sin can prepare the field for more sins of this type, or as a cause *per accidens,* by a set of consequences. One has committed a crime and then discovers one has to kill some witnesses in order to protect onself. At the level of material causality[36] one sin can prepare others. Fights in a marriage can lead to divorce and mental suffering in the children. As to final causality, the desire to commit a sexual aggression upon children can be the reason why one abducts them. Lastly, if one commits lewd acts in order to lay hands on the money of one's partner, this taking of the money is the formal cause of the sin of being unchaste (**article 4**).

THE CAUSES OF SINS IN PARTICULAR (QQ. 76 - 84)

After considering the causes of sin in general Thomas now studies them in detail. His complete treatment points to the interest of the theme for moral theology. Although part of what he writes belongs to theology, most is of a purely rational nature. The arguments will be rendered in a shortened form. Thomas first studies the causes of sin in ourselves. Next, a series of questions deals with possible causes outside of us which might bring us to sin, while Q.84 asks to which extent one sin can be the cause of other sins. In a concluding section Thomas studies the effects of sin.

The causes of sin in ourselves: ignorance (Q. 76)

Aristotle discusses the effect of ignorance upon the degree of responsibility for our actions, developing his view in contrast to the opinion of Socrates who held that all wrongdoing is the product of ignorance. In the *Nicomachean Ethics* II, c. 2 he shows that there is an ignorance which does not do away with the blameworthy character of an act. A person who commits a fault through a vice has no regret about what he has done. His vice prevents him from getting a clear view of why his act is bad. But if one regrets what one has done, because one

---

[36] Aquinas means the object with which sin is concerned (the *materia circa quam*).

did not know that it was wrong one is thought to have acted out of ignorance. Aristotle mentions the different aspects of an act done out of ignorance.

Ignorance is a cause *per accidens* of a bad act in that it removes what otherwise impedes one from performing this act[37]. This can occur in two ways, sc. by not knowing the general rule for our duties or by not knowing a concrete circumstance, e.g. that a person in the room is affected by the smoke of my cigarettes. If in these cases one would have carried out the respective act all the same, even if one had known the general rule or the particular circumstance, the ignorance is no excuse but merely accompanies the wrong action (**article 1**).

Is ignorance itself sinful? Aquinas first stresses the difference between a simple not knowing (*nescientia*) and ignorance. Ignorance is a privation of knowledge one could have or should have[38]. Sometimes we have an obligation to possess this knowledge, sc. if without it we cannot act or work correctly. Thus everyone must know the fundamentals of law and justice relative to his position. But one is not obliged to know certain other things, such as the conclusions of the sciences. Whoever fails to learn what he should know commits a sin of neglect. But he is not responsible for what he cannot know, for this ignorance in involuntary. Therefore, no invincible ignorance is sinful (**article 2**)..

If one acts in ignorance but so that if one had known that the act was wrong, one would nevertheless have done it then this ignorance is not the cause of the sinful act and does not excuse it nor does it make the act involuntary. If, on the other hand, one would not have acted if one had known (and one was not obliged to know it), then such an act is not a sin, for it is involuntary (**article 3**). In the final article of this question Thomas asks whether ignorance can make an act less sinful. This is the case when this particular act is less voluntary. An ignorance because of which an act is entirely involuntary, makes that this act not to be a sin at all. Ignorance which accompanies a sinful act, without being its cause, does not extenuate its sinfulness. Ignorance which causes one to commit a sin, can be the result of one's own fault and, if so, this makes the sin more serious. When it is only indirectly willed, ignorance can diminish the sinful character of an act. If a student neglects to study regularly, without realizing that his conduct is wrong, and obtains thereby poor results, this effect is less willed than if he had been more aware of his fault (**article 4**).

The sensory appetite as a cause of sins (Q. 77)

In the eight articles of Q. 77 Aquinas examines the widely held opinion that passions lead to sin. A fundamental question here is whether the sensory appetite

---

[37] "Non quælibet ignorantia est causa peccati, sed illa tantum quae tollit scientiam prohibentem actum peccati".

[38] St. Thomas uses the expression "aptus natus", which means a natural aptitude and, in this case, an inclination to this knowledge.

can exercise influence on the will at all. Since the will is an immaterial faculty, which has as its object the good presented to it by the intellect, a direct influence upon it of the lower faculties is excluded. But the will can be influenced indirectly in two ways, sc. if through intense activity of the sensory appetite the will, which is rooted in the same soul as these sensory powers, loses strength and concentration or, secondly, when disorderly representations in the imagination or the estimative power hamper the formation of the right judgment in the intellect and so influence the will. In their representations and "judgments"[39] the imagination and the estimative power follow the passions. As a result the intellect in its judgments may adapt itself to the one or the other of the passions (**article 1**).

Is it possible that under the influence of the passions and emotions the intellect forms a wrong judgment, which it knows to be wrong? Socrates believed that no one ever acts against his insight and knowledge. If one acts wrongly one does so out of ignorance[40]. He taught that one chooses always what one considers best. If this choice is wrong, it is so because of ignorance. Thomas observes that, up to a point, Socrates was right. If the will chooses something bad, this must in some way be seen as good by the intellect, since otherwise the will would not direct itself to it. Experience, however, shows that Socrates' position as such is wrong since many people sin, although they know that what they do is not right. The solution of this difficulty[41] is that in order to act morally we are led by a double knowledge, sc. a general and a particular knowledge. A defect in either one of them is sufficient to make an act bad. An example will illustrate it: a person knows in general that one should not commit a sexual irregularity, but it happens that he does not see that a particular sexual act must be avoided. His will may not follow this general knowledge but the judgment about this concrete case. Moreover, the general judgment remains in the background as habitual knowledge but is not taken into consideration in this concrete case[42]. So one can act against one's better insight.

That in individual cases one does not take into account what one knows habitually can be the result of a lack of attention and of being in a poor mental or

---

[39] This judgment is a quasi-judgment; it connects a representation with a subject and so prepares the judgment of the mind.

[40] See *E.N.* VII, c. 3. 1145^{b}22 ff; Plato, *Protagoras* 352 B ff. Cf. James J. Walsh, "The Socratic Denial of Akrasia", in G. Vlastos (ed.), *The Philosophy of Socrates*, Garden City, N.Y. 1971, 235-263; Kevin McTighe, "Socrates on the Desire for the Good and the Involuntariness of Wrongdoing. *Gorgias* 446 A -468 C", in Hugh H. Benson (ed.), *Essays on the Philosophy of Socrates*, New York 1992, 263-297.

[41] One must keep in mind what was said in chapter two about the acts leading to a choice, sc. the distinction between the knowledge of the good and the judgment before the choice is made which is directed to a particular object. See also q. 71.

[42] It is impossible that one has at the same time an actual knowledge of this general rule and a judgment contrary to it.

physical condition. A strong emotion may also impede one from reaching the judgment that a certain act is to be avoided. This may happen in three ways, a) through intense emotion the will may lose strength, b) through a passion making us incline to something which is directly opposed to the insight of reason, c) through the state of the body hampering the functioning of the mind, e.g. when one is asleep or drunk. Through insane love or great anger one may lose the use of one's reason (**article 2**). This is a weakness since one does not submit one's actions to the control of reason (**article 3**).

As has been shown, a choice results from a syllogism which has the form of a general proposition (a rule of conduct) plus a concrete act under this rule, drawing the conclusion that the act is to be performed. When one performs a wrong act, this general rule of conduct is being set aside and replaced by another general rule. But if the original rule of conduct did not remain present in some sense the choice would not be sinful. So Aquinas says that according to Aristotle there are four propositions in such a syllogism[43]. A simple example will illustrate what is meant: I must take care of my health and stop smoking; however, (in a second general judgment I feel that) a man needs occasional, small pleasures; a cigarette will provide me such a pleasure. Therefore I now light a cigarette.

In a well-known text St. Augustine writes that selfish love leads to disrespect for God and so builds up the city of Babylon[44]. Every sinful act, in fact, results from a disordered inclination to a transitory good which one seeks because one loves oneself in a wrong way. True love of oneself means that one wishes oneself a real good (**article 4**). In this connection we may also mention a sentence in the New Testament, according to which whatever is in this world is either desire of the flesh, the lustful eye or pride in one's possessions[45] (**article 5**).

Is an act less sinful when it is performed out of passion? Sin consists essentially in a free choice, which is an act of our reason and will, whereas a passion is a movement of the sensory appetite. If it precedes the choice, it can, as was said above, pull reason and will along with it and in this way reduce the voluntary character of a sinful act. This is particularly so since by a passion one directs oneself to some transitory good, while what is most typical of a sinful act is that one turns away from one's true end. But a passion which is consecutive to a choice of an object by the will makes this particular object to be willed more and this is a sign that one really wants what one is about to do (**article 6**).

A passion suppresses the sinful nature of an act only when it makes the act entirely involuntary. If because of a vehement passion the act which one performs is no longer controlled by the will, one is nevertheless responsible if this passion arose and developed with one's consent. But if its cause is involuntary, e.g. illness, the act which one performs is no longer voluntary nor, hence, a sin.

---

[43] Art. 2 ad 4. See *E.N.* VII, c. 5.
[44] *De civitate Dei* XIV, c. 28.
[45] *1 John* 2, 16.

Quite frequently what actually happens will lie somewhere between these extremes, for instance when it was possible to repress a developing passion, but one failed to do so. In such cases one is not entirely without blame (**article 7**).

Since a passion can diminish the sinfulness of an act, can we still commit a serious sin when acting under the influence of a passion? One commits a serious sin when one turns away voluntarily from the last end of human life. This aversion will not be a serious sin if our reason and will were unable to deliberate about the act, something which may happen when there is a sudden surge of a passion. However, when after a lapse of time one begins to act under the influence of a passion this act is no longer entirely all of a sudden. Reason and will can intervene and oppose this passion. Therefore, crimes committed out of passion, such as murder and adultery, are usually serious sins (**article 8**).

Perversion as the cause of sins (Q. 78)

A final but most decisive internal cause of sins is the perversion of the will, which makes one willingly love a transitory good more than what right reason and the law of God tell us to do. Aquinas explains it as follows: according to the natural order man aims at the good. That he directs himself to some evil is the effect of a disorder in his reason, will or sensory appetite. Ignorance can cause such a disorder in the intellect and a passion provoke it in the sensory appetite. This disorder is also found in the will when it loves what is less good more than what is better. It happens that one tries to acquire some temporal good at the expense of a spiritual one. In such a case one sins because of a certain perversion, in other words, one sins intentionally. The evil is not willed because of itself, but indirectly in so far as needed to reach some good. The perverse attitude of the will can either be habitual or happen just in one case (**article 1**). Is acting out of a vice acting out of an inner perversion? Aquinas points out that a habitus can be present in us without that our acts are caused by it, for it is proper to a habitus that one can use it when one wants to[46]. A person beset with vices may sometimes act morally. When in acting one is moved by a vice the action is performed because of a perversion. What agrees with this vice becomes in a way natural to the agent or a sort of second nature. The object which agrees with this vice, excludes a spiritual good. So one chooses a spiritual evil to obtain a good conformed to a vice. But this is acting out of perversion or malice (**article 2**).

Aquinas pushes his analysis one step further. The will directs itself to the good in agreement with right reason. If it directs itself to what is wrong this may happen because a) there is in this person a disorderly disposition which makes him tend to something bad which appears to him as fitting, this disorderly disposition being either a vice acquired by habituation or based on a sickly disposition

---

[46] "Habitus est quo quis utitur cum voluerit".

of the body, e.g. an inclination to certain sinful acts, or because b) what prevented him from committing a sin disappears. Someone wanted to commit a certain sin but as long as his parents were alive he refrained from it. This shows that a sin which originates from a perversion within a person always presupposes some disorder, although this disorder need not always be a habitus (**article 3**).

A sin committed out of such an inner perversion is worse than one committed out of passion. This is because a) that the will's share in it is greater, since it directs itself to what is wrong, whereas in the case of a passion the will is pushed from without, b) a passion disappears quickly, but a habitus which leads to sin is a permanent state, which makes a conversion difficult, c) whoever acts because of a perversion in himself is not adjusted to his true end, which is a serious defect (**article 4**).

The external causes of sins (QQ. 79 - 83)

When one considers the unimaginable amount of evil which people in the course of history have done and are still doing, one might wonder whether outside factors play a role in the genesis of wars, genocide, the murder of millions of unborn children, torture and violation of human rights, criminality and corruption. A first question is whether God is responsible for all this (**Q. 79**). In his *Iliad* Homer speaks of a divine power which blinds some people so that they commit excesses to which Achilles and Agamemnon fall victim[47]. Some texts of Holy Scripture seem to suggest that God surrendered certain people to their sinful inclinations[48]. In fact, however, God is in no way a cause of human sins. It is impossible that he be a direct cause of sins, since he directs all things toward himself and cannot make things deviate from this order. Neither is God indirectly responsible for the sins committed by man when he does not impede them. In such cases he leaves people to their own responsibility (**article 1**).

A sin is an action having a defect. The entitative content of this act is caused by God, as is that of all activities, processes and movements in the universe[49], but the defect in it is the effect of the human will which removes itself from the order established by God. An example illustrates this to some extent: if a man

---

[47] *Iliad* XIX 86 ff.. Cf. W. Jaeger, *Paideia. The Ideal of Greek Culture*, I, Oxford 1954, pp. 48 ff.

[48] *Romans* 1, 28 and the often quoted text of *Jesaiah* 45, 7 ("Deus... creans malum").

[49] As is argued convincingly in Thomistic metaphysics, whatever is a real being exists by participation in subsistent Being which is necessary by itself. Cf. *S. Th.* I, 104, 1 ad 2: "Intantum enim indiget creatura conservari a Deo inquantum esse effectus dependet a causa essendi"; "Solus Deus est ens per essentiam suam, quia eius essentia est suum esse, omnis autem creatura est ens participative, non quod sua essentia sit eius esse".

limps, it is not his power to move which causes this limp but a defect in his leg (**article 2**).

Can *demons* make man sin? (**Q. 80**). Several religions attribute a considerable influence to invisible, personal powers outside man. Traditional Christian theology says that the devil seduces people. However, a direct causal influence by such beings on the human will would be impossible. But they could propose some object that calls forth in the will a desire for it. Anyone proposing such an object, suggesting that it is a real good, could be considered an indirect cause of a sinful choice. But the will is not necessarily moved by such an object and remains free in its choice (**article 1**).

Questions 81, 82 and 83 discuss the transgression of a commandment of God by the first men, described in *Genesis* 3, in so far as this is the cause of our sins, a theme which is treated in Christian theology. From a purely philosophical point of view one can say that the widely diffused inclination to commit crimes, the ease with which individuals and countries time and again become involved in conflicts, the concessions many make to the pursuit of excessive pleasure and rampant dishonesty, the worries and suffering of so many, the transitoriness of human undertakings, the prevalence of sickness and death all point to a disturbance of the order of things. In this connection Thomas prefaces these questions with the remark[50] that according to the faith of the Catholic Church the sin of the first human couple passes to later generations.

Sin as the cause of other sins (Q. 84)

Can a sin which one commits lead to further sins? Vices are dispositions which lead us to acts contrary to the real end of our life and are opposed to what our nature demands from us. The one or the other vice is often considered the source of several sins. A first question is whether concupiscence or desire can be called the root of all sins. If one understands concupiscence as a disorderly inclination of man's fallen nature to transitory things then all sins fall under it. If one means by concupiscence love of money, then it is also the source of other sins. "For we see that by riches man is in a position to commit whatever sin there is and can satisfy his desire to commit whatever sin he wants". People remain free, however, in their choices and act without being forced (**article 1**).

The book *Ecclesiasticus* at 10, 15, calls pride the beginning of every sin. In so far as one understands by pride despising God and refusing to observe his commandments one takes the word as meaning a general sinful attitude. If one uses the term to denote this attitude inasmuch as it flows forth from our fallen nature then it is in fact the beginning of all sins. However, pride can also mean a misplaced belief in one's own excellence. In this sense it is a special sin, but it is

---

[50] Q. 81, art. 1

nevertheless the root of other sins in the order of intention, since one makes one's own prestige the main goal, something which plays a role in all sins. The love of money is the root of other sins at the level of execution, since it provides the means to satisfy all sinful desires (**article 2**).

Capital sins are vices from which other sins flow forth, in particular in so far as they are final causes and direct and lead people to other sins (**article 3**). Any sin can be a disposition to other sins, but here something special is meant. Among the different vices an ancient tradition considers the so-called capital sins the source of many other sins. Cassian[51] names eight such capital sins, sc. gluttony, lust, unchastity, anger, greed, sadness[52], sloth (*acedia*)[53], vanity or pride. John Climacus mentions seven capital sins[54] St. Gregory the Great also lists seven of these sins: vanity, jealousy, anger, melancholy, avarice, gluttony, unchastity[55]. Thomas takes over his list but combines vanity with pride. Both in Q. 84 as in the *Quaestio disputata de malo*, q. 8, a. 1, he presents a synthesis. One sometimes commits a sin to attain the object pursued by some vice. Thus one practices fraud in order to enrich oneself (greed). What one tries to obtain in a disorderly way through a vice is, a) one's well-being and excellence of the mind, which one pursues in the wrong way out of vanity, b) one's bodily well-being, in preserving one's life and health either seeking to attain this in a disorderly way by gluttony or, as regards the powers and acts which have to do with the perpetuation of mankind, by unchastity, using these powers in the wrong way. c) external goods by avarice leading us to acquire and have them in a way not conformed to the order of things.

It also happens that one abandons what is good because of an evil which is connected with it. The vice behind this attitude is a certain laziness or inertia. One does not want to make an effort with one's spiritual faculties on account of the work involved. When one envies someone else for what he has, because one does not have it oneself, we speak of jealousy or envy. Many people think that they are as good or capable as others and sometimes envy is even seen as meritorious. If one wants to cause damage to others, it is anger which moves us to do so. These vices are usually the cause of new sins but may sometimes originate from other sins. With regard to sins committed because of ignorance, laziness is their general cause, since one does not take the trouble to gather the necessary knowledge (**article 4**).

---

[51] *Collationes*, V, c. 10.
[52] Meant is a guilty trend to depression and spleen.
[53] The term *acedia* means an aversion from effort and spiritual work.
[54] *Scala paradisi*.
[55] *Moralia* XXXI, c. 45 (*PL* 76, 620).

THE CONSEQUENCES OF SINS (QQ. 85 - 87)

In the next part of his treatise on sin Aquinas examines the consequences of our sins before discussing (QQ. 88 and 89) the difference between minor and serious sins.

Sin affects the good which man possesses by nature (Q. 85)

When Thomas speaks of damage done to the good man has by nature, he does not mean that sin causes damage to what is essential in man and his faculties, for there is no such damage done. He means that man's natural inclination to virtuous acts[56] grows weaker through sin. When one performs certain acts an inclination is shaping up to more acts of this type. Since by sinning one moves in a direction contrary to virtue, the inclination to perform good acts according to this virtue diminishes[57] (**article 1**). It might seem that if one continues in this direction the natural inclination to virtuous actions will almost entirely be taken away. But this is not the case. Sin cannot undo man's nature, by which he is able to act rationally and his rational capacity remains the same. But the obstacles are multiplied which impede this inclination to become effective (**article 2**).

The way in which a good number of people behave shows that such faculties as the will and the sensory appetite do not always follow right reason, just as the intellect itself also is not always reaching the truth and easily becomes a prey of all sorts of errors[58]. Plato described in a telling way the conflicts which occur in life and the risk that reason loses control[59]. Aristotle for his part saw moral life as reaching the mean between the extremes of the passions (**article 3**). Yet another effect of sin is that it reduces our inner equilibrium and the wholesome pressure of our natural inclination toward the good as well as to the virtues. Although sins do not impair the fundamental good of human nature they deprive us of the virtues and of acting in an orderly way (**article 4**).

Are death and bodily defects an effect of sin? Aquinas first points out that the one who sins does not have the intention of becoming a victim of sickness and death, but in a secondary way sin can be their cause since it removes what pro-

---

[56] See q. 51, a. 1 and q. 63, a. 1.

[57] Cf. the words of Socrates at the beginning of Plato's *Republic*, 350 D: Unjust actions cause such a dislocation in our innermost that we are hardly able to do the good.

[58] In Christian theology one speaks of the consequences of the Fall of the first human pair, sc. the wound of ignorance in the intellect, the wound of a certain malice in the will, that of weakness in the irascible and of concupiscence in the concupiscible appetite.

[59] In particular in his *Phaedrus*. Cf. *Republic* 571 B and the commentary by J. Gould, *The Development of Plato's Ethics*, Cambridge 1953, p. 187: "We have thus come as far as we may from the ideal individual matched with an ideal society; we have reached the spectacle of a man dictated to by passions that he cannot control and in a perpetual state of war, not only with his fellow men but even with himself".

tects one against them. According to the traditional interpretation of *Genesis* 1-3 man in his original state was shielded from sickness and death but, by his sin, lost this privilege and was left to himself[60]. But are death and defects of the human body natural? Thomas answers that one can consider transitory things in two ways, sc. by examining their place in the world or by considering the proper nature of these things. If one considers the essential nature of things, their corruption is against their being which is ordered to self-preservation. But seen in the context of the world as a whole (*natura universalis*) the corruption of things makes sense. Dying beings yield their place to new generations. Dying it is also in agreement with the material principle in them which must be determined now by this and then by another form. Their formal principle, on the other hand, is ordered to building up their being and to preserve it, even if it cannot attain this permanently because of its union with matter. In man the situation is different[61]. Our rational soul is not entirely subject to matter nor immersed in it, but has an independent activity of its own. Therefore, considered from the point of view of the human soul, incorruptibility is more natural for man than it is for other material beings. But since man's being comprises also matter, man is mortal[62] (**article 6**).

The stain caused by sin (Q. 86)

We speak of a stain or blot when the wholeness or beauty of a thing is affected. Clothes become dirty, silverware gets black. In those who act virtuously one notices a radiation of their reason in them and the lustre of a harmonious life. But if a person acts against right reason and attaches himself in a wrong way to transitory things this lustre disappears. This flaw remains, even if the action belongs to the past, as long as a person keeps acting at variance with the rule of reason (**articles 1 & 2**).

GUILT AND PUNISHMENT

Introduction

Punishment is an evil imposed on one because of a fault one has committed. Expressing himself concisely Aquinas writes that if the evil is freely chosen we

---

[60] Q. 85, 5 ad 1: "Sic igitur, remota originali iustitia, natura corporis humani relicta est sibi".

[61] "Et quamvis omnis forma intendat perpetuum esse quantum potest, nulla tamen forma rei corruptibilis potest assequi perpetuitatem sui, præter animam rationalem".

[62] Aquinas adds that God had removed this mortality from the first human beings.

speak of sin, if it is imposed against one's will, it is punishment[63]. So the treatise on sin is followed by that on punishment. Several articles of Questions 87 - 89 deal with theological themes but those dealing with philosophical subjects are summarized in the following pages.

In daily life punishment is widely applied, both in the education of the young at home and at school as well as in society. The Greeks at first saw punishment as retribution or retaliation indifferently, but Aristotle distinguishes between the two[64]. Punishment is a means to restoring right order, but Aristotle also speaks of the effect of compensation[65]. Ulpianus defines punishment as retribution for an evil one has committed[66]. The *Digesta* 48, 19, 20 mention the correction of the culprit as a goal of punishment. St. Augustine considers punishment (*malum poenae*) an evil one suffers, in contrast with the *malum culpae*, a sin one commits[67]. As we shall see, Aquinas connects punishment with a particular human inclination to undo damage done to oneself or to others. Grotius, for his part, following the ancient tradition, defines punishment as *malum passionis quod infligitur ob malum actionis*[68] and distinguishes between personal revenge and punishment applied according to the principles of public law.

Opinions vary with regard to the goals of punishment, although there is agreement about the fact that transgressions can only be punished when those who commit them are responsible for what they do and are guilty. Is any violation of natural law whatever sufficient reason for punishment or can one only be punished by the state for crimes and misdemeanors formulated as such by the law? In a deterministic vision of man, as one may find it in certain, particularly in Marxist countries, a citizen does not do evil by his free choice. Rather, he is wrongly programmed, so that re-education takes the place of punishment proper[69].

Punishment can only be applied if the person to be punished did wrong voluntarily and knew that he was liable tp punishment. As regards the aims of punishment we mention a) re-establishment of the violated order; b) prevention of future crimes by removing the culprit from society; c) correction and rehabilitation of the culprit so that he can function again in the framework of civil soci-

---

[63] *Q. d. de malo*, q. 1, a. 4: "De ratione culpæ est quod sit secundum voluntatem, de ratione autem poenæ est quod sit contra voluntatem".

[64] *Rhet.* I, 10, 1369^{b}12-14: ἡ μὲν γάρ κόλασις τοῦ πάσχοντος ἕνεκα ἐστιν ἡ δὲ τιμωρία τοῦ ποιοῦντος ἵνα πληρωθῇ.

[65] *E.N.* 1104^{b}13.

[66] *Digesta* 50, 16, 131 (*noxae vindicta*).

[67] *De libero arbitrio*, I, 1; *Contra C.. Adimantum manichaeum*, disc. 26 (*PL* 42, 169: "Dupliciter enim appelatur malum: unum quod homo facit, alterum quod patitur; quod facit peccatum est, quod patitur poena".

[68] *De iure belli et pacis*, II, 20, n. 1.

[69] For a survey of the different theories of punishment see *Historisches Wörterbuch der Philosophie*, X, 208-261.

ety. - Certain authors deny that the purpose of punishment is to restore the order of the law that has been violated. But their view is contradicted by experience and current praxis: war-criminals in hiding who are discovered many years after they have committed their crimes and who no longer constitute any danger to others are nevertheless prosecuted in court.

Punishment supposes guilt and liability. One distinguishes between moral responsibility and juridical liability. The latter concerns the transgressions of positive laws which are not always perceived as moral obligations[70]. Moral guilt originates when our acts are not in agreement with our moral obligations and the end of our human life. Feelings of guilt are, *inter alia*, the awareness of having perturbed the order one had to respect by actions for which one is responsible. The culture one grew up in, the education one received, the religion one professes are important factors which can favour, resp. reduce feelings of guilt. Certain contemporary trends of thought seek to identify "the others", sc. society, wealthy people and nations or international business conglomerations as guilty. Sometimes people have an aggressive attitude and seem to transfer latent or repressed feelings of guilt[71] to persons or institutions which they consider dangerous or inhumane. To these factors one must add that nowadays the means of communication in an alarming way provoke desires, desires which are experienced as needs, and needs which are seen as rights to certain things. One who opposes himself to this is seen as guilty. One also witnesses attempts by some organizations to present unacceptable forms of conduct (such as homosexual practices, abortion, active euthanasia, adultery, sexual promiscuity) as licit or normal, while a systematic propaganda is waged against maxi-capitalism, dictatorships and certain structures of society. Persons who consider themselves wronged or placed at a disadvantage, no longer feel themselves guilty, but consider "the others" responsible. Certain authors go so far as to call the society in which modern man lives guilty and to speak of an ontological guilt[72].

Punishment (*Q 87*)

A first question is whether being punishable is the result of an evil one has done. To explain punishment Aquinas refers to a phenomenon we observe in nature, where something which exceeds its right measure provokes a reaction in what is opposed to it. Important changes in temperature call forth reactions in nature

---

[70] In a more remote sense, however, they are. The accurate observance of even minor rules contributes to enhance respect for the law in general.

[71] This feeling of guilt may result from wrong moral behavior, such as disorderly marital or homosecxual unions, promiscuity, continued contraception, wasting one's time, drug abuse, but may also be caused if a type of work and an environment are not fitted for certain persons.

[72] For a more detailed study see L. Elders, "Le sentiment de culpabilité d'après la psychologie, la littérature et la philosophie modernes", in *Nova et vetera*, 1984, 271 - 297.

meant to mitigate the effects of such changes. Trees along the seacoast incline so as to withstand prevailing winds. Something similar happens in education. Children who all the time disturb the conversation of adults are reprimanded and put in their proper place. They are expected to conform to a certain order as it prevails at their home and in school. Thomas sees a natural inclination in us to put others who rebel in their proper place and make them step down[73]. What applies to smaller communities holds also for every well-ordered society: those who belong to it form a certain unity in respect of the principles on which the society is based. Whoever opposes himself to these principles will be corrected by the leader or the group as such, because he opposes himself to the goals of such a society.

A text of the *Summa contra gentiles* explains this further. As long as natural things observe the right order in their activities they preserve their goodness and continue to exist, but if they abandon this order they decay[74]. This shows that persons who act against man's proper goals will suffer drawbacks. Applying to human conduct what one sees in nature is acceptable, since the goals of man are natural goals, which he must try to attain by his free choices. The moral order concerns our natural inclinations. This way of presenting the considerations about punishment shows that the transgression of the moral order has consequences for the acting person, although the text of the *Summa contra gentiles* does not stress that a punishment is inflicted. This point is brought out in the *Summa theologiae*: a well ordered society or its leaders put the culprit back in his proper place[75]. This "putting one down" (*deprimere*) has the sense of making one undergo something against his will[76].

Man is placed in three states, a) he must obey the order indicated to him by his intellect, b) furthermore, he is a member of a civil society and sometimes also of a spiritual society, c) finally he is subject to the divine government of the world. - One can act against one's own reasonable insight, transgress the order established in society or, finally, sin against the law of God. This results in a threefold punishment: remorse, a punishment inflicted by the civil authorities and a punishment measured out by God. The three states or structures mentioned by Aquinas allow us to distinguish between the moral order, the order of law, and the order which comes with religion.

Punishment is consecutive on sin in so far as sin is a disorderly act. No one wants evil for the sake of evil, and so incurring punishment is not intended by the one who performs bad acts. But a punishment is not directly caused by sin. Sin makes the person who sins guilty (**article 1**). Must the fact that as the result

---

[73] "Unde in hominibus hoc ex naturali inclinatione invenitur, ut unusquisque deprimat eum qui contra ipsum insurgit".

[74] *O.c.*, III, c. 140.

[75] "... ut ab ipso ordine vel principe ordinis deprimatur".

[76] *S.C.G.* III, c. 140: "... dum contra voluntatem suam homo aliquid pati cogitur".

of a sin one committed one sometimes perpetrates other sins be considered a punishment for the first sin? Formally speaking this is not the case, since sinful acts are freely willed, while punishment is imposed precisely against the will of a culprit. But in an indirect way subsequent sins are a punishment for the evil one has done inasmuch as because of the sins one commits one exposes oneself to further disorderly actions and can more easily become a prey to one's passions. Sin can also render us depressed and downcast (**article 2**).

While the next three articles take up some theological matters **article 6** raises an interesting question, sc. how to make reparation for a sin one committed, especially with regard to the moral and religious order? To re-establish the perturbed order - one has followed one's desire more than was right - one must now either willingly or forcibly undergo something contrary to what one likes. As to a transgression of the order established by God, one must try to approach God by bearing patiently the set-backs and difficulties of life as a punishment inflicted by God or by voluntarily imposing some form of punishment on oneself. In this line of thought Thomas argues that just as one can pay a debt for someone else so one can make reparation for a friend on account of one's friendship (**article 7**). Apart from this case the punishment for a certain transgression concerns the one who committed it and so everyone is punished for his own faults. However, in so far as a punishment is a means of correction it can also affect other persons. To give an example, a family undergoes some painful consequences if the father loses his job because of dishonesty. But if the man's wife and children approved of what he did then their difficult situation can also be considered their punishment. However, Aquinas vigorously rejects the view that children are punished for the sins of their parents, except in so far as through a bad example they may more easily resort to wrongdoing themselves (**article 8**).

The division of sins (QQ. 88 & 89)

The final question of this treatise on vices and sins deals with the division of sins into grave and minor sins, in theological language mostly called mortal and venial sins. This distinction is explained as follows: sin is a sort of weakness or illness of the soul. When it causes irreparable damage, i.e. if by sinning man turns away from his last end -, one speaks of a serious sin. One may compare this to an argument, the premisses of which are wrong. A minor sin, on the other hand, concerns the means which lead to the end, but does not affect one's being directed to it. This means that this division into serious and venial sins is an analogous division (**article 1**). But venial sins can create dispositions which eventually lead to greater sins (**article 2**).

In **Q. 89, article 6** a question is discussed which is not without importance. Before a child reaches the years of discretion and acquires the full command of his reason and free will there cannot be a question of great sins. But after acquiring this control a human person must reflect on how to organize his life (*deliberare de seipso*) and direct himself to the right end[77]. But the choice of the last end will often be veiled and take the form of what one sees one's parents do or of what is the pattern of life of persons one admires. It shows how important parents are for the moral education of their children. Aristotle points out that a virtuous person is a sort of criterion and yardstick for all sorts of good actions. He refers to a passage in Plato's *Laws* 653 AB where we read that parents must help their children to rejoice in what is good and be saddened by what is bad[78]. Aquinas ends his considerations by stressing the importance of a good education in the virtues as the best means of avoiding vices and sins.

---

[77] Q. 89, a. 6 ad 3: "Primum enim quod occurrit homini discretionem habenti est quod de seipso cogitet ad quem alia ordinet sicut ad finem. Finis enim est prior in intentione".

[78] *E.N.* 1104^{b}12. In his commentary *In III Ethic.*, lesson 1, St. Thomas notes: "In potestate nostra est esse decentes, id est bonos, secundum habitum virtutis, et pravos secundum habitum vitii".

CHAPTER IX

LAW IN GENERAL.
THE ETERNAL LAW, NATURAL LAW, HUMAN LAW

A previous chapter explained in what sense virtues are internal principles of the moral acts. Our behaviour, however, is also determined by rules, obligations or recommendations imposed or proposed from without. Questions 90 to 108 are concerned with law and rules of conduct. Methodically as usual Aquinas first discusses law in general (QQ. 90 - 92) before considering the different kinds of rules and laws. This treatise on law is of fundamental importance for the moral and juridical order. It has laid the foundation for later studies and presented an original and unsurpassed synthesis of natural law ethics.

The essence of law (Q. 90)

A law is a rule and measure of conduct of an obligatory character directing us to perform certain actions or refrain from them[1]. In a broader sense one can also speak of the laws of nature, such as the law of gravitation, and similar laws in the field of physics and biology on which human life depends. In addition our life is regulated by the rules, ordinances and laws of the civil society in which we live. The original meaning of the term "law" is that of an obligatory rule of conduct for the citizens of a political community. Taking this definition as his starting-point Thomas shows how in the different sectors of human life and also in the supernatural order one can speak of laws. In this respect the treatise elaborates the analogous relationship between the natural and supernatural order with regard to this point.

The sources used by Aquinas when composing his treatise are authors of classical antiquity such as Aristoteles, Cicero, Augustine and Isidore and the *iurisperiti*, i.e. the authors who wrote commentaries on Roman law as codified by the emperor Justinian[2]. Thomas's doctrine of law has been studied exhaustively in the twentieth century. Some doubts remain as to the extent of its dependence on Aristotle. A. Dempf considers this doctrine a synthesis of the ethics of Aristotle[3], but M. Wittmann believes that it is not related to Aristotelianism[4].

---

[1] Art. 1: "... regula et mensura actuum secundum quam inducitur aliquis ad agendum vel ab agendo retrahitur". Cf. art. 2: "Ad legem enim pertinet praecipere et prohibere"
[2] The *Digesta* (an extract from juridical books between 100 and 400) are part of what was codified. These *Digesta* were discovered again in the first half of the twelfth century in Bologna. What the *Digesta* are for civil law, the so called *Decreta* of Gratianus (middle of the twelfth century) are for canon law. See O.H. Pesch, *Deutsche Thomasausgabe*, Bd. 13: *Das Gesetz (I-II 90 - 105), Heidelberg / Graz / /Wien / Köln* 1977.
[3] *Sacrum Imperium*, pp. 388 ff.

The French philosopher Jean-Jacques Rousseau loathed rules and laws[5]. Similar views are proposed in the existentialism of Jean-Paul Sartre. In reality, however, most rules and laws are meaningful and in many respects even necessary. Moreover, man must himself formulate basic rules of conduct, sc. the precepts of natural law.

A law is a rule regulating our human acts[6]. The Greek word for law, νόμος, originally signified established properties and possessions, rule, custom, whereas the Latin word *lex* had the meaning of calling a levy or mobilization but came to signify later a decree and law[7]. Thomas observes that our reason is the rule and measure of our actions and directs them to the end we have chosen. Therefore, a law is essentially the work of reason[8] and not an expression of an inclination of the will, unless in this sense that a rule or command of reason requires a previous act of the will, from which it derives its ordering power. Moreover, a law is addressed to the intellect of those for whom it is destined and who learn from the law which acts are ordered to their real good[9]. The aim of civil laws is to bring the citizens to the desired goal, in analogy to the way God leads people to the end he himself is by what we call the eternal law (*lex aeterna*[10]), .

One can direct things and people to certain goals by guiding them and by means of rules. While in general things have an inclination to certain actions and activities by virtue of their nature, man, who is endowed with reason, is aware of the presence of some fundamental inclinations in himself. In other beings similar rules of conduct are materially, but not formally present. As our speculative intellect possesses a set of first principles which enable it to know reality, to formulate general statements and to draw conclusions, one also finds a number

---

[4] *Die Ethik des heiligen Thomas von Aquin*, pp. 366ff. O.H. Pesch , *o.c.* in note 2, gives a survey of the sources used by Aquinas.

[5] *Du contrat social*, ch. 1: "L'homme est libre et partout il est dans les fers". Rousseau believes that individual man is oppressed by society and the ideas prevalent in his environment and so is hampered in his development.

[6] See O. Lottin, "La définition classique de la loi", in *Revue néoscolastique de philosophie* 27 (1925), pp. 119-145 and 243-273, published again in "La loi en général. La définition thomiste et ses antécédents", in *Psychologie et morale aux 12ᵉ et 13ᵉ siècles*, tome II: *Problèmes de morale*, Louvain-Gembloux 1948, 11-100.

[7] The etymology proposed by Aquinas (*lex* as derived from *ligare*) is not correct.

[8] In his commentary *In V Ethic.*, lesson 11, n. 1009, Thomas adds to Aristotle's text the words that law is a *dictamen rationis*. Suarez, on the other hand, sees the law as an act of the will (*electio*), consecutive to a judgment of reason (*De legibus*, lib. 1, c. 4).

[9] *In II Sent.*, d. 41, q. 1, a. 1 ad 4: "Lex dirigit sicut ostendens qualis debeat esse actus proportionatus fini ultimo".

[10] See below, Q. 93.

of first principles in the practical intellect[11] which have the character of rules or laws[12]. One may quote such insights as that we must respect our parents, we must look after our own well-being and live together peacefully with other people, etc. These laws are a product of reason (**article 1**).

Reason makes laws in view of an end to be reached. There are, in fact, many particular goals[13], but these are directed to the well-being and happiness of people. The first principle of all our actions is no other than the last end to be reached. Therefore, the law must primarily be directed to that end, sc. the common good of all. Accordingly rules and laws possess the character of a real law only when they are directed to the common good[14]. Particular goals the legislator is aiming at, such as the protection of our natural environment or safety on the roads (diverse as such goals may be) are directed to the well-being of all[15]. So laws are formulated within the framework of human society and in the light of the common good (**article 2**).

This point is explained in greater detail in the next article. Since the law in its proper sense concerns primarily the common good, issuing laws is the task of the entire society or of those who are governing it. An individual person, all by himself, does not make rules, except in this sense that, as a member of a comprehensive community or as a citizen of the world, he can draw up rules of conduct for himself, e.g. by formulating the precepts of the natural law[16]. In his answer to the second objection Aquinas points out another property of the law, sc. its obligatory character. A private person can recommend others to behave well, but cannot effectively oblige them to do so. Only the body politic of the citizens (*multitudo*) or those in authority can effect this with the help of sanctions. Within civil society there are smaller communities, such as the family, but these cannot reach their well-being by their own efforts alone and are ordered to the good of the state which is a perfect society. Rules and regulations which are valid in these restricted communities do not have the character of laws in the strict sense of the term[17] (**article 3**).

---

[11] I.e. the intellect in so far as it is moved by the will as an efficient cause to perform certain acts, while the will itself is formally determined by the object presented by the intellect.

[12] Art. 1 ad 2: "Et huiusmodi propositiones universales rationis practicae ordinatae ad actiones habent rationem legis".

[13] Cf. *E.N.* 1111ᵃ24: "Actions are concerned with individual things" (*actiones sunt in particularibus*).

[14] Art. 2: "... quodcumque aliud præceptum de particulari opere non habet rationem legis nisi secundum ordinem ad bonum commune".

[15] *Ibid.*, ad 2.

[16] Art. 3 ad 1: "Et hoc modo unusquisque sibi est lex, inquantum participat ordinem alicuius regulantis".

[17] Ad 3: "... ita etiam et bonum unius domus ordinatur ad bonum unius civitatis, quae est communitas perfecta. Unde ille qui gubernat aliquam familiam, potest quidem facere aliqua præcepta vel statuta, non tamen proprie habeant rationem legis".

In order to be able to obey the law, the citizens must have knowledge of it. For this reason the law must be promulgated. Its promulgation is a necessary condition for its being obligatory[18]. So the definition of a law comprises four elements: a regulation by reason, directed to the common good[19], issued by the person charged with the government of the state and duly promulgated. As was pointed out above, according to Aquinas the law is the work of reason and not of the will alone. This excludes arbitrariness and points already to the treatise of the natural law in Q. 94.

The different kinds of law (Q. 91)

After his introductory remarks, having defined the law, St. Thomas now proposes a classification of the main types of laws[20]. This is not a division of a genus into its species: the different kinds of laws realise the definition each time in a different, analogous way. This distinction between the different kinds of law is important. What is at stake is the cohesion between the ontological and moral order, a connection Thomas makes in his treatment of the eternal law and of the natural law.

The first and most fundamental law is the eternal law. Basing himself on a truth, argued for in his metaphysics, metaphysics, that the world is governed by divine providence[21], Aquinas states that all things are directed to the end that God has set for them. This plan of divine providence directing all things exemplifies and fulfills the definition of law. Even promulgation is not lacking in so far as man see this binding orientation from the behavior of things. This plan of God which directs all things to their good is called the eternal law, *eternal* since God's thought is eternal, comprehends all times and history, knows no succession and sees future events as present[22] (**article 1**).

The eternal law encompasses all beings, directing them by their natural activities to their ends. But man is a case apart since he can, in a sense, participate in God's providence by taking care of himself and others. This is a participation in the eternal law which is called the *natural law*. The natural light of man's reason by which he sees what is good and what is not good, is a participation in

---

[18] Gratianus writes: "Leges instituuntur cum promulgantur". O. Lottin, *o.c.*, notes that Alexander of Hales had a different view in respect of this point.

[19] On the significance of the common good in the ethics of Aquinas, see the appendix attached to this chapter.

[20] According to V.L. Brady, "Law in the *Summa fratris Alexandri*", in *Proceedings of the American Catholic Philosophical Association* 24 (1950), 133-146, Alexander's division would have influenced that of Aquinas.

[21] See *S.Th.* I, 22, 1 & 2 and parallel texts.

[22] See our *The Metaphysics of St. Thomas Aquinas in a Historical Perspective*, Leiden 1991.

God's knowledge. In his *Commentary on Psalm 4* Aquinas writes that this participation is as a light which shines in us and by which we know what is morally good and what is wrong. - In the second objection raised in this article it was argued that man is free in his choices and that, for this reason, there cannot be a particular inclination to a predetermined end. But in his reply Aquinas explains that every act of the intellect and of the will has its origin in inclinations which are in conformity with our nature[23]. Any and all reasoning depends on principles which are naturally known, and each inclination to things which are means directed to a goal depends on the natural inclination to the last end. The natural law consists of the first principles of the practical intellect, which knows them immediately through our fundamental inclinations. Differently from animals, man has an intellectual knowledge of his obligations which we may call a law. This conclusion is important since it says that the order man must conform to is based on his human nature and that therefore ethics is based on the ontological order[24]. For this reason A. Dempf considers the treatise on law as the metaphysical center of Aquinas' ethics (**article 2**).

The first principles of the practical intellect, which are the basis of the natural law, are general. In order to know what one must do in particular situations and fields of activity, applied rules of conduct are necessary. Our *positive laws* owe their origin to this fact. Thomas does not mean the choices which individuals must make in their private life with the help of the virtue of prudence, but rules concerning our living together in the political society. Because of the great variety of circumstances and of developments in the course of time these man-made laws can vary considerably. They must nevertheless remain related to the principles of the natural law which is their immutable foundation, while human laws are changeable (**article 3**). The following article of this question deals with divine positive law by means of which God directs man to his supernatural end (**article 4**).

The effects of the law (Q. 92)

In the *Nicomachean Ethics* II, ch. 1 Aristotle writes that legislators of the different political societies aim at making people better men and citizens by means of laws[25]. According to this view the law must prescribe a rule of conduct accord-

---

[23] "... omnis operatio rationis et voluntatis derivatur in nobis ab eo quod est secundum naturam".

[24] Cf. U. Kuhn, *Via caritatis. Theologie des Gesetzes bei Thomas von Aquin*, Göttingen 1965, 106.

[25] In *E.N.* V, c. 3, 1129^{b}19 Aristotle explains this by saying that the law commands people to do what a courageous person does (e.g. by not abandoning one's post in a war), to practice self-control, not to commit adultery, not to offend others, to show friendliness, etc. If the law

ing to the virtues, or, at least, prescribe actions which are useful for man. Nowadays individualism has become very strong and legislators generally exclude the private moral life of the citizens from what the law should regulate[26]. They do not consider themselves to be competent in this field. In the most favorable case the legislator wants to offer a certain protection to generally acknowledged values, such as that of the family or unborn human life, without however excluding the opposed practices. Legislators justify this by pointing to what they call a development in the moral thinking of the citizens. People now tolerate certain forms of conduct which only half a century before were condemned by public opinion. But this vision is not without danger. It happens that public opinion is to such an extent influenced by emotions or by the media, that it even condones murder, genocide and cruel oppression. In particular circumstances the "moral sense" of the people is far removed from being a safe criterion for judging the goodness of certain forms of behavior. One needs objective laws, as Cicero stated in an impressive way[27]. It is true, though, that modern legislation is often more compassionate than certain laws issued in the past, in so far as nowadays those factors which diminish the moral responsibility of persons are acknowledged. The punishments which are meted out are also more humane. Similarly contemporary jurisprudence makes it possible to enforce a minimum of social solidarity.

Nevertheless the view that the law must make the citizens act virtuously is classic. According to Plato the state and its laws are the indispensable means of educating the citizens and thus making their life better. Inspired by this conviction Plato attempted to sketch the outlines of an ideal society. Aristotle, for his part, notes that whatever form a state's constitution has, it must help the citizens to reach their true end.

Agreeing with Aristotle Aquinas writes that the legislator attempts to accustom his subjects to performing virtuous actions by means of ordinances and sanctions[28]. He does so either in general[29] or indirectly (*secundum quid*). If the

---

is correctly formulated, it will also prescribe acts according to the other virtues and prohibit following one's vices.

[26] This is evident when one considers recent legislation in some countries permitting, within certain limits, the use of soft drugs, abortion or euthanasia along with civil acknowledgment of homsexual partnerships.

[27] *De legibus* I, 16, 43: "Quodsi populorum iussis, si principum decretis, si sententiis iudicum iura constituerentur, ius esset latrocinari, ius adulterare, ius testamenta falsa supponere si haec suffragiis aut scitis multitudinis probarentur... atqui nos legem bonam a mala nulla alia nisi naturae norma dividere possumus, nec solum ius et inuria natura diiudicatur, sed omnino omnia honesta et turpia"

[28] *In II Ethic.*, l. 1, n. 250 f.

[29] Cf. *S.C.G.*, III, c. 116: "Quia vero intentio divinae legis ad hoc principaliter est ut homo Deo adhaereat,.... necesse est quod intentio divinae legis principaliter ordinetur ad amandum (Deum)".

legislator seeks the true good, sc. the common good, the laws he issues will help make the citizens good persons. In cases where the law prescribes something which has only a certain usefulness, those who observe these laws will become better only in some respect. But if the legislator establishes laws as they should be, he will prescribe a line of conduct according to the virtues, or impose at least the performance of certain actions conducive to man's end. If, on the other hand, a legislator imposes measures which are in conflict with human rights, such as the prohibition of professing one's religion or the obligation of sterilization of a mother after her first or second child then we no longer have to do with real laws. However, such perverse rulings may still show some of the characteristics of an authentic law since they are promulgated by civil authorities and impose sanctions, etc.[30] **(article 1).**

How does the law attain the goal for the sake of which it was promulgated? It does so by prescribing and prohibiting[31]. While virtuous acts are prescribed and bad actions forbidden, the law is neutral with regard to indifferent actions. Aquinas means by the latter actions which show only a minimal amount of goodness of badness. By threatening with punishment the law sees to it that its subjects obey. If one objects that the law must make the citizens better but that it not very virtuous to do something out of fear of punishment, then one may reply that by getting people accustomed to do what is good they will finally act for the good by themselves. Some authors suggested that the legislator should offer rewards for good behavior, but Thomas replies that this would not be convenient, since rewards may be offered by all sorts of institutions, while imposing sanctions is reserved to the legislator **(article 2)**.

THE DIFFERENT KINDS OF LAWS (QQ 93 - 108)

The series of questions which now follows deals with the different kinds of laws, such as the eternal law, natural law, human positive law and the laws of the Old and New Testaments. We examine only the first three in philosophical ethics.

The eternal law (Q. 93)

One has sought the origin of the theory of the eternal law in Stoic philosophy, which teaches that an absolute, divine law determines all process and activities in the universe. The laws of nature and the principles of man's moral life have

---

[30] Art. 1 ad 4: "Dicendum quod lex tyrannica cum non sit secundum rationem, non est simpliciter lex, sed magis est quaedam perversio legis. Et tamen inquantum habet aliquid de ratione legis, intendit ad hoc quod cives sint boni, scilicet ut cives sint bene obedientes".

[31] "Prohibiting" is also a form of prescribing, so that when used in a broader sense the term prescribing is typical of all laws.

this divine plan as their source and their foundation. The idea agreed with the doctrine of creation and was used by the Christians. St. Augustine, for his part, defines the eternal law as "God's plan or will which commands that the order of nature be preserved and prohibits that it be perturbed"[32]. The eternal law is immutable and engraved in our souls[33]. Positive law must be in agreement with it[34]. According to O. Lottin the Franciscan masters in Paris were the first to stress the importance of the theme of the eternal law[35]. Alexander of Hales reminds us that God governs all things by his eternal law on which the natural law depends in its entirety[36].

St. Thomas placed this theme in a more comprehensive perspective. It is noteworthy that he does not mention the eternal law in his *Summa contra Gentiles*. The reason why he brought it up here is probably that he wanted to give a theological foundation to his treatment of natural law and to bring together the different kinds of laws in one synthesis. Since the law aims at making man morally good and at helping him reach his last end, and since God, man's last end, governs everything, all laws must have their basis in God. As he writes at the beginning of his question, by "the eternal law" is understood the plan of divine wisdom by which God orders and governs all creatures[37]. Metaphysics shows that God, the creator of all things, regulates all created activities. The groundplan of all things lies in God's essence and divine wisdom moves them toward their assigned goals. This divine government satisfies this definition of a law (**article 1**). In his voluntaristic approach Duns Scotus sees the eternal law as a decision of the divine will, which could have been different[38]. He takes this as implying that moral laws oblige because of an arbitrary decision of God's will, and that the natural law as such has no compelling justification.

Some object that the theory of the eternal law introduces a factor which cannot be verified and that its concept has no significance for man's life. To this Thomas answers that all of us have a certain, mediated knowledge of the eternal law. It is true that nobody here on earth knows God's plan of the government of the world as it is in God himself[39], but rational creatures experience a certain reflection of it, since God is known from the things he has made. Whatever knowledge we have about the truth of things and their order is a participation in

---

[32] *Contra Faustum* 22, 27: "Lex æterna est ratio divina vel voluntas Dei, ordinem naturalem conservari iubens, perturbari vetans".

[33] *De diversis quaestionibus* 53, 2.

[34] *De libero arbitrio* I, 6, 14.

[35] *Psychologie et morale aux XIIe et XIIIe siècles*, tome II, 52-63.

[36] *Summa theologica* III, p.2, inq. 1, c. 7, a. 4.

[37] "Lex æterna nihil aliud est quam ratio divinæ sapientiæ secundum quod est directiva omnium actuum et motionum".

[38] *In IV Sententiarum*, I, 1. d. 35.

[39] While living on earth man cannot know the divine essence.

God's truth and in the eternal law[40]. Everyone knows at least the principles of the natural order of things. The better one understands the truth of natural things and their order, the better one knows the eternal law. One could consider this knowledge, which we acquire by observing and studying nature, a sort of promulgation of the eternal law (**article 2**). To Aquinas the eternal law is the transcendental foundation of all moral principles.

He even goes one step further and shows that every law is derived from the eternal law. This thesis is not so surprising as it seems to be at a first sight. In ancient times all nations and tribes have attributed a divine origin to the precepts about moral life valid in their respective societies. According to Heraclitus all men must submit themselves to the universal *logos* which nourishes all laws[41]. Cicero proclaims that the laws come from God[42]. Thomas sees God's plan and causality at work in all created activities, since the First unmoved Mover is the primary cause of all movements in the universe. This agrees with what we see in our environment, sc. the laws and commands of higher authorities are applied at lower levels as, e.g., the plans of an architect are carried out in their details by the contractor and his helpers. Thus one can say that all laws known to us are an application of God's eternal law, in so far as they rest on right reason[43]. The second objection reminds us that certain laws are bad and cannot come from God. Aquinas answers that a law which deviates from right reason is no longer a law, but a violation of it. A final objection against the thesis of this article suggests that our laws often permit things which cannot be in accordance with the will of God. In his answer Aquinas observes that in the order established by God our laws cannot prescribe everything that is good or forbid whatever is bad. This order says that our laws must not interfere in certain things ("non se intromittat de his quae dirigere non potest") which, according to the law of God, are immoral. The situation is different when man-made laws approve of immoral behavior (**article 3**).

The eternal law extends to whatever is subject to the divine government, i.e. to all of creation. All processes are necessarily subject to it (**article 4**). No one makes a law, in the strict sense of the term for oneself, nor for irrational things

---

[40] This is shown in metaphysics. Aquinas illustrates the doctrine of the participation in God's eternal law by a reference to the *De vera religione,* c. 31, of St. Augustine: "Conditor tamen legum temporalium, si vir bonus est et saliens, illam ipsa consulit æternam, de qua nulli animæ iudicare datum est, ut secundum eius incommutabiles regulas, quid sit pro tempore iubendum vel vetandum, discernat. Æternam igitur legem mundis animis fas est cognoscere, iudicare non fas est".

[41] Fragm. 114 (Stobaeus, *Anthol.*, III, 1, 179).

[42] *De legibus*, II, 4, 8-10: "Lex vera atque princeps, apta ad iubendum et ad vetandum ratio est recta summi Iovis".

[43] "Unde omnes leges, inquantum participant de ratione recta, intantum derivantur a lege æterna".

subject to his power. However, the latter are governed by God's law. As man makes rules for his subordinates, so God places in all natural things the principles in virtue of which they act[44]. All processes and activities in the physical world are subject to God and irrational beings participate also in God's law. Even defects occurring in nature are not subtracted from divine providence (**article 5**).

Man is subject to the eternal law a) in so far as he has certain principles for his activities in common with the other created things, such as his natural inclinations, which are the basis and framework of his activities, b) in so far as he possesses reason to guide his life, since reason is also a participation in the eternal law. Regrettably, both ways of being subject to God's law can become blurred: the knowledge of the good we must do can be obscured and the natural inclinations toward virtuous acts corrupted. But we preserve nevertheless a certain knowledge of the good and experience always its attractive power[45] (**article 6**).

M. Rhonheimer uses the category of participation in the eternal law in order to find an objective foundation for our moral obligations[46]. He believes that our reason cannot derive these from our natural inclinations and that ethics is not dependent on or not connected with anthropology and ontology. Man's practical reason grasps directly the *bonum rationis* which lies in our mind. It does so by participating in the eternal law. - It is certainly true that the moral law is a participation in the eternal law, but we need to be clear about the intelligibility of our moral obligations intelligible and to indicate their foundation. To do so there is no other way, it would seem, than St. Thomas's doctrine of natural law. In Rhonheimer's theory this basis is obscure.

Natural law (Q. 94)

Thomas's treatment of natural law is one of the pivotal chapters of the entire *Summa theologiae* and in the history of philosophy it is rightly considered a fundamental account and justification of human basic duties and rights. It surpasses texts by later authors such as Suarez, Grotius and Pufendorf. For the historical background of this doctrine we must go back to the Greece of the fifth century B.C., where the insight dawned that there are unwritten fundamental laws with regard to our obligations as human persons, laws which have more

---

[44] Thomas sees an analogy between the way in which God places the principles of their activities in the natural things and the promulgation of laws in civil society.

[45] "... notionem legis æternæ aliquo modo habet... ; modus quodammodo corruptus in malis, in quibus et inclinatio naturalis ad virtutem depravatur per habitum vitiosum et iterum ipsa naturalis cognitio boni in eis obtenebratur per passiones et habitus peccatorum".

[46] *Natur als Grundlage der Moral. Eine Auseinandersetzung mit autonomer und teleologischer Ethik,* Innsbruck / Wien 1987.

weight than ordinances promulgated by governments or upheld by established customs[47]. The Sophists saw an opposition between nature and man made-laws and customs. Aristotle did not yet elaborate a systematic treatise of natural law. He considers the fact that people are citizens of a state a basis for certain conclusions on how they should live and reach happiness. Furthermore he distinguishes between particular, positive laws, made for those living in a certain community, and laws which are valid for all[48]. In his *Nicomachean Ethics* he speaks of a component of justice which rests on conventions and a second which has the same value for people in the entire world[49].

According to the Stoa the whole world is one huge political society and the divine *logos* determines the nature of individual things as well as the order of the whole. Man can know the law which is active in all things; it is his duty to live in agreement with it. The Stoic philosophers saw no difference between the laws in physical nature and the fundamental moral law of man, whose task it is to live consistently with himself and in agreement with nature (ὁμολογουμένως [τῇ φύσει] ζῆν). They mention a fundamental inclination to preserve one's own life, to respect and care for one's parents, to look after one's children. This inclination toward what belongs or is related to us (οἰκείωσις) is ordered to what comes first for us according to nature. Cicero also subscribes to this theory. Man is placed under an eternal law which is independent of what people think. It is an unwritten and inborn law which we do not learn or receive from others but which we draw from nature itself[50]. The *Digesta*[51] define natural law as what nature has taught all living beings, since this law is not proper to mankind, but governs all living beings which live on earth and in the sea.. In this definition Ulpian, a Roman jurist who died in 228, makes his own the Stoic theory of a general law at work in things, but he pays less attention to another aspect of Stoic doctrine, sc. the participation in the universal Logos. Ulpian makes a connection between natural law as proper to man and the law of nations (*ius gentium*) developed by the Romans, while the jurist Gaius affirms that both are identical. Isidore of Sevilla no longer speaks of a natural law common to man and animals[52].

Some critics said that later in his life St. Augustine abandoned a natural law theory in favor of a Christian vision in which grace stands in the center[53], but this interpretation is not right. During his whole life he taught that there is in

---

[47] Cf. Sophocles, *Antigone* 454 ff.; Euripides, *The Trojan Women* 886 ff.
[48] *Rhetorics* 1373^{b}4.
[49] *E.N.* 1134^{b}18 - 21.
[50] *Pro Milone* 4, 11: "Est igitur haec... non scripta sed nata lex, quam non didicimus, accepimus, legimus, verum ex natura ipsa arripuimus".
[51] I, I, I, 3:"... quod est omnibus animantibus commune".
[52] *Etym.* V, c.4.
[53] G. Fassò, *La legge della ragione*, Bologna 1964, p. 46.

man an inborn natural law which all know[54]. Moreover one encounters the same idea in the Church Fathers: natural law is given together with reason[55]. However, authors such as Origen, Irenaeus and Justin hold that the knowledge of it has been obscured in man by sin, but that it has been promulgated clearly in Holy Scripture and restored in Christ. The commandment of love belongs to it. Some Fathers of the Church distinguish between a primary law of nature, proper to man before the Fall, and a second natural law for fallen human nature which stresses the insights obscured by sin. In this way they tried to establish a relation between the natural law and the commandments taught in biblical revelation. Thomas, on the other hand, emphasizes the lasting ontological order on which the natural law rests.

In the Latin Middle Ages Hugh of St. Victor deals *in extenso* with the natural law. He distinguishes between three periods in its knowledge and observation, sc. the time prior to Moses, the period of the Old Law and the time of the grace which dawned with Christ. The commandments of the Decalogue make up immutable natural law[56]. Peter Lombard states that the natural law, which is the same for all men, is prior to the commandments of Moses[57]. Gradually a transition takes place in the study of natural law to a more philosophical approach. Natural law is seen as the order established and prescribed by natural reason. Our reason discovers in our nature what is needed to live morally, formulates it and considers it as binding. Obviously these requirements of our nature have their origin in God, the Maker of human nature[58]. St. Bonaventure lists three definitions of natural law: according to Gratian it comprises what is taught in the Old Testament and in the Gospel, according to Gaius and Isidore the natural law is a law which all the nations have in common, according to Ulpian the natural law is what nature teaches living beings[59]. Albert the Great underlines the rational character of the natural law, defining it as the knowledge of how to act which is given us according to the nature of our reason[60]. His doctrine that laws derive from the insight of reason was novel and, for his day, a pioneering step forward. Albert argued that reason formulates the different natural inclinations and expresses them in the precepts of natural law. Against Ulpian he up-

---

[54] Cf. *De div quaest.*, q. XXXI, 1 (*PL* 40, 20); *De sermone Domini in monte*, II, 11, 32 (*PL* 34, 128): "Quis enim scripsit in cordibus hominum naturalem legem nisi Deus?". See R. Pizzorni, *Il diritto naturale dalle origini a S. Tommaso d'Aquino*, Rome 1978, 109 ff.

[55] Pizzorni, *o.c.*, 127.

[56] *De sacramentis legis naturalis et scriptae* (*PL* 176, 18 ff.).

[57] *In epist. ad Romanos*: *PL* 176, 18 ff.

[58] See O. Lottin, *Le droit naturel chez Saint Thomas d'Aquin et ses prédécesseurs*, Bruges 1931.

[59] *In IV Sententiarum*, d.33, a. 1, q. 1.

[60] *De bono* V, q. 1, a. 2: "Ius naturale est lumen morum impressum nobis secundum naturam rationis".

held that the knowledge of natural law is exclusive to man[61]. In his *Commentary on the Nicomachean Ethics* he writes that, by analogy with the first principles of being in the speculative intellect, there have to be first principles for our actions in the practical intellect[62].

The doctrine of St. Thomas will be dealt with in the following pages. For Aquinas the nature of things is the source of their first movements which aim at their perfection. Ockham taught that the precepts of the law are not based on rational insight. God could also have prescribed the opposite of the Ten Commandments. In his absolute power God is entirely free to modify whatever law there is, but in the present order of things (according to God's *potentia ordinata*) he invites man to obey certain laws and commandments[63]. Suarez, on the other hand, accepts the identification of the natural law with the human mind, but there has to be a legislator in order to have a law[64].

In the following centuries opinions about the natural law varied. Thomas Hobbes holds a pessimistic view and sees primarily the animal in man. Natural law is not inborn. Political authorities must make laws to create some order. David Hume discarded the assumption that moral obligations can be derived from the ontological structure of the human person, despite the fact that in the eighteenth century many considered human nature the beacon one should follow. During the last hundred years such movements as historicism, positivism and existentialism rejected the existence of unchangeable norms, based on human nature. Some understand the terms "natural law " in a pejorative sense as referring to man's biological nature and argue that appealing to it degrades man to the animal level. On the contrary, man should shape his own rules in total liberty.

According to Aquinas natural law is nothing other than a participation in the eternal law present in man[65]. Natural law is the order of our tasks and obligations as acknowledged by reason. It is not inborn as such, but only in the sense that its principle is given with human nature. It is also natural in this sense that by spontaneous acts reason formulates its first principles on the basis of the fundamental inclinations and demands of human nature. Natural law comprises more than the commandments formulated by reason, for it extends also to the

---

[61] *De bono* V, q. 1, a. 3: "Ius naturale nihil aliud est quam ius rationis sive debitum secundum quod natura est ratio".

[62] See S. Theron, "The Interdependence of Semantics, Logic and Metaphysics as Exemplified in the Aristotelian Tradition" in *The International Philosophical Quarterly* 42 (2002), 63-93, p. 80.

[63] See G. Lagarde, *La naissance de l'esprit laïque au déclin du moyen-âge*, tome VI, Paris 1946, p. 77.

[64] *De legibus. Opera Omnia*, vol. V, pp. 100-105.

[65] *S.Th.* I-II 91, 2: "Et talis participatio legis æternæ in rationali creatura lex naturalis dicitur".

moral obligations which one can deduce from these principles, ordering our other inclinations to reason[66]. Since natural law has its roots in human nature, it is universal and permanent. Not man's natural inclinations as such, but the obligations derived from them as they are formulated by reason in view of the end of human life constitute the natural law[67].

Certain moralists, such as G. Grisez, J. Finnis and J. Boyle, while upholding the precepts of natural law, deny that these have their basis in man's natural inclinations. They subscribe to David Hume's position that it is illicit to deduce the "ought" from the "is". For Finnis the inclinations are morally neutral. What happens is that man experiences certain objects as good (such as eating what he needs and likes). Finnis distinguishes some six or seven[68] of such goods (which he calls basic and pre-moral). Since these goods contribute to human fulfilment, directing oneself to them becomes morally good. The difference from Thomas's position is that for Finnis these "basic goods" are somehow man's own projection, whereas for Aquinas the objects of the basic moral commandments are connected with man's natural inclinations[69]. All those things to which man has a natural inclination are naturally apprehended as good and, therefore, are objects of pursuit. It is cause for wonder why authors such as Finnis shy away from an "ought" based on the "is", since the "is" obviously is the order of creation, and one can hardly think of a better way to live morally than conforming oneself to this order. Giving an example, Finnis argues that it is utterly impossible to derive a commandment such as the injunction not to lie from a natural inclination. But the answer is quite simple: we instinctively know (because of our inclination to live in a community) that living together with people as we want to do demands truthfulness and, also, that the natural function of language is to express our thoughts, so that lying distorts a natural function.

In the first article of this question Thomas discusses the ontological status of natural law. Is it a faculty or power, an emotion or a habitus? In his answer he argues that it is something constituted by reason ("aliquid per rationem constitutum"), as a sentence is a product of reason. This explains why it is not a habitus in the sense of a determination of a faculty by means of which one acts. In so far, however, as the natural law is something permanent, which one actually becomes aware of, but which stays in the background, it is a disposition or habi-

---

[66] Cf. Ph. Delhaye, *Permanence du droit naturel*, Louvain / Lille / Montréal, 1960 (Analecta Namurcensia, 10).

[67] I-II 94, 2. Some critics accept that natural law is based on man's specific nature, but argue that its stipulations remain general, so that a more existential approach is needed to know what one must do.

[68] J. Finnis, *Natural Law and Natural Rights*, Oxford (several reprints); *Aquinas. Moral, Political and Legal Theory*, Oxford 1998.

[69] Cf. I-II 94, 2" "et secundum hanc inclinationem pertinent ad legem naturalem ea per quæ vita hominis conservatur".

tus. Aquinas himself speaks of a habitus of the first principles[70], but he does not mean that the propositions of the natural law, i.e. their content, are a habitus, but that with regard to the principles which contain them a habitus is formed. One may compare this with a scientific insight which as such is not a habitus but which can form part of a science which is. This remark has its importance in so far as it shows that what is essential in natural law is that as a law it is stated by the intellect (**article 1**).

This point is elaborated in the next article. Aquinas assumes that there is an analogy between the relation of the precepts of natural law to the practical intellect and that of the first principles of being to the speculative intellect. Not everyone knows immediately a great number of these first speculative principles and, likewise, not all the precepts of the natural law are known at the start of one's moral life. There is a certain order of the principles of being, e.g. one first understands that being is not not-being[71], that is that "this thing is not that thing". Analogically there is a first principle of the practical intellect. As the concept of being is the first concept to enter the mind, "good", viz. being as the object of our desires, is what is known first by the practical intellect, directed as it is to action. Every agent works for a goal which must have the nature of a good. The intellect formulates the inclination to the good as a first principle: "the good must be done, what is evil avoided"[72]. On this principle all other precepts about what one must do or avoid are based. All things to which one has a natural inclination are seen as good and desirable, what is opposed to them as to be avoided. This means that the order of the precepts of the natural law corresponds to that of our natural inclinations.

A first inclination of man, which he has in common with all existing things, is directed to the good of his being. Every substance tends to preserve its existence according to its nature. On account of this inclination whatever preserves man's life and prevents the opposite falls under natural law. - Furthermore, like other living beings man has an inclination to be active in certain fields. As regards this inclination, whatever nature teaches all living beings comes in under the natural law, such as sexual intercourse, the education of one's children. In the third place, there is in man an inclination to those things which agree with his rational nature, such as the inclination to learn the truth about God and to live in a community with others. Therefore, the acquisition of knowledge and the peaceful coexistence with others belong to natural law. These first principles of the practical intellect together form a set, called *synderesis*. As is the case with the first

---

[70] I 58, 3; I-II 53, 1.

[71] One cannot at the same time affirm something and deny it.

[72] This text and a passage of *In epist. ad Romanos*, c.7, lesson 1, are the only ones where St. Thomas explicitly mentions this most fundamental principle of the moral order. The expression "ad bonum faciendum" is frequent in Thomas's works.

principles of the speculative intellect, those of the practical intellect always remain present in a latent way.

The use of the term *synderesis* by the medieval authors goes back to St. Jerome[73], who writes that the Greek philosophers speak of an act or a power of the soul which they call synderesis[74]. St. Jerome understands it as conscience. At the beginning of the XIIIth century some authors considered synderesis part of the intellect: it makes us avoid what is bad. According to Albert the Great synderesis has its seat in the intellect and contains the general principles of moral action, but according to Bonaventure it is located in the appetite. Albert holds that the fundamental principles of the moral order form a habitus[75]. While in earlier works Aquinas frequently uses the term synderesis, in this part of the *Summa theologiae* he seems to avoid it. This led M. Crowe to suggest that Thomas's thought with regard to natural law underwent some changes[76]. But surprisingly these first principles of our moral acts are mentioned six times in the *Commentary on the Nicomachean Ethics* which dates to the same years as the Second Part of the *Summa theologiae*. It is possible that Aquinas speaks less of these principles in the *Summa* since he wants to stress that reason must be active and formulate each time afresh what one must do[77].

The different precepts of the natural law form a unity in so far as they are based on one first commandment, and are all regulated by reason. In his *Summa contra gentiles*[78] Aquinas writes that certain actions are as such becoming to man since they agree with his nature. Man must live in a community and refrain from what is detrimental to it. He must use the things he needs for his life with moderation, since otherwise they become harmful. He must take care of his body and the lower faculties in such a way that his mind is as unhindered as possible in its work. Finally, whatever brings man closer to God is good. If one raises the question whether polygamy is good or not[79], then the consideration of what is naturally good allows us to conclude that it is contrary to at least some demands of a worthy human life[80] (**article 2**).

---

[73] See his *Commentary on the prophet Ezechiel* 1, 10 (*PL* 25, 22 BC). He calls this synderesis a spark of conscience in Cain.

[74] It is possible that συντήρησις was confounded with συνείδησις. See M. Waldmann, "Synteresis oder Syneidesis? Ein Beitrag zur Lehre vom Gewissen", in *Theol. Quartalschrift* 119 (1938), 333 -371.

[75] See O. Lottin, *Psychologie et morale aux XIIe et XIIIe siècles*, vol. II, 1, pp. 103 - 349.

[76] *The Changing Profile of the Natural Law*, The Hague 1977, p. 140.

[77] William of Auxerre mentions these three fundamental inclinations, *Summa aurea*, II, tract. XII, q. 1 (fol. 65 vb). See Pizzorni, *o.c..* p. 204.

[78] III, c. 129.

[79] Cf. *In IV Sent.*, d. 33, q. 1, a. 1.

[80] Cf. J. M. Aubert, *Le droit romain dans l'œuvre de saint Thomas*, Paris 1955, p. 98.

All that to which man has a natural inclination belongs to the natural law. There is in every human being an inclination to act according to the virtues, so that one can say, in a general way, that acting according to the virtues belongs to the natural law. However, individual virtuous acts do not fall under the natural law, since there are many virtuous acts which man performs with the help of knowledge he gained much later and to which nature did not move him at first. An example is the foundation of an organization or society with a social purpose. Thomas sees a certain difference between first fundamental obligations and rules of conduct formulated later, which do not belong to the natural law, even if they are a sort of prolongation of it. The latter rules are not equally good for everyone. A married woman who visits sick people in her neighborhood does a good work, but if for this reason she leaves her small children alone at home, then it may cease to be a good deed. In article 6 this distinction between primary and secondary precepts is worked out further.

How one applies these principles depends also on the circumstances One must obey one's parents, but not when they ask us to do something morally bad. Enforcement of property rights clearly depends on the circumstances too. Acting according to the principles of natural law can be hindered by the passions when they prevent the intellect from applying moral principles to concrete acts (**article 3**).

Is the law of nature the same for all? The question has great importance. The Stoics gave a positive answer. Not just the Romans or the Greeks but all men as members of the human community, whether they are free citizens or slaves, have the same basic rights and duties. Before the Stoics Aristotle had mentioned a *iustum naturale* which obliges everywhere[81]. Isidore of Seville summarizes this in a fine definition to which Thomas refers, viz. "The naturally right is common to all nations and everywhere happens in virtue of a natural inclination and not by a constitution, (as) that men and women unite, that children are born and educated, that all possess in common all things, that all enjoy the same liberty and can acquire whatever is captured in the air, on earth and in the sea"[82]. The "possessing in common" probably means that the world with all her treasures is at the disposition of all. St. Thomas takes the words to mean that nature did not introduce the distinction between what is privately owned and what oth-

---

[81] *E.N.* 1134^{b}19: φυσικὸν δίκαιον μὲν τὸ πανταχοῦ τὴν αὐτὴν ἔχον δύναμιν. In this connection Aristotle writes that familiarity with other cultures and customs has led some to see natural law as something relative. In our time similar doubts have been voiced. Cf. the theory about moral rules and customs of the anthropologist Margaret Mead in her earlier works.

[82] *Etymologiae* V, c. 4: "Ius naturale [est] commune omnium nationum et quod ubique instinctu naturæ non constitutione aliqua habetur, ut viri et feminæ coniunctio, liberorum successio et educatio, communis omnium possessio et omnium una libertas, adquisitio eorum quae caelo, terra marique capiuntur".

ers claim to possess, nor did it destine some people to the state of submission in which happen to live. People have introduced these rights or rules themselves because of the advantages connected with them[83].

Speaking of natural law St. Isidore mentions the right of nations as a kind of application of it[84]. Commenting on this Aquinas explains that in its principles the natural law is the same for all and is known by all[85], but that conclusions drawn from it in particular cases are not the same for all. There are cases where a general rule is suspended. Thus one does not return somebody else's property, if it is a dangerous weapon which at this moment the owner is going to use for a bad purpose. That a general rule cannot be applied happens more frequently in the field of concrete actions. It is for this reason that Aquinas writes that not all have the same insight and the right knowledge with regard to what they are doing. Because of bad habits to which people have grown accustomed and which are common in a certain community vices as. drunkenness, theft, corruption, abortion or homosexual behavior, are no longer seen as morally wrong. But the principle remains that every human person must act according to right reason and that all desires and urges must be governed by the intellect.

This explanation does justice to the differences which may occur when one applies the first principles. Thomas does not set up a rigorous system but draws attention to possible developments in the knowledge of the natural law and notes that there may be obstacles which make it difficult to formulate our first principles.

Jacques Maritain speaks of progress in the awareness of our moral obligations[86]. In many societies progress has been made in the acknowledgment of human rights, the equality of men and women and the way the weak should be treated. On the other hand, the awareness of certain norms may also be obscured, like theft seems to have been acceptable among the Germanic tribes (**article 4**).

The previous article mentioned possible obstacles one encounters when applying the principles and precepts of the natural law. Sometimes people have insufficient knowledge of what is contained in them. The question which Aquinas now raises is whether the natural law can change objectively. Can parts of it be rendered inoperative? There is no doubt that certain elements of natural law have been made more explicit by human laws. Examples are social legislation and the prohibition of child labour. But can certain precepts be suspended? It is

---

[83] I-II 95, 5 ad 3.

[84] *Etymol.* V, 6, 1: "Ius gentium est sedium occupatio, ædificatio, munitio, bella, captivitates, servitutes, postlimina, foedera pacis, indutiæ, legatorum non violandorum religio..., et inde quia eo iure fere omnes gentes utuntur".

[85] "... dicendum quod lex naturæ, quantum ad prima principia communia, est eadem apud omnes et secundum rectitudinem et secundum notitiam".

[86] *On the Philosophy of History*, pp. 82-83.

impossible that the first principles change or be cancelled, since they are intimately tied to man's unchanging nature. However, with regard to precepts derived from them it may happen that they are not applied because of particular circumstances[87]. Thomas knows the distinction some theologians made between precepts of the First Table and those of the Second from which God was thought to be able to dispense[88]. In his *Quaestio disputata de malo*[89] he proposes an answer in this sense, but in the present article a different solution is advanced[90]. The natural law consists of moral precepts which are formulated by reason. In certain circumstances an obstacle can make the application of a precept impossible, as may happen in the case of the restitution of some one else's property. As regards the three cases recorded in the Old Testament[91] he writes that God, the Creator of human nature, can make known that a particular act no longer comes in under the law as man has formulated it and that what obliges man need not oblige God. Thus killing an innocent person is a crime, but daily thousands of people die because of natural causes which, in the last analysis, depend on God's will. No one can claim the right to live long. Secondly, created causes are subject to divine causality, and so in the chain of causes a human being can also be inserted as causing the death of someone[92].

The argument also holds for material goods. Material possessions are primarily God's property[93]. As regards the behavior of the prophet Hosea a similar answer applies. The rights connected to marriage are subject to God's will. God can assign a woman to a man even outside marriage,

If one objects that this seems quite arbitrary, as if on the one hand God imposes rules of conduct which are anchored in our nature, while on the other he suspends them, the reply would be that what God does constitutes in a sense the nature of things. Thomas points to the example of water which because of its nature, spreads equally over a flat surface, but which can become a tidal wave under the influence of the sun and the moon. This is not against the nature of

---

[87] Medieval theologians debated about certain passages of the Old Testament (*Genesis* 22, 2; *Exodus* 12, 35 and *Osea* 1, 2) which appear to say that God himself suspended some precepts or at least suspended some people from them.

[88] *In I Sent.*, d. 47, q. 1, a. 4 ad 3 & ad 4.

[89] Q. 3, a. 1, ad 17.

[90] In I-II 100, 8 he writes that the commandments of the Decalogue "sunt omnino indispensabiles".

[91] See note 86.

[92] See II-II 104, 4 ad 2: "... Deus nihil potest præcipere contra virtutem quia in hoc principaliter consistit virtus et rectitudo voluntatis humanæ quod Dei voluntati conformetur et eius sequatur imperium quamvis sit contra consuetum virtutis modum"

[93] In his answer to the third objection (the Hebrews stealing the gold and silver vessels from the Egyptians) Thomas writes that private property and certain situations in which people are subject to others have not been instituted by nature, but by man himself because of their apparent usefulness.

water. In this way an effect caused by the One on whom the natural activity of a thing depends is not against its nature[94]. The finality of things remains intact at a higher level. Thomas preferred this solution to that proposed elsewhere which explained the exception by the subtraction of the matter of a particular commandment from the rule[95].

One is dispensed from observing a precept of the law when under the circumstances obedience to the law would be against the intention of the legislator. For precepts which are formulated in such a way that they express explicitly the intention of the lawgiver, no dispensation is possible[96]. But Aquinas adds that it happens that in some cases mentioned in the Old Testament something no longer falls under the law, because it lies outside what the Legislator intended to formulate and the person concerned knows by a divine intervention that a particular act he is about to perform no longer falls under the general rule, so that this act will not be one of murder, theft or adultery.

Duns Scotus, who distinguishes between the Decalogue and natural law argues that God cannot dispense from the commandments of the Decalogue, but may intervene in the order of things by suspending the natural law. Good and evil would have been different if God had created a different world. For this reason murder, theft and similar crimes are not immoral as such. - Were Scotus right, then the precepts of natural law would be actually quite arbitrary and it would be difficult to explain why one is requested to faithfully observe the commandments. Moreover, the distinction Scotus makes between the precepts of the natural law and the Decalogue can hardly be defended (**article 5**).

The question whether we can lose the knowledge of some precepts of the natural law belongs also to the theme of possible changes in the natural law. In the course of history there have been frequent changes in the norms which people and states apply. In his response Aquinas distinguishes between very general precepts which are known to all and other, secondary rules which go into details and are thus conclusions derived from these precepts or principles[97]. The first group of precepts can never disappear from our mind, although it happens, as we saw, that, hampered by a passion, a person is blinded and does not apply a general rule to a concrete situation[98]. However, the secondary precepts can be wiped from our consciousness, e.g. by wrong opinions (as one can also

---

[94] I, 105, 6 ad 1: "Cum igitur naturalis ordo sit a Deo inditus, si quid præter hunc ordinem faciat, non est contra naturam. Unde Augustinus dicit, XXVI *Contra Faustum*, c. 3, quod "id est cuique rei naturale, quod ille fecerit a quo est omnis modus, numerus et ordo naturæ". Cf. also *Q. d. de potentia*, q. 1, a.3 ad 1.

[95] *In III Sent.*, d. 37, q. 1, a. 4 ad 3 & ad 4.

[96] I-II 100, 8: "Et ideo præcepta decalogi sunt omnino indispensabilia".

[97] O. Lottin points to such a distinction in the works of William of Auvergne. See his *Psychologie et morale*, II, 76.

[98] I-II 77, 2.

be mistaken in one's theoretical studies) or by perverse customs (which may prevail among certain groups). In our modern society certain customs prevail, concerning which many citizens are not aware, or are not able to see, that they are opposed to natural law. Conversely, in former centuries the natural rights of women, wage earners and children, which nowadays all in the West agree upon, were not always acknowledged (**article 6**).

With regard to the later history of the doctrine of natural law the school of Duns Scotus propagated the view that the law is mainly an act of the will. In his absolute power God can impose conduct which goes against natural law, but according to his actual will, in the order of things established by him (by his *potentia ordinata*), he does not act in this way. William of Ockham goes beyond this position and argues that good and evil are exclusively a question of God's will. Luther's idea of man's total incapacity to do the good has pushed the doctrine of natural law into the background, but in sixteenth century Spain a renaissance took place of the theory of natural rights, in particular in the teaching of Vitoria. Suarez, for his part, rejects the position of those who identify natural law with man's nature. On account of his voluntaristic approach Suarez thinks that natural law is a real law because God, the supreme legislator, imposed it. Suarez influenced Hugo Grotius who, however, detached the natural law from the will of God[99]. Other important authors are Samuel Pufendorf and John Locke. While positivism and subjectivism undermined interest in theories of natural law, totalitarian regimes provoked a reaction. People began openly to defend inalienable human rights and the need for universally acknowledged norms. We must always keep in mind that for Thomas natural law is not a command imposed upon us from without but a natural insight of our mind that shows us the way to our real end.

APPENDIX

Aquinas's view of the human rights

What we call human rights are entitlements derived from the natural law[100], of which they are sometimes a further development formulated in positive laws. Rights are relative to duties: if children have a right to be nourished and educated by their parents, the latter have a duty to nourish and educate them. Nowadays human rights are conceived as claims which individual citizens or groups put forward. People insist on their right to be respected, to have suitable jobs and job security, to shorter working hours, to vacations and social assistance. Human

---

[99] *De iure belli et pacis*, Prolegomena : "... etiamsi daremus...non esse Deum".
[100] Cf. John Locke's *Second Treatise of Civil Government*, in which he derives man's natural rights from the law of nature.

nature is the foundation of the more basic rights, even if in contemporary theories about human rights this foundation is not always apparent. The advocates of human rights appeal rather to the declarations of human rights, promulgated by common consent. In this connection natural law ethics has the important task of clarifying the basis of these rights, defining them more precisely and showing what the duties are corresponding to these rights. Implementing human rights will be possible in proportion to the state of development and organization of a society. Several hundred years ago it would not have made much sense to assert the right to a job which the government should provide.

Basic human rights are characterized by the following properties:
a) They are universal and apply to all men. This axiom is based on the fact that we all share the same human nature[101]. b) They must be immediately evident because they are derived from the first principles of the natural law[102]. c) They do not change and cannot be totally erased from our mind[103]. Certain human rights now widely acknowledged, at least in the Western World, were at one time not recognized by all. Examples are the rights of working people, of women and of ethnic minorities. The question is connected with that of the mutability of the natural law discussed in the preceding section and with a pervasive influence of Christian doctrine.

Sometimes conclusions are drawn from these rights which are obviously wrong. For instance, the right to express one's views is interpreted by the media as the right to publish whatever they want and to use any means to get access to what - in terms of circulation numbers and profit - reporters and editors consider important. A further issue where natural law ethics has an important role to play is that of the relationship between the individual and the state, and that between individual countries and political umbrella structures such as the European Union. Natural law ethics, based on the principles outlined by Aquinas, establishes that what an individual person or a particular group can do by himself or itself should not be regulated by the state or other comprehensive structures. Natural law ethics can also help determine our obligations with regard to our natural environment. While it defends the right of man to use minerals, plants and animals for his benefit it pays attention to the rights of different nations and of future generations. It also plays role in the analysis of the right of aliens to enter and to settle in other countries and the possible duties which the host country may have in this respect.

---

[101] St. Thomas, *In V Ethicorum*, lesson 12.
[102] I-II 100, 1.
[103] *Quaestio disputata de malo*, q. 2, a. 4 ad 4 & ad 13.. See Jesús García López, *Los derechos humanos en Santo Tomás de Aquino*, Pamplona 1979, pp. 66 ff.; S. Theron, in *Anthropotes* 1991, 171-189.

Positive or human law (Q. 95)

Natural law consists of the principles and the general norms of man's moral life, but it must be further determined in order to give those who live in a political society concrete rules for conduct. This further determination is achieved by means of positive laws, which regulate the different aspects of human life in society[104]. Most positive laws are not norms which are deduced from the precepts of natural law by way of a conclusion, but are often indirectly connected with them as further determinations which, in other circumstances, could have been different[105]. If a positive law contradicts a precept of natural law then it is no longer a law in the proper sense of the term. The natural law is the basis and the condition for the validity of positive laws.

In ancient Greece the positive laws of the various city states were the pride of the citizens. Heraclitus compares them with the city walls protecting the inhabitants[106]. They made the difference between the life of free citizens and that of the barbarians, among whom abuse of power and sheer arbitrariness were rampant. Despite his unjust condemnation Socrates respected the laws of Athens and observed them until his death. The Sophists, however, sometimes criticized the laws, since they were artificial and were abused by the powerful. According to Plato laws which do not serve the common good are no real laws.

In so far as they are an application of natural law to concrete and changing situations positive laws can easily be altered. St. Augustine stressed the contrast with the unchangeable natural law, pointing out that the legislator draws his inspiration from the eternal law applying its unchangeable norms in the different periods of history[107]. Aquinas observes that the general principles of the natural law cannot be applied to all cases in the same way because of the great variety of situations in which people live[108].

The introductory article of this question explains that man must develop by his own efforts what nature has given him. He does so by devising ways of nourishing and protecting himself. Nature provides him with the basic things he needs in order to do so, sc. his mind and his hands. Experience shows that man, as an isolated individual, does not get very far and that he needs the support of others, since he is made to live in a community. As regards acquiring the virtues

---

[104] Natural law is the source and origin of the positive laws. Cf. *In V Ethic.*, lesson 12, n. 1023: "omnia iusta positiva vel legalia ex iusto naturali oriuntur".

[105] However, in Article Two Thomas says that human law sometimes consists in conclusions drawn from natural law. In such cases it no longer has a purely positive character.

[106] Fragm. 44.

[107] *De vera religione* I, 31, 58: "... ut secundum eius incommutabiles regulas quid sit pro tempore iubendum vetandumque discernat".

[108] I-II 95, 2 ad 3: "Principia communia legis naturæ non possunt eodem modo applicari omnibus propter multam varietatem rerum humanarum".

which are essential for his happiness, he has a natural aptitude for them, but practice is necessary in order to become a virtuous person. Since people tend to take the easiest way and to seek to experience as much pleasure as possible, especially when they are young, some measure of discipline is necessary. For young people with a good character the example and the authority of their parents may be enough to bring them to a life according to the virtues, but for others who are more inclined to lust and other vices, the pressure of laws is needed to keep them on the right path..

From this summary one can see that St. Thomas treats positive law from the point of view of man as on the way (*in via*) to his final destination, viz. happiness. Law is primarily considered from the viewpoint of its usefulness for man's moral life. In his answer to the first objection he writes that persons with a natural inclination to the virtues profit more from admonishments than from enforced rules, while those with a tendency to vice need the goad of the law. A second objection argues that the law is cold and impersonal and that it is better to leave the promotion of rights and justice to actual persons than to a rule of law. In his reply St. Thomas writes that it is easier to find a small number of wise people to make good laws than to find the great number of persons who would be needed to judge all the individual cases. Furthermore, while elaborating and drawing up projects of laws those in government usually are able to discuss them at leisure, whereas in jurisprudence, where there are no set rules, one must each time reach a new decision in a some haste. Thomas does not want the judges to decide what is right. Only individual cases, for which there is no law, must be left to the discretion of the judges (**article 1**).

In order to be just a law must agree with right reason, i.e. with natural law. Hence a positive law possesses the character of law in so far as it is derived from natural law. If in some respect it deviates from it, it is no longer a law but a distortion of what a law should be. Positive laws can be deduced from natural law in two ways: a) by drawing conclusions from it, e.g. that while driving a car one may not endanger the life of others; b) by adding concrete details which further determine the general rule, as an architect who builds a house can give different shapes to its essential structure (foundation, walls and roof). The punishment for homicide, for instance, can be determined in different ways by different countries. The laws in this the second group are valid because they are issued by the legislator, while those of the first type get their validity directly from natural law (**article 2**).

Thomas now presents a definition of positive law by reducing a long and laborious description of it by St. Isidore[109] to three main points. a) The law must be adjusted to the end, b) As any well conceived undertaking the law must correspond to a plan, here. the law of nature and the divine law, c) The law must be

---

[109] *Etymol.* V, c. 21.

useful. Point b) includes the requirement that the law be adjusted to what is possible for different persons and that it must take into account the differences between people as well as changing circumstances (**article 3**).

After having determined the nature of positive law Aquinas now proposes a division. a) In so far as positive law consists of conclusions drawn from natural law it is called the law of nations (*ius gentium*) which obliges all men and is effective everywhere in the world. Inasmuch as positive law is a determination of the natural law we speak of civil law, which can differ from country to country[110]. b) Positive laws are also divided according to the different categories of citizens working for the common good, such as government officials, the military and ministers of religion, since there are laws proper to them. c) Positive laws are divided according to the constitutions of the different states, which determine their form of government. Thomas mentions various forms of government as Aristotle had distinguished them, such as monarchy, oligarchy and democracy. d) Laws are finally divided according to the types of activity they regulate (**article 4**).

The authority and the range of positive law (Q. 96)

The Latin title of this question reads *De potestate legis humanae*. The meaning of the term *potestas* is both that of "power to oblige" and "scope of action". In the age of Socrates some doubted the value of the civil laws. The different city states had widely varying laws and this seemed to indicate that all laws are relative[111]. But both Plato and Aristotle defended the need for positive laws and for objective criteria. In this question Aquinas further asks if the law must go into details and, moreover, if it must be such that the citizens will accept it.

---

[110] This division corresponds to the text of *E.N.* V, c 10, 1134^{b}19 ff., which speaks of τὸ φυσικὸν δίκαιον that everywhere has the same validity and does not depend on subjective opinion, in contrast with positive laws. Aristotle acknowledges that the natural law can also undergo minor changes. In contemporary theories of law the term "the law of nations" means primarily the treaties between states, i.e. international law. Spanish scholastics such as Francisco de Vitoria, Dominic de Soto, Gines de Sepúlveda and Suarez, and somewhat later Hugo Grotius, are the founders of the theory of international law. In the Roman Empire *ius gentium* signified the rights of those who were not Roman citizens, although they lived within its boundaries. In St. Thomas's works the meaning of the term is moving towards that of human rights. Commentators differ on whether the *ius gentium*, as mentioned in the text, must be placed under the natural law or under positive law (as nowadays the term "international law" undoubtedly refers to positive laws). According to Vitoria it is a law which is in the middle between the natural and the positive law. See A.F. Utz, *Thomas von Aquin. Naturgesetz und Naturrecht*, Bonn 1996, p. 209.

[111] Cf. the theory of Callicles in Plato's *Gorgias*. See also *Laws* 889 E and F. Heinimann, *Nomos und Physis. Herkunft und Bedeutung einer Antithese im griechischen Denken des 5. Jahrhunderts*, Basel 1945.

It is the general conviction of jurists that laws are made to regulate what takes place often, but are not made in view of what happens exceptionally. As Aquinas explains, a law must be adjusted to its end, i.e. to the common good. But the common good comprehends both persons and things and demands that a law be valid for a long period in order to be effective. Privileges and exemptions, on the other hand, concern only individual persons. The answer to the second objection reminds us that a law does not make sense if it regulates only one isolated action. This is the task of the virtue of prudence (**article 1**).

The observance of a law must be possible for the citizens. But people are different. What is acceptable in the behavior of children may be blameworthy in that of adults. Since laws are destined for a great number of people, many of whom do not possess a high degree of virtue, laws cannot prohibit all less good or even all wrong actions, but only the more serious offences, which the great majority of the citizens can avoid, and in particular those acts which inflict damage on others. The criterion of what the law should or should not prohibit is whether actions threaten the life of people or the well being and existence of the community. If such acts were not forbidden by law the society concerned would be destroyed. These are acts as homicide, theft etc. Even if the civil law does not punish some actions which are morally wrong, these are nevertheless opposed to the natural law. The conclusion is that positive law cannot prohibit all that is forbidden by natural law. Can the level of morality of a people restrict the legislative activity of governments? Can the law still forbid certain things, such as graft or euthanasia, when a considerable part of the citizens consider it licit? Thomas replies that a law cannot contradict the natural law but, on the other hand, need not forbid all that is morally wrong (**article 2**).

Positive laws do not forbid all vices nor do they command total virtuous behavior, but they regulate those acts which concern the common good. Actions can be related to the common good directly or indirectly. Directly related to it are acts which make it possible for the state to function. They concern matters of justice and national defense. Indirectly related to the common good are those acts which concern the life of the citizens in a society, such as the protection of the elderly and the sick, the respect for people's privacy, education of the young. In general, positive laws promote the virtuous life, but do not force the citizens always to act virtuously (**article 3**).

A related question is to what extent positive laws oblige. Does one observe them out of fear of sanctions or out of personal conviction? If such laws are just, Aquinas writes, they oblige in conscience because of their connection with natural law which as needing to be further determined by positive laws. Laws are just a) if they aim at the common good, b) if the legislator does not exceed his competence, c) if their contents are good, e.g. when they equally divide the necessary impositions.- If in a country which considers itself a democracy there has been considerable deceit during the elections and the newly "elected" government makes laws then these conditions are not fulfilled. It also happens that a government wastes public money or tries to steer the country in a direction the majority of the citizens do not approve of. If tax-burdens are very unjustly divided or if a law no longer aims at the common good then such legislation becomes unjust and oppresses the people[112]. These laws do not oblige in conscience, unless in those cases in which one must bear with some injustice in order to avoid greater evils. Laws which are contrary to the law of God, e.g. the interdiction to be a Christian, should not be passed or observed at all. Thomas acknowledges the right and the duty of the citizens to examine critically what the legislator wants to impose. Their appraisal of a law, however, must be based on its contents rather than on the way it was made and promulgated[113] (article 4).

Is everyone subject to the laws in the same way? A law has two characteristics, sc. it is a rule regulating a citizen's conduct, and it is accompanied by sanctions. As for the first point, all who are subject to a legitimate authority are bound to observe the law which it issued. This implies that a person is not bound by the laws of some other country which are not recognized in one's own country and one is not bound either if one has been dispensed by a higher authority rom the observance of a law issued by officials at a lower level. In classical antiquity and in the Middle Ages it was thought that an emperor or king was not obliged to observe the law that he had himself proclaimed[114]. However, in our democratic regimes the king or governor who issues a law, must observe it himself. Aquinas notes that even if a king is not affected by the sanction attached to the law he issues, he must nevertheless take the law as a rule for his own conduct. To obey a law can mean that one feels oneself under coercion. However, righteous and virtuous people do not feel themselves under such compulsion, since they comply out of their own accord with what the law commands (article 5).

A final question is whether a citizen can sometimes feel himself dispensed from observing a law. It happens, Thomas says, that the observation of a law which is useful in general brings great disadvantage with it on certain occasions. A legislator cannot take into account all possible situations and he makes laws so that they apply to most cases, since he aims at promoting the common good. In a particular situation, however, observance of a law can cause harm to the common good. If that is the case then one need not observe it. However, one must not too easily resort to such exceptions. It is the task of the legitimate authority rather than of individual citizens to suspend the law in question. Only if an immediate danger threatens and it is not possible to postpone an action,

---

[112] "Huiusmodi magis sunt violentiæ quam leges".

[113] Utz, o.c., p. 221.

[114] This is also the opinion of Thomas Hobbes. See his *Leviathan*, c. 26.

will a person not be subject to the law. Whoever in such a situation acts outside the law, does not pass a judgment on the law itself but understands that at this time the letter of the law should not be followed. He or she concludes that the legislator did not intend to impose the law for this kind of situation. In a final remark Aquinas writes that situations are so widely different that no one can foresee everything that can happen and lay down in one text what should be done in all possible circumstances. The legislator considers only what happens in most cases (**article 6**).

The conditions for modifying human laws (Q. 97)

One might think that laws which are derived from unchangeable natural law precepts could not change. For what is just and right, remains so and in fact, rules should be changed as seldom as possible. However, history shows that laws which were good at first have had to be modified later on. Seen from the point of view of human reason as making the laws, changes are possible where in the course of time one comes to understand better which precepts will serve the common good, just as there is progress in the sciences. Regarding those for whom a law is destined, changes may occur in their life which demand other laws. It is a fact that changes in the economic order or in the international situation and developments within their particular countries have forced governments to modify existing laws or to issue new ones. Nowadays increasing criminality and terrorism demand adaptations of the laws in order to better protect the citizens. It goes without saying that the ideal is the stability and permanence of the laws, but in our present situation, in which so much is changing, a total immutability of the laws is not possible. As for the objection that what was once just, remains so Thomas replies that the question of whether a law is just is also determined by its usefulness for the well-being of all and this does not always remain the same (**article 1**).

Laws can be changed when the common good demands this. But making such modifications always has disadvantages, since the observation of a law, prevalent custom is of great importance. If a law is modified, its observation, in so far as it is based on custom, is interrupted[115]. For this reason laws should be changed only if this yields a considerable and evident advantage, for instance, if an existing law has become positively bad or if keeping it is to the disadvantage of the majority of the population. If we modify laws too easily then solid customs fall into abeyance and confusion arises. As Aristotle says, laws get most of their coercive power from custom[116] (**article 2**).

---

[115] "Quando mutatur lex, diminuitur vis constrictiva, inquantum tollitur consuetudo".
[116] *Politics* II, c. 5, 1269ª20.

Obviously prevailing customs are an important factor when issuing laws and in observing them. For this reason Aquinas determines the relation between custom and law in the following way. What people think and want to have or to do shows in what they say and undertake. If new ideas and new needs emerge then rules and laws may need to be modified. Acting consistently and repeatedly in a certain manner can also lead to the modification of a law, especially when a custom takes shape. Custom can even become a rule of conduct which has the force of law. It may become an interpretation of a law or cause a law to fall into disuse. It is understood, however, that no custom, which depends on the will of man, can ever prevail over the law of nature or divine law. One might wonder how a custom can develop which goes against an existing law. Aquinas replies that a law sometimes admits of exceptions, dispensing people from its observance and if such cases multiply because of new circumstances or of changes in the conduct of the citizens then a new custom will begin to prevail. If so, it becomes clear that the law is no longer useful. But if the reason why the law was issued remains valid then the custom must yield to the law. It is, in fact, not easy to bring about changes in the conduct of the great majority of people. In particular in a democratic state, where the citizens can make laws (through an elected parliament), customary law has great authority. As F. Utz notes, in this sort of situation it is not so much a question of the objective goodness of a law as of its applicability, considering the way of thinking of the majority of the people and the prevalent or emerging customs[117]. One may hope that in the long run better insight will prevail over bad custom, as Thomas suggests in his answer to the first objection (**article 3**).

Can the government dispense from the observance of laws? The word, *dispensation* means that one adapts or assigns what is common or general to what is particular. In this general sense a dispensation from a law shows how individuals must relate to general precepts. It happens that a precept which in most cases serves the good of society is not fitting for some particular persons and would have a bad effect or would prevent something better from coming about. However, it would be dangerous to let individual citizens judge such a matter, unless at moments of an evident and sudden danger. For this reason those who govern a nation or a community have also the power to dispense from a law which falls under their authority and to decide that certain persons do not have to obey the law in question. If in doing so they proceed in an arbitrary way then they are imprudent and unfaithful to their task of promoting the common good. A dispensation from the general precepts of the natural law is not possible, but it can sometimes be given with regard to precepts which are conclusions from its principles (**article 4**).

---

[117] *O.c.*, p. 215.

APPENDIX

St. Thomas's doctrine of the common good

Laws must be ordered to the common good. But what do the words "the common good" mean precisely, an expression Aquinas uses some 370 times in his works? Leaving aside the statements which say that God is the common good of the universe and of man, we will consider the meaning of the words in connection with human society. A human society has its own end which is denoted by the terms "the common good". Within the political society there are societies or communities which pursue a non-comprehensive goal, such as cultural activities, the promotion of economic ventures or sports. The state is considered the perfect society which makes it possible for man to fully develop his capacities. Man is a social being and a political animal who can reach his full existence only together with others and with the help of others, and so owes his well being and level of culture to the community.

This entails that one cannot oppose the good of the individual citizen to that of the community, since the good of the individual can only be reached within the community. Moreover, according to his very nature, man lives together with others and wants to treat them well and help them.

The well-being or the common good of the society does not have an existence of its own apart from that of the citizens. It is a unity of order which is rooted in the good of its members and consists of many elements. As the good of all who live in a certain society, it is the comprehensive end of their activities. This end does not exist from the very beginning in its entirety but it is pursued and only partially realized. A community can exist only when its members tend to the common good. This is obvious when one considers what makes it up, viz. a) the life and health along with the bodily and spiritual development of its members, b) the activities of the members in view of the common goal at the level of social and political life, c) the sum of institutions, laws, ordinances and material goods which are necessary or beneficial to the life of all.

The common good is an end and gives each society its meaning. Thomas even goes so far as to say that the individual members of a community, in accordance with their nature, love the good of the whole more than their own good[118]. This must be understood of the original order in which the first man was placed. In the present situation of fallen man many pursue their own, limited well-being more than the good of the whole society. A number of people even experience an opposition between their personal well-being and the goals of the community. In fact, however, people cannot act in favour of or against the common good without promoting or damaging their own private interests. When one works in

---

[118] I-II 109, 3.

favour of one's interests within the framework of the community, doing what is just then one makes a contribution to the common good.

The common good is a difficult concept since it seems to denote something ungraspable, sc. a comprehensive end, made up of concrete components, whereas it is itself not palpable. In addition to its concrete components it comprises also the collaboration of the individual citizens in view of the security and well-being of all. The well- being of the individual is reached only when it is incorporated into that of a comprehensive community. The text means a community in which one is really at home.. Modern states, however, have developed a great number of complex rules and laws which often alienate the citizens. This renders it more difficult to understand Aquinas' view of the common good[119]. Moreover, the rise of individualism makes people wonder to what extent they are social beings and must direct their activities to the common good. This phenomenon goes back to the later Middle Ages, when a transition began to take place toward a more individualistic way of thinking, which both found its expression in nominalism and was promoted by it. Individualism sees man as an isolated being and stresses the rights of the individual over and against those of others. The image of a world in which a fixed place had been assigned to man, was replaced by that of a universe expanding indefinitely in which man no longer felt at home. Because of political, social and economic changes such social institutions as the guilds were abolished. The feeling of belonging to one universal Church was shaken by the Protestant Reformation and the wars of religion. People were no longer aware of belonging to a universal community. Many came to believe that the sole purpose of the state is to protect them.

These changes can be observed in the views one had of rights. In the ancient tradition as well as for Aquinas a right signified in the first place the right cause (*res iusta*), and secondly the knowledge by which one knows what is right, and finally the right that is administered. But in modern thought a right is seen as the power one has over what belongs to one, i.e. the power to dispose of things and persons. Thomas Hobbes even identifies natural right with freedom[120]. John Locke elaborated the theory of the individual who as such is unconnected with life within the political society. He argues that the individual citizen can acquire wealth in an unlimited way, without being concerned with others.

Aquinas's concept of the state as the perfect political society and that of the citizen as a person are different from concepts held by some modern authors using the same terms. Jacques Maritain, for instance, sees the human person as an autonomous subject with rights of his own, prior to society. Influenced by

---

[119] See L. Elders, "Algemeen welzijn als doel- en ordeningsprincipe van het maatschappelijk leven", in E. De Jonghe en L.J. Elders (eds.), *De beginselen van de sociale leer van de Kerk*, Leuven / Amersfoort 1994, 93 - 109.

[120] *Leviathan*, I, ch. 14: "The Right of Nature, which writers commonly call *ius naturale*, is the Liberty each man has to use his own power as he wills himself".

modern individualism some authors even say that historically and logically the individual precedes the state, whereas Thomas considers man from the point of view of his final end, sc. ecause of his nature man is destined to a life in the community. But for many modern authors the state is an institution which depends on the free decision of the citizens and has as its only task to organize human cohabitation[121]. When favourable circumstances for the life of the individual citizen have been attained, the state has accomplished its mission. Thomas, on the other hand, argues from man's social nature and sees man as he is placed in the natural order of things. Man is not a bearer of rights prior to and independently from his incorporation into the state. Thomas considers man in relation to his moral perfection and sees him within the society called to belong to the chosen people of God. Society is not only a requisite for the greater well being of the individual citizens, life in the human community leads to the perfection of those who live together. The state and the laws which concern society as a whole are not a product of the free choice of individual citizens but are derived from the social nature of man. For this reason one cannot reduce the common good to a means of promoting the interests of the individuals nor to the sum of material goods. The view-point of individualist ethics must be left behind.

---

[121] See A. F. Utz, *Thomas von Aquin. Deutsche Thomasausgabe*, Band 18bis, Bonn 1987, 448-498.

CHAPTER X

PRUDENCE

INTRODUCTION : THE CARDINAL VIRTUES

In the general introduction the question was raised whether one can assemble from the theological writings of Thomas Aquinas the principles of a philosophical ethics. The answer was affirmative. When dealing with the cardinal virtues a similar question arises: in the second volume of Part II of the *Summa theologiae* St. Thomas studies the infused supernatural virtues, as appears from the context of this treatise and its location after the discussion of the three theological virtues, faith, hope and love.. He does not explain the difference between the virtues we acquired in a natural way and the infused virtues[1], but his analyses and arguments concerning the nature and division of the virtues are at the level of natural reason. This means that Aquinas sees an analogy and coherence between the natural and the infused moral virtues. The nature and operation of the infused virtues must apparently be studied in the light of the acquired virtues. The acquired virtues, in fact, are taken up into the supernatural virtues. Their practice helps Christians on their way to their supernatural end. For this reason a considerable part of the treatise on the infused moral virtues consists of explanations at the level of natural reason. This justifies presenting the insights of St. Thomas about the cardinal virtues in a study of philosophical ethics. In the following chapters his main conclusions will be put forward.

Chapter VII proposed some general remarks on the virtues. However, the detailed study of the individual virtues must use the principles of the practical intellect. This explains why the treatment of them follows the chapter on natural law. Aquinas considers them in the *Secunda Secundæ*. Our chapters ten to thirteen discuss the moral virtues in some detail, following the account of Aquinas in the second volume of Part II (the *Secunda Secundae*) of the *Summa theologiae*. QQ. 47 - 56 of this Part study prudence, the virtues assisting it and the opposite vices. This is discussed in our present chapter. In following chapters justice, fortitude and temperance will be examined. Because of the sheer size of Aquinas's treatise we can present his doctrine only in a concise form.

---

[1] See E. Schockenhoff, *o.c., 334 ff.*

PRUDENCE

Prudence considered by itself (Q. 47)

In most manuals of moral theology published between 1600 and 1920 the treatise on the moral virtues was absent and no special attention was paid to prudence, although this virtue holds a central place in man's moral life. Q. 47 of the *Secunda Secundæ* has 16 articles, eight of which deal with this virtue as such, while the following articles illustrate certain aspects of it. The Bible and ancient Christian authors are important sources, but nevertheless the *Nicomachean Ethics* holds a central place in Thomas's text. In our time interest in the virtue of prudence is not very great. For some of our contemporaries it is not obvious at all that one needs a virtue to act wisely, others think that a prudent person is someone who is clever in working for his own interest[2].

As has been shown in Chapter VII prudence has its seat in the intellect in so far as it deliberates and is moved by the will to regulate our actions. Its field of operation comprises our entire life (**articles 1 & 2**). Since our acts concern individual objects and situations and must be ordered with a view to our final end, prudence must both know the general principles and be able to assess the concrete situations to which these principles must be applied. Thomas differs from Aristotle in so far as he argues that both the knowledge of general principles and their application fall under prudence (**article 3**). Prudence is a virtue since it makes our actions agree with the fundamental inclinations of our nature, so that they are directed to the good end. At the level of the intellect it produces proper insight (**article 4**); it is distinguished from the other moral virtues by its association with the intellect, but since it is directed to man's activity, it differs from such intellectual virtues as wisdom and the knowledge of the first principles (**article 5**).

While prudence applies general principles to concrete actions, it does not assign goals to what we do: these goals have already been chosen and so it is the task of prudence to help find and determine what leads us to these goals (*ea quae sunt ad finem*)[3] (**article 6**). This means that in everyday life prudence helps us reach some balance (the mean) in our actions (**article 7**). Its task comprises examining, deliberating over and judging the different options and, next, indicating what is to be done. For Aquinas this last function is an essential part of

---

[2] Cf. David Hume, *A Treatise of Human Nature*, III, last part. See also B. Waltz, *Genitrix virtutum. Zum Wandel des aristotelischen Begriffs praktischer Vernunft*, Münster (Lit-Verlag), 1986.

[3] One finds the expressio in *E.N.* 1144^{a}8 and parallel texts (τὰ πρὸς τὸ τέλος) : the moral virtues ensure that we direct ourselves to our true ends, prudence makes us use the right ways and means in order to reach these ends. The expression *ea quae sunt ad finem* has a broader sense than the word "means".

prudence, which includes more than deliberations alone which would not really engage us[4] (**article 8**).

Energy and thoroughness[5] are characteristic of the prudent person. As Aristotle writes, thorough and even time-consuming deliberation is needed first, but then one must carry out rapidly what one has decided to do[6]. St. Augustine for his part stresses this thoroughness one must proceed with[7]. To be prudent involves much more than circumspection (**article 9**). One might think that the major task of prudence concerns one's private life exclusively. In fact, Aristotle writes that people usually consider a person prudent who takes good care of his own interests[8]. But Thomas notes that this opinion is against love and right reason. Since our personal goals and our happiness are part of the common good[9], which is at a higher level than our own well-being alone, prudence is also directed to the good of society. Whoever promotes the well-being of the community promotes also his own good[10] (**article 10**). Since the common good, the good of smaller societies or communities and one's own well-being are distinct goals, pursuing them requires distinct forms of prudence (**article 11**). Prudence in governing a community is especially proper to those in positions of leadership, although everyone must possess some of this type of prudence (**article 12**).

Some people deliberate carefully in order to attain bad ends. In such cases their behaviour shows some external likeness to the virtue of prudence, although they do not have this virtue itself. It also happens that a person acts with prudence in view of some limited goal, e.g. a businessman taking good care of his affairs, but fails to place his work in the context of the whole of his life and obligations. If so then he lacks the perfect form of prudence, something which is also the case when one carefully deliberates but does not execute what prudence suggests. The authentic virtue of prudence gives counsel in view of the end of one's entire life, as has been argued above[11].

---

[4] Q. 47, a. 8: "Et est tertius actus eius præcipere; qui quidem actus consistit in applicatione consiliatorum et iudicatorum ad operandum. Et quia iste actus est propinquior fini rationis practicæ, inde est quod iste est principalis actus rationis practicæ et per consequens prudentiæ".

[5] In this context the Latin word *sollicitudo* has the meaning of the careful and energetic carrying out of a task. Referring to the etymology Isidore gives of the word Thomas writes that sollicitude means that one "ex quadam solertia animi velox est ad prosequendum ea quae sunt agenda".

[6] *E.N.* VI, c. 10, 1142^b4..

[7] *De moribis Ecclesiae*, c. 24.

[8] *E.N.*, c. 9, 1142^a1 ff.

[9] See the appendix to the previous chapter.

[10] Art. 2 ad 2: "Qui quaerit bonum commune multitudinis, ex consequenti etiam quærit bonum suum".

[11] "... quæ ad bonum finem totius vitæ recte consiliatur, iudicat et præcipit". Cf. I-II 58, 5.

In **article 13** Aquinas enquires whether the virtue of prudence is given together with sanctifying grace, while in **article 14,** speaking of acquired prudence, he points out that, as is the case with the other virtues, prudence is caused by repeated prudent actions. If so then youthful persons cannot yet possess this virtue. But are there not people who are circumspect because of a natural disposition? He replies that the knowledge of first principles, from which general rules for our moral behavior are deduced, is given us by nature, while as regards prudence in our concrete activities, Aquinas distinguishes between goals and what leads to such goals. There are people who have a natural inclination to their true goals and so form a correct judgment about them. But concerning the roads which lead to these goals, the situation of different persons and the type of work they do shows a great variety. Here nature has not determined anything, although it happens that one person understands more quickly what should be done than does another (**article 15**). Since prudence is active in following our natural inclinations and is not a matter of knowledge alone, oblivion will not so easily occur, because these fundamental inclinations always remain. But intervening passions can hamper our forming judgments according to the first, basic principles (**article 16**).

The virtues accompanying and assisting prudence (Q. 48)

Before going into details on the functioning of prudence Aquinas proposes some distinctions. The Stoics mentioned subordinate virtues which accompany the main virtues[12]. They assigned five or six of these virtues to prudence. Before their time Aristotle had discussed some of them[13]. Cicero speaks of *partes prudentiae*[14], an expression also used by Aquinas, who gives a survey of the different ways in which one can speak of virtues subordinated to prudence or assisting it:
a) Certain parts taken together constitute a whole, as do the parts of a house. These are called integral parts *(partes integrales)*. Prudence has some such integral parts.
b) Other parts are juxtaposed to the main virtue and belong to the same genus. So we distinguish between prudence in respect of private affairs and prudence in the direction of a community. These juxtaposed virtues are called *partes subiectivæ* (what is meant is the division of a genus into species).
c) Finally there are auxiliary virtues which concern secondary aspects and are called *partes potentiales*..

---

[12] *SVF* III 264 (Stobaeus, *Eclogae*, II, 60, 9).
[13] *E.N.* VI, c. 9, 1142^{a}32 ff.
[14] *Rhetorica* II 53.

With regard to a) Aquinas found in the works of Aristotle[15], Cicero[16] and Macrobius[17] a good number of valuable suggestions as to virtues active in a prudent deliberation and decision.. He distinguishes eight stages in the exercise of prudence, which are discussed in Q. 49, article 1. - The classifications proposed in b) are relatively straightforward. To c) belong the ability to take counsel (*eubulia*), knowledge of what happens normally (*synesis*) in similar cases or in a particular fields and insight (*gnome*) which allows us to project on an act the light of higher principles, so we do not have to follow the usual views of the majority of people.

The elements of a prudent decision (Q. 49)

Q. 49 has eight articles which successively discuss the eight stages or components of a prudent decision. A first step is remembering what normally happens in similar cases. For this experience is required, which can be gained only in the course of time and is stored in one's memory. At this level remembrance is of great importance. In his answer to the second objection Aquinas notes that one can train one's memory and offers a method of doing so (**article 1**). Next he discusses *intellectus* by which he means the right insight into and evaluation of a self evident principle. An example will illustrate what is meant. At work one must do one's duty. However, to attend a party until the early hours of the morning is an impediment to good work during the day, so one should leave earlier (**article 2**). Willingness to learn from others (*docilitas*) is another component of prudence. In view of the enormous variety of situations and possibilities an individual person cannot easily reach an overview of everything involved, and certainly not within a short time. For this reason he must allow others to help him and in particular seek the advice of elderly, experienced people[18]. In this connection Aquinas stresses also the importance of consulting diligently, frequently and respectfully the writings of one's predecessors and warns us not to neglect or despise them out of laziness or pride (**article 3**).

Another quality which helps to form prudent judgments is called *solertia*. This is the ability, zeal and accuracy which help us find with ease and rapidly the required means for reaching a given goal (**article 4**). Aquinas often distinguishes between *intellectus* and *ratio*. Both belong to prudence. In this connection he understands by *intellectus* a direct intellectual knowledge of the principles. Deliberating in order to reach certain insights is the work of the mind as *ratio*. The human mind cannot in one act understand and penetrate everything, in

---

[15] *E.N.* VI, c. 5, 1143^{b}5.
[16] *Rhetorica* III, c. 16; *De senectute*, 78.
[17] *In Somnium Scipionis*, I, c. 8.
[18] Cf. Aristotle, *E.N.* VI, c. 11, 1143^{b}11.

particular as regards concrete events. It must compare and draw conclusions[19] (**article 5**). As has been said above, it is the task of prudence to arrange what can be ordered to the end in such a way that the end is reached. Past events are now definite and cannot be changed, but what lies in the future and will not necessarily happen can be ordered to the end. This is done by the act of *providentia*, foreseeing what lies in the future and directing what one does now in regard to it. It goes without saying that, in order to do this, deliberation and a right judgment are required. The terms "forethought" and "prevision" express this function of prudence (**article 6**). Forethought and prevision often go together with circumspection. The end and what is ordered to the end must be good, but it happens again that what as such is good becomes undesirable or even bad because of certain circumstances. Circumspection makes us take into account the situation and the circumstances (**article 7**). What is good is often accompanied and hampered by something bad. It also happens that what is bad presents itself under the appearance of a good. For this reason great caution is required (**article 8**).

The different kinds of prudence (Q. 50)

As has been mentioned in Q. 48 the virtue of prudence is like a genus which comprises several species. The first and most striking kind of prudence is the one everybody must use in organizing his own life. Thomas now discusses the prudence needed to govern a state or community. The reason why a particular kind of prudence is required to do so is that wherever a special way of administering and governing is found a special form of prudence is needed. As is obvious, governing a country and a whole people and directing them to the common good is one of the highest forms of prudence for which the virtue of justice is a foremost requisite. Now this is the prudence which those who hold high positions in government ought to have (**article 1**). On the side of the citizens there should be willingness to cooperate and the sense of belonging to the community so that the government can carry out its task in a meaningful way. One may consider such an attitude part of the prudence proper to the individual citizens (**article 2**).

The family stands between the political society and individuals. In order to direct the family a special form of prudence is required (**article 3**). In addition there is a particular type of prudence concerning military matters. What we do with deliberation and art, he explains, agree with what happens in nature, as God has established it. For nature not only sees to it that things maintain and develop themselves but also that they ward off outside influences which attack and harm

---

[19] Thomas stresses that *intellectus* and *ratio* are not different faculties or powers but different operations of the same intellect. "Nomen intellectus sumitur ab intima penetratione veritatis, nomen autem rationis ab inquisitione et discursu".

them. Hence animals too are equipped with a second appetitive power, the irascible faculty, by which they can oppose aggression (**article 4**). It is thus Thomas's understanding that organizing oneself against a hostile threat or waging military campaigns demands a special form of prudence.

The virtues which assist prudence (Q. 51)

The title of this question is "the *partes potentiales* of prudence". The words mean virtues or habitus which help prudence. The first of these assisting virtues mentioned is *eubulia*, the aptitude for consideration which makes one find the right way to the intended goal within a reasonable time without protracting deliberations and without much hesitation. It is proper to a virtue to make our actions good[20], so that the power of deliberation which perfects them with regard to our human life and our true end (*ad finem virtutis*) must be called a virtue. People can possess this virtue less than perfectly so that it would not always extend to certain fields of human activity, such as organizing the economy of a country (**article 1**). But if we understand the virtue of deliberation in this way, is it not identical with prudence itself? No, because where there is a different type of goodness we have to do with a different virtue. Since deliberating well, judging correctly and giving the right commands all differ, the respective virtues responsible for these acts also differ. Aquinas considers commanding the performance of a particular act to be the most proper task of prudence, while deliberation and evaluation prepare for this command (**article 2**). It happens that a person is able to deliberate, but does not succeed in reaching a judgment or evaluation, if hampered by a poor condition of the sense-power called common sense (*sensus communis*)[21]. This sense depends partly on our natural dispositions and partly on the way one uses them while it is strengthened by practice. To form a correct judgment it is important that one is not afflicted with worthless or irrelevant sense impressions. A correct disposition of the appetitive faculties can be of some help (**article 3**). Sometimes a good judgment is not carried out unless perhaps in a negligent way. The command to execute an act is the task of prudence itself, a task which is described by Aquinas as the specific work of prudence[22]. -

---

[20] In his answer to the second objection Aquinas observes (against those who doubt whether the gift of deliberation should be called a virtue) that whatever has to do with man's activities must be perfected by some virtue: "Oportet enim circa omnia humana perfici per virtutem". He re-affirms that the virtues cover the entire field of human actions.

[21] The sense power of common sense collects, puts together and distinguishes the impressions of the external senses, a function which St. Thomas sometimes calls "judging". Cf. *In IV Sent.* d. 44, q. 2, a. 1 ad 3; *S. Th.* I, 57, 2 and this article.

[22] Art. 3 ad 3: "Et ideo post virtutem quae est bene iudicativa, necessaria est finalis virtus principalis quæ sit bene præceptiva, scilicet prudentia".

The last virtue assisting prudence is *gnome*[23]. Aristotle uses this term in the sense of a correct understanding of what is equitable, in particular by taking into account the position of other people. Thomas sees this virtue as a prolongation of *synesis*[24], by noting that sometimes one must evaluate an act in the light of higher principles and do something that goes beyond the rules for ordinary human conduct. An example can illustrate this: those who, despite great risks for their own and their family's safety were sheltering Jews in Nazi occupied countries, did so in the light of higher principles (**article 4**). For such behaviour a higher insight is required. This conclusion lays the ground for the theological study of the associated gift of counsel in q. 52.

THE VICES OPPOSED TO PRUDENCE

Imprudence (Q. 53)

Following his standard method Aquinas, after having studied a virtue, discusses the vices opposed to it. A text of St. Augustine's[25] distinguishes between vices which are clearly opposed to the virtue of prudence and others which show a certain resemblance with it, although in reality they are contrary to it. Faults of the first group fall under imprudence. A first question is whether imprudence is a fault or a sin. When the term means just the absence of a virtue, it need not be a sin. Imprudence becomes a sin when one does not possess the virtue of prudence one should have, since one has made no effort to act prudently. In this case a lack of disposition is meant, but it also happens that before performing a particular action one does not deliberate and does nothing of what a prudent person would do. In this case one deviates from the standard rules which make our behaviour wise. This too is sinful (**article 1**).

What sort of sin is this imprudence? It is a general sin inasmuch as prudence is involved in the practice of all virtues and consequently its opposite, imprudence, has a repercussion on whatever one does. In every sin one commits there is some fault in the act of reason directing to the act[26]. Imprudence can also be called a general vice inasmuch as it comprehends several vices, which correspond to the subdivisions of the virtue of prudence. These concern one's own personal life, the direction of the affairs of one's family, the government of the

---

[23] *E.N.* VI, c. 11, 1143ª19. The term γνώμη has the general sense of a realistic appraisal of a question. In rhetoric it determines the real meaning of what is said.

[24] Knowledge of what normally happens in similar cases. See above Q. 48, c).

[25] *Contra Julianum* IV, c. 3 (*PL* 44, 748)): "Omnibus virtutibus non solum sunt vitia manifesta discretione contraria, sicut prudentiæ temeritas, verum etiam vicina quodammodo, nec veritate sed quadam specie fallente similia, sicut ipsi prudentiæ astutia".

[26] "Nullum enim peccatum accidere potest nisi sit defectus in aliquo actu rationis dirigentis".

community. Furthermore the following vices are opposed to the virtues assisting prudence: superficiality in one's judgments, rashness, thoughtlessness, inconstancy and carelessness. Other vices are reduced to these, such as unwillingness to learn from others (**article 2**).

In order to reach a prudent decision one has to pass through several stages, such as remembering what happened in the past in similar circumstances, making a correct appraisal of the present situation and foreseeing how things will develop in the future One must compare the different options, be willing to learn from older or more experienced people. If one of these stages is omitted, one acts with precipitation, i.e. one is unwise. Acting with precipitation is sometimes caused by the impetuosity of the will or by the passions. People can be so impetuous or proud that they neglect to pay attention to what leading authorities say (**article 3**). Another vice leads to wrong judgments. This vice is consists in a failure to take into account those factors which contribute to a correct evaluation[27] (**article 4**).

Another factor is the lack of resoluteness and constancy in carrying out what one has seen to be the correct way to do something. This lack derives from the will. People may discontinue acting in a certain way which they previously considered to be the right way, once now another course of action has become more attractive. Reason gets involved and errs by rejecting what it had at first seen as good. This is obviously imprudent, i.e. there is a lack of steadfastness opposed to prudence (**article 5**). Finally Thomas attempts to identify the roots of imprudence. In order to reach a prudent judgment one must not be carried away by representations and impressions of the sensory powers. Desire for pleasure may easily make one neglect wise deliberation about a situation and a careful evaluation of all the factors involved[28] (**article 6**).

Negligence (Q. 54)

In discussing the virtue of prudence Aquinas mentions carefulness and zeal, which makes one execute a decision without hesitation. Negligence is a vice since it makes us omit an action which reason has deemed to be correct. Negligence can concern all sort of actions but as such it is contrary to the circumspection and attentiveness which should characterize the work of reason[29]. It results from a lack of constancy and tenacity in the will. The objects of negligence are the good actions one should perform but which are abandoned or only per-

---

[27] "Inconsideratio maxime opponitur rectitudini iudicii".

[28] Art. 6, ad 3: "Vitia carnalia intantum magis extinguunt iudicium rationis inquantum longius abducunt a ratione".

[29] Vices in the field of reason have a repercussion on all our actions , for "quilibet actus rationis se extendit ad quamlibet materiam moralem".

formed in part[30] (**article 1**). This negligence is contrary to prudence, to which thoughtfulness, energy and constancy belong (**article 2**). When the will slackens our reason is not moved to command what it should or to do it in the right way. Quite often this kind of negligence will not be a serious sin. But it is a serious sin when what are at stake are questions of the utmost importance such as concern about one's final end (**article 3**).

Vices falsely resembling prudence (Q. 55)

In the first two articles of this question Thomas, referring to a text of St Paul about the *prudentia carnis*[31] , discusses the case of people who make the inclinations of what our lower appetitive faculties desire their final goal (**articles 1 & 2**). When our deliberation has a merely apparent good as its object or when, in order to reach a particular goal, one uses cunning means, then one proceeds in a way which can appear prudent, but in reality is no more than astuteness (**article 3**). Finding crafty means of reaching a goal is the work of astuteness, but when one actually resorts to them we speak of ruse (*dolus*). Deceitfulness shows in particular in one's words (**article 4**). If one passes to action we have to do with deceit (**article 5**).

The next two articles deal with exaggerated solicitude for temporal things. Cf. *Matthew* 6, 31: "Do not be worried about what you will eat or drink or where to find clothes". This solicitude goes too far when one considers temporal goods as man's main goal. Moreover, there is a risk that one becomes concerned exclusively with these things, so that no time is left to occupy oneself with things spiritual. Finally, the Gospel saying could also mean that one should not be needlessly anxious about lacking what is really needed (**article 6**). The words "Be not concerned about to-morrow" (*Mt* 6, 34) mean that one should not be unduly preoccupied with what may come at a later moment, for each day has its own tasks and worries[32] (**article 7**). All the vices we have discussed suppose a certain use of our reason, something which is not always the case with sins at the level of sensuous passions. One uses one's reason correctly when one acts according to justice. A wrong use of our reason originates when one acts against justice. Especially avarice and love of money may lead to such injustice (**article 8**).

---

[30] Cf. art. 2 ad 3: "... negligens autem per defectum promptae voluntatis".
[31] *Romans* 8, 7.
[32] "Unicuique enim tempori competit propria sollicitudo".

CHAPTER XI
JUSTICE

Much of what concerns us, our social obligations, our work and contacts with others, has to do with justice. We speak of just wages, a fair division of tasks, an unfair treatment, violence, corruption, violation of human rights, just and unjust wars, equal rights for all and so on. The numerous cases in which we use the terms just and unjust show that justice has many aspects[1].

As Joseph Pieper writes[2], in Thomas's treatise on justice[3] our Western tradition concerning justice and injustice received an exemplary expression. One does indeed find in Western classical literature a considerable interest in everything that has to do with rights, justice and injustice. The first book of Plato's *Republic*, the fifth book of the *Nicomachean Ethics*, texts of Cicero in his *De officiis* and *De finibus*, book XIX of Augustine's *De civitate Dei*, these are eloquent witnesses to the general conviction of the importance of the virtue of justice for social life. In his study of justice Thomas uses this ancient tradition but also avails himself of the writings of medieval jurists.

In the preface to this long treatise, of which we only present here the main conclusions and leading statements, Thomas surveys the themes to be treated: justice as a virtue, its different parts, including auxiliary virtues and, finally, the gift of piety related to justice and some corresponding biblical precepts in its respect. We shall discuss justice itself, its parts and auxiliary virtus.

On rights (Q. 57)

Justice has to do with what is right. A quality or a virtue is determined by the object to which it is essentially directed. Therefore, Aquinas first explains what "right" (*ius*) is, since we can only know what justice means, when we know what "right" implies. This first part of the treatise ends with q. 60 which discusses the administration of justice, i.e. the task of judges to determine what in inter-human relationships is right and what not. Thomas gives a simple but profound explanation of the term "right". "Right" or "just" is a quality of our actions in so far as they are directed to others, whereas in contrast with justice the other three cardinal virtues move us to acts concerned with ourselves. Justice brings about a certain equality, as the word "just" derived from *iustum* suggests[4]. What is right and just in our actions also depends on the other person with

---

[1] Cf. *In V Ethic.*, lesson 1: "Multiplicitas iniustitiae manifestat multiplicitatem iustitiae".
[2] *Über die Gerechtigkeit*, München 1953, 13.
[3] *Summa theologiæ*, II-II, qq. 57 - 122.
[4] Aquinas refers to the verb *iustari* in Vulgar Latin. We use the verb *adjust* in the sense of "to make conform or suitable to" something.

whom we are dealing. "Right" is not so much what is fitting to ourselves as what is adjusted and is due to the other. This can be a thing, such as a house or one's wages, but also an action to be performed. We encounter here a fundamental fact of human life, sc. certain things are due to people. Since man is placed in the middle of nature and lives in the company of his fellow men, he can and must consider certain things as due to himself and to others.

While for Aquinas "right" is in the first place something objective, given with the way things are, concerning inter-human relationships, later on "right" was seen in the first place as something one can claim and of which he can dispose[5]. Thomas himself drew attention to a certain shift in the meaning of the Latin term. While *ius* (right) originally meant a just cause, it later came to signify also jurisprudence, the science which helps determine what is right in particular cases. The knowledge or science which determines what is "right" and the rules or laws codifying it are also called "right"[6]. While "right" concerns things which belong to people, the law is a statement of the intellect which tells us which actions must or must not be performed in order to promote or protect the common good. Thomas finally notes that we can never give God in an appropriate way what is due to Him. For this reason man's obligations with regard to God are not denoted by the word "right". It is sufficient if we do what we can and submit ourselves totally to God[7] (**article 1**).

As the scholastic method demands, the definition of "right" is followed by a division. This division of rights depends on the different ways in which something is due to other persons[8]. This being due can be a) on account of the nature of the thing in question (*ex ipsa natura rei*). One has borrowed something and must return it. This is called natural law[9]. This right does not depend on the state nor on egoistic or altruistic inclinations of particular people. It may happen, however, that this right is suspended because of changes taking place in the rightful claimant[10]. b) Something can be due to another person in virtue of a transaction (*ex condicto*) or a decision of the community. In an agreement between particulars a person can acquire a right (e.g. by contract). The community

---

[5] Cf. Th. Hobbes, *Leviathan*, I, c. 14: "The right of nature which writers commonly call *ius naturale* is the Liberty each man has to use his power as he wills himself".

[6] At least in Roman law.

[7] Art. 1 ad 3: "Sufficit Deo ut impleamus quod possumus. Iustitia tamen ad hoc tendit ut homo, quantum potest, Deo recompenset, totaliter animam ei subiiciens".

[8] The now customary classification of law as private law, public law, commercial law, criminal law etc. comes in under the divisionion mentioned by Aquinas.

[9] Thomas opposes Gratian's religious interpretation of natural rights as that which "in lege et evangelio continetur" (Gratian, *Decretalia, D.* 1). At the same time he rejects the positivist view.

[10] E.g. when because of physical or mental insufficiencies a person is placed under guardianship and can no longer freely dispose of his belongings.

or the government can also decide what belongs to a person (social benefits, distribution of land, etc.). This distinction goes back to Aristotle[11].

Regulations at the level of positive law may never be contrary to natural law[12]. If some regulation is contrary to natural rights then it is not valid[13]. Agreements between people also create rights[14]. Before an agreement has been reached on a particular point one is free. Once it has been reached, if it is in agreement with natural law, one must observe it[15]. (**article 2**). On a positivist approach rights are derived only from the way people actually live in a society. According to this view what one declares a right is a right.

If the division of what is just into natural rights and positive rights covers the entire extent of justice, where to place international law? Some see the law of nations as a subdivision of natural law, but Thomas distinguishes between what is directly given with our nature, such as what is due to a man and what to a woman, and conclusions derived from it by further deliberation, which are fitting to all. As to the first class of rights, man may have some of them in common with the animals, such as matters relative to sexual intercourse[16], while the rights of the second group are exclusively proper to man and are acknowledged in the entire world[17]. Only rational beings can draw conclusions and compare them with their basis in natural law[18]. These conclusions are so evident that there is no need to formulate them in special laws. They constitute the law of nations. Aquinass gives two examples to illustrate the relationship between what belongs to natural law and what to the law of nations. Considered as such a piece of land has no particular relation with the person who is its owner[19]. The same can be said about certain relations within society and differences between ranks and positions in life. Differing from Aristotle Thomas writes that there is

---

[11] *E.N.* V, c. 7, 1134^{b}18.

[12] To pay for abortions out of public funds, for example, is contrary to the natural law.

[13] Art. 2 ad 2: "Si aliquid de se repugnantiam habeat ad ius naturale, non potest voluntate humana fieri iustum".

[14] Art. 2 ad 2: "Voluntas humana ex communi condicto potest aliquid facere iustum in his quae secundum se non habent aliquam repugnantiam ad naturalem iustitiam".

[15] *E.N.*, V, c. 7, 1134^{b}18.

[16] "... quod omnibus animalibus commune est".

[17] Gaius, *Digesta*, I, i, leg 9: "Quod naturalis ratio inter omnes homines constituit, id apud omnes gentes custoditur, vocaturque ius gentium". See above, Chapter IX, q. 94, article 4.

[18] "Considerare autem aliquid comparando ad id quod ex ipso sequitur est proprium rationis.

[19] With this remark Thomas deviates somewhat from Aristotle who in *Politics* II, c. 5, seems to connect the right of private ownership more closely with natural law. In his *De officiis* I, 7, 21 Cicero writes "Sunt autem privata nulla natura, sed aut vetere occupatione, ut qui in vacua venerunt, aut victoria, ut qui bello potiti sunt, aut lege, pactione, condicione, sorte". See A.F. Utz, *Thomas von Aquin. Recht und Gerechtigkeit. Deutsche Thomasausgabe*, vol. 18bis, pp. 351-400.

no basis in human nature why one person should be serving to others. But it happens that because of the advantages it can have, the weaker person becomes subservient to others[20] (**article 3**). It is noteworthy that Thomas mentions first the advantage of this situation for the weaker person.

One can only practice the virtue of justice in relation to someone else, if this person is capable of acting[21]. One's own child, even if it should be treated as a human being according to the principles of justice and has a claim on certain things its parents must provide it with, does not belong to the juridical sphere in the strict sense of the term, the relationship is different[22]. In an analogous way the rights and duties of married persons have a particular character, since here the otherness (*alietas*) required for a strictly juridical relationship is only present in a limited way[23] (**article 4**). There is a difference between a relationship based on law and one based of the friendship between two persons, in which this otherness (*alietas*) disappears since one identifies oneself with the other person.

Justice (Q. 58)

After having established what right, as the object of justice, is we can now pass to a consideration of this cardinal virtue itself. In twelve articles Aquinas discusses the nature and the effects of justice and determines its place among the virtues. In the *Digesta*[24] justice is described as the steady and permanent will to give everyone what is due to him. This definition expresses well the properties of the virtue of justice, provided one does not understand "the will to give everyone what is due" as an incidental act but as a habitual disposition. The object of justice is indicated by "to everyone what is due to him", its virtuous character by "the steady and permanent will". The definition agrees with what Aristotle teaches[25]. In order to possess this virtue one must not act with justice only occasionally, but be disposed to do so always and everywhere (**article 1**).

---

[20] Art. 3 ad 2. Aquinas states explicitly that this situation of subservience must be to the advantage of the weaker persons ("inquantum utile est huic quod regatur a sapientiori et illi quod ab hoc iuvetur"). The advantage to the weaker person has precedence over the use the higher placed person derives from it.

[21] "Necesse est quod alietas ista quam requirit iustitia, sit diversorum agere potentium".

[22] "Et ideo patris ad filium non est comparatio sicut ad simpliciter alterum et propter hoc non est ibi simpliciter iustum, sed quoddam iustum, scilicet paternum". Some see in this position a relic of Aristotelian thought and of the Roman view of the rights of the *pater familias*. See Utz, o.c., 298.

[23] Animals are not legal persons, although man, from his side, has the obligation to treat them reasonably.

[24] I, 1, tit, 1, leg 10.

[25] *E.N.* V, c. 5, 1134^{a}1.

Justice, we saw, concerns actions directed to other persons. This means that there are always persons involved, capable of independent behaviour[26]. In a metaphorical sense, however, one can speak of a just treatment of one's own body or of one's faculties. In fact, actions which concern ourselves and our emotions are ordered by the other moral virtues, while justice takes into account what these actions mean for others (**article 2**).

Justice is a virtue since it submits our actions related to others to the rule of reason and makes them morally good. If one treats other persons in a just way one does not do them any special favor, but gives them only what is due to them. One can, however, also speak of an advantage of justice for ourselves in so far as it makes us do spontaneously and willingly what we have to do (**article 3**). Justice does not aim at making us think correctly, but at making us act in a just way in that we give others what is due to them. The appetitive faculties are the proximate principles of our actions. Therefore, justice has its seat in them. But only reason and not the senses see what is due to someone and therefore the will (as corresponding to reason) is the seat of justice (**article 4**).

In so far as the other person to whom justice addresses itself is a member of civil society the due which one gives him is at the same time for the benefit of the community. This is also the case with the acts of the other virtues by which one makes oneself a better person. To strengthen his argument Thomas writes that man is a member of society and that whatever a member has can be ordered to the good of the whole. This does not mean that the human person is in everything subordinated to the state, but that the good he does is advantageous to the society. This doctrine excludes any extreme subjectivism. In this sense justice is a general virtue[27].

In so far as the government of a state but also the citizens give the community (and hence its members) its due the justice they act with is *iustitia legalis*, i.e. justice as directed to the society, also called social justice (**article 5**). Since the common good is the object of this virtue, social justice has its own specific character. But according to its effects it is a general virtue inasmuch as it directs the acts of the other virtues to the common good. It is to be found more in those who govern than in the individual members of a society (**article 6**).

Besides this social justice there is kind of justice by which one gives individual persons their due, something that social justice does only indirectly. The two virtues are different since their objects are different, sc. the common good and the good of individual persons (**article 7**). This particular justice has an object of its own, sc. what is due to the individual persons[28] (**article 8**). Because the proper object of justice is actions directed to what lies outside us, justice does

---

[26] Cf. the adagium "actiones sunt suppositorum".

[27] Compare II-II 122, 1: "Utrum praecepta decalogi sint praecepta iustitiae".

[28] If one objects that not only justice but also certain passions are directed to other persons, the answer is that not so much the passions themselves as their effects are directed to others.

not address our passions. However, just actions are accompanied by a certain pleasure (**article 9**). According to Aristotle a virtuous action lies in the mean between excess and deficiency. While this is true as regards the virtues regulating our emotions it seems difficult to indicate what the mean might be for justice. In a sense one can nevertheless speak of a mean in so far as what is due lies in the middle between "more" (one gives more than due out of generosity) and too little, when one acts unjustly (**article 10**).

Having arrived at the end of this question St. Thomas repeats the definition of justice: justice is the virtue which makes us give everyone his due. Some other virtues such as pity and generosity accompany justice, which is a main virtue Justice is primarily concerned with the exchange of goods between persons, but it also extends to whatever can be the subject of a right. To cause damage to someone, for instance, is an unjust act (**article 11**). Justice is of a higher rank than the other moral virtues. This is evident in so far as social justice is concerned, but particular justice shares this position, since it has its seat in the will (which is a higher faculty than the sensory appetite), is directed to the good of others and extends to all. Our way of speaking confirms the conclusion. A person is called a good man because he is a just person[29] (**article 12**).

Injustice (Q. 59)

A primary vice opposed to legal justice is the neglect of the common good. Another vice violates the relations between persons by taking advantage of others and seeking one's own profit without being willing to share the burdens (**article 1**). This second way of acting makes one take for oneself more than is right. If this is done without the intention of being unjust then such an act need not result from the vice of injustice but would rather be unjust only *per accidens*. A vice is present when one commits an injustice willingly and with a certain pleasure, i.e. performs acts in opposition to that to which our nature is inclined (**article 2**).

One may perform unjust acts willingly but one suffers them unwillingly. It may happen that one causes damage to others without wanting to do so. But when one inflicts damage on oneself one is not unjust in the strict sense of the term. However, in so far as one is a member of society one wrongs the community when causing serious harm to oneself (e.g. by committing suicide) (**article 3**). In a final article Thomas determines the degree of malice of various sins against justice. To commit an injustice means to cause damage to a person, and so it is opposed to benevolence[30]. It is a serious evil, unless when it concerns small matters which the other person considers insignificant (**article 4**).

---

[29] Cicero, *De officiis*, I, c.7: "In iustitia virtutis splendor est maxima, ex qua boni viri nominantur".

[30] From the Christian and human point of view (which is that of St. Thomas) being unjust to others is against love (*caritas*).

The administration of justice (Q. 60)

As was announced in the preface to this treatise the last question to be discussed in the general introduction is that of the administration of justice. In concrete cases a judge determines what is just. In order to be able to do so the judge must possess the virtue of justice. That is why Aristotle writes that people have recourse to a judge as a sort of living justice[31]. His verdict and sentence are an act of reason[32], the virtue of justice inclining him to reach a just judgment. The virtue of prudence assists the judge in his task. Since the acts of the other virtues refer to ourselves and not to others, we do not go to a judge when there are difficulties in these fields, but at best to wise and virtuous persons to ask them some advice (**article 1**). To be just a verdict must satisfy three conditions. It must proceed from the virtue of justice, be a statement of the competent authority and observe the rules of prudence. If a judge commits himself similar offences as those for which he condemns others then he shows by his conduct that he deserves to be condemned also (**article 2**).

People are sometimes under suspicion of having committed an offence or a crime. We become suspicious about a person, because of our own wickedness which makes us attribute bad actions to others. A suspicion may arise from the fact that we find someone unattractive or even have an active aversion against him. However, suspicions may also rest on objective indications. One is unjust, though, if one suspects someone else or condemns him on minimal indications only (**article 3**). Without a compelling reason (*sine causa cogente*) one may not suspect others, but must interpret possible signs of malice for the better (*in meliorem partem interpretare*). It is preferable to be mistaken a few times than to be unfair by suspecting others unjustly[33]. When we emit an opinion about things this is different. Whether we appraise the value of a house correctly or not, does not make a difference to the house, but only to ourselves. When we have only a faint suspicion concerning certain persons, we must choose the interpretation which is most favorable to them[34] (**article 4**).

The judge must determine what is just in a particular case. What is "right" depends on the nature of things (the natural right) or the rules which are accepted in a community (positive law). Both are formulated by the law. The judge must adhere to what has been decided by law. It is possible that in some cases one cannot judge according to the letter of the law, but must determine

---

[31] *E.N. V, c. 4, 1132ᵃ20:* ... δίκαιον ἔμψυχον.

[32] The Latin term *iudicium* is also used - as in English - to denote any judgment of the intellect.

[33] The *in dubio pro reo*, since time immemorial a principle in English justice, has been widened in its application by the treaty of Rome (1950) to the assumption of innocence (art. 6, 2).

[34] "... in meliorem partem interpretando quod dubium est".

what is equitable[35]. In this case one assumes that the legislator would have issued a different law, if he had known the circumstances now prevailing (**article 5**). The one who administers justice interprets the law in a particular sense by applying it to particular cases. But making and interpreting the law is reserved to the competent authorities governing the citizens of a country. One cannot usurp this competence nor can one force the citizens to obey laws that have not been issued by the legitimate authority (**article 6**).

On how the virtue of justice is divided into its parts (Q. 61)

As became clear in the study of prudence, Aquinas distinguishes between parts of a virtue which are, in a sense, species within a genus, parts which belong to a virtue (the integral parts) and finally the auxiliary virtues (*partes potentiales*). These various parts of justice are treated successively in questions 61 to 80. With regard to the first division of justice, sc. into its species, Aquinas distinguishes between distributive justice and commutative justice (concerned with exchanges between people and barter). The first is the virtue persons in government must possess, by which they give each member of the community proportionally what is due to him. Commutative justice, on the other hand, regulates the relations between the citizens as they exchange goods and services among themselves. - Surprisingly at this point Thomas does not mention legal justice discussed in q. 58, articles 5 & 6, which directs the activities of the citizens to the common good. The reason probably is that commutative justice will make people take the right attitude toward the common good and that all just acts are directed to the common goal of the community (**article 1**). In commutative justice the mean which the virtue must attain is the precise quantity of what is due. In distributive justice this is different because the government must take into account the rank of persons and their place in the state (**article 2**).

Both virtues may concern the same things, e.g. objects for use or of value. But the acts differ. In commutative justice these acts involve an exchange between two persons, in distributive justice things are assigned (**article 3**). After a description of the different ways in which justice can be done and injustice committed in inter-human relationships, Aquinas mentions the concept of reciprocity (*contrapassum*): one who has inflicted damage on somebody else must himself suffer the same damage. This reciprocity also applies to what the citizens must do for the community and what they receive from it. But in certain cases the

---

[35] *E.N.* V, c. 14, 1137ᵃ31 ff. Aristotle calls τὸ ἐπιεικές an ἐπανόρθωμα νομίμου δικαίου, that is a correcting of what according to the letter of the law is just. If the law is not clear, the verdict of the judge must remain within the framework of the law. If certain texts are at variance with one another, his verdict must be in agreement with the principles of the law.

equality is not mathematical. Wealthy persons should contribute more to the community than they receive from it (**article 4**).

Restitution (Q. 62)

At the beginning of Q. 61 Aquinas observes that restitution comes in under commutative justice. For this reason it is studied immediately after the general discussion of the species of justice. The term *restitutio* means that something belonging to a person is given back to him. One may be keeping a thing which belongs to someone else, with or without the latter's consent. In the strict sense of the word restitution consists in the same thing being returned to its owner, but often it will be something else of equal value (**article 1**). To return what one has taken away illegitimately from someone is a serious obligation in justice. When restitution in the strict sense of the term is not possible, as in the case of defamation, something of approximately equal value should be given back (**article 2**).

One can also cause damage to others by violence and threats. It is up to the judge to impose a punishment in such cases. If one is condemned, one must both make restitution and undergo the imposed punishment (**article 3**). When because of our fault the other party loses what it possessed, full restitution is required. But if the other party's claim concerns the loss of expected revenue because of our interference then the restitution of the amount the man supposedly lost is not necessary, since expected revenue is not the same as real income (**article 4**). Restitution is to be made to the person who suffered the prejudice or to his heirs, unless restitution at this moment is prejudicial to the owner[36]. If with the owner's consent one uses for a while some of his belongings or property, compensation should be given if these have been lost. If one receives a deposit of money or other goods and this gets lost without one's fault then no restitution is required. The text suggests that if someone buys in good faith a stolen object, he must return it to the owner (**articles 5 & 6**).

Those who help steal the possessions of others are also obliged to return what is stolen. Even the person who does not impede a theft, while he could easily do so, has a duty to compensate the owner. This applies also to governments when their policies lead to an increase in thefts. Finally, one must restore stolen goods as soon as possible, since when one keeps them against the will of the owner the latter is deprived of their use and cannot enjoy the benefits of them (**articles 7 & 8**).

---

[36] Aquinas writes that whatever one possesses must be to the advantage of the owner (omnia enim quae possidentur sub ratione utilis cadunt). For this reason one may postpone the restitution of a weapon to its owner who at this moment might harm himself or others with it..

OFFENCES AGAINST JUSTICE

Favoritism and respect of persons (Q. 63)

The first question of this treatise examines offences against distributive justice while questions 64 to 78 deal with those against commutative justice. A frequently occurring form of partiality is the attribution of offices and positions to certain persons, not because of their suitability and competence, but for other reasons such as family relations, graft or expected benefits. Such favoritism is against commutative justice since it does not respect the required proportion between the aptitude of candidates and the requirements for a post. This does not concern, of course, totally free gifts and assignments, because everyone can give away one's own according to one's discretion. When deciding whether someone is suitable for a certain position then this person's qualities, competence and moral life must be taken into account. In elections one chose the candidate considered best suited for this service to the public good (**articles 1 & 2**).

Homage is paid and honors are awarded on account of a person's excellence. But one can also be honored because of the work of others: leaders of a country may receive such honors as due to their country. In this field awards are not always deserved, while others who deserve special homage, go unnoticed. Even the judiciary sometimes favors certain persons unjustly (**articles 3 & 4**).

Homicide (Q. 64)

Dealing with offences against commutative justice Aquinas first discusses those that the injured person suffers in a unsought exchange and then those occurring in willed exchanges (QQ. 77-78). Homicide, which belongs to the first category, is the most serious violation of rights possible. By way of introduction the question is raised as to whether one may kill living beings. The answer is that one may use things for the purpose for which they are made or have been destined. In nature beings of a lower rank are for the sake of what is higher, so that one can say that in general plants are for animals to use and plants as well as animals for man. The fact that plants and animals are irrational means that they are subordinated to rational beings. If man needs them as food then he is allowed to kill them (**article 1**).

Is it right to apply capital punishment in certain cases? Basing himself on the doctrine that man as part of society must serve this society Aquinas concludes that when some individuals threaten or greatly damage the community they can be removed by execution. Criminals act against the order of reason and in this way lose their human dignity. But the amount of punishment must correspond to the seriousness of the crime[37], protect society and have a deterrent effect. The judiciary, taking into account factors which reduce the responsibility of the criminal, can apply other penalties instead of capital punishment, such as banishment or a life sentence[38]. In our contemporary society, marked by individualism, some activists and religious leaders argue that the right to life of the criminal is inviolable. The society, which they consider as being based upon a contract between the citizens, can protect itself sufficiently against serious criminals by imprisoning them for long periods. In countries where capital punishment is applied the execution of criminals falls under the competence of the authorities having the care of society and the security of citizens (**articles 2 & 3**).

Another question nowadays debated question is whether suicide is permitted, that is a positive or negative action by which one willingly ends one's own life. Aquinas mentions some of the reasons which may bring people to commit suicide (dishonor, the avoidance of pain and illness, sadness and depression). By committing suicide people seek to free themselves from what they experience as an unbearable situation. Suicide is opposed to our natural inclination to keep ourselves alive as well as against the love we must have for ourselves. Moreover, man is part of a society which he harms by killing himself. Finally, Thomas writes, our life is a gift of God which we cannot freely dispose of[39]. These arguments apply also to recourse to active euthanasia in those cases in which it might or could be considered that human life had lost its meaning due to perhaps serious health problems, great pain or deterioration of one's faculties (**article 5**).

A further question is whether one can ever kill innocent persons. While the execution of a criminal may be desirable or even necessary for the protection and promotion of the well-being of society, the life of innocent persons is, on the other hand, of the greatest importance for the community[40] (**article 6**). This conclusion is applicable also to the killing of unborn babies or of a deformed foetus. **Articles 7 & 8** deal with self-defense and involuntary manslaughter. The morality of our acts is determined by what one seeks to accomplish and not by what is not intended[41]. An act of self-defense can have a dual effect, viz. preservation of one's own life and the death of the aggressor. One must aim only at the first effect. Obviously in defending oneself one must not use greater force than necessary. The case of soldiers and the police is different, since the government has assigned to them the task of protecting the country and maintaining public order and security. In this respect they can directly intend to fight aggressors and

---

[37] Cf. the axiom of Roman law: poena debet commensurari delicto.

[38] Cf. I-II 87, 3 ad 1.

[39] Ad 3: "Transitus de hac vita ad aliam feliciorem non subiacet libero arbitrio hominis, sed potestati divinae".

[40] "Vita autem iustorum est conservativa et promotiva boni communis quia ipsi sunt principalior pars multitudinis".

[41] See above I-II 72, 1.

criminals. Finally there is the case when one unwillingly causes the death of someone else. A person can be held responsible if he effects this by immoral acts, e.g. by selling hard drugs or by a lack of caution as when causing a fatal accident by drunken driving.

Theft and robbery (Q. 66)

After discussing offences against the life of other persons Thomas now considers sins concerning other people's property. A first question is whether we can ever have property rights over certain things. **Article 1** considers man by himself and argues that without any doubt man has the right to use for himself things in his environment. In this sense possessing certain things is natural for all men. However, this right is not unlimited, since natural things are at the disposal of all and the society is prior to its individual members[42]. The **second article** goes one step further. Man has the power to acquire things for himself and to use them. Thus people will work harder and be more careful in their use of things when these belong only to themselves than they would if they were public property. In such a case people would avoid efforts to look after them, leaving that to others. Moreover, due to the fact that people own private property an ordered situation arises and so we avoid the chaos of everyone trying to grab whatever is within reach or what suits him or her best. Finally, a situation of private ownership promotes peace between people. Dissension and quarreling are frequent when possessions are held in common. With regard to the use of things, however, one should not consider the right to property as exclusive. In emergencies one should be willing to share with others. One can acquire property rights to things by one's own work, but for Thomas this right is less absolute than such authors as John Locke believe it to be, who place themselves in the tradition of "possessive individualism"[43]. Nevertheless the right to private property is a natural right, as long as it does not prevent certain goods from being accessible to all[44].

Theft is contrary to justice inasmuch as it consists in taking away what belongs to others. Theft concerns things and not the person of the owner. Theft is characterized by the secrecy with which it is carried out. Receiving stolen goods also falls under theft (**article 3**). Theft, both in itself and in acts of violent robbery, deprives the owner of his goods (**article 4**). From a moral point of view theft is a serious offence which causes damage to another person. Moreover by frequent thefts civil peace is jeopardized[45] (**article 5 & 6**). The right to private

---

[42] I.e. in the order of final causes.

[43] See C.B. MacPherson, *The Political Theory of Possessive Individualism*, Oxford 1962.

[44] Cf. a. 7: "Res quas aliqui superabundanter habent, ex naturali iure debentur pauperum sustentationi".

[45] "Si passim homines sibi invicem furarentur, periret humana societas".

property does not do away with the fact that natural things serve for keeping everyone alive and allowing them to reach a certain well-being. But how one respects this and looks after the destitute is left to the discretion of the property owners. A single person can never alleviate the misery of all the poor, even with his entire fortune[46]. If someone is starving and thus in urgent need, he may take someone else's belongings to nourish himself in so far as necessary (**article 7**). The public authorities can in some cases use force to repossess or requisition property illegally acquired (**article 8**).

Injustice in court procedures and jurisdiction (QQ. 67 - 71)

Q. 67 concerns the competence and the conduct of judges. The verdict of a judge is like a law for concrete cases and, therefore, must have a coercive power. The judge must have jurisdiction over the persons to be judged and be competent in the question under dispute (**article 1**). In investigating a case he must let himself be guided by the law and by what he learns during the process more than by what he knows as a private person[47] (**article 2**). The judge who, in the words of Aristotle[48], is the interpreter of justice can only pronounce a sentence if an accusation has been made (**article 3**). Since a judge does not administer justice in his own name but on behalf of the public authorities he cannot acquit the accused if in doing so the rights of the prosecution and the interests of the state are violated. The supreme authority in a state can remit a punishment if this can be done without harming the common good (**article 4**).

Dealing with unjust accusations Aquinas distinguishes between denunciation and accusation (**Q. 68**). The first should lead to reprimands or criticisms meant to make the person who has been denounced change his conduct. When a crime has been committed which endangers society[49] one is obliged to lodge a complaint or an accusation, provided one has sufficient evidence. If a crime is not important or one does not have sufficient evidence then filing a complaint or accusation is not necessary, for no one is obliged to undertake something which he cannot bring to an end in the required way (**article 1**). For the sake of greater accuracy and certainty the acts of a process must be put in writing. Thomas adds that in the course of a process the declarations witnesses initially made may dif-

---

[46] Thomas weakens Augustine's words who says that what people have in abundance belongs to the poor.
[47] "If there is a doubt he must examine the accusations critically, but "si eas non possit de iure repellere debet... eas in iudicando sequi".
[48] *E.N.*, V, c. 4, 1132ᵃ20.
[49] "Si crimen fuerit tale quod vergat in detrimentum reipublics, tenetur homo ad accusationem... "

fer from what they will say later[50] (**article 2**). An accusation must serve the common good. Besides false accusations one can also commit an offence by using crafty means to prevent the punishment of the culprit. A judge must disprove false accusations which are based on wrong information or motivations (**article 3**). A false accusation which might have got the accused person condemned, must be punished in proportion to the punishment which was going to be imposed on the innocent person[51] (**article 4**).

Q. 69 deals with what the accused can or must do. Is he allowed to tell a lie by denying that he committed the offence of which he is justly accused? The judge has the right to ascertain the truth in such cases. Therefore, the accused is obliged to speak the truth conformably to the law's intention. But if the judge goes beyond what the law (*ordo iuris*) allows him to ask then the accused need not answer or may answer evasively, although he may not tell lies (**article 1**). The accused may defend himself by concealing what he is not bound to disclose. However, it is not lawful to deceive (**article 2**). If for good reasons the accused person thinks that a judge was too strict in sentencing him or arrived at a wrong verdict then he can appeal to a higher court. If he does this to postpone his punishment then he acts unjustly, since he renders the task of the tribunal more difficult and impedes the other party from obtaining satisfaction (**article 3**). One who is condemned to death can oppose this punishment only when he has been falsely condemned. Thomas has tyrannical governments in mind here. Opposing oneself to them is the same as fighting off robbers[52] (**article 4**).

Q. 70 examines the duty of witnesses. Aquinas first determines when one must testify. If in questions belonging to law and order (*secundum ordinem iuris*) the competent authorities demand that one testify then one must obey. This does not apply to things which are hidden (*in occultis*) and not known publicly. If one is requested to testify by an authority to which one is not legally subject then one only has to do so if in this way one can shield an innocent person from harm or punishment. In things relative to a condemnation one only need testify when obliged to do so according to the juridical order in force (**article 1**). In the field of human actions absolute certitude cannot be reached and a strong probability is sufficient, i.e. one which in most cases sees the facts of the case correctly but can sometimes be mistaken. This probability is reached when several witnesses are heard. If witnesses of the same social rank and in equal

---

[50]"Multi eadem verba audientes, si interrogentur, non referrent ea similiter, etiam post modicum tempus".

[51]"Unde iustum est ut ille, qui per accusationem aliquem in periculum gravis poenæ inducit, ipse etiam similem poenam patiatur"

[52]"Et ideo, sicut licet resistere latronibus, ita licet resistere in talibus casibus malis principibus".

number contradict each other then the judge must decide in favor of the accused[53]. If witnesses differ among themselves then the judge must try to find out whom to believe (**article 2**). Thomas discusses next what invalidates or nullifies the testimony of some witnesses, e.g. of criminals and mentally disturbed people (**article 3**). A false testimony is a serious offence since one lies and violates the oath one has sworn that one will testify truthfully. In giving testimony what is doubtful must be presented as such. However, anyone who is unintentionally mistaken because of a failing memory or for some similar reason has no guilt (**article 4**).

The final question of this treatise (**Q. 71**) discusses the task of lawyers. In the thirteenth century the task of lawyers was not so well organized according to standards set by the profession as it is today, and well-known, reputable citizens could act as defense counsels in court. In medieval Christian society the question arose whether lawyers and physicians must always be at the disposal of those who need their help. St. Thomas answers that one cannot help all the poor[54], but must care for those with whom one is more closely related because of circumstances of time and place, in particular when the indigent cannot expect support from elsewhere (**article 1**). Whoever lacks sufficient knowledge or does not hear well cannot undertake the defence of persons accused. Certain other tasks or a poor reputation can also be an impediment to the exercise of the function of a lawyer, except in emergencies (**article 3**). To collaborate in an immoral undertaking is sinful. A lawyer counsels his client but acts wrongly if knowingly he defends an unjust cause. If successful in such a case then he is obliged to give restitution to the opposite party for the damage it suffers because of his plea. One may admire his competence and ability, but he uses his talents for something bad[55]. In a patently unjust cause Thomas considers legal aid, which aims at getting the defendant acquitted, forbidden. But if a lawyer defends a cause, not knowing it is unjust then he is not guilty[56] (**article 3**). A lawyer may ask compensation for the assistance he gives. The same applies to a medical doctor. But in determining the amount of this compensation he must moderate himself and take into account the financial capacity of his client, the nature of the case and the amount of work he did, as well as local custom. To demand an excessive fee is against justice. Judges, because of their neutral position between the parties

---

[53] "Quia facilior debet esse iudex ad absolvendum quam ad condemnandum".

[54] "Nullus enim sufficit omnibus indigentibus misericordiae opus impendere".

[55] Art. 3, ad 1: "Quamvis enim laudabilis videatur quantum ad peritiam artis, tamen peccat quantum ad iniustitiam voluntatis, quia abutitur arte ad malum". But in a just cause he may hide material that could be damaging to his client.

[56] A physician, in contrast, may continue his efforts in favor of a sick person whose situation is hopeless, since he does not cause harm to anyone.

must be paid out of public revenue. Witnesses may ask compensation for their expenses, time or work (**article 4**).

Injustice caused by the spoken word (QQ. 72 - 76)

Contumely, in the strict sense of the term, means that one publicly humiliates or damages the honor of a person (**Q. 72**). This is usually done by words but can also be done in other ways. Considered as sounds words do not cause damage, unless one speaks very loud, but as signs expressing things they can do so, in particular by making known what is contrary to a person's honor (**article 1**). When judging contumely and offensive words we must take into account the inner disposition of the offending person. As an offence, contumely or destroying another's honour can be as bad as theft. People attach at least as much value to their honor as to their possessions. But a few unfriendly words are not contumely (**article 2**). The virtues of patience and forbearance help us to bear offences, but on certain occasions we must refute contumely, sc. in order to restrain the brutality of others, so that they do not go on with their attacks, and, in the second place, in order to avoid that the work we do for others suffers because of false accusations (**article 3**). Anger easily leads to contumely, for it makes one want to revenge oneself. Pride is an occasion for abuse, sc. when one considers oneself better than others (**article 4**).

Contumely and offensive speech are uttered in the presence of the offended person, but slander and speaking ill of others is done in their absence (Q. 73). Thomas compares contumely and slander with robbery and theft. The first is done openly, the second in secret. Anyone who speaks evil of someone in secret damages his reputation (*fama*), in particular when he does so in the presence of several people[57]. Anyone who speaks badly of others aims at giving them a bad reputation (**article 1**). However, personal reputation is one of the most important of temporal goods. If it has been damaged, one is impeded from doing much good one could otherwise have done. Intending to destroy someone else's reputation is a serious sin. But it may happen that one says something against a person's reputation for other reasons, and in such cases it can be without guilt. If one has damaged the reputation of others then one is obliged to make restitution (**article 2**). Such crimes as homicide and adultery, which affect people's bodily existence, are worse than slander, which concerns only external things. But on the same scale slander is worse than theft. One must, however, take into consideration that words are easily spoken and one does not always have the intention of harming the other person (**article 3**). Out of fear of what others will say by-

---

[57] Thomas distinguishes between honor and one's good name (*fama*). The latter term denotes the reputation a person has in the place where he is living while honor signifies the dignity one has and ascribes to oneself.

standers sometimes do not refute those who slander someone. In this way they may themselves incur some guilt (**article 4**).

QQ. 74 - 76 discuss ear whispering, which seeks to set a person against someone else, and cursing people. Since friends occupy the highest place among external goods and one needs friends, such scandalmongering is a serious offence. To determine the immorality of pouring ridicule on someone, we must take into account the intention of the speaker. Does he really want to belittle others and treat them as negligible or is he joking and speaking about defects of little or no importance?

Fraud in buying and selling. Interest on loans and usury (QQ. 77 - 78)

With regard to commerce and doing business, fixing the prices of products and services and charging interest on loans have always raised important questions. Aquinas had no knowledge of the economic system in force today, but he draws attention to a number of fundamental truths which deserve to be considered. A first question is (**Q. 77**) whether it is licit to sell things at a higher price than they are worth. The principle is simple: to cheat, in so far as one requests a higher price than the value of a product, is utterly reprehensible. Aquinas explains his answer as follows: if we leave aside deceit, we can speak in two ways of buying and selling. a) The practice of buying and selling has been introduced because of the advantage it has for both parties. Now, what has been instituted for both may not favor one party more than the other, so that in a transaction the value and the counter-value must be equal. The value of articles for people's use is stated in their price expressed in money. When the price exceeds the value, or *vice versa*, there is no equality. To sell something for too high a price, or to buy it too cheaply is unjust. b) One can also speak of selling and buying in so far as something more useful for one person or its loss more disadvantageous to another, due to extraneous circumstances, e.g. when the buyer urgently needs something, while the vendor will suffer a serious inconvenience when he no longer has that thing. In such a case the price not only depends on the objective value, but also upon the inconvenience the vendor suffers. For this reason he may sell the object in question for a higher price. But if the one who sells will hardly miss the object in question while the buyer will derive considerable benefit from it then it should not be sold for a higher price, even if it is equitable that the buyer of his own accord makes a proportionate payment. Since the law cannot prohibit everything that is unjust, but limits itself to what undermines the society, unfair practices in buying and selling are often not punished, unless deceit and swindle are involved (**article 1**).

There is deceit when the product sold is not the one that the parties negotiated about, secondly, when the agreed quantity is not delivered or, thirdly, when the product shows defects. In such cases the vendor, even if the defects have escaped his attention, must pay compensation (**article 2**). If the vendor does not make known a product's hidden defects and does not lower the price accordingly then he acts unjustly. Defects which may become dangerous for the buyer, must be made known[58], but if compensation for other minor defects has been deducted from the original price then they need not be brought to the buyer's knowledge (**article 3**). May one sell things for a higher price than one has paid for them? Referring to Aristotle[59], Aquinas notes that business can be conducted in a twofold way, sc. a) by barter or *in natura* with regard to things needed for daily life. Thomas wants to preserve these things from speculation (as governments sometimes fix the price of products of primary necessities in order to protect low income groups), b) secondly, as business in the sense of buying and selling things not needed for daily life, money changing, etc. What is meant is buying something in order to sell it at a higher price. Aristotle rejects this second form of doing business, since it does not have a decent purpose. Cicero, for his part, writes that a businessman only makes money by lying[60]. But Aquinas notes that even if making a profit as such is not a decent goal, it is not positively bad, but rather something indifferent. It may be directed to a good goal, such as the subsistence of one's family or looking after others. One can become entitled to sell something for a higher price by such things as improvements of the merchandise, market trends[61], risks incurred during transportation of the merchandise, etc. (**article 4**). It is not difficult to apply these principles to contemporary trading.

Q. 78 discusses the immorality of usury and the question whether one may charge interest for lending money. The term usury some kind of despicable practice, but here it has a broader meaning and signifies also what is now called interest on loans or investments. In **the first article** Aquinas, following Aristotle, presents some fundamental considerations regarding lending to others[62]. With regard to certain things one places at the disposition of others, using these things means consuming them, as is the case with comestibles. In other cases property rights and use remain separate, for instance, when one rents a house. Money was invented in order to facilitate the exchange of goods. The natural and most proper use of money is to spend it in order to acquire things. One cannot separate money from its use. For this reason it is illicit to demand a compensation for lending it just as one does not pay extra when buying wine for "using it" later on. If one does, one demands a compensation which has no basis in re-

---

[58] "Dare alicui occasionem periculi vel damni semper est illicitum".
[59] *Politics*, I, c.3, 1257ª9.
[60] *De officiis* I,42, 140.
[61] Aquinas speaks of "secundum diversitatem loci et temporis".
[62] *E.N.* V, c. 5, 1133ª29 and *Politica* I, c. 3. 1257ª6.

ality[63]. But it is licit to request a bonus for the service one renders by lending. One can also ask a compensation for the disadvantage one suffers when one can no longer dispose oneself of one's property. Such a compensation is not a payment for the use of this sum of money. In case one lends money to others to start a business, one has the right to claim part of the profit. One remains the owner of the money and can ask a compensation for the risk one took (**article 2**). The situation described by Aquinas is what often happens in our economic system, e.g. with savings accounts, bank loans and shares in companies. What the first article of this question rejects concerns the lending of money against interest when one would have kept this money in an unproductive way[64].

For things the use of which the use is consuming them no extra rent is due in addition to the price one agreed upon. However if the owner suffers some damage by putting goods at the disposition of others, his loss must be compensated. If one requested a piece of land as interest for a loan, then the person who lent the money is obliged to return the yield of the land to the owner (**article 3**). It is not illicit to borrow money from someone who wrongly requests interest, if one really needs it. One should not make others sin, but one may use the wrong attitude of others to reach an honest goal (**article 4**).

The parts of justice (Q. 79)

As Aquinas does in his treatment of prudence, he now raises the question whether in acting according to the virtue of justice we must distinguish between various acts. The answer is that justice consists primarily in giving the others what is their due. In commutative justice the others are one's fellow men, in distributive justice they are the society to which both government and the citizens must give its due. "Giving to the other what is due to him" is the center of justice. Parallel to this, the will must positively avoid what harms the other (**article 1**). If one causes damage to others then one commits a transgression, as one also does when one omits what one is obliged to do for them. However, no one is obliged to do the impossible, a principle which has its application in cases of restitution, where one must always do what one can[65]. Generally speaking, acting directly against justice is a more serious offence than omitting to perform what one is obliged to do (**articles 2, 3 & 4**).

---

[63] D 5: "Exigit pretium eius quod non est".

[64] For a more detailed discussion of the licitness of interest on loans see A.F. Utz, *op. cit.*, p. 432 ff.; *La Somme théologique des jeunes. La justice*, 3, p. 338 and the literature mentioned.

[65] In art. 3 ad 2 Thomas refers to the rule that positive commandments are not always obligatory ('non obligant ad semper sed ad tempus') while negative commandments oblige always.

Virtues which are subordinate to justice and the opposed vices (QQ. 80 - 120)

As prudence has subordinate virtues such as *eubulia, synesis* and *gnome*, there are also virtues which are connected with justice as agreeing with it in one respect while differing in another. All virtues whose acts are directed to other persons belong to justice, even if they differ from it in so far as a) they fall short of it in bringing about the required equality, or b) there is no question of a legal obligation. The virtues which concern our relation to God and to our parents, sc. religion and piety, belong to the first group, for we can never return to God or our parents in equal measure what we have received from them. With regard to the virtues of the second group Thomas distinguishes between legal and moral obligations. Legal obligations come in under the virtue of justice in the strict sense of the term. As regards moral obligations, one can distinguish degrees in such obligations. Certain acts are required in order to be just, while others contribute to it without however being really necessary. Thomas has in mind kindness, generosity, friendliness. As regards the first group he distinguishes between moral obligations we have to others, such as that of truthfulness, and a kind of obligation to ourselves to have our dignity respected when people are unjust to us, sc. that we claim our rights. In his discussion of these virtues Aquinas uses material from Aristotle, Macrobius, Cicero, Isidore and others.

The virtue of religion and the opposite vices (QQ. 81 - 100)

The discussion of the virtue of religion, its effects and what is opposed to it covers a considerable part of the pages devoted to the discussion of justice. We limit ourselves to the main points.

Q. 81 discusses the virtue of religion (*religio*) which orders our relations with God who is our origin and the goal to which we must direct our actions[66]. Good acts are virtuous acts. To render God the homage due to him is a good and noble act and, therefore, religion which makes us do so is a virtue. Religion is a particular virtue since it makes us honor God as the cause of the world which he governs. (**articles 1 - 3**).

Since God surpasses by far all created beings, special homage is due to him, and so religion is a particular virtue. But this virtue does not suffice for reaching God as he is in himself[67]. God is not the material object of acts of religion, but their end[68] (**article 4 & 5**). Since religion makes us approach God more than do the other virtues it is of a higher value. Man must lift up his mind to God with

---

[66] The account Aquinas gives presupposes the conclusions reached in metaphysics about God and creation.

[67] This is the work of the theological virtues, faith, hope and love.

[68] Art. 5: "Deus non comparatur ad virtutem religionis sicut materia vel obiectum sed sicut finis".

the help of sensible things[69] and for that reason the virtue of religion makes us perform, not only internal but also external acts. In order to turn to God one must free one's mind from what is at a lower level and rest in him in unshakable firmness. The term "holy" (*sanctus*) signifies this, Thomas says (**articles 6 - 8**).

In the following questions Aquinas studies the acts of religion. In **Q. 82** he mentions the will to place ourselves without hesitation in the service of God. This attitude will put its stamp on our entire life. Meditating on our dependence on God and on God's being makes us devout. When we reflect on God's goodness, we are filled with joy, although our own shortcomings and insufficiency may be a cause of sadness (**articles 1 - 4**).

Q. 83, which comprises 17 articles, is devoted to prayer. Prayer is an act of reason, since reason understands that for certain things one needs the help of others. Aquinas stresses that prayer is not intended to change God's plan but to obtain what God has decided to give us because of our prayers (**articles 1 & 2**). After devoutness prayer is the most important act of religion. Next St. Thomas discusses what we should ask from God in prayer. Prayer is proper to beings endowed with reason, who acknowledge someone else who stands above them to whom they can address themselves with their requests. Finally he mentions some properties of prayer: it must be attentive, at least as regards the intention one has when one begins to pray. It must last as long as is necessary to bring one into the right mood. Finally one can distinguish prayer of petition and prayer of thanksgiving.

Another internal act of religion is adoration (**Q. 84**), whereas offering a sacrifice demands both internal and external acts. Aquinas explains the general religious custom of mankind of offering sacrifices to the divinity by pointing out that people's natural reason moves them, in accordance with a natural inclination, to show in their own way their submission to the One above them, i.e. they use sensible signs and symbols to express their inner disposition. This means that bringing sacrifices is one of man's natural rights and duties (**Q. 85, article 1**). This inner disposition and willingness to offer sacrifices is obligatory upon all, but not everyone is bound to all forms of external sacrifices (**articles 3 & 4**).

QQ. 86 & 87 explain why one should both offer gifts and contribute to the support of ministers of religion. **QQ. 88 - 91** study such acts of religion as taking vows or swearing oaths, invoking the name of God to confirm one's statements and using God's name to praise God. Sins against the virtue of religion are examined in **QQ. 92 - 100**. One sins against this virtue by doing too much or too little. If a person expresses his religion in a manner and at a moment which are inconvenient, he indulges in the vice of superstition and exaggerated religiousness (**QQ. 92 - 93**). To render to creatures the homage due to God is to

---

[69] This is a central thesis of the metaphysics of Aquinas: our natural knowledge of God is exclusively acquired from what our senses let us know about the world.

commit an act of idolatry which is a form of superstition. Special homage is due only to God (**Q. 94, articles 1 & 2**). Misplaced expressions of religiousness result from ignorance (**article 3**). What brings people to commit idolatry are their attachment to sensible things, ignorance about God and the fact that they attribute too much value to some creatures (**article 4**).

Divination is another practice contrary to authentic religion, sc. if one tries to predict the future in a wrong way[70] (**Q. 95**). Thomas mentions different forms of divination and the means often used to this effect (**articles 3 & 4**). One of them is astrology, which in the Middle Ages was practiced by many. Are the celestial bodies the causes of certain events on earth? A direct influence on the human intellect and will must be excluded, but Thomas believes that the celestial bodies can possibly provoke certain reactions in the human body. A good number of people usually follow their bodily inclinations and this explains why certain predictions may come true (**article 5**). Who resorts to natural causes to determine what the future may bring does nothing illegitimate (**article 6**). But presages of coming events are in no way their causes (**article 7**). In **Q. 96** recourse to divination and the use of charms are rejected.

QQ. 97 - 100 examine actions proceeding from a lack of religion. A first one, mentioned in **Q. 97**, is tempting God, understood as testing God's knowledge, power and will. One tempts God when, in order to find out if God can do something, one requests something from Him (**article 1**), a way of acting which shows a lack of both knowledge of and respect for God (**article 2**) and is which contrary to the virtue of religion (**article 3**).. - **Q. 98** deals with perjury. The purpose of taking an oath is to confirm our words. To tell a falsehood under oath is directly opposed to this purpose (**article 1**). One involves God in a lie and so in reality one despises Him (**articles 2 & 3**). If in ordinary intercourse with people one requests that the other part confirms his words under oath then one shows a lack of trust. Public authorities, however, can demand that people confirm what they say under oath (**article 4**). Any form of disrespect for sacred matters or sacred persons is considered a sacrilege (**Q. 99, article 1**). Since behaving in this way has a deformity of its own, it is a special sin[71]: something sacred is desecrated and a lack of respect for God is shown (**article 2**). The nature of a sacrilege depends on the consecrated person or sacred object or ceremony one treats thus without respect (**article 3**). Even to objects and persons belonging to a cult which is not that of our own religion we must show respect since these are sacred to others. Finally, in **Q. 100**, the buying and selling of sacred offices (simony) is discussed.

---

[70] Art. 1: "Quando sibi indebito modo usurpat prænuntiationem futurorum eventuum".

[71] Art. 2: "Ubicumque invenitur specialis ratio deformitatis, ibi necesse est quod sit speciale peccatum".

*The virtue of piety, respect for persons of a higher rank
and paying one's due to them (QQ. 101-103)*

On the preceding pages our duties with regard to God were considered. In the next three questions our obligations towards our parents and persons placed in authority are dealt with. Behind the treatment here lies a view of human society and its organization which differs from the contemporary, more democratic order of family and society life. **Q. 101** concerns piety which determines our relation to our parents and relatives as well as to our country. Since, after God, these are our greatest benefactors (**article 1**) we must respect and help our parents when, because of illness or poverty, they need our support (**article 2**). Since our duties with regard to our parents and our country have a particular character among analogous obligations a special virtue, sc. piety, is needed to fulfil these duties[72] (**article 3**). With regard to a possible conflict between what religiosity asks from us and what piety demands Aquinas notes that no virtue stands in conflict with another, but that virtuous acts are subject to limits and have a certain measure. If one goes beyond these, they turn into a vice. Even if the obligations resulting from the virtue of religion have a certain priority, they may not prejudice one's duties with regard to one's parents (**article 4**).

Persons in leading positions deserve to be treated with respect, an attitude resulting from a virtue which Aquinas calls *observantia* (**Q. 102**). The reason is that these persons share the task of our parents who are the origin of our existence, education and way of life and are also the cause of whatever belongs to the perfection of human life[73]. For an analogous reason persons in authority, teachers and military commanders are entitled to respect (**article 1**), which consists in the acknowledgment of their dignity and a willingness to follow their guidance (**article 2**). Honouring those who work for the well-being of the country is an act of piety, but if one does so because of their particular qualities, honoring them results from respect. Piety toward one's own parents and relatives has precedence over piety with regard to public authorities (**article 3**).

St. Thomas finally mentions homage (*dulia*) (**Q. 103**). Human beings show their respect for others by external signs. These marks of honor make that the honored person will be generally respected. A good name results from such homage[74] (**article 1**). Even if the persons honored are generally speaking not better than others, homage is due to them because of some good quality they

---

[72] Thomas points out the difference between justice as directed to society and piety. Justice aims at the common good, the second at one's country inasmuch as one owes, in a sense, one's existence and culture to it.

[73] Art. 1: "... pater est principium et generationis et educationis et disciplinæ et omnium quæ ad perfectionem humanæ vitæ pertinent".

[74] "Quia ex hoc quod testificamur de bonitate alicuius, clarescit eius bonitas in notitia plurimorum".

have (**article 2**). Especially those who are in a subordinate position or in the service of others should pay homage to their superiors (**article 3**).

Obedience, gratitude and contrary vices (QQ. 104 - 108)

As there is leadership in nature, so also in human life. People should follow the directions given by their leaders as a requirement of the order established by the natural law. Yet rational man does not obey merely by a natural inclination but by free choice. Obedience can be virtuous if it is freely chosen (**article 1**). To follow up and carry out the commands of one's superiors is a particular form of homage and a virtue of its own, the object of which is the command or order a superior gives us (**article 2**). By obeying one submits one's own will to someone else, a difficult but meritorious act (**article 3**). The next article speaks of obedience to God. Concerning the question whether one should always obey one's superiors, Thomas writes that obedience bears upon external acts. He sees two exceptions to our duty to obey, sc. when an order contradicts a higher obligation or when a superior gives an order outside his field of competence. Moreover, such matters as taking care of oneself and contracting a marriage do not fall under what superiors can command us to do. Finally, Aquinas reminds us that all men are equal by nature[75] (**article 5**). The Christian faith does not do away with the natural order[76]. Therefore, Christians must obey civil authorities in so far as justice demands. Illegitimate authority and unjust commands have no claim on our obedience, unless for secondary reasons, such as in order to avoid civil strife (**article 6**).

The refusal to obey the orders of persons in authority is an expression of disobedience (**Q. 105**) and an offence against the moral order. This vice may originate from pride which makes us not want to follow orders. It is understood that those in authority must not deluge their subordinates with so many precepts that they cannot possibly observe all of them (**article 1**). Disobedience becomes the more serious the higher the authority which issued the orders and the more outspoken its will to oblige us (**article 2**).

Religion, piety and the virtue of respect are accompanied by gratitude towards God, our parents, teachers and those in authority. There is also a particular form of gratitude towards persons who have helped us in special ways. In such cases there is no duty in strict justice, but one of what is fitting (*"ex solo debito honestatis"*) (**Q. 106**). The greater the benefits bestowed on us, the greater the gratitude demanded from us (**article 1 & 2**). Basing himself on the axiom of metaphysics that every effect returns to its cause[77], Thomas writes that natural

---

[75] "Quia omnes homines natura sunt pares".
[76] "Per fidem Christi non tollitur ordo iustitiæ sed magis firmatur".
[77] The explanation is that every agent directs what he effects to the end he seeks to attain.

reason demands that one who receives some help or a present from someone else show gratitude to his benefactor. In general, gratitude is shown by expressing one's appreciation. In certain cases gratitude urges us to help a benefactor who now finds himself in difficulties (**article 3**). Our attitude must be such that as soon as we receive a gift or help, we want to show our gratitude. But as for expressing it, it is sometimes better to wait for a more convenient occasion for our benefactor. If it is some help which we received or a gift given us out of sincere friendship or benevolence then in expressing our gratitude we must also take into account the feelings of our friend and benefactor. Thomas even believes that true gratitude will urge us to return something of greater value to our benefactor than what we received from him (**articles 4, 5 & 6**).

Being grateful is the act of a virtue. If it is impossible to show our gratitude we are excused, provided we have the lasting will to be grateful. However, we are ungrateful if we forget what others did for us (**Q. 107, article 1**). One can act also against gratitude by being grateful in an exaggerated way which is not becoming, but in most cases the vice of ingratitude consists in doing too little, e.g. by not acknowledging the help or the gift one received, by not thanking for it or by refusing to do anything in return. Ingratitude can be a lesser or more serious offense. If someone continues to refuse to acknowledge the gifts and help he received, he does not deserve to be given more (**articles 2, 3 & 4**).

Q. 108 deals with a particular attitude towards others, sc. *vindicatio*, which consists in punishing others to revenge oneself. Revengefulness, i.e. the attitude of one who is totally fixed on the evil someone did or does to him and sees nothing else, is wrong since one sets one's mind on the wrongdoing of someone else. That a person did something against us is no good reason for causing harm to him[78]. If, however, there is hope that by punishing him one can bring him around to a better attitude or protect others, revenge can be a virtue. If a whole group has acted wrongly, one may sometimes punish the leaders in order to deter the others from repeating what they did. Vindication can, therefore, be an act of a special virtue. This is also manifest because all natural inclinations are accompanied by virtues[79]. There is a natural inclination to defend ourselves against offences and damage inflicted on us and to inflict punishment, not so much in order to injure as to remove what is harmful. Vindication is good in so far as it contributes to curb bad behavior (**articles 1 & 2**). A punishment is a kind of equalizing: one who in injuring others did his own will must now undergo some punishment against his will. Furthermore, punishment can contribute to making people better by letting them realize the evil they did and by deterring them from committing further offences. Respectable people are sometimes afflicted by

---

[78] In his answer St. Thomas quotes the maxim of the Gospel not to render evil for evil.

[79] Art. 2: "Ad quamlibet inclinationem naturalem determinatam ordinatur aliqua specialis virtus".

life's trials without any fault on their side. This happens in order to make them spiritually better persons. On the other hand, nobody is harmed in spiritual things without his own fault (**article 3**).

Truthfulness, lying, hypocrisy, boasting and irony (QQ. 109 - 113)

It is right to tell the truth and so truthfulness is a virtue (**Q. 109**). When telling the truth, excesses may occur when one says things which are true, but at the wrong moment or tells them to people who should not know about them. There is a deficiency, on the other hand, when one hides what one is supposed to communicate. What one says must agree with reality. The love of truth is a special virtue, since it has its own object, sc. words and deeds as signs of what is expressed by them (**articles 1 & 2**). Truthfulness is one of the virtues assisting justice, sc. it is ordered to others and brings about a certain equality between words and gestures on the one hand and what is signified by them on the other. A meaningful cohabitation of people is not possible when they cannot trust each other[80]. Truthfulness differs from justice in so far as what is due to others under trustfulness is not a legal obligation but rests on virtue[81] (**Article 3**).

The first vice opposed to truthfulness according to Aquinas, is mendacity (**Q. 110**). What is typical of mendacity is the will to be untruthful. Mendacious people often want to mislead the person to whom they speak. When one believes oneself to be lying but is actually telling the truth then one is nevertheless untruthful. When lying a) one can exaggerate or understate in telling something (irony), or b) one can be more or less guilty in deceiving someone else. Sometimes the one who lies wants positively to harm others, but one can also tell an untruth jokingly and one can ly in order to avoid difficulties or harm, and, according to a classification of St. Augustine, c) lying is distinguished according to the goals one pursues, e.g. lies against God (in order to cause harm to the Christian faith), against one's fellow men or sometimes with the intention of helping someone else with our lies. Furthermore there are lies told because of the pleasure lying gives, while other lies proceed from the vice of mendacity. There are also lies one tells when in trouble and lies told jokingly. The greater the good one seeks to reach by lying, the smaller the offence (**articles 1 & 2**).

Because of their very nature our words express our thoughts. It is wrong (*indebitum*) when someone expresses something different by his words from what he thinks, because it is a disturbance of right order. It is illicit to do something wrong in order to obtain a good. So one may not tell lies even to save others from danger. The degree of malice of lies depends on the extent to which they

---

[80] "Non autem possunt homines ad invicem convivere nisi sibi invicem crederent tanquam sibi invicem veritatem manifestantibus".

[81] "Non enim hæc virtus attendit debitum legale, quod attendit iustitia, sed potius debitum morale, inquantum scilicet ex honestate unus homo alteri debet veritatis manifestationem".

are opposed to the love of others and inflict damage. Lying about things of little importance is less serious (**articles 3 & 4**).

Q. 111 discusses hypocrisy and dissimulation. It belongs to truthfulness that one presents oneself as one is. This applies to our words, but also to what we do. Hypocrisy consists in presenting oneself in words and actions differently from how one is, e.g. by pretending that one is a good and reliable person. Hypocrisy is contrary to truthfulness (**articles 1, 2 & 3**).

A person is boasting when he presents himself as better than he really is. Boasting is opposed to truth by excess. It may proceed from pride but also from vanity. If by praising oneself one injures others or if such boasting proceeds from pride, then it can even be a serious sin (**Q. 112**). To scoff at oneself (called *ironia*, understood in this particular sense) consists in presenting oneself as less good than one really is or in denying some of one's good qualities. Boasting out of ambition will often be a more serious offense than this "irony" (**Q. 113**).

Friendliness, flattery, quarrelsomeness (QQ. 114 - 116)

People must live together with others in a becoming way, both in what they say and in what they do. To do so a special virtue is required, sc. friendliness. Friendliness does not go so far as friendship, but leads to a friendly attitude toward others. In particular a wise person will be friendly with regard to others, even if sometimes he must be strict and severe[82]. This kindness belongs to the virtue of justice since it concerns our relation with others. Obviously there is no question here of a legal obligation, but of what it is better to do (**Q. 114, articles 1 & 2**).

Flattering people is wrong because it is contrary by excess to the virtue of kindness. By unduly complimenting others or gratifying their possible vanity one exaggerates by an excess of kindness. If we praise someone then we should do so in the proper way and in the right situation. If one praises in another what is positively bad or if one wants to inflict damage on the other by one's flattery then one sins against love (**Q. 115, articles 1 & 2**).

Quarrelsomeness makes one contradict others. This may happen through a lack of unanimity, but also out of aversion for a certain person. This vice is contrary to friendliness, which makes intercourse with others pleasurable. Often quarrelsomeness is a greater evil than flattering (**Q. 116, articles 1 & 2**).

---

[82]Witnesses who had personally known St. Thomas declared that his face always had a kind expression.

Liberality, greed and dissipation (QQ. 117 - 119)

Liberality is a virtue which makes us help others. One uses one's possessions not just for oneself but also for the good of others. However, it would be wrong to give away so much that nothing is left for one's own needs. The virtue of liberality lies not so much in the amount of money given as in the intention of the spender, which constitutes the act of this virtue. The sum of money involved is the external object (**Q. 117, articles 1 & 2**). When one is supporting huge undertakings, e.g. a hospital, a museum, a college, we speak of patronage (*magnificentia*). It belongs also to this virtue that one administers one's possessions wisely so that one can use them for good ends. To do so one needs prudence (**article 3**). Liberality is not a subdivision of justice, since one has no obligation to give away part of what one has, but there is a certain correspondence between liberality and justice, inasmuch as the acts of both virtues are directed to others and concern material goods (**article 4 - 6**). Greed makes us lose the right measure in acquiring and possessing external goods, because it makes us want more than is becoming. Practically, this implies that less will be left for others. Moreover greed makes us concentrate on material things and for that reason it is a vice (**Q. 119, articles 1, 2 & 3**).

Greed can make people act against justice. It is also contrary to liberality. Greed is active in people's innermost, since a greedy person finds pleasure in having money. In so far as greed leads people to commit other offences, it is called one of the capital sins. The following sins may proceed from it: hardness of heart and harshness which exclude all pity, unrest since one is all the time preoccupied with acquiring more money, violence, ruses and deceit as means by which one attempts to increase one's wealth (**articles 4 – 8**). Finally, in connection with managing one's money, Aquinas mentions the vice of dissipation(**Q. 119**), which is the opposite of greed. A spendthrift is not attached to the possession of money and is not concerned to administer his possessions in a prudent way. One can throw away one's money to buy more carnal gratification but other motives may also active here. Dissipation is wrong because it does not keep the mean typical of virtues. But considered by itself dissipation is a lesser vice than greed, for by throwing one's money around one does something useful for others. Moreover, a cure is easier, for when nothing is left to spend dissipation will stop (**articles 1, 2 & 3**).

Epikeia (Q. 120)

Closing his treatise on justice St. Thomas deals with *epikeia*. Since human acts concern concrete situations which may vary endlessly it is not possible to establish rules and laws which cover all cases. It can be against justice or against the general interest to apply a law in a particular case. In such a situation one must ascertain what justice and the common good demand. To this effect we apply *epikeia*, a sort of equitableness. It does not mean that one condemns the law, but judges that a particular case does not fall under it. *Epikeia* is part of justice.

APPENDIX

There are some themes which are not treated by Aquinas under the virtue of justice but elsewhere in his works, although they are related to it. Since they are of great importance we summarize what he writes about them..

War

Thomas inserts the theme of war in his treatise on (supernatural) love. War is the counterpart to love. Everybody desires to safely possess his belongings and to live in peace, i.e. to reach his goals without being hindered (**II-II, q. 29, article 2**). Quarrels, disputes, fighting and revolt are contrary to peace, as is war, which is a matter of fighting against an army from outside the borders of one's country and which involves a considerable number of soldiery (**Q. 42, article 1**). In **Q. 40** Aquinas begins his analysis with an obvious question. Is war a breach of peace? Is waging a war always morally wrong? Confronted with the horrors of war and the damage which the warring parties and also many innocent people suffer one is tempted to consider war an abominable evil.

Aquinas mentions three conditions which can make a war just. a) In the first place public authority must declare the state of war and enlist men for military service. For it is the task of the government to protect its subjects and their belongings. This is done at a local level by the police, if necessary with the use of weapons, but for the country as a whole by the military. b) In the second place a just and sufficient cause is required. Thomas does not explain this point further, but it is obvious that one must compare the evils a war will cause with the injustice committed against one's country. Many have pointed out that the disastrous consequences of a nuclear war exclude ever being justified in waging one, although the possession of nuclear weapons in order to maintain a balance of power, is not self-evidently condemnable. c) In the third place the parties at war must have the right attitude and intention, sc. to obtain a good or to avoid an evil. It may happen, Thomas says, that a war, started on just grounds and declared by the competent authority, becomes unjust because of the wrong intentions of the parties who want to destroy each other or to revenge themselves in a cruel way or want to overpower the opposite party out of an implacable hatred.

Aquinas refers to a Gospel text which tells us not to oppose those who use violence against us, but he observes that even if, for our part, we must always be prepared not to offer resistance or to defend ourselves in some cases we must sometimes act differently for the sake of the common good or also that of those who commit an injustice against us or with whom we are involved in a fight[83]. The goal of a military campaign must always be to reach a situation of lasting peace.

With regard to the question of what means one can use to wage a war, Thomas is very succinct. One may use ruses or dissimulate one's own plans but deceit by lies is immoral (**article 3**). Acts of war on religious holidays are not forbidden. If a medical doctor is allowed to help his patients on such days then one may also defend the well-being and security of a country, so that untold misery for the citizens is avoided (**article 4**). From the above it appears that waging a war can be a moral act, accompanied by such virtues as prudence, justice and fortitude.

Concerning fights between private persons we read that one may defend oneself in the right measure against those who injustly attack one. However, one should avoid harboring grudges and feelings of hatred (**Q. 41, article 1**). A revolt by which a group of citizens rebels against the government or against other groups of the population causes great damage to the common good and is for that reason morally wrong. Aquinas supposes here apparently that a just order reigns in the country concerned. If the country is governed by a tyrant then there no longer is any question of a just order. A tyrant does not work for the well-being of the general public but for his own advantage. Opposition against such a government is not a revolt. However, such opposition must not lead to greater evils than those the country is now suffering from. Thomas concludes his exposé with the remark that a tyrant is himself a rebel because he creates dissensions among the citizens in order to secure his regime (**Q. 42, article 1& 2**).

Labour

Labor lies at the intersection of our physical and spiritual life. It is an expression of our human existence. In order to work one must have an idea and a plan one is going to carry out. The material with which one works often offers some resistance. While the medieval tradition considered work as aiming at the accomplishment of things[84] and so of man himself, Hegel made work part of the human mind, an expression of the movement of the spirit which returns to itself. The negation, which constitutes man's being, now passes into the object which is changed and so "annihilated". This is not so for the work a slave carries out

---

[83] He probably means that an enemy out on conquest deserves to be punished so as to show that, in the long run, unjust actions are not advantageous. Connected to this point is the question whether a state or an alliance of states has the duty to oppose an enormous injustice, such as genocide, committed in a different country, although there is no immediate danger for oneself.

[84] Cf. II-II 32, 5: "Actiones quae transeunt in exteriorem materiam magis sunt actiones et perfectiones materiae transmutatae".

but applies only to the person who works for his own goals[85]. Marxism underlined the degrading character of labor in industrialized societies, but correctly described labor as the way in which man enters into relation with nature and as serving also to promote solidarity among workmen. On account of the fact that the workmen are not themselves owners of the workshop or factory Marx thinks that they are alienated from themselves by the work they do for the owners.

Aristotle thought that manual labor was an obstacle to intellectual work, a widespread idea in the ancient world. Cicero writes that persons of good standing must take no interest in the manner in which laborers provide what is needed for life[86]. As Christianity spread, however, a more positive view of human labor began to impose itself. St. John Chrysostom, St. Augustine and other Christian authors stressed the value of manual labor for spiritual discipline and pointed also to its use for society. So manual labor was no longer considered an inferior activity. St. Benedict prescribed several hours of daily manual labour for his monks so that they could themselves provide what they needed without bothering others and had a surplus to feed those in need.

Thomas considers spiritual work of greater value than manual labour. The latter finds its terminus in what lies outside man. When we work we actualize certain possibilities hidden in material things. In order to do so one must have sufficient force, possess some experience and overcome the resistance of the material one is working with[87]. Work is carried out by a human person endowed with reason and will and therefore it is a human action (*actus humanus*). An animal does not work because it does not think. The necessity to work appears from the fact that one must provide for oneself and others what is necessary for life. To do so man disposes of the members of his body and he has in fact been placed in an environment in which he can work[88]. An individual person by himself can hardly provide all the things he needs so that collaboration with others and team work are necessary. Labour, therefore, has an eminently social character. This does not mean that everyone must engage in manual labour or that all should do the same type of work.

Even if spiritual work and the contemplative life as such are of higher value[89] yet manual labour is necessary because of our daily needs[90]. Moreover manual

---

[85] See B. Lakebrink, *Studien zur Metaphysik Hegels*, Freiburg i.Br. 1969, 120 ff.; 128.

[86] *De officiis* I, 42: "Illiberales et sordidi quaestus mercenariorum omnium quorum opera, non quorum artes emuntur".

[87] *Q. d. de potentia*, q. 3, a. 4 ad 16.

[88] *Quodl. VII*, q. 7 ad 17: "Sicut autem ex ipsa dispositione corporis patet, homo naturalem ordinem habet ad opus manuale propter quod dicitur *Job* 5, 7: "Homo ad laborem nascitur sicut avis ad volandum"."

[89] Cf. *Summa contra gentiles* II, c. 1: "(operatio intellectus praecedit). Quod quidem in rebus humanis manifeste apparet: consideratio enim et voluntas artificis est et ratio aedificatio-

labour may help calm down the passions and so promote the virtuous life[91]. Elsewhere Thomas writes that the purpose of manual labour is threefold, sc. to avoid idleness, to acquire control over one's own body and to provide the necessities of life[92]. From this third purpose of labour it follows that it is prescribed by the natural law[93]. Manual labour is our human way of dealing with nature and the world.

With regard to the different species of manual labour Aquinas notes that as our hands are instruments of the intellect. So every sort of work that is done with some tools in view of providing what one needs for one's livelihood is to be considered manual labor[94]. Between contemplation on the one hand and manual labor on the other there is what is called intellectual work, of which the value is higher the greater the share of reason in it[95]. Those who serve the common good by intellectual work are entitled to be supported by the other citizens[96],

Aquinas points out that there must be a correct relationship between the usefulness of the work done and its remuneration. The salary must be equivalent to the quantity of work one has done, its quality and value, the degree of laboriousness and the situation of the worker[97]. Justice must determine the amount of compensation to be given. Since work demands effort and one is easily distracted, one needs such virtues as fortitude and temperance. The goal of work is rest. Definitive rest will only be found in afterlife. But at set times work must be interrupted since we need rest for both body and mind[98]. In fact we cannot use our spiritual faculties without becoming tired, due to our mind's necessary dependence on the body, which does become tired[99].

---

nis".Cf. L. Elders, "Vida activa y vida contemplativa según santo Tomás de Aquino", in *El Cristiano en el mundo*, Pamplona 2003, 429 - 442.

[90] II-II 182, 1: "Secundum quid tamen et in casu est magis eligenda vita activa propter necessitatem praesentis vitae".

[91] II-II 182, 3.

[92] II-II 187, 3: "Secundo ordinatur ad otium tollendum ex quo multa mala oriuntur".

[93] *Quodl. VII*, q. 7, a. 1: "Nec solum in praecepto legis positivae, sed etiam iuris naturalis. Illa enim sunt de iure naturali ad quae homo ex suis naturalibus inclinatur"

[94] II-II 187, 3: "... per opus manuum omnis operatio intelligitur de qua aliquis victum licite potest lucrari".

[95] Cf. Sylvester M. Killeen, *The Philosophy of Labor according to St. Thomas Aquinas*, Washington D.C. 1939.

[96] II-II 187, 4.

[97] Cf. *In I Cor.* 3, lesson 2: "Ubi potior est labor, ibi sit potior merces".

[98] II-II 168, 2.

[99] II-II 142, 1 ad 2.

CHAPTER XII

FORTITUDE

As was argued in Chapters VI and VII virtues are stable dispositions which make that our acts are morally right. The good of man consists in the agreement of his actions with the right insight of reason. Thanks to the intellectual virtues the mind can do its work in a manner which is perfects it. The virtue of justice helps the will regulate our relations with others. But there are obstacles which may make the will deviate from what reason sees as our good, sc. when one improperly lusts after pleasures. The virtue of temperance helps us to avoid these aberrations. One can also shrink from the difficulties which one encounters when trying to live a virtuous life. Fortitude assists us in overcoming such difficulties.

The virtue of fortitude (Q. 123)

One must not confuse fortitude with certain attitudes which show an external resemblance to virtuous acts, but do not proceed from the insight of the mind and a decision of the will characteristic of authentic virtue. When someone confronts a dangerous situation in a temerarious way without realizing the dangers or caring about them he does not act out of fortitude. This is also the case when out of sheer optimism one is confident of being able to overcome threatening dangers or when one is driven by some passion when confronting dangers or when one hopes to gain financial advantages by a rash temerity[1]. - Obviously Aquinas does not view fortitude as a matter of physical strength. For him, rather, fortitude has an intellectual component presupposing a direction to the right end (**Q. 123, article 1**). The virtue of fortitude is to be distinguished, therefore, from a courageous attitude. Such an attitude is helpful for practising this virtue but it is not yet fortitude, which is a further development of this attitude and enables us to stand firm in the face of great dangers. These dangers are the proper matter to which fortitude addresses itself[2] (**article 2**).

In the following article the object of fortitude is determined more precisely. In the first place fortitude allows us to overcome the fear which makes us recoil from difficult and dangerous tasks and deviate from the right insight of reason. Fortitude moderates or even suppresses fear so that this emotion cannot have a paralyzing effect, i.e. it makes us resist fear in a reasonable way (*moderate*). On the other hand, fortitude also keeps audacity within bounds (**article 3**). This

---

[1] Q. 123, 1 ad 2.
[2] Thomas quotes Cicero's definition, *Rhetorica* II, c. 54: "Fortitudo est considerata periculorum susceptio et laborum perpessio".

means that by fortitude our will holds to a course of action which our reason presents as good, in particular when we must confront the greatest of all evils, death. In times of war fortitude allows us to engage ourselves in defending others even at the risk of our own life. The nursing of the victims of contagious diseases, the defence of the weak and innocent against the powerful, standing up for justice and human rights against criminal organizations and tyrannical regimes also fall under the object of fortitude. From this it appears that standing firm and holding one's own is the principal act of fortitude, more than actively opposing evil. The numerous difficulties and countless obstacles which we encounter in the course of life are the field where fortitude has to carry out its task[3]. We hold on and stand firm, not out of recklessness but by directing ourselves to the right end (**articles 4, 5 & 6**). Despite the surrounding dangers and the effort this standing firm may cost, fortitude can give us inner joy (**article 8**).

When there is an occasion to practise the virtue of fortitude a passion such as anger can be of some use, provided it remains under the control of reason. Anger will be helpful when one has to resist a threatening evil[4]. Since on many occasions in life we must suffer pain, confront dangers and stand firm in the face of opposition, the virtue of fortitude is indispensable. It is even a cardinal virtue (**article 11**). In so far as fortitude makes us direct ourselves to a good which reason presents as right and helps us to make an effort to reach and keep it, fortitude is, after prudence and justice, the most important of the moral virtues (**article 12**). One can distinguish degrees in this virtue according to the nature of the difficulties and dangers which we face when following the right insight of reason. The highest form of fortitude is the willingness to suffer martyrdom in order to bear witness to the truth (**Q. 124**).

The vices opposed to fortitude (QQ. 125 - 127)

Fortitude is weakened or rendered impossible by fear, fearlessness and audacity. Fear is produced when a good we like threatens to get lost. Fear can be right when it makes us flee what reason we tells us to avoid, but it is wrong when it makes us flee from what we should support or suffer. The emotion of fear can remain limited in us to the sensory appetite but may also influence the will and so become the vice of cowardice. If so then the will may act moved by fear, but nevertheless remains free. If in this case the choice of the will is contrary to our obligations, fear is the cause of a sinful act, even if what one does out of fear is not fully voluntary (**Q. 125, articles 1-4**). Fear originates from our love of certain things and persons that we are afraid to lose. Everyone wills his own life

---

[3] As St. Augustine writes in *De civitate Dei* XIX, c.4, the need for fortitude proves that there is evil.

[4] Art. 10: "Assumit iram ad actum aggrediendi".

and whatever is ordered to it. This love, however, should develop in the right way, so that one does not lose from sight what is ordered to one's last end. No one, not even a person who commits suicide, is entirely devoid of this self-love[5]. But it happens that out of dullness, pride or because of a lack of natural love of oneself one does not fear dangers and threats. It is not right either not to care at all about the loss of one's possessions, since these are needed for living a humane and moral life[6] (**Q. 126, article 1**). Fearlessness affects the right measure of emotions which normally should make us anxious, even if we have the virtue of fortitude. A fearless person no longer fears what he should fear (**article 2**). Audacity as rashness is also contrary to fortitude since it makes us lose the sense of the right measure in matters where one should feel some fear. For this reason it is opposed to the virtue of fortitude (**Q. 127, articles 1 & 2**).

The parts of fortitude and its auxiliary virtues (Q. 128)

As was explained in the chapters on prudence and justice, Aquinas distinguishes within the principal virtues parts or general conditions for their practice which he calls the integral parts of a virtue. Secondly, such a virtue is subdivided into species (its *partes subiectivae*) and finally there are assistant virtues, the *partes potentiales*. In the case of fortitude there is no division in species since the matter of this virtue is already particular. But there are some integral parts, which one may consider its principal acts, sc. to stand firm and to attack opponents or enemies (*aggredi*). In order to perform these two main acts some assistant virtues are required. To attack one needs confidence[7], which makes us think that we can succeed. But perseverance is also needed in order not to give up when we are half way in what we are doing. Patience, for its part, helps us not to become afflicted by threatening dangers or difficulties. These virtues can also function on their own, but when associated with fortitude itself they become its auxiliary virtues.

The sources of St. Thomas exposé on fortitude are the *Nicomachean Ethics* and *Rhetoric* of Aristotle, the *De affectibus* of Macrobius and the *Rhetorica* of Cicero. Some of the assistant virtues played an important role in Stoic ethics[8]. The virtues to be discussed on the following pages can be represented schematically as follows:

---

[5] Q. 126, art. 1: "Unde etiam qui seipsos interimunt ex amore carnis suæ hoc faciunt quia volunt a præsentibus angustiis liberari".

[6] Ad 3: "Non autem debent contemni bona temporalia inquantum instrumentaliter nos iuvant ad ea quæ sunt divini amoris et timoris".

[7] Thomas speaks of *magnanimitas*.

[8] See R. Gauthier, *Magnanimité*, Paris 1951.

ASSISTANT VIRTUES FOR STRIKING OUT	OPPOSITE VICES
Self-confidence and magnanimity	By excess: audacity, ambition, vanity
	By deficiency: pusillanimity
Generosity and patronage	By excess: dissipation
	By deficiency: scantiness
ASSISTANT VIRTUES FOR STANDING FIRM	OPPOSITE VICES
Patience	No opposite vice
Perseverance	By excess: obstinateness
	By deficiency: laxity

Magnanimity (Q. 129)

Aristotle devotes much space to the study of this virtue which allows us to distinguish ourselves by noble actions in political society. The magnanimous man knows his own value and desires to be honored. At a first glance this attitude seems at variance with the Christian virtue of humility. The three commentaries on the *Nicomachean Ethics* from the period 1280 to 1310, studied by Gauthier[9], see such an opposition here and argue that magnanimity cannot be a virtue. Siger of Brabant answered that humility is a form of modesty, a virtue mentioned by Aristotle[10], but this does not solve the difficulty since for Aristotle this modesty is the attitude of those who do not deserve great honors. For St. Thomas humility is the virtue which makes us acknowledge our condition as creatures and act in agreement with it. A person can be at the same time magnanimous and humble. In his *Commentary on the Nicomachean Ethics*[11] he interprets the description of the magnanimous man in such a way that it becomes acceptable for Christians. In the *Summa theologiæ* he transposes this virtue to a different level so that it becomes an important element of our moral life. As its name indicates this virtue is a disposition of the mind which enables us to undertake great things. Now, among man's external goods honor is most important, for it is a testimony to his virtue and value. People go to great length to avoid indignity and to be honored. Magnanimity enables one to perform important actions so that one can be honored[12] (**articles 1 & 2**).

Magnanimity is a virtue since it applies the measure, indicated by reason, to an important matter. In his answer to some of the difficulties Thomas mentions as characteristic of the magnanimous person a dignified carriage without undue

---

[9] "Trois commentaires sur *l'Éthique à Nicomaque*", in *AHDLMA* 16 (1947-1948).
[10] Cf. St. Thomas, II-II 161, 4.
[11] *In IV Ethicorum*, lesson 10.
[12] Ad 2: "Ad ea tendit magnanimitas quae sunt magno honore digna".

haste and not speaking with a shrill voice. Magnanimity can go together with humility since one is magnanimous owing to God's gifts, but humble because of one's own faults. Replying to the fifth objection Aquinas explains a somewhat strange and shocking attitude which Aristotle attributes to the magnanimous person, sc. that he does not like to be reminded of the support and gifts he has received from others. When Aristotle calls the magnanimous person cautious and reserved it is because such a person does not meddle with all things placed before him, but only with what is important. In short, in all things the magnanimous person gives precedence to what is noble over what is useful[13] (**article 3**). Since magnanimity leads us to find the right measure in receiving homage it is a virtue with an object of its own (**article 4**), related to fortitude and resoluteness in the midst of dangers. Magnanimity makes us strong, but with respect to easy things such as honor (**article 5**). Confidence of succeeding in an important undertaking is also an effect of magnanimity (**article 6**). The feeling of security which expels despair belongs to magnanimity, while possessions and success in business help us to acquire it (**articles 7 & 8**). One should not underestimate the importance of this virtue in public life. It has a great value for those who have to direct others and who because of their wealth are in a position to accomplish important undertakings.

Vices opposed to magnanimity (QQ 130-133)

A first vice mentioned by Aquinas is self-conceit or presumption by which one believes oneself to be better than one really is. This sort of conceit goes against the natural order since one's actions must be adapted to one's capacity. But this does not mean that one should not attempt to improve one's capacities (**articles 1 & 2**). Secondly, ambition is identified as a vice. Ambition makes us seek honors to which we are not entitled, but also makes us ascribe the good we have or do exclusively to ourselves or, if we should be honored, makes us neglect the opportunity given to be useful to others (**Q. 131**).

Vanity is a further vice opposed to magnanimity. It is not wrong to acknowledge one's own value and to hope that others will also acknowledge it. But when one wants to be honored without having deserved it, or seeks praise from people who cannot judge one's merits or is not prepared to direct the honor bestowed on one to a good end, then we have to do with the vice of vanity. The good end to which one should direct the honor received is that, strengthened by the praise of others, one perseveres in doing what is good and hopes that others will do the same (**Q. 132, article 1**). Desire for honor which we do not deserve

---

[13] D 5: "In omnibus præponit honesta utilia". In art. 6 ad 1 Thomas explains Aristotle's words that the magnanimous person does not need others and their support (*E.N.* IV, c. 3, 1124^{b}17) by adding the words "in the human manner", i.e. he needs the help of God and, as a social being, of his fellow men.

is vanity, opposed to magnanimity (**article 2**). Often vanity is not a serious sin (**article 3**), even if St. Gregory the Great calls it a capital sin. In fact various vices may come from a disorderly desire for honor, such as boasting, pretending to be someone special, hypocrisy, self-conceit, stubbornness, quarrelsomeness etc. (**article 4 & 5**). As a final vice contrary to magnanimity Thomas mentions pusillanimity and gives this explanation. Whatever is opposed to a natural inclination is wrong. While all things are inclined to act in conformity with their natural capacity, pusillanimity prevents people from trying to do what lies within their reach. This attitude is contrary to magnanimity[14] (**Q. 133, articles 1 & 2**).

Supporting great undertakings (magnificentia) and the contrary vices (QQ. 133 - 135)

In the Greek city states the patronage of public works was of great importance, as it is in the United States with regard to the support for schools, museums, philanthropical and religious organizations etc. Thanks to Aristotle this virtuous attitude came to be studied in ethics[15]. In performing this sort of liberality one must be guided by reason. This virtue is not so much directed to spending great sums of money on oneself, e.g. by building a conspicuous palace-style house, as to doing something great for the community[16] (**Q. 134, articles 1 - 4**). If one is too small-minded to do something great, although one has the means for it, one suffers from the vice of extreme thriftiness, which wants to avoid all expenses[17]. This vice is not the same as a lack of liberality, for it makes one refrain from supporting important undertakings (**Q. 135, article 1 & 2**).

Patience, perseverance and contrary vices (QQ. 136 - 138)

Thomas gives a beautiful analysis of what the virtue of patience means. For this effect he could make use of what classical authors and Church Fathers had written on this subject. The virtues one possesses make us continue to seek the good, as determined by reason, amidst conflicting emotions and external challenges. Sadness, pessimism or a tendency to depression make it more difficult to live in conformity with the good as reason presents it. Our human life brings us many reverses and disappointments and so we need a virtue which helps us to maintain the direction which reason sees as good for us and to bear with equa-

---

[14] "Pusillanimus ex animi parvitate se retrahit a magnis".

[15] *E.N.* IV, c.2.

[16] Art. 2 ad 2: "Intendit aliquod magnum... in aliquo opere factibili".

[17] Q. 135, art. 2: "Intendit minus expendere quam dignitas operis requirit".

nimity the difficulties we encounter[18] (**Q. 136, article 1**). Patience helps us to practice the other virtues, since it disarms what discourages us (**article 2**). Aquinas adds that one bears suffering and reversals in view of the end one hopes to reach. To possess the virtue of patience to its full extent one must sustain the difficulties of life on earth in order to reach God (**article 3**). Thus patience is one of the virtues assisting fortitude (**article 4**).

Wherever we encounter a special difficulty in acting towards the end of our life a special virtue is required. To accomplish something difficult over a long period of time demands a special virtue, i.e. is a disposition which enables us to persevere in the good wherever we encounter difficulties (**Q. 137, article 1**). This perseverance is connected with fortitude (**article 2**). While perseverance enables us to practice the virtues over a long period of time and despite various difficulties, constancy or firmness makes that we persevere when we are threatened by difficulties from outside ourselves (**article 3**).

Aquinas finally mentions two vices which are opposed to perseverance, sc. in the first place a certain weakness which makes us give up as soon as difficulties appear. Those who are always out for comfort and pleasure, easily fall victim to this vice (**Q. 138, article 1**). The other vice, stubbornness (*pertinacia*), is at the opposite extreme, where one never gives in and maintains under all circumstances one's preconceived plan (**article 2**).

Having dealt with the virtue of fortitude Aquinas makes an important observation, viz. it is impossible to give many precise indications as to how we our acts might express this virtue, inasmuch as fortitude is to be distinguished from patience and perseverance. Fortitude concerns our behavior when we encounter great difficulties which demand that we act prudently and with circumspection, ourselves determining what we must do[19]. This means that in the exercise of this virtue there is considerable room for one's own liberty and responsibility. Circumstances must always be taken into account[20].

---

[18] Cf. St. Augustine, *De patientia*, c.2 (*PL* 40, 611): "Patientia hominis est qua mala æquo animo toleramus".

[19] II-II 140, 2.

[20] See J. F. Groner, *Deutsche Thomasausgabe*, Bd 21, p. 426. On the virtue of fortitude in general, see J. Pieper, *Die Tapferkeit*, Kösel-verlag.

CHAPTER XIII

TEMPERANCE

Since time immemorial temperance has been considered one of the most important virtues of our moral life as being the fourth of the cardinal virtues. Its function is to help us control emotions and passions which might impede our intellect from reaching a correct judgment. In his preface to the treatise on fortitude Thomas writes that the cardinal virtues enable us to reach the right insight (*rectitudo rationis*) with regard to what we must do. Temperance does so by keeping us, when we are driven by the desire for what is pleasurable, from following a course of action contrary to what reason tells us to do.

The treatise on temperance comprises twenty two questions. The division of the text is the same as that applied in the analysis of the other cardinal virtues. Thus a definition of the nature of temperance is followed by a consideration of the contrary vices (QQ. 141 - 142). Next, temperance is subdivided. Thomas discusses first the virtues which are, in a sense, components of temperance (QQ. 143 - 145). After that he distinguishes different forms of temperance (QQ. 146 - 154) mentioning finally its auxiliary virtues (QQ. 155 - 160). After each virtue or group of virtues the contrary vices are identified and discussed.

Temperance (Q. 141)

A first question is whether temperance is a virtue. In his answer Aquinas places the treatise as a whole in the genral framework of his ethical theory. Temperance does not mean self-vexation nor is it a condemnation of pleasure. The good of man is the goal to be attained, and this is to live according to right reason[1]. The virtues are dispositions by which we are inclined to do what is in agreement with right reason. Temperance, which means "keeping the right measure" inclines us to this also. Therefore, it is a virtue. Implicitly the collaboration of the virtue with reason is intimated.

However, there is a difficulty. By their very nature human beings seeks pleasure and delight. So temperance and self-control seem to go against the grain of our nature and should not be called virtues. In his answer Aquinas recalls that man is a complex being. Certain inclinations of our sensitive nature can make us withdraw from the control of reason, whereas our specific human nature comprises our entire being in so far as it is directed by reason. In this understanding controlling one's desire for pleasure is not at all against human nature. Temperance is always rational, enabling us to determine when it is reasonable to give in

---

[1] The text of Dionysius is quoted again: "bonum hominis est secundum rationem vivere" (*De div. nom.*, c.4).

to a desire for pleasure. On the other hand, renouncing excessive pleasure need not always be an act of temperance. One may also do so out of thriftiness. Some persons have a natural disposition for an imperfect form of the practice of some virtues, but in order to perform perfect acts of a virtue one must possess all the virtues (**article 1**).

Through the whole of our life we must keep the right measure. Temperance has the function of keeping within reasonable limits what attracts most the sensory appetite. It gives us inner rest and opens the mind for higher values (**article 2**). However, the object of temperance must be further determined. The good which the sensory appetite seeks to attain is, as such, not opposed to the order of the intellect, but rather serves it. But when the appetite seeks to reach such a good in an unreasonable way it must be restrained and subjected to a rule. This means that the primary object of temperance are the passions which are concerned with sensible things and also with the sadness which may result when one does not reach or have these goods. By controlling these passions, temperance also exercises a regulating influence on the other emotions (**article 3**).

People seek pleasure in different fields. Which of these are the object of temperance? In order to formulate his answer Thomas compares the proper object of temperance with that of fortitude. As fortitude is concerned mainly with great dangers and serious difficulties, temperance will also concentrate on the greatest pleasures[2]. Pleasure or pleasure is the greater the more closely it accompanies activities intimately connected with human nature, such as eating and drinking in order to stay alive and sexual intercourse as providing for the survival of mankind. The accompanying delight consists in feelings of the sense of touch. Therefore, temperance is in the first place concerned with the pleasure the sense of touch gives us. Inasmuch as the pleasure one experiences in the activities of the other senses is connected with the sensations of the sense of touch, such pleasure is a secondary object of temperance. In fact, the activities of the other senses can also cause pleasure. The eye is caressed by seeing objects which impress it agreeably and this applies also to the ear and the sense of smell, so that here too one can speak of an experience of delight[3]. However, the objects of these senses are not immediately needed for the preservation of one's life. The delight which seeing gives us is for this reason not invasive. Pure spiritual pleasure does not have any important effect on the sensory appetite and is as such conformed to reason. It can only in an indirect way become an obstacle for reason if it keeps us away from other tasks we must carry out (**article 4**). Taste, however, is more intimately connected with the sense of touch than the other senses and so it also falls in under the object of temperance, as is the case with

---

[2] The proper object of a virtue is that to which it is directed in its highest degree.

[3] Aquinas notes that an animal brings these experiences in connection with its primary necessities.

whatever in fragrances, colors and sounds contributes to increase lust when one is eating and drinking or in having sexual intercourse (**article 5**).

In the preceding articles Aquinas mentioned repeatedly the order which reason must impose on our activities and emotions, but he did not yet explain how reason itself finds its orientation in these matters. To attain certain ends nature has attached considerable delight to the activities ordered to these ends. The urgency of these ends is called by Aquinas the *necessitas huius vitae*[4]. This fundamental statement is an approval of man's striving for the delight connected with these essential functions, but within the limits of the principle of finality. This point is further elaborated in the answer to the second and third objections. What is simply necessary for human life can be used without restriction by a person possessing the virtue of temperance. This comprehends also what is needed to live as is becoming to one's rank and the circumstances of the moment. Elaborate meals on feast days come in under this rule. However, we must always avoid what causes damage to our health. What does not can be used in a moderate way, taking into account what accords with one's social position (**article 6**). Temperance has a regulating effect, as have the other virtues. Its task is to give us a certain reserve in performing those natural activities which produce the greatest pleasure. But the desire for pleasure remains always present in man (**article 7**). Since the virtue of temperance concerns the sphere of private activities, it is of lower rank than justice and fortitude which fulfil important functions in respect of society (**article 8**).

The vices contrary to temperance (Q. 142)

By helping us to keep the right measure virtues establish the mean between excess and deficiency thus avoiding vices. Following Aristotle, Aquinas names insensitivity with regard to pleasure as the first vice in the field of temperance. To refuse any kind of pleasure or delight is against our human nature and, therefore, not right. One can, of course, forsake one kind of pleasure for some good purpose. A simple example is refraining from smoking or from eating sweets for medical reasons or using periodical abstinence in a marriage to avoid dangerous complications which a further pregnancy might cause. This is not to deny the significance of delight, but means that one renounces certain of its forms in view of a higher end (**article 1**). The other extreme, sc. excess, is intemperance and insobriety. Aristotle calls intemperance a childish attitude, since one seeks pleasure without listening to what reason tells us[5]. To this one may add that concupiscence gets stronger when one does not resist it. It becomes a sort of habit

---

[4] Literally, "what is necessary for this life".
[5] "Puer autem non attendit ad ordinem rationis", Thomas explains.

which pushes and forces us[6]. If one resists and represses the craving for pleasure it is reduced to reasonable proportions. At the end of this article St. Thomas notes that when limiting oneself to the pleasure connected with certain activities based on what nature demands from us one does not sin unless one wants an excess of pleasure. But where people frequently overstep the mark is in their quest of means devised to titillate and to stimulate, such as the adding of all sorts of spices when preparing meals and methods designed to enhance the mutual attraction of the sexes and increase pleasure in intercourse (**article 2**).

To explain in greater detail the nature of intemperance Aquinas compares it with timidity and cowardice. Intemperance is a more serious vice than the latter. It is more positively willed because timidity and cowardly behavior can be explained by fear which one feels for one's own life[7]. Intemperate people seek pleasure in particular fields, for nobody wants to be intemperate in all respects. Therefore, in order to triumph over one's intemperance one should not busy oneself opposing whatever causes pleasure. In the case of cowardice things are different, since in the individual situations which give occasion to it cowardice is less willed than lust. There is just the general will to save one's life by fleeing from danger (**article 3**). Finally Aquinas raises the question whether, as Aristotle says[8], intemperance is the most reprehensible vice. He agrees with Aristotle inasmuch as intemperance concerns the lust which human beings have in common with animals and is, for this reason, further removed from what makes for human dignity. Moreover, in people who are affected by this vice one sees least of the splendor of reason, which constitutes the beauty of the virtues. In order to comply with one's daily duties one has to use one's reason, while surrendering to the desire for pleasure does not require much reflection. This does not mean, however, that intemperance is the worst behavior possible (**article 4**).

The components, species and auxiliary virtues of temperance (QQ. 143 - 162)

Q. 143 gives a survey of the parts of the virtue of temperance. As with the other cardinal virtues temperance also has three kinds of parts. Thus its integral parts are the stages which an act of temperance goes through or are factors[9] which belong to temperance. In the case of prudence, experience of what happened in the past under similar circumstances, a keen eye for the present situation and prospecting the future are such integral parts. As to temperance these integral

---

[6] Thomas refers to St. Augustine, *Confessiones* VIII, c. 5: "Dum servitur libidini, facta est consuetudo, et dum consuetudini non resistitur, facta est necessitas".

[7] Cf. ad 2: "Amor conservationis vitæ propter quam vitantur pericula mortis, est multo magis connaturalis quam quæcumque delectationes ciborum vel venereorum, quae ad conservationem vitæ ordinantur".

[8] *E.N.* II, c. 10, 1118^{b}2.

[9] Thomas speaks of "conditiones quae necesse est concurrere ad virtutem".

parts are the feeling of shame (which makes us avoid what is unbecoming or is at variance with this virtue and decency) and moral integrity (*honestas*) which make us appreciate the beauty of right measure. In the second place temperance is divided into species, its *partes subiectivae*, according to the division of its object. If keeping the right measure concerns eating and drinking we speak of abstinence and sobriety, if it concerns sexual matters we speak of chastity and modesty. The third division is into the auxiliary virtues (*partes potentiales*), which are concerned with other forms of temperance. Every virtue which in some way regulates our inclination to pleasure and the craving for it can be said to assist temperance. Such virtues are self-control (*continentia*)[10], humility and meekness which have a moderating influence on the passions. They prevent the will from being carried along by unbridled desires and make one avoid offending others by one's presumption or unreasonable self-confidence. Moreover, they also restrain anger and the desire of revenge. These virtues also concern the manner in which one treats one's own body such as caring for one's appearance and resorting to entertainment and physical exercise. They affect the way we relate to what lies outside ourselves which must be regulated and make us feel content with what is essential (*sufficientia*)[11] and avoid what is exaggerated (*simplicitas*).

The components of temperance (QQ. 144 - 145)

The two components of temperance are the feeling of shame and decency (*honestas*). The first (*verecundia*) is not a complete virtue in its own right. It consists in the fear of doing something blameworthy in the eyes of other people. Who has the virtue of temperance, will not be seduced by the shameless conduct of others, but will nevertheless experience a feeling of shame when confronted with it. This feeling may be of help in acquiring temperance (**Q. 144, article 1**). People are ashamed of the evil they have done, especially if others come to know about it. But whoever acts virtuously does not fear being blamed (**article 2**). One is above all ashamed in front of people in one's own environment, especially when they are virtuous, for one is afraid of losing the good opinion they have of one (**article 3**). However, totally criminal or immoral people lose this feeling of shame. Elderly people are generally far removed from shameful behavior and so for them there is no reason to be ashamed and the same applies to the very virtuous (**article 4**).

Conduct is called decent if it is praiseworthy and it is praiseworthy if it is virtuous. For this reason modesty coincides in general with virtuousness. De-

---

[10] Aristotle did not consider self-control a virtue (*E.N.* VII, 1). A person who must as yet make an effort to control himself, does not yet possess the virtue of temperance. According to Aquinas, however, self-control is an imperfect virtue.

[11] Aquinas adds that in this connection Andronicus speaks of *parcitas* (thriftiness).

cency regulates human behavior so as to make it agree with the order of reason and gives it a certain dignity and nobility which are opposed to what is unbecoming and shameless. Temperance makes us reject what is unbecoming or indecent, in particular violent and unbridled passions. What is decent is by its nature agreeable to us, for everyone likes what is adapted to him[12]. Decency is a component of temperance in that it brings us to a fitting behavior (**Q. 145, articles 1 - 4**). In his exposé of temperance and its associated virtues Thomas relies on Aristotle, Cicero and St. Augustine and stresses that decency has a certain spiritual beauty and is a condition or a first beginning of temperance.

Abstinence, sobriety and the opposed vices (QQ. 146 - 150)

As announced in Q. 143 temperance is subdivided according to the ways of keeping the right measure in eating and drinking or of using one's reproductive faculties. As a first form of temperance Aquinas mentions abstinence (with regard to food). Obviously he does not mean total abstinence from food, but our regulating by reason the amount and quality of the food we eat. If a physician prescribes a diet, observing it is not yet a virtue, but when on the basis of one's inner disposition one brings eating food into agreement with the insight of reason, one possess the virtue of abstinence. Reason indicates the right mean between too much and too little. One should be cheerful while observing restrictions (**Q. 146, article 1**). The delight which eating certain types of food can cause, may make a person lose sight of what is reasonable (**article 2**).

Q. 147 discusses fasting, an act of temperance which has a threefold goal: repressing lower desires; liberating the mind for the study of higher things; doing penance for the evil one has done. Right reason does not approve of such fasting as would make one's health suffer damage or of eating so little as to be unable to carry out one's duties (**Q. 147, articles 1 & 2**).

The vice opposed to abstinence is gluttony, which gives us an unreasonable desire for food. To eat much or even too much is not a sin provided one thinks one needs this quantity of food. This comes rather from a lack of experience. One is gluttonous when one exceeds the right measure because one likes certain kinds of food (**Q. 148, article 1**). We need food and it is not always easy to determine the correct quantity for ourselves, which gives us a certain excuse. On the other hand, gluttony can lead to other sins (**article 3**). Thus by excessive eating one hampers the work of reason, rejoices in inanities, begins to speak too much and may use coarse or lewd language, says Aquinas. One's bodily health likewise does not improve (**articles 5 & 6**).

The virtue of sobriety makes us keep the right mean in the use of alcoholic or other stimulating beverages. By drinking too much the use of reason is impaired.

---

[12] Art. 3: "Honestum est naturaliter homini delectabile".

What St. Thomas writes applies even more to drug abuse (**Q. 149, article 1**). Because of the special threat intoxicating drinks constitute for the activity of the intellect and the will, a special virtue, sobriety, is required to make us keep the right measure (**article 2**). This does not mean, however, that the use of alcoholic beverages as such is illicit: for no food or beverage is bad as such[13] Only when one exceeds the right measure, which can differ for different persons, does the consumption of alcoholic beverages become sinful (**article 3**). Aquinas thinks that women and young people are at greater risk of yielding to the pleasure of drinking. The elderly must also be careful not to lose control of their intellectual powers by excessive drinking (**article 4**).

Drunkenness and dipsomania are contrary to sobriety. Drunkenness may result when a beverage one is drinking is much stronger than one thought it was, but usually it is caused by immoderate drinking. In this sense it comes in under gluttony (**Q. 150, article 1**). Drunkenness is sinful when one knew that by continuing to drink one would become intoxicated. To deprive oneself willingly of the use of reason (the faculty which allows us to act virtuously) and to expose oneself to the danger of immoral acts is a serious sin. In particular, continued abuse is immoral, since one then knows better about the consequences (**article 2**). Thomas observes, however, that there are more serious sins than drunkenness, such as acting directly against what reason tells us to do. One is not responsible for what one does while drunk, except when drunkenness is voluntary, as will often be the case (**articles 3 & 4**).

Chastity and the opposite vices (QQ. 151 - 154)

Chastity is a virtue because it curbs unruly passions and, by virtue of a decision of the will, makes us keep the measure according to right reason in the use of our bodily powers. Its object as a particular virtue is the pleasure which accompanies the use of our sexual power (**Q. 151, articles 1 & 2**). As was explained above, chastity differs from abstinence, since its object is different. Thomas draws attention to the fact that desire for sexual pleasure is stronger than that for pleasure in eating and drinking. For this reason, a greater measure of discipline is required in this field. Finally the virtue of modesty is mentioned, which is concerned with external indications of sexual differences and with whatever can provoke sexual desire. Modesty is the more necessary as the sexual organs do not obey the control of reason in the way other members of the body do (**articles 3 & 4**).

Q. 152 deals with virginity. The question whether a celibate life is licit had been raised by some Averroists of the Faculty of the Arts in Paris in St. Thomas'

---

[13] "Nullus cibus vel potus secundum se consideratus est illicitus".

time[14]. They referred to Aristotle who teaches that one who avoids all pleasure is insensitive[15]. Aquinas defends the licitness and goodness of virginity as follows. Human acts are wrong if they abandon the path of right reason. Right reason tells us to use the means to reach a specific end to the extent that the means are conform to this end. Since the good which man seeks to reach is multiple and the spiritual, contemplative life occupies the highest place, a person can renounce what is directed to bodily goods and pleasure, in order to devote himself entirely to what is higher. One may compare this with people who in view of their health renounce the use of certain types of food or drink. St. Thomas argues that not every individual person must care for all needs so that not every human individual has the duty to generate children. Enough people will see to the continued existence of mankind by procreation. This view contains a difficulty insofar as one could say that an orderly and moderate sexual activity contributes to a balanced spiritual life. Aquinas's answer to this objection is that one must see virginity in a theological perspective, which places the sublimity of man's last end, viz. the vision of God, in the foreground and takes into account that in the actual situation of mankind (after the Fall) the desire for sexual pleasure can become an obstacle to an intense spiritual life[16] (**Q. 152, article 2**).

The following four questions discuss unchastity and the related vices. The Latin word for unchastity, *luxuria*, signifies licentiousness in what has to do with people's conduct in respect of sexual activity. Far from condemning man's sexual life Aquinas writes that right reason indicates that one uses things in a manner which agrees with their end, provided this end is good. It is definitely a great good that mankind continues to exist. The use of man's sexual powers is directed to this, so that this use can be absolutely without sin, if it is practiced in the right manner in accordance with what is fitting for human procreation. The great pleasure by which sexual intercourse is accompanied, preserves the virtuous mean, if intercourse takes place according to reason (**Q. 153, articles 1 & 2**).

The more important an activity is, the greater must be our solicitude that the order shown by reason is observed. If in an activity as important as sexual intercourse the order of reason is abandoned such conduct becomes unchaste. The use of man's sexual powers must be such that the purpose it serves is guaranteed (**article**). Unchastity is a capital sin since it is the occasion of a number of other sins, injures our spiritual life, hampers us in following right reason, slackens the will to accomplish our work and can lead to a reckless blindness (**articles 4 &**

---

[14] See article 210 of the 219 articles condemned by bishop Tempier. Cf. R. Hissette, *Enquête sur les 219 articles condamnés à Paris le 7 mars 1277*, Louvain / Paris 1977, p. 299.

[15] *E.N.* II, c. 7, 1104^{a}22.

[16] Cf. the answer to the second objection in Q. 153, art. 2: "Hoc tamen quod concupiscentia et delectatio venereorum non subiacet imperio et moderationi rationis, provenit ex poena primi peccati".

5). Unchastity is found in various forms according to the objects of the actions one performs. The purpose of the sexual powers is frustrated by intercourse performed in unnatural ways or by sexual union outside the stable bond of marriage, since this, for one thing, jeopardizes the education of the children[17]. Next adultery, violation and incest are rejected. Such acts do not respect the rights and dignity of the women involved (**Q. 154, art. 1**).

Fornication is a serious sin. Aquinas argues this point by saying that the good of the child must be guaranteed[18]. In order to care for children and to educate them a stable bond between the parents in a monogamous marriage is required. In particular the presence and role of the father is important. He must protect the child, instruct and assist it while it is growing up. A casual coming together of a man and a woman is against the nature of human beings[19]. Since the good of the community is involved in these matters, the lawgiver makes legally binding rules for marriage. In exceptional cases a father or mother alone must take care of the children, but the law deals with what happens in most cases. Fornication is opposed to the good of the child and is a more serious offence than theft (**articles 2 & 3**).

With regard to the morality of touching, embracing, etc. Thomas writes that as such these are not sinful, in particular where local custom or some good reason makes them desirable. When they are done in order to provoke sexual desires, outside marriage, they become sinful (**article 4**). With regard to losing the seed, if this is a spontaneous natural process, e.g. during one's sleep, it is not sinful. This is different when it has been provoked by images one took pleasure in before going to rest[20] (**article 5**).

Violation of a virgin is a much more serious crime than unchastity, because of the injustice committed and the consequences for this woman. Abduction adds a special degree of malice (**articles 6 & 7**). Sexual intercourse with a woman married to someone else offends against chastity and against the good of children who might be born out of this union. Moreover, adultery violates the fidelity the partners promised to each other. Incest, however, is a special offence against chastity. St. Thomas rests his argument on what classical authors and St.

---

[17] The argument can also be applied to contraception, which frustrates the main purpose of sexual intercourse. In other texts St. Thomas points out that the community of man and wife constitutes the highest degree of friendship (*S.C.G.* III, c. 123: "maxima amicitia"), which means that the union of man and woman is not only directed to procreation but includes also a high degree of benevolence, unity of thought, mutual support, pleasant togetherness, etc. See below Chapter XIV on friendship.

[18] Cf. also *SCG* III, c. 122.

[19] "Et ideo contra naturam hominis est quod utatur vago concubitu, sed oportet quod sit maris ad determinatam feminam, cum qua permaneat, non per modicum tempus sed diu vel etiam per totam vitam"

[20] Cf. *SCG* III, c. 122.

Augustine say who reject sexual intercourse between relatives on account of the respect they must have for each other. It also renders normal contacts between parents and their children much more difficult, increases the desire for pleasure and disturbs normal friendly relations. - In this question Thomas follows the traditional view, not as aware as we now are of the dangerous biological and the extreme psychological consequences of sexual intercourse between close relatives within the family. Finally he mentions the situation of persons who obliged themselves by vow to a chaste life. When they have intercourse with others, they commit the additional sin of sacrilege (**articles 8, 9 & 10**).

The last two articles deal with sins against nature as they were called. A new form of unchaste behavior results consisting in a special deviation from right reason. All sins of unchastity are actions which go against the order of reason, but when they go against the very nature of the sexual act, there is question of acts against nature. This may happen in different ways as by self-gratification, intercourse with animals, homosexual acts, grossly deviant acts of sexual intercourse between men and women. Since these forms of unchastity go against what nature has established, they constitute the most serious offenses against the virtue of chastity (**articles 11 & 12**)[21].

THE AUXILIARY VIRTUES OF TEMPERANCE AND THE OPPOSITE VICE S (QQ. 155 - 162)

Self-control and incontinence (QQ. 155 - 156)

We have already drawn attention to Aristotle's view according to which self-control (ἐγκράτεια) is not a virtue, since the really virtuous man no longer needs to make an effort to control himself. There are persons who show a certain degree of self-control but follow nevertheless their passions[22]. But, differing on this point from Aristotle, Christian authors considered self-control a virtue. So it is not surprising that among the 219 articles condemned by bishop Tempier in 1277, there is a statement which says that continence is not a virtue[23]. However,

---

[21] Some argue against this doctrine that man can freely use his own natural bodily powers, as he does with external nature. As long as no damage is done to others, one has an ample field of freedom. It is also argued that for some people an inclination to homosexual contacts is natural. The answer to this objection is contained in the philosophical anthropology of St. Thomas, who considers man as a unity, so that one cannot create a distance between one's own body and the use one makes of it, as if the sexual faculties were just a tool. As was shown in the chapter on the natural law, man must follow the *basic* inclinations of his nature.

[22] Cf. *E.N.* VII, cc. 1-4. The text deals actually with the question of whether one always sins out of ignorance. Aristotle rejects the view of Socrates and stresses human weakness. See James J. Walsh, *Aristotle's Conception of Moral Weakness*, New York 1963.

[23] Art. 208. See Hissette, *o.c.*, p, 297.

what is meant by self-control and continence? St. Paul uses the term in the sense of chastity. but for Aristotle it is a disposition by which one opposes the bad inclinations one is suffering from[24]. This disposition resembles somewhat a virtue, inasmuch as reason understands that one's passions pull one in the wrong direction, but the sensory appetite is not yet fully subject to reason. St. Thomas adds that when one uses the term in a broad sense, self-control can be called a virtue since it leads to good actions (**Q. 155, article 1**).

Self-control is primarily concerned with those passions which pull us into a certain direction, and not with those which make us recoil. Passions are the stronger, the more powerful the natural inclinations are they are connected with such as eating, drinking, sexual activities. The pleasure connected with these are experiences of touch, so that self-control must regulate the sense of touch[25]. Both people who have self-control and those who have not are exposed to the same surges of the sensory appetite. This implies that self-control cannot have its seat in this appetite. A person who possesses self-control, decides not to follow his passions. This means that self-control has its seat in the will, which makes such a decision. Understood in this sense, self-control is not at the same level as chastity (**articles 2, 3 & 4**).

As for the vice contrary to self-control, one should not look for it in the body and among the passions, but in the soul. If one gives in to the passions, one knows that this is wrong, even if one brushes this knowledge aside. Since a person who cannot control himself deviates from what reason sees as right and surrenders to sensual pleasure, his way of acting is wrong. Using the term "incontinent" in a broader sense, a person can also be said to be incontinent in seeking honours, material goods, etc. This form of incontinence is sinful because it does not follow the measure of reason (**Q. 156, articles 1 & 2**). In view of the fact that the incontinent person sins on account of a choice, but the unchaste on account of a deep-seated vice, the acts of the latter are worse. A deep-rooted vice makes the intellect go on formulating wrong judgments, whereas in the case of the incontinent person this happens only incidentally. Incontinence in one's sensual desires is in many respects worse than a lack of self-control when one is angry. The former lies at the level of the senses, whereas anger has more to do with reason. The angry person wants to revenge an injustice done to him; moreover, anger often arises spontaneously from one's character and so one deserves forgiveness more than does the person who is incontinent with regard to sensual desires (**article 3 & 4**).

---

[24] See texts referred to in n. 22 and *E.N.* VII, c. 9.
[25] Art. 2 ad 4: "Delectationes venereorum sunt vehementiores quam delectationes ciborum. Et ideo circa venerea magis consuevimus continentiam et incontinentiam dicere quam circa cibos".

Clemency, meekness and the opposite vices (QQ. 157-159)

Anger because of an injustice we have suffered may induce us to inflict a heavy punishment on others. Now, the virtue of clemency makes us reduce this punishment. Meekness (*mansuetudo*), which moderates the intensity of anger, leads to the same effect. Both clemency and meekness are virtues because they impose the control of reason on feelings of revenge and anger. St. Thomas does not see a contradiction in the fact that severity can also be a virtue, sc. when inflexibility in the application of the punishment decided upon, follows the guidance of reason[26]. Likewise one cannot say that by reducing a punishment out of clemency one abandons the just mean, for clemency lies beyond the passions, so that the question of the mean does not immediately apply (**articles 1 & 2**).

Clemency and meekness are accompanied by a certain moderation. Clemency reduces the punishment that was imposed, meekness restrains one's anger. For this reason both are auxiliary virtues of temperance, even if their matter is different. With regard to the reduction of the inflicted punishment, this must always be in keeping with the intention of the legislator, even if in some cases it does not follow the letter of the law. Clemency must guided by the rules of *epikeia*. In this respect moderating our feelings is also important, so that we do not use all of the power we have when inflicting punishment. This moderation is typical of clemency[27]. Clemency and meekness, considered for what they are, are not the most important virtues, since they do not directly aim at reaching a good for ourselves. But both occupy an important place among the virtues which regulate our less noble feelings. By reducing these meekness shows a considerable measure of self-control, while clemency, by reducing punishment, is in close accord with a love for one's fellow men (**articles 3 & 4**).

Q. 158 deals with irascibility and becoming angry[28]. Both are presented as opposed to meekness. Some passions, such as jealousy, always seem to be ignoble, but anger can have good reasons[29]. In this case the will can accept the movement of anger in the sensory appetite[30]. But a movement of anger must keep the right measure. If one gets angry rashly, without any deliberation then this can affect the task of reason unfavorably. But if anger is consequent upon what reason tells us to do, it can be right[31], even if to some extent it would im-

---

[26] In his answer to the second difficulty Aquinas observes that clemency is for severity what *epikeia* is for distributive justice.

[27] St. Thomas refers to Seneca, *De clementia*, c. 3: "(Clementia) est temperantia animi in potestate ulciscendi".

[28] *Iracundia* irascibility) is used to express both irascibility and growing angry.

[29] St. Thomas decidedly opposes the Stoic view which considers all passions as wrong.

[30] See *Q. d. de malo*, q. 12, a. 1.

[31] It helps one to carry out energetically what one has decided to do.

pede reason in its work[32]. It is also right when one who is angry seeks satisfaction in conformity with what is reasonable, but this is no longer the case when the punishment one wants to impose is unreasonable or unjust, or if one pursues a wrong end thereby. Moreover, one must always keep the right measure when angry. A first movement of anger can be spontaneous, so that one has no control over it, even if in theory one can repress any emotion[33] (**articles 1 & 2**).

When driven by anger one can seek unjust retribution. When one becomes angry in an unreasonable way such anger is sinful. If one's anger is greatly opposed to love then it is a serious sin. Compared to sins of hatred and jealousy anger is less serious, because one only wants to inflict an evil on others in the form of what one considers, at least subjectively, a just retribution (**articles 3 & 4**).

To become or be angry can be subdivided into irascibility which on the slightest occasion explodes in anger, anger which remains for a long time since one cannot forget the injustice one has suffered and, thirdly, vindictive anger. Character plays an important role in all these attitudes. Thus there are quarrelsome, embittered and vindictive persons. Anger offers an opening to several other vices. What one wants to do when one is angry has quite some pull and impetuosity can hinder reason in its work, so that it makes wrong judgments[34]. It is difficult to quiet anger down and someone who is mad with anger can hardly be persuaded to stay calm, precisely because he thinks he is in the right. Thomas adds that sadness over the evil done to us can be the cause of anger[35] (**articles 5 & 6**). Anger provokes indignation and brings one to make plans for revenge. It also leads to furious altercations, insolence and cursing. Anger usually tends to exact excessive punishment or retribution. But if the sensory appetite does not react at all to an injustice inflicted on us then we are suffering from a deficiency of this feeling. Aquinas is convinced that the movement of the will, refusing this injustice, should be followed by an emotion[36]. This deficiency is also wrong. Anger as well as the other passions are useful inasmuch as they make one execute more quickly what reason prescribes (**articles 7 and 8**).

---

[32] If, on the other hand, one were to interrupt the execution of what one was doing to deliberate anew, this would really slow things down.

[33] Art. 2 ad 3: "Et ideo motus qui præveniunt iudicium rationis non sunt in potestate hominis in generali, ut scilicet nullus eorum insurgat, quamvis ratio possit quemlibet singulariter impedire ne insurgat".

[34] Art. 6, ad 3: "Ira dicitur esse ianua vitiorum per accidens, scilicet removendo prohibens, id est impediendo iudicium rationis per quod homo retrahitur a malo".

[35] Art. 6 ad 1: "Illa tristitia ex qua oritur ira ut plurimum... (est) passio tristitiæ quæ consequitur ex iniuria illata".

[36] Art. 8: "Et hic quidem motus ex necessitate consequitur in homine ad simplicem motum voluntatis quia naturaliter appetitus inferior sequitur motum appetitus superioris, nisi aliquid repugnet".

Cruelty is contrary to clemency (**Q. 159**), since it is opposed to a gentle and forgiving attitude. Wanting to inflict too severe a punishment results from a certain cruelty and harshness. Clemency merges with pity inasmuch as both detest the misery of others. Clemency reduces the amount of punishment, pity relieves misery by supporting others. Cruelty goes together with mercilessness. Cruelty seeks a justification for too much severity, but savagery does not consider at all what is just but finds pleasure in cruel behavior and is indeed something bestial (**articles 1 & 2**).

Unpretentiousness, humility and pride (QQ. 160 - 162)

In the introduction to Q. 155 modesty was described as one of the auxiliary virtues of temperance. Temperance subordinates strong desires to the rule of reason. However, there are less important movements in us for which some moderation is desirable. For this yet another virtue is required since man's entire life must be regulated by virtues[37]. This virtue of modesty is subordinated to temperance. It plays a role in four fields of activity. Thus the desire to excel is regulated by humility, the desire to acquire knowledge by studiousness (which is opposed to curiosity), the desire for much exercise as in sports must also be regulated, as is the case, fourthly, with caring for one's appearance. The dispositions to do so these things fall under modesty, but do not differ from each other as do the parts of justice (**Q. 160, articles 1 & 2**).

In order to acquire a good which is difficult to reach (*bonum arduum*) two virtues are necessary, sc. on the one hand a virtue which restrains us from seeking higher goals than are becoming for us, this is the task of humility, and, on the other, a virtue which boosts our resolve against discouragement and makes us continue to accomplish difficult tasks, magnanimity. This shows the nature of humility which presupposes the knowledge of our own limits and of what is lacking in us. But the virtue of humility as such has its seat in the appetite which it regulates. St. Thomas sees no opposition between the possession of humility on the one hand and accomplishing something great with high-spiritedness, with confidence in God, on the other. This dialectic of something both restraining one from an undertaking and pushing one to do it is also proper to fortitude which strengthens us against fear and bridles rashness and audacity. Humility does not demand that one deny the talents one has. Even if we are aware of our shortcomings and scanty merits we need not crawl before others but rather discourage them from thinking that our merits are very important (**Q. 161, articles 1, 2 & 3**). Since humility imposes certain limitations it falls under temperance, in par-

---

[37] Art. 1: "Oportet quantum ad omnia vitam hominis secundum virtutes regulatam esse". In the chapter on the virtues it was pointed out that these govern man's entire moral life. The reason is that acts of the same kind cause the corresponding virtues. This shows also that one must possess all virtues in order to be virtuous.

ticular under modesty. After prudence and justice humility is the most important virtue since it makes us find our right place in all matters (**articles 4 & 5**).

The vice opposed to humility is haughtiness or pride (*superbia*). Pride makes us try to seem more than we really are. But doing so is contrary to what is fitting for us. To this extent pride is morally wrong and is directly opposed to humility, as pusillanimity is to magnanimity. As a disorderly quest of own's own excellence[38] pride has a particularly sinful character. Pride seeks something difficult, sc. to show off one's excellence and to make others recognize it. So that pride has its seat both in the irascible appetite and in the will, inasmuch as the will directs itself to what is difficult. There are degrees of pride, sc. ascribing to one's own merits what one has received from God or from others, believing that one obtained something from God because of one's merits, boasting of possessing something that one does not actually have, placing oneself in the foreground while not respecting or even despising others (**Q. 162, article 1 - 4**).

While humility leads us to submit ourselves to God pride, on the contrary, can be the cause that we do not submit ourselves. St. Thomas adds that, considering what a proud person wants[39], sc. to make known to others and to force upon them the knowledge of his excellence, pride is not the most serious sin. There are other things more opposed to the good of the virtues. In respect of the fact that the proud person turns away from God, the source of all the goods one has, pride is a serious sin. The proud person refuses to submit himself to God[40]. It is not so easy to avoid pride, since this vice may even flow forth from the fact that one acquires the virtues, and so it hides behind good works. But one who is aware of one's own weakness and of God's immensity can avoid this pitfall. The influence of pride is far reaching since it brings with it an aversion from God (**articles 5 - 8**).

Studiousness and curiosity (QQ. 166 - 167)

Working with zeal requires one to direct one's mind to a determinate object. One must first acquire knowledge and next apply the mind to what this knowledge is concerned with. For this reason zeal and application (*studium*) refer in the first place to knowledge and next to what we must do with this knowledge. So the virtue of studiousness implies acquiring knowledge. In no field can a person accomplish anything, if he is not guided by reason as ordering things. Moved by his very nature man desires to know. Studiousness promotes this de-

---

[38] Q. 162, art. 4: "Superbia importat immoderatum excellentiæ appetitum".

[39] Aquinas distinguishes between a dual aspect in sinful actions, sc. turning oneself to a limited and transitory good, and turning away from God who is the imperishable good (art. 6).

[40] A quotation from Cassianus, attributed to Boethius, throws some light on it: "Cum omnia vitia fugiant a Deo, sola superbia se Deo opponit" (*De institutione coenob*. XII, c. 7: PL 49, 434.

sire and regulates the effort to acquire knowledge. As an auxiliary virtue of temperance studiousness is not an intellectual virtue but influences the will which moves the intellect to acquire knowledge. This virtue is needed since because of his physical limitations man easily succumbs to the temptation of avoiding strenuous intellectual efforts (**Q. 166, articles 1 & 2**).

Studiousness is not directly directed to knowledge but addresses itself to the zeal needed to acquire it. The knowledge of the truth as such is always good, but it can be used in a wrong way. However, the desire for acquiring knowledge can be either good or bad. It is bad when something bad is connected with it or when it is disorderly. This happens when one seeks to know useless things and so is hampered from learning what is necessary[41]. A further deviation, for Thomas, consists in applying oneself to the study of created things while remaining blind for their dependence on God. Finally, one acts wrongly when one seeks to know things which are clearly beyond one's power (**Q. 167, article 1**). - A further question is whether curiosity, as a vice, is concerned with the study of sensible things. In his answer S. Thomas points out that sense-cognition is absolutely necessary for our life on earth and that man's sense-cognition is directed to intellectual knowledge. But when one collects information about trivial things in a manner that keeps us from studying what is useful, or when sense-cognition is used for what is sinful then one is yielding to the vice of curiosity. But if one uses the data the senses provide in an orderly way then the application and zeal needed for acquiring them are praiseworthy (**article 2**).

Moderation in sports and play as well as in caring for one's appearance
(QQ. 168-169)

It is the task of the virtues to order what we do according to our best insight. Some activities of our body as well as caring for our appearance are also subject to the order of reason. Beauty and dignity in this respect consist in one's doing what is fitting according to one's particular personality, age and sex. Although virtues are inward, what we show on the outside is a sign of them[42]. In order to do what is becoming in caring for our appearance we must control our passions (**Q. 168, article 1**).

After this introduction Aquinas examines the proper theme of q. 168, sc. the place of sports and play in our life. Not just the body needs rest, our mind (soul)[43] also gets tired when it does exacting work dependent as this is upon the

---

[41] Much of what the means of communication present to us, may render serious study.difficult.

[42] A quotation from St. Ambrose confirms this conclusion: "Habitus mentis in corporis statu cernitur... vox qædam animi est corporis motus (*De officiis*, I, c. 18

[43] Thomas uses "soul" meaning the principle of life which is the source of the sensitive and intellectal activities.

organs of the body. This applies to the acquisition of knowledge by the senses, but also by the intellect, in particular when one studies things which lie beyond the level of what is perceptible by the senses. By activities in which practical reason is involved the body gets tired, but a sort of spiritual weariness also results. This bodily weariness disappears when one takes a rest and tiredness of the mind also must be combated by rest. One must abstain for a while from study and look for some relaxation in play and distraction But one should not entertain oneself with unbecoming and harmful things. One should always keep a certain seriousness, and the relaxation we choose should fit our person, the place and time, our state in life and other circumstances. Reason tells us what to do and in this it is helped by this particular virtue of moderation (**article 2**).

What in relaxation and amusement goes beyond good measure (in behavior, in words or in relation to the circumstances of place and time of the particular persons), is in conflict with the virtue of temperance. On the other hand, a lack of distraction and play is also wrong. When irritable one becomes displeasing to others. When one does not take part in a game, one can be isolating oneself unduly from the others[44] (**articles 3 & 4**).

The last auxiliary virtue mentioned by Aquinas is the disposition which makes us try to have a presentable appearance (**Q. 169**). Some Fathers of the Church and spiritual authors were quite severe in their judgment about what they considered exaggerated ways of dressing and make up, probably on account of certain patterns of behavior they observed among the higher classes of society in that time. Thomas writes that there is nothing wrong with such things as ornaments or jewelry which some people use, but that one may exceed the right measure here. This "right measure" here depends in part on what in a certain environment is generally accepted. But one should never be passionately attached to such things as ornaments or luxurious clothes, nor seek other people's praise for what one is wearing nor spend too much time in taking care of one's appearance.

However, there is also the possibility of doing too little for one's appearance. Some even boast about neglecting it. Aquinas concedes that ornaments and similar aids to beauty care are not nature itself, but writes that reason requires us to take good care of our appearance. Obligations, however, can differ according to people's position (**Q. 169, article 1**). With regard to the care women give for their appearance the same applies as above. Women should take good care of how they look, so as to please their husbands so that the latter are not attracted to other women (**article 2**).

---

[44] A quotation which Thomas (mistakenly) attributes to Seneca tells us that we must behave ourselves in such a way that no one finds us annoying or considers us a worthless companion.

CHAPTER XIV

LOVE AND FRIENDSHIP

Books VIII and IX of the *Nicomachean Ethics* deal with the theme of friendship, as the effect and fulness of a virtuous life. Aquinas wrote an extensive commentary on both books and, in several of his works, he paid much attention to this question[1]. Ethics studies all human acts in view of man's end. Friendship is most necessary to attain the goal of human life. We need to be surrounded by friends. No one who is endowed with what belongs to normal human nature wants to live without friends, not even when he possesses all other remaining goods. The rich and the poor, the young and the elderly, all need friends. Wealthy people are often helped by their friends to preserve and increase their possessions. If one becomes poor, friends are a support. Friends can help the young not to go wrong, while the elderly and those who need to be cared for receive the necessary help because of friendship[2]. Natural friendships such as those between parents and their children or between the citizens of the same country are the most important assets of community life and create concord in political society[3].

As has been argued in Chapter IV love is the first and fundamental act of the appetite. The object of love is the good and the desirable[4], for love is directed to the good. Now being itself in so far as it is the object of the appetite is good. It follows that the appetite is directed to being[5]. The object presented by the cognitive faculties, provokes a movement in the appetite which approves the object. In a sense this object becomes present in it as that to which its inclination is directed. In Aquinas's treatise on love as the primary passion in the *Prima Secundæ* of the *Summa theologiæ* he mentions as the effects of love to be together, to go beyond oneself (inasmuch as love is directed to its object) and the intensification of all activities. As will appear these effects are found in a surpassing way in friendship.

---

[1] Many studies have been published on the importance of the theme in classical antiquity. For a survey and bibliography see F. Dirlmeier, *Philos und Phila im vorhellenistischen Griechentum*, München 1931; J. Voelke, *Les rapports avec autrui dans la philosophie grecque d'Aristote à Panaetius*, Paris 1961; J.-C. Fraise, *La notion d'amitié dans la philosophie antique*, Paris 1974.

[2] *E.N.* VIII, c.1, 1155ª9 ff. In this context Aristotle uses the concept of friendship (φιλία) in a broad sense: it means dealing in a friendly way with others and looking after their well-being as parents do regarding their children, teachers their pupils and relatives one another.

[3] *In VIII Ethicorum*, lesson 1.

[4] Cf. *In Dionysii De divinis nominibus*, c. 4, n. 266: "Cum bonum sit quod omnia appetunt, quaecumque de se important appetibilis rationem ad rationem boni pertinere videntur".

[5] This point is forcefully made by M.C. Donadio Maggi, *Amor y bien. Los problemas del amor en santo Tomás de Aquino*, Buenos Aires 1999.

Aquinas distinguishes between the sensory appetite and the will. Both faculties have the good as their object. In the sensory appetite this inclination is always directed to what is good for the bearer of this faculty[6]. What is loved by this love of concupiscence is not loved because of itself but for the sake of the person who desires it in view of some use or pleasure he hopes to find in it. As for the appetite which follows the intellect, sc. the human will, here also the love of desire is found, but also a pure objective love which wills the good for the sake of the good itself. The latter inclination is called love of benevolence or love of friendship[7]. In another text St. Thomas writes that concupiscent love does not have its terminus in what is loved, but turns back to the person or things for whom or for which one wills the good of this object, whereas the love of benevolence has its terminus in what is loved[8].

Is unselfish love possible ?

Since the concupiscible appetite is directed to one's own well being, the question has been raised whether a totally unselfish love is possible at all. P. Rousselot[9] argued that according to Aquinas every love must be directed to one's own good, but his thesis has been contested[10]. Rousselot believed that Aquinas taught the unity of the love of desire and the love of friendship[11]. He points to the fact that although man can place himself in a wider horizon, he must nevertheless always seek his own good in whatever love he has. To see better what the problem is about, we must distinguish between spiritual love and sensual love. The latter is directed to what is pleasing and to pleasure. Because of the prospect of the pleasure which reaching or acquiring the loved object will give, man and animals are moved to perform certain natural functions, some of which are in fact to the advantage of other persons, as is the case in procreation.

---

[6] The sensory appetites are signified by the terms *concupiscibilis* and the *irascibilis*. The word *concupiscence* can denote any inclination (I-II 71, 6 arg. 2). Man has the sensory appetite in common with animals but his is more noble(I-II 25, 2 ad 1).

[7] *In Evang. Ioan.*, c. 15, lesson 4: "Sciendum est quod amor concupiscentiae non est rei concupitae sed concupiscentis, sed amor amicitiae est potius rei amatae quam amantis, quia diligit aliquem propter ipsum dilectum, non propter ipsum diligentem".

[8] *In III Sent.*, d. 29, q. 1, a. 3: "Amor iste (sc. concupiscentiae) non terminatur ad rem quae dicitur amari, sed reflectitur ad rem illam cui optatur bonum illius rei;....amor benevolentiae ad rem ipsam terminatur".

[9] *Pour l'histoire du problème de l'amour au moyen âge. Beiträge zur Geschichte der Philosophie des Mittelalters*, Bd. VI, Heft 6, Münster i.W., 1908.

[10] See above all L.-B. Geiger, *Le problème de l'amour chez saint Thomas d'Aquin*, Montréal / Paris 1952.

[11] Only in the mystics may one find an ecstatic love which make them love God for the sake of God.

Spiritual love depends on the intellect which knows what the good is (*ratio boni*)[12]. In this way the love which follows on intellectual knowledge, is in the first place love of the good as such and so the will seeks the good before looking for pleasure[13]. One may wish for oneself the good as such present in a concrete good as its formal core (*ratio formalis*) but one can also let the movement of the mind halt at this good, love it for itself and/or wish it for some one else. In this last case we speak of the love of friendship[14]. This "pure" love is a sort of staying inwardly with a good or with a person one loves. This love is unselfish and does not reduce the good to one's own well being, as Rousselot thought that love always does.

Given that love of the good as such is possible it is also possible to love God more than onself. The basis for this love is the fact that all created things share in God's goodness. God is the universal good and the source of all goodness[15]. Each creature, with whatever it is and possesses, belongs to the whole of which it is a part, and even more so to God, who is its origin and cause[16]. This implies that every creature, and also man, love God with a natural love more than themselves[17]. This need not (yet) be a conscious and explicit love of God[18]. What is meant is that man, in whatever he seeks to attain, strives in reality for the universal good, in which this particular good partakes[19]. If one objects that a part loves the good of the whole only insofar as this suits it, the answer will be that even so it does not subordinate this good to itself, but directs itself to the good of the whole. Thomas adds a theological argument. A Christian must love God above all. However, this commandment cannot be contrary to human nature,

---

[12] The object of the will are goods which falls under the general concept of the good, as it is known by the intellect (II-II 25, 4: "... sub communi ratione boni prout est apprehensibile ab intellectu").

[13] I-II 4, 2 ad 2: "Et ideo, secundum appetitum sensitivum qui est in animalibus, operationes quaeruntur propter delectationem. Sed intellectus apprehendit universalem rationem boni, ad cuius consecutionem sequitur delectatio, unde principalius intendit bonum quam delectationem".

[14] What is meant is virtuous and noble friendship, not friendship for a person because he is useful or his company pleasurable.

[15] This point is argued in metaphysics. See our *The Philosophical Theology of St. Thomas Aquinas in a Historical Perspective*, Leyden 1991; II-II 26,3: "Super communicationem autem bonorum naturalium nobis a Deo factam, fundatur amor naturalis".

[16] The being of creatures is a continued participation in divine being.

[17] I, 60, 5: "Unumquodque autem in rebus naturalibus, quod secundum hoc ipsum quod est alterius, principalius et magic inclinatur in id cuius est quam in seipsum".

[18] In the present situation of fallen human nature this inclination can easily be obscured.

[19] The act by which we direct ourselves to a determinate good is the same as the act by which we direct ourselves to what is formal in this object: seeing light is the same act as seeing a color of the light (II-II 25, 1).

because the supernatural order does not destroy nature but perfects it[20]. So there must be a basis in human nature for such a supernatural love of God. In Chapter I it was argued that even for our imperfect happiness on earth our highest good lies in the knowledge of God. God must be loved above all things as the cause of our happiness[21].

Aquinas lays down the order which obtains in things we love (*ordo amoris*), God, ourselves, our fellow men in view of the good of their souls, then those with whom we are more closely connected[22]. In his answer to such questions as "Should one love one's parents more than one's children?", "one's wife more than one's parents?", Thomas uses a twofold criterion, sc. being the cause of our being good and being connected with us. According to the first criterion a person will love his parents more than his wife, according to the second, he loves his wife or she her husband more and they their children. A closer relationship makes love more intense[23].

The love of friendship

It lies in our nature to will our own well being. In fact we are closest to ourselves. Love for ourselves is the form and model for the love of friends, to whom we relate as to ourselves[24]. The love for others originates, say Aristotle and Aquinas, in the following way. By sharing in the same human nature[25], the same nationality or family and by working or traveling together with others we observe the good in them..

Benevolence is defined as wishing someone well[26]. The starting point for this benevolence is man's social nature. We live together with others in a family, in a village or city, a tribal community or a country as well as in freely chosen associations. We need each other and this explains why for the sake of our needs we seek the vicinity and help of others. This allows Thomas to draw the conclusion that we have the duty to be helpful and to do good, but taking into account the

---

[20] I, 62, 5; *In IV Sent.*, d. 2, q. 1, a 4 B.

[21] II-II 26, 2: Cf. A. Wohlman, "Amour du bien propre et amour de soi dans la doctrine thomiste de l'amour", *Revue thomiste* 81(1981), 204-234.

[22] II-II 26, 1-12.

[23] II-II 26, 8: "Intensio autem dilectionis ex coniunctione dilecti ad diligentem".

[24] II-II 25, 4: "... est forma et radix amicitiae. In hoc enim amicitiam habemus ad alios quod ad eos nos habemus sicut ad nos ipsos".

[25] In *E.N.* VIII, c. 11, 1159^{b}27 Aristotle uses the term κοινωνία which in the Latin translations becomes *communicatio*. The Greek word for *benevolentia* is: εὔνοια.

[26] In the strict sense one does not wish anything for God; one loves God with a simple act of love (*In I Sent.*, d. 17, q. 1, a. 5).

right time and place[27]. We cannot help everyone, but we must be disposed to do good to others, when the occasion presents itself.

Benevolent love goes one step further. Benevolence is not an emotion but an act of the will, by which, in virtue of a judgement of reason, we want the good of another person[28]. "When two people resemble each other, since they seem to have the same character[29], they are in a sense one in this regard, as human beings are one in their specific nature. For this reason our love for someone is directed to him as to a person who is one with ourselves, and we want the happiness of the other as our own happiness"[30]. Thomas stresses that the love of oneself is the root of friendship and gives form to it: we feel friendship for others because we relate to them as to ourselves[31]. However, we are more one with ourselves than with others and so we love ourselves more[32]. He notes that in a noble friendship one loves a friend in a twofold way: one loves him and wants what is good for him; secondly, one also loves the good which one wishes the other to have[33]. This benevolent love becomes friendship when the other has the same disposition as his friend, because for friendship mutual love is required.[34]. Therefore benevolent love is the starting-point and the beginning of friendship[35]. Friendship demands mutual love and sharing what one has and does[36]. What holds for any real friendship is that it consists more in loving one than in being loved[37].

Is friendship a virtue ?

Love is not the act of a particular virtue. As the basic movement of the appetite a noble love is active in of every virtue, as disorderly love is present in every vice[38]. In his introduction to Book VIII of the *Nicomachean Ethics*, which deals with friendship (as does Book IX), Aristotole writes that friendship is most nec-

---

[27] II-II 31, 2: "... pro loco tamen et tempore; omnes enim actus virtutum sunt secundum debitas circumstantias limitandi".

[28] II-II 27, 2: "... ex solo iudicio rationis".

[29] Thomas uses the term *forma*.

[30] I-II 27, 3.

[31] II-II 25, 4: "Amor quo quis diligit seipsum est forma et radix amicitiae. In hoc enim amicitiam habemus ad alios quod ad eos nos habemus sicut ad nosipsos".

[32] II-II 26, 4: union is stronger than association.

[33] II-II 25, 2.

[34] II-II 23, 1: "Benevolentia non sufficit ad rationem amicitiae, sed requiritur quaedam mutua amatio". Cf. *E.N.* VIII, c. 2, 1155^{b}53.

[35] *In III Sent.*, d. 29, q. 1, a. 7: "Benevolentia est principium et radix amicitiae".

[36] I 20, 2 ad 3: "Reamatio et communicatio in operibus vitae", also under difficult or painful circumstances.

[37] II-II 27, 1: "Magis existit amicitia in amare quam in amari".

[38] II-II 125, 2.

essary for human life, for if a one possesses all the other things one needs, one would nevertheless not want to live without friends[39]. He adds that friendship is a virtue or connected with virtue[40]. Thomas's view is on this point is subtle[41]. In a certain respect friendship is a virtue, since it regulates our actions with regard to others. The virtue of justice does so according to what is due to them under the law (*ratione debiti legalis*), friendship on account of a friendly or moral "obligation" (*ratione boni gratuiti*) . In this respect friendship goes beyond justice. Justice needs friendship as a supplement, but where there is real friendship, justice becomes superfluous[42]. On the other hand, friendship is not a special virtue, since there are several kinds of friendship[43]. A friendship is good only when it is based on the virtues, which regulate the inter-human relations, such as the virtue of piety. Benevolence, the starting-point and beginning of friendship is found in some of the virtues which were discussed in Chapter X, on justice. For this reason friendship results from the virtues rather than being itself a virtue[44]. Because one is virtuous one likes other virtuous persons[45]. The love with which a friend answers our love is not a virtuous deed of our own. Finally, whatever in ourselves or in our friends goes against virtue is an impediment to the development of friendship[46]. According to Aristotle perfect friendship is found only between small numbers of people. Thomas suggests that this applies to those who answer to our benevolence. People will only do so when they are sufficiently good. While real and vigorous friendship extends to few persons, benevolence can nonetheless embrace many[47].

---

[39] In this treatise Aristotle often uses the word φιλία in a broader sense in cases where we would speak of mutual love, such as the love between parents and their children.

[40] *E.N.* VIII, c. 1, 1155ᵃ3: ἔστι γὰρ ἀρετή τις ἢ μετ' ἀρετῆς.

[41] II-II 23, 3.

[42] *In VIII Ethic.*, lesson 1.

[43] St. Thomas divides friendships according to their goals in profitable, pleasurable and noble friendships. As for the having of things in common and the exchange characteristic of the different types of friendship he distinguishes between consanguinity, sharing the same citizenship and certain common undertakings (ii-II 23, 5).

[44] II-II 23, 3.

[45] *Q. d. de virtutibus*, q. 1, a. 5, ad 5: "Amicitia proprie non est virtus, sed consequens virtutem. Nam ex hoc ipso quod aliquis est virtuosus sequitur quod diligit sibi similes". Cf. *ibid.*, q. 2 ad 2: "Ex hoc ipso quod aliquis habet virtutem et amat bonum rationis, consequitur ex ipsa inclinatione virtutis quod diligat sibi similes, scil. virtuosos".

[46] II-II 106, 1 ad 3.

[47] *Q. d. de virtutibus*, q. 2, a. 4 ad 11: "Amicitia perfecta non habetur ad multos, ita quod ad unumquemque sit ratione sui ipsius, sed quanto amicitia est perfectior ad unum ratione eius, tanto ad plures se posset extendere ratione ipsius. Et sic caritas quia perfectissima amicitia est, ad Deum se extendit et ad omnes qui possunt percipere Deum, et non solum ad notos sed etiam ad inimicos". Thomas had to confront this question since he argued that supernatural love (*caritas*) is friendship, and this love must extend even to the enemies of God. Aristotle, for his

Division, properties and effects of friendship

Aristotle describes friendship as a mutual benevolence, which makes one wish that a friend fares well and in which one knows of the feelings one has for him or her. This benevolence is based on the advantages resulting for both, on pleasure this friendship gives and on virtue and spiritual values[48]. Essential to a friendship is the mutual love of friends. According to the nature of this love we distinguish (a) forms of friendship which aim at advantages or pleasure and where the friend is not loved because of himself, even if in this sort of friendship a mutual love is possible; b) perfect friendship which is found only among good people, for the bad and wicked have nothing for which they could be loved by others, unless for certain things which are useful or give some pleasure[49]. Both Aristotle and Thomas point out that by not being together and by lack of contact friendships grow weaker and languish, in particular friendships of the first group[50].

This is a division according to the goal of friendships, but one can also subdivide friendships according to what one has in common with a friend and the kind of relationship on which a friendship rests[51]. Each type of friendship refers primarily to that in which the good is found which the friends share and on which their friendship is based. A natural friendship such as that between parents and their children is primarily based on consanguinity[52]. Comradeship between soldiers is based on their common military service and campaigns. Friendship brings with it a certain equality. Friends give each other equal rights and share equally what they have[53]. In friendships where a certain inequality prevails, as between parents and their children, teachers and their students, the latter need only return something equal in an analogous way. Where there is no proportionally equal exchange friendships are in danger of dying out[54]. It is to be expected that a friendship based on the advantage it brings will disappear when this advantage or pleasure vanishes. In such friendships friends are not loved

---

part, stresses the necessary proximity of a friend and the continuous exchange of thought, feelings and plans which is proper to a friendship.

[48] *E.N.* VIII, 2, 1156ª3.

[49] *In VIII Ethic.*, lessons 3 & 4.

[50] *L.c.*, lesson 5. Cf. also *Super Evang. Ioannis*, c. 8, lesson 5: "Omnis amicitia in coniunctione fundatur"; II-II 23, 1: "Nihil enim ita proprium amicitiae est sicut convivere amico"; II-II 24, 10: "Multas amicitias inappelatio solvit".

[51] II-II 23, 5; 26, 2.

[52] II-II 26, 2; 7.

[53] *Summa contra gentiles* III, c. 124: "Amicitia in quadam aequalitate consitit".

[54] *In IX Ethic.*, lesson 1: "Amicitia conservatur per recompensationem proportionalem".

because of themselves. A noble friendship is endangered when one of the friends no longer lives a virtuous life[55].

Aristotle has a broad idea of friendship. Wherever there is a certain community or togetherness he sees a possibility of friendship. Friendship is necessary since it makes relations between people more humane and so it is the crown of a life according to the virtues. According to his broader vision Aristotle compares different forms of political relationships to the different types of friendship. As a king governs his subjects, a father directs his family. But under a perverse political regime such as a tyranny, friendship between the government and its subjects is not possible.

Aristotle mentions five properties of friendships[56] : one wants a friend to stay alive, to be doing well. One wants to do good to him and desires to be together in a pleasant way. Finally, one wishes to have the same ideas and feelings. Thomas stresses the same points[57]. One may add to these properties that because of the friendship one cherishes for someone one loves also those who are related to him[58]. Another property mentioned by Aquinas is willingness to render services to a friend. The explanation is that one wants to comply with a friend's wishes, for one wishes his good[59]. In fact, every friendship is strengthened and made to continue by expressions of love[60]. The greater a friendship, the stronger and more durable it is. One sees this in the relationship between husband and wife, which Aquinas calls the greatest friendship of all[61].

One can also speak of the effects of friendship (*opera amicitiae*). We like to do something for a friend, even if this requires some work[62]. One expects a friend to accept what one does for him. One wants the good of a friend for the sake of the friend himself. To this one may add a good deal of unanimity which is shown in being together, in thinking and liking the same things, in being sad or joyful about the same things and in sharing the same undertakings[63].

On account of his social nature man must live together with others and collaborate with them in many fields of activity. There is no doubt that it is better to live together with friends than with enemies. The ideal is that people treat each other with kindness, are interested in others and are ready to help them. In order

---

[55] *In IX Ethic.*, lesson 3.

[56] *E.N.* IX, c. 4, 1166^{a}3 ff. See St. Thomas, II-II 25, 7. With regard to the past property mentioned by Aristotle he writes: "Concordat cum ipso quasi in iisdem delectatus et contristatus".

[57] II-II 29, 3 ad 3. The text refers to Cicero's "amicorum est idem velle et nolle".

[58] II-II 23, 1 ad 2.

[59] *S.C.G.* III, c. 95.

[60] II-II 82, 2 ad 2.

[61] *S.C.G.* III, c. 123: "maxima amicitia".

[62] *In IX Ethic.*, lesson 7: "Illa quae laboriose fiunt, magis diliguntur".

[63] *O.c.*, lesson 6: "Concordia est circa operabilia".

to live happily one must find pleasure in what is done in agreement with virtue[64]. Often we can judge better what another does than what we ourselves do. Since a friend is an *alter ego*, one rejoices in what he does and so one's own joy becomes greater. Moreover, a friendship makes us become more intensely aware of one's own existence and one's thoughts and feelings, since one experiences these also in a friend. In this way friendship is the fulfilment of a life according to the virtues and part of the happiness possible during our life on earth[65].

---

[64] *In IX Ethic.*, lesson 10: "Requiritur ad felicitatem quod felix delectetur in opere virtutis"

[65] The Christian virtue of *caritas* realizes this benevolent love on a higher level and a new motivation.

INDEX NOMINUM

Abelard, Peter	5, 86	Eberle, A.	13
Andronicus	283	Elders, L.J.	17, 31, 79, 162, 179, 193, 227, 270
Anscombe, G.E.M.	90		
Aeschylus	13	Epicurus	14
Alain of Lille	15	Eudoxus	41
Albert the Great	36, 75, 97, 208, 212	Euripides	207
Alexander of Hales	16, 35, 200, 204		
Ambrose, St.	16, 160, 204	Fassò, G.	207
Anselme, St.	32, 35	Festugière, A.-M.	90, 172
Aubert, J.-M.	212	Finnis, J.	210
Augustine, St.	14, 16, 40, 57f., 71, 79, 101, 107, 120, 140, 147, 188f., 174, 192, 204, 207, 210, 236, 251, 269, 282	Flamant, J.	102
		Freud, S.	305
		Gaius	207, 241
Avicenna	58	Galenus	94
		García López, J.	218
Belmans, Th.C.	72, 75	Gauthier of Bruges	5
Bernard, St.	79	Gauthier, R.A.	16, 60
Blomme, R.	15	Geiger, L.-B.	298
Boethius	42, 50, 102, 293	Gerald of Abbeville	56
Bonaventure, St.	79, 82, 208, 212	Gornally, L.	44
Bourke, V.J.	17, 22	Gould, J.	190
Boyle, J.	210	Grabmann, M.	35
		Gratianus	240
Cajetan	79, 143	Gregory, the Great, St.	131
Cassianus	293	Groner, J.F.	277
Chrysippus	94, 114, 166	Grotius	192, 206, 221
Cicero	17, 40, 50f., 94, 99, 116, 160, 166, 169, 177, 197, 205, 207, 233, 239, 258, 269, 271	Grisez, G.	210
		Gründel, J.	51
		Guindon, R.	35
Cleanthes	70		
Clement of Alexandria	162, 166	Hardie, W.F.R.	19, 28, 38, 164
Cope, E.M.	109	Hedwig, K.	17
Crowe, M.	212	Heinimann, F.	162, 221
		Heraclitus	205, 219
Dagonet, F.	33	Hiltbrunner, O.	160
D'Arcy, E.	85	Hissette, R.	286
Delhaye, Ph.	12, 210	Hobbes, Th.	223, 240
Deman, Th.	22, 43	Homer	187
Dempf, A.	197	Huby, P.	14
Descartes	94	Hudson, W.D.	91
Dewey, J.	34	Hugh of St. Victor	208
Dirlmeier, F.	297	Hume, David	230
Diogenes Laertius	69f., 78		
Dionysius, Ps.	75, 85, 105, 173, 279	Isidore, St.	197, 207, 213, 220, 258
Donadio Maggi, M.C.	21, 297	Jaeger, W.	187

307

Jaffa, H.J.	38	Plato, *passim*	
Janssens, L.	89	Plotinus	162
Jerome, St.	78, 176, 212	Pohlenz, M.	70, 94, 166
Joachim, H.H.	70	Pope, S.J.	8
John Chrysostome, St.	16, 269	Posidonius	94
John Climacus	189	Protagoras	13
John Damascene, St.	48, 50, 62, 96	Pufendorf, S.	206, 217
John of Salisbury	15	Pythagoras	40
Jolif, Y.	60		
		Ramirez, J.-M.	22
Kenny, A.	38, 59	Rhonheimer, M.	206
Kidd, I.G.	94	Rist, J.M.	70, 114
Killeen, S.	270	Robert Grosseteste	16
Kluxen, W.	20	Rousseau, J.-J.	198
Kuhn, U.	201	Rousselot, P.	298
Lakebrink, B.	269	Sartre, J.-P.	72, 198
Lagarde, G.	209	Schockenhoff, E.	135, 229
Leclercq, J.	54	Schwartz, E.	14
Liebard, J.	14	Scotus, Duns	78, 216
Locke, John	217, 227, 250	Seneca	15, 167, 290
Lottin, O.	15, 84, 160, 198, 204	Sepulveda, G. de	221
		Sertillanges, A.-D.	23
MacIntyre, A.	145	Socrates	69, 90, 182, 219, 288
MacPherson, C.	13, 250	Sophocles	207
Macrobius	162, 233	Soto, Dominic de	22
Maimonides	15	Spanneut, M.	218
Maritain, J.	12, 214	Suarez	198, 206, 221
McInerny, R.	22		
McTighe, K.	184	Theron, S.	8, 37, 150, 209, 218
Meier, M.	94	Thracy, Th.	70, 164
Nemesius	48, 63, 67, 96, 102, 118, 131	Ulpian	192, 207
		Utz, F.	30, 221, 225, 228, 241, 257
Nisters, Th.	51		
		Walsh, J.J.	172, 184, 288
Ockham, William of	75, 209, 217	Waltz, B.	230
Osborn, J.H.	14	Weiss, R.L.	16, 71
		William, B.	38
Pegis, A.	44	William of Auvergne	35, 216
Pesch, O.H.	135, 197	William of Auxerre	16, 212
Peter Lombard	35, 71, 147, 208	Wittmann, M.	23, 135, 197
Pieper, J.	22, 145, 239, 277	Wohlman, A.,	300
Pinckaers, S.	82, 88, 145		
Pizzorni, R.	208	Zeno	70, 94.

INDEX RERUM

Abstinence	281, 284	*consilium*	63
according to nature	30	*Corpus Hippocraticum*	164
according to reason	30	courage	1228ff.
accusation	251	criteria of morality	70
acedia	118	cruelty	292
acts, human -,	47 ff.	curiosity	293
origin of free -,	47	custom	225
morally neutral -,	73, 78		
principles of our -,	135ff.	Decalogue	209, 216
actus hominis	18	deceit	285
actus humanus	18	decency	283
adultery	287	*Decrees of Gratianus*	197
amor benevolentiae	298	deliberation	62, 234
anger	130, 254, 291	despair	225f.
consequences of -,	132	*dilectio*	104
animals	242	*dilige et quod vis fac*	71
appetite, sensitive -,	95	dispensation	215, 225
concupiscible -,	298	dissipation	266
		docilitas	233
Barter	256		
beati ut homines	44	*Ea quae sunt ad finem*	230
benevolence	104, 300	election	60
bonum honestum	121	emotions	97
- *intentum*	121	end	74f, 77
- *rationis*	206	final -,	37
- *utile*	121	more than one - ?,	37, 59
		epikeia	266f., 290
Capital punishment	248	equitableness	267
caritas	104	*ethica docens*	16
chastity	285	- *utens*	16
choice	60	ethics	13
Church Fathers	15f	history of -,	13ff.
circumstances	50, 73, 80	division of -,	18
clemency	290	method in -,	23
command	66	nature of -,	18
common good, the -,	226f, 243	intellectual character of -,	29
common sense	235	importance of -,	31
commutative justice	246f	- and the virtues	32ff.
concupiscence	49, 183f, 189	ethics as a practical science	69
conformity with God's will	87	*eubulia*	235, 258
connaturality	103	euthanasia	249
conscience	82f	*exercitium actus*	56
erroneous -,	82		
- and prudence	85	Faculties	149
- in theoretical intellect	83	favoritism	248
consent	64	fear	49, 125, 272

309

causes of -,	49, 125, 272	irascibility	290
effects of -,	127	irony	264
finis operantis	73	*ius gentium*	209
- *operis*	73	*iustitia legalis*	243
forethought	234	*iustum naturale*	213
fortitude	271		
fraud	255	Joy	57ff.
free choice	65	judge	245, 252
friendship	297ff	justice	168, 239ff.
types of -,	303	parts of -,	246, 257ff.
division of -,	301	administration of -,	245f.
frui	57		
		Labour	268
Generosity	258	law	197ff.
good and bad	54	eternal -,	198
goodness and badness	71ff.;	kinds of -,	200
- of actions	36, 74, 81	effects of -,	105f.
- of external actions	87f.	positive -,	219
gnome	236, 182	natural -,	17, 82, 206ff.
gratitude	262	lawyer	253
greed	262	*Liber de bona fortuna*	17
guilt	191	licentiousness	286
		like seeks like..	104
Habitus	136ff., 148	love	103ff., 297ff.
happiness	35ff., 58	effects of -,	105f.
imperfect -,	22, 42f.	- of God	299
hatred	107	unselfish love	298
homicide	248	lying	264
homosexuality	111		
honor	254	Magnanimity	274
hope	122ff.	manual labour	263
human rights	???	*materia circa quam*	72
humility	274, 292	mean, the -,	164ff.
hypocrisy	264	means	230
		meekness	290
Idolatry	260	method in ethics	23ff.
ignorance	49, 182	modesty	285
imprudence	236	*modus compositionis*	23f., 26
inclination	103, 211	*modus resolutionis*	23
incontinence	288	morality of actions	71ff.
indifferent acts	78	motive	74
individualism	227		
intellectualism	90	Name, good -,	254
intemperance	281	*natura non tendit nisi ad unum*	39
insensitivity	281	natural inclinations	67, 211, 288
intentio finis	28	natural rights	240
intention	58, 86, 89	nature does not direct to what is bad	29
interest on loans	255	*necessitas huius vitae*	281

negative commandments	???	- the measure of morality	30
Neoplatonism	14	reciprocity	246
Nicomachean Ethics	19 *et passim*	*recta ratio agibilium*	15, 177
noluntas	54	*- factibilium*	152
norma normata	84	relaxation	295
		restitution	247
Obedience 262		revenge	263
object of human acts	74, 77f.	rights	239
observantia	261	robbery	250
offence	254		
ordo amoris	147, 300	Sadness	110
ornaments	295	causes of -,	119
otherness	242	effects of -,	119
		salary	270
Partes integrales, - subiectivae, -		secundary precepts	213
potentiales of the virtues	232	self-conceit	275
passions	93ff.	self-confidence	283
classification of -,	96	self-control	154, 279, 283, 288
moral qualification	98f.	self-defence	268
origin of -,	98	sensory appetite	183
relation between -,	100	sensual desire	49
- as illness of the soul	94	sin	171ff.
patience	276ff.	capital -s,	189
Peripatetics	17, 99	distinction between sins	175
perseverance	277	causes of sins	181ff.
perversion	186	consequences of sins	190
piety	258, 261	division of sins	195
play	295	sobriety	284
pleasure	57, 109, 279ff.	*sollicitudo*	231
positive commandments	257	Sophists	13, 231
positivism	217	specification of acts	18
potentia ordinata	209	sport	294
pre-moral acts	89	studiousness	293
primary precepts	213	suffering	116
principles, first -,	24, 211	suicide	249
private property	250	*synderesis*	82, 211ff.
prayer	259	*synesis*	236, 258
pride	292		
		Temperance	279ff.
prudence	168, 229ff.	components of -,	283
punishment	191, 193, 263, 290	auxiliary virtues	282
purpose	74	truthfulness	264
		tyrant	268
Quarrelsomeness	265		
		Unchastity	286
Ratio	84	usury	256
ratio boni	299	*ut in pluribus*	24
reason	99, 167		

311

Vanity	275	-s and passions	155
via caritatis	201	*vis instrumentaria*	58
violation	287	voluntary	47
vice	93, 171ff	involuntary	47
violence	49	mixed -,	49
virginity	285		
virtue	147	War	267
definition of -,	147	will	47
distinction between -s,	157	what moves the -,	54
intellectual -s,	151	internal actsw of the -,	81
moral -s,	150	witness	252
seat of -s,	149	work, see labour	

INDEX OF GREEK WORDS

ἀδίκημα	90	ἦθός	13
ἀκολασία	90	ἠθικός	13
ἀκρασία	90	θυμοειδής	93
ἁμαρτία	90	κόλασις	192
ἀπαθεία	94	λογιστικός	93
ἀρετή	145	μαλακία	90
ἀταραξία	70	νόμος	198
ἄτη	171	ὀρμή	146
ἀτύχημα	90	οἰκείωσις	207
βούλησις	60, 63	ὁμολογουμένως ζῆν	70, 207
ἐγκράτεια	288	ὄρεξις	108
ἑκούσιος	47	ὁρμή	146
ἑκών	93	οὐχ ἑκών	93
ἐπανόρθωμα	246	πόνος	116
ἐπιεικές	246	προαίρεσις	60
ἐπιθυμητικόν	13	σοφία	146
ἐπιθυμία	108	τὰ πρὸς τὸ τέλος	230
ἐτός	13	τιμωρία	192
εὐδαιμονία	35	φιλία	297, 302
ἡγεμονικόν	166	φρόνησις	146

www.ingramcontent.com/pod-product-compliance
Lightning Source LLC
Chambersburg PA
CBHW031408290426
44110CB00011B/304